*Violet*

TO RODNEY

JESSICA DOUGLAS-HOME

# *Violet*

*The Life and Loves of*
*Violet Gordon Woodhouse*

## THE HARVILL PRESS
LONDON

First published in Great Britain in 1996
by The Harvill Press,
84 Thornhill Road,
London N1 1RD

2 4 6 8 9 7 5 3

A CIP catalogue record for this book
is available from the British Library

ISBN 1 86046 269 3 (hbk)

Extracts from *Noble Essences* by Osbert Sitwell, courtesy of David Higham Associates

Extract from *Little Dark Magician of the Clavichord* by Sacheverell Sitwell,
courtesy of David Higham Associates

Extract from *Blighters* by Siegfried Sassoon, courtesy of George Sassoon Esq.

Chapter head decorations by Jessica Douglas-Home

Designed and typeset in Caslon at
Libanus Press, Marlborough, Wiltshire

Printed and bound in Great Britain by Butler & Tanner Ltd
at Selwood Printing, Burgess Hill

# CONTENTS

# ACKNOWLEDGEMENTS

I am very grateful for all the help I have received from members of the Labouchère, Tollemache, Barrington and Drinkwater families, who have taken time to recall their ancestors' memories of Violet Gordon Woodhouse, and have lent me photographs and documents. I am especially indebted to Bill Barrington's great-nephew, Robin Alderson, for lending me his store of Violet's letters to Bill dating from the beginning of their love affair in 1899.

Isabel Armitage generously shared with me her perspective on Violet from her unique position as a friend and neighbour since the day that Violet first moved to Nether Lypiatt Manor in 1923; it was she who, more than anyone else, was responsible for putting me in touch with so many who were connected with Violet's story.

Richard Luckett helped me immensely in a host of issues connected with Violet's music. I thank, too, Ruth Dyson, Richard Troeger, Noel Malcolm, Raymond Glaspole, Christopher Hogwood and Robin Holloway for their help in musical matters; Alfred Brendel for listening to Violet's recordings; Alan Vicat for so tirelessly compiling the discography; and Liz Wood for sharing her limitless knowledge of Ethel Smyth.

There have been many who, through their patience in answering questions on historical detail, or commenting on the manuscript, have helped me more than they know over a long period of time. I thank Angela Huth, who, by herself seeing the fascination of Violet's life, encouraged me; Peter Adamson, Mark Almond, Valda Aveling, Diana Baring, Simon Blow, Julia Caffyn, George Clive, Anne de Courcy, Carl Dolmetsch, Christopher Gibbs for being a living *Almanach de Gotha*, Michael Gough Matthews, William Harcourt-Smith, Sabrina Harcourt-Smith, John Higgins and David Jennings; TRH Prince and Princess Michael of Kent, the present owners of Nether Lypiatt, for letting me, amongst other things, revisit the house; Moira Kennedy; Colin Leach for reading and correcting the entire text; James Lees-Milne, HRH Princess Margaret, David McKenna, Paul Mirat, Nicholas Mosley, David Pryce-Jones, John Purvis, Steven Runciman, Roger Scruton, Reresby Sitwell, Arthur Stanton, Christine Stone, Jean Strutt; Richard Eeles and Vanessa Williams-Ellis for cataloguing my father's and Violet's books. My grateful thanks also to my editors – Ruth Thackeray, who gave encouragement and help before I sent the book to Harvill, and Alex Maccormick and Toby Buchan, who brought it to fruition.

Others, too, have helped me by supplying a vital fact or insight or by correcting an error: Primrose and Christopher Arnander, Detmar Blow, Simon and Alice Boyd, Sarah Bradford, Crystal Brown, Rachel Butt, Margaret Campbell, Mary Clive, Fiona Fraser, Hazel Gage, Peter Groom, Shusha Guppy, Priscilla Gwynne Longland, Gaynor Heathcoat Amory, Paul Johnson, John Keegan, James Knox, Candida Lycett-Green, Roland Pym, Peter Reid, Alan Rubin, Norman Stone, Lucilla Warre-Cornish, Philip Ziegler and Alastair Sampson; and John Byrne for tracking down Violet's portrait by Roger Fry.

I must thank Susan Clifford for her optimistic and undaunted attitude to typing and retyping the book so many times, and also Joanna Hooley and Anne Martin for their help with the typescript.

At times I have almost lived in the London Library and I would especially like to thank everyone who works there, even if my particular gratitude is due to James Edmunds and Guy Penman for their help. Other libraries have also proved vital sources of information: Westminster Music Library; the Bodleian Library; the British Library; Helmingham Archives; Tate Gallery Archives; University Library of Michigan; and the Harry Ranson Humanities Research Center, University of Texas at Austin.

It is not an overstatement to say that this book would not have come into existence but for Rodney Leach. For the past eighteen months he has helped greatly with the research and devoted painstaking and meticulous care to making improvements, revisions and additions. He was largely responsible for the section dealing with the First World War. Countless difficulties in arriving at the facts were resolved with his help and it has been of the greatest importance for me that he tolerated – and enjoyed – discussing and analysing all the people who feature so prominently in the book.

# INTRODUCTION

From the moment when I first went to live at Nether Lypiatt, at the age of six, I was enthralled by the possessions of my great-aunt, Violet Gordon Woodhouse, from whom my father had inherited the house. Her letters, photographs, music, books and furniture – even her hats, scarves, and curtain materials – etched themselves into my childhood memories. At first these things lay as she had left them, creating a self-contained world of evocative colours, shapes and images – as if upon her departure from life she had somehow preserved her personality, in the form of a collection of enchanted keepsakes.

That Nether Lypiatt was haunted was taken for granted in the neighbourhood. In the precipitous wood below the garden stood an obelisk – memorial to a horse whose galloping hooves could be heard in the early hours of the morning every January. Another ghost was that of a blacksmith who had forged a deliberate mistake in the wrought-iron gates of the forecourt and had cursed the house when he was sentenced by its owner, a judge, to be hanged for sheep-stealing. But for me it was Violet who haunted Nether Lypiatt: her presence in those years after her death kept a hold on the occupants of the house, as if to command them to choose one of their number to set down the record of her extraordinary life.

My mother kept many of Violet's letters and papers (meticulously catalogued by my brother), hoping herself to tell the story one day. My aunt, Kit Ayling, went a step further, giving Violet pride of place in a history of the Gwynnes, which she never published; my great-aunt Dorothy, Violet's sister, kept a diary for seventy years; Osbert Sitwell wove a brief biography of Violet into his own memoirs; and of course there were scattered memorabilia in the hands of others. As time passed, however, many of those who had known her died, and it became increasingly clear that if the last surviving first-hand memories of her were to be recorded, I had to act quickly. Otherwise the true story of Violet's life and powers would fade, the evidence would be dispersed and lost beyond recall, and only a few isolated legends and anecdotes would remain.

I began with the idea of writing a short book in the form of an extended memoir. I half expected that the spell which Violet had cast on so many of those who had met or known her would fail to stand up to close scrutiny, and assumed that I would find that, as a musician, she was not much more than a highly gifted amateur. But as I dug deeper she grew in stature. Spending hours in libraries, sifting through papers, reviews, letters and old music, making new and unexpected contacts with scholars and with people who had known Violet and heard her play, I followed the trail of her encounters with Casals, Tertis, Busoni, Sarasate, Diaghilev, Picasso, Rubio, Wilfred Owen, Bernard Shaw, the Sitwells and Arnold Dolmetsch. And what leapt from every page was that in the eyes of her peers she was one of the great artists of her time.

As for the four "husbands" with whom she lived simultaneously, I found that these were original and cultivated men who had willingly forgone families and an independent position in society in order to devote themselves, until their own deaths, to Violet, whom they set on a pedestal far above ordinary mortals. Crisis came for this tight-knit group in the First World War, when three of them went to the trenches, and here I met with another surprise. Delving in the regimental histories in the Imperial War Museum, I was able to retrace in minute detail their heroism in action during the most awful battles – at Loos, in the swamps of Mesopotamia, on the Somme and at Passchendaele.

As if this were not enough, as the book progressed I came across convincing proofs (of which previous accounts had contained hardly a hint) that women were often as enamoured of Violet as men, perhaps even more so. The composer Ethel Smyth, the radical feminist, music critic and playwright Christabel Marshal, and the lesbian novelist, Radclyffe Hall, were but three among many women to fall in love with Violet.

Strong and unusual characters attract tales about them, of which some are true and some apocryphal. Stripped of their context, it is hard to know what to make of such anecdotes. So it was important to establish a historical framework if I was to reconstruct Violet's life with honesty. Here, too, I was in for a pleasurable surprise. Again and again, details were corroborated and stories of which I had initially been suspicious proved to be not only accurate, but clues to a richer understanding of her personality and of her relations with the musical and cultural world of England in the first half of the twentieth century.

Through the help of many people, there were landmark moments: the unearthing of an unknown Roger Fry painting of Violet; the discovery in a Suffolk attic of the correspondence between Violet and the love of her life, Bill Barrington; the appearance of letters written to or about Violet by Delius and by Edith, Sacheverell and Osbert Sitwell. Soon it was possible to date and place in their proper context all the papers which she had left behind in boxes, but whose full meaning had initially been so difficult to decipher. A last-minute discovery, made by the eminent musical scholar Richard Luckett, was that one of Violet's deepest musical instincts had been correct: contrary to all received opinion, Scarlatti did indeed, as she sensed he must have, intend some of his sonatas for the clavichord.

Life-enhancing people are rarely perfect – their flaws are part of their vitality and their fascination. Violet possessed an exquisite selfishness, and despite her well-deserved reputation for generosity, friendship and warmth, she could also be cold and critical. Yet those who loved her forgave her everything, while to her servants she was as much a friend as an employer.

A performer of music, unlike a painter, a writer or a composer, lives in the same artistic half-world as an actor. Shakespeare needs a Burbage as much as Scarlatti needs a Violet Woodhouse, but unless the work of such interpreters is recorded it dies with them. I hope the scale of importance of Violet's service to Bach and Mozart, to the early English composers, to folk music, and above all to Domenico Scarlatti, will now be recognized, as well as her contribution to restoring the harpsichord and clavichord to the mainstream repertoire. The twentieth century's changed attitude towards early music might well have come about anyway, but it needed the beauty of Violet's playing to alter people's preconceptions, and so lead the music-loving world to rediscover a lost universe.

I feel a sense of profound relief that Violet's papers and letters have been sorted, their messages decoded, and her life finally written down. If this book depicts something not only of her artistic stature but also of her significance as a friend of artists, an independent spirit and the most feminine of early feminists, I hope it will place her firmly in her rightful position alongside other women of genius.

x

*Violet*

# I

## *Family Secrets*

IT WAS WHISPERED during her lifetime, among the very few who were in the know, that Violet Gordon Woodhouse, or Violet Gwynne as she was born, owed her magical musical powers to a dark family secret: her mother's Indonesian ancestry.

At the end of the nineteenth century the suspicion that an Englishwoman of otherwise impeccable stock had traces of mixed blood might well have devastated her prospects; and the marriage of Violet's maternal grandfather, William Purvis, to the granddaughter of a Sumatran ranee, or tribal princess, had created a connection, however remote, that was dangerous enough to call for dissimulation, and if necessary camouflage.

Throughout Violet's life gossip was deflected by vague allusions to her "Spanish origins", which seemed to explain her jet-black hair, dark brown eyes and gypsy looks, as well as her flashing temperament, rapturous relationships and flamenco sense of rhythm. But even this suggestion was no more than a hint by Violet's mother, May, for Latin blood, if less appalling than East Indian, was nevertheless distinctly too foreign for May's husband, and Violet's father, James Gwynne. Indeed, it is unlikely that May ever dared to spell out to James the real truth about her ancestry.

Violet's grandfather came from an enterprising Scottish family of merchants and traders with business interests from Alabama to Indonesia. Inheriting the family's taste for adventure from his father, who had made a fortune in cotton in the United States, William Purvis joined the navy as a young man. In 1822 his travels took him to Padang on the west coast of Sumatra, where he accepted an invitation to dine as guest of honour with the Dutch Resident[1], Theunis In'tveld, and his wife Anna. The In'tvelds' beautiful fourteen-year-old daughter Cornelia, who had just returned from school in Calcutta, took the place at dinner of her older sister, who was

1 The district colonial officer.

unwell. That same evening William fell in love, and less than a year later he made Cornelia his wife.

The secret which was to haunt the respectability of the Gwynnes, when they became linked by marriage to the next generation of Purvises, was that Cornelia's mother Anna was half Indonesian. Theunis In'tveld had sailed from Holland to the East Indies in his youth and, like so many Dutchmen before and after him, had fallen under the spell of the islands. He settled eventually in Padang, one of the oldest Dutch colonial towns, founded by the Dutch East India Company in 1606. There the expatriates lived comfortably, with numerous servants, in big, stolid one-storey houses, inter-marrying freely with the natives and often wearing local costume. The little town itself, overlooked by the Ape mountain, was laid out formally with squares, wide streets and churches. The heat was intense and in the wet season the rain fell in torrents. Beyond the sea wall, shoals of fish gave the clear water the appearance of a rainbow.

Inland, tucked in the valleys below the great mountain chains with their volcanic peaks, flowed wide, hidden rivers, their banks half covered by trop-ical growth spreading out from the tracts of still unexplored rainforest. There lurked in these undiscovered parts, amid the jungle of ebony and camphor, mahogany and sandalwood, oak and chestnut, tigers, rhinoceroses, lemurs, elephants and rare snakes. Cornelia had grown up among brilliantly coloured birds and vivid sweet-scented flowers, of which she spoke longingly in later life, when her destiny took her to live under the grey Scottish skies.

In this mysterious country, with its mixture of peoples of Polynesian, Arab, Indian, Chinese and Portuguese descent, there was a deep belief in magic and in spells, and most Europeans living there felt the potency of that belief at one time or another. Although the Muslim, Hindu and Christian religions had all left their mark on the people, they had not replaced the primitive faiths which had existed long before the conquerors came to the islands. Spirits and ghosts, some benign, some sinister, played an important part in the daily lives of the people, to be invoked against the invaders, or to ward off sickness or ensnare a loved one. Indonesian women, legendary for their beauty and their piercing gaze, were reputed to possess strong and secret powers in matters of hatred and desire. The contrast with the sober struggle of the Netherlands against the cold North Sea was an irresistible attraction to Theunis In'tveld. He became a pillar of the community, marrying a dark-skinned local girl, Anna Carels, and eventually rising to the position of Resident in Padang, where he lived and died, never to return to Europe.

Theunis In'tveld's wife Anna was the daughter of a Dutch settler, but it was from her mother, a Sumatran ranee, that she inherited the wonderful looks which she passed to her daughter, Cornelia, who in turn passed them on to Violet's mother, May. As for Cornelia, her letters reveal a woman of spirit, who was only too well aware that the two-year silence, during which her husband received not a single word from his relations in Fife, signalled their displeasure at his marriage to the daughter of what they would have called a half-caste. Cornelia describes herself as "an Indian"; and in fact nowhere in Indonesia is the ancient Indian influence stronger than in Padang.

For eleven years William and Cornelia Purvis stayed in Sumatra. His trading ventures prospered and he became a very rich man. But in 1833, his liver weakened by the climate, he decided to return home; his health apart, he did not wish to bring up his children in the Far East. Cornelia made what she knew must be her last farewell to her parents and set sail with William for Scotland. Their arrival was spectacular. Landing from his own vessel with the ravishing Cornelia and their six children, William also disembarked several of her nephews and nieces, accompanied by three servants in turbans, earrings and tunics, who were baptized on the quayside. As they came down the gangplank the colourful group jangled and shone, the children and the servants decked from top to toe in gold anklets, brooches and bracelets, a testament to William's reluctance to pay customs duty.

William and Cornelia settled in Edinburgh where, in 1841, Violet's mother Mary (known as May) was born to them, the last but one of ten children. It was impossible to escape being charmed by Cornelia, even if the Purvises still could not entirely warm to a woman of questionable descent in their ranks. The atmosphere at home was affectionate and relaxed, and Cornelia saw to it that the house was full of music, two of her daughters, Elizabeth and Anne, being exceptionally gifted pianists. Cornelia taught May to sing and was herself a fine soprano – May used to speak nostalgically to Violet of her childhood memories of her mother pouring out notes "like wonderful rich velvet". Cornelia's looks were at one with her voice. Glimpsing her across the auditorium at the opera in London, King William IV gazed at the dark beauty in black velvet with diamond stars in her hair and a hint of bronze in the colour of her skin, and sent his equerry to invite her to his box. When she refused, the King sent the equerry back just to ask her name. Her portrait shows her with perfect shoulders, eyes set wide apart, classic features and the shadow of the serene smile of a woman sure of being loved.

In 1854, after almost thirteen years of contented domesticity, William Purvis died of pneumonia. Heartbroken, and now more exposed to the cold-shouldering of the Purvis family, Cornelia was unable to face the prospect of a lonely existence in Scotland. Leaving behind her two youngest daughters, Kate and the thirteen-year-old May, to live with her oldest son Robert and to be educated in Edinburgh, she repaired to Leiden in Holland to seek solace in the companionship of her third daughter, Anne Vijgh, and her In'tveld relatives nearby in The Hague – they, at least, were not embarrassed by her Indonesian origins. There, in 1857, at the age of forty-nine, Cornelia died, her flight from Scotland and her death breaking a crucial link in the chain of evidence that connected her descendants to their ancestry. Her children dispersed, some back to the Dutch East Indies, some to North America, some to the Netherlands, so that in the end only Kate and May remained to keep alive in Britain the half-remembered, romantic, but far from welcome truth about their lovely Sumatran great-grandmother.

In 1859, by then a young woman of eighteen, May Purvis met the twenty-seven-year-old James Gwynne on one of his regular biannual visits to Edinburgh to stay with his maternal uncle and aunt, Henry and Margaret Anderson. James was on the lookout for a wife, and his mother, who would have preferred a Scottish girl, made sure that the Andersons introduced him to the daughters of suitable fellow Scots like the Purvises. May dazzled him. Not only was she extraordinarily beautiful, but, like her mother Cornelia, she was able to inspire love at first sight. Despite the soft Scottish lilt in her voice there was a seductive hint of something foreign about her. Admittedly their temperaments were very different, and May might perhaps have kept her distance had she not been devastated by the loss of both her parents, and miserable at having to live with her sister-in-law. But she, too, was anxious for marriage. James was ardent and good-looking, he had the self-confident air of a successful man, and he represented the reassuring prospect of wealth and children. May gave enough encouragement for him to make a formal proposal of engagement to her on the last day of his Scottish stay , which she accepted.

The Purvises and the Gwynnes had a fair amount in common. Both families had their larger-than-life characters; both were well-to-do, the Purvises from trading abroad, the Gwynnes from engineering. James's mother, born Agnes Anderson, was from good Scottish professional stock. Her father had owned the first steamship on the Clyde, and one of her brothers, Sir James Eglinton Anderson, physician to Queen Adelaide, the wife of William IV, had been the surgeon in attendance at a duel fought by the seventh Earl of Cardigan, notorious for his part in the Charge of the Light Brigade at Balaclava in 1854, during the Crimean War. James's father, John Gwynne, had been mechanically inventive, having built Britain's first centrifugal pump, a major technological advance developed for the expanding business of reclaiming flooded land. With the financial backing of a friendly merchant banker and tea trader, Herbert Twining, John Gwynne combined manufacture with property investment – the site for his first factory, off the Strand in London, was largely chosen for its prospect of capital appreciation when the Thames Embankment was built.

James, the eldest son, was involved in Gwynne & Co. from its inception in 1849. Two years later, at the age of nineteen, he organized the firm's stand for the 1851 Great Exhibition in the Crystal Palace in Hyde Park, and on John Gwynne's death in 1855 he became the managing partner. He was a mere twenty-three, but he was shrewd and, since nearly everything he touched made money, he came to believe himself infallible in matters of business early in his career. Morally, too, he was sure of his judgement, perhaps too sure. His younger brother George had "gone wrong" in Gwynne & Co. and had been packed off to Australia to avoid a financial scandal. James was determined not to put up with any such nonsense when he started his own family.

The Gwynnes had strong genes and, as a family, ran to explosive tempers, a stubborn streak, and considerable willpower. Their opinions tended to the conventional in all but the fierceness with which they were held, a family characteristic which had come down in full measure to James. His tunnel vision about his pump business, a topic about which May had no curiosity whatsoever, struck her as unromantic. At the start of their long engagement, however, she diplomatically disguised her lack of interest, and his letters to her are full of pride in his firm's products. During the summer of 1862 he wrote to her frequently about the second Great Exhibition at the Crystal Palace, where the firm again had a large display: "The great Centrifugal Pump is ours . . . it worked six and a half hours yesterday, this shows what I have already obtained, as other days it did not work more than one half hour".[2]

Fluent in French, well-read, musical and literate, May was much the more cosmopolitan and broadly educated of the two. She had her mother's sparkling, playful personality and, like her, she was surrounded by laughter and incapable of harbouring a grievance. By contrast, James's serious and uncompromisingly Anglo-Saxon mind was set on engineering, finance and the management of the family firm. The seeds of future incompatibility were there to be seen, but James was in love. He wrote poems to May, he

2 It was critical that the Gwynne Pump should be shown to the best advantage. James quotes to May from a letter to *The Times:* "There would be no more beautiful sight in the building than to watch the great Centrifugal Pump and other pumps at work, if they only had steam enough at their command to produce the effects of which they are capable."

felt intensely protective towards her, and he was determined to go through with the marriage in the face of what was turning into a wall of concerted opposition from his own family.

James's mother was a woman of resolute character who, after her husband's death, lived with her three sons and her daughter in a Regency house in Hanover Terrace in London. From the day James brought May to see her, the engagement met with her relentless hostility. The first battle arose, at least nominally, over religion, for the Gwynnes were strict Presbyterians while the Purvises were Episcopalian; yet however important these sectarian differences, they seem an inadequate explanation for the violence of Mrs Gwynne's antagonism. May's looks, like her temperament, had a touch of the Mediterranean – or could it be the East? – about them, and it is impossible to avoid the conclusion that James's mother guessed from her appearance, and subsequently confirmed through the Andersons, that there must be something other than Scottish and Dutch blood in her veins. After all, Cornelia had made no secret of it, and there were still plenty of Purvises, In'tvelds and Vijghs around. Admittedly, the hard facts were beginning to be lost in the mists of time; perhaps there were traces of Spain in May's ancestry, for the histories of Spain and Holland were intertwined? But May's father had been married in Sumatra, and everyone knew the sort of things that went on out there. Nothing explicit was proved, but Mrs Gwynne's suspicions could not be assuaged.

James's mother writes in one of her letters of "our happy family life, now destroyed", and the vehemence of her campaign to prevent May from becoming her daughter-in-law is brought sharply to life in James's correspondence:

> My own, own darling, I am so sorry my Mother has written you the letter she has. It is not such as I expected or could justify. I feel it is not written in the kind of spirit I expected, and I cannot blame you, my own, if it has annoyed you.
>
> I do think, my pet, you have tried for peace, and I cannot ask you to make the concessions I am willing to submit to with my own mother. I do not justify her. *I do honestly believe she is diseased on this subject.*

In another letter, James writes:

> My dearest, you are unkind when you say I have gone against you. This I have never done. I fearlessly can assert, I have always taken your part, have always stood by you, and O May it is not kind to turn against me. I know you have in this matter yielded to my feel-

ings and wishes, and I thank you from my heart for doing so. I would willingly have done the same for you in a like case. What would you not have done, or what would you not do for your dear departed Mother if she was back with you again?

May, you do me again, my own, great injustice: is it necessary to ask me "Am I to understand that if your Mother wished it, you would have put off fulfilling this engagement?" This I think should never have been asked me. I can only refer to *the past*, and ask you, has my conduct justified such a question?

By the last weeks before the marriage James was no longer on speaking terms with any member of his family. His two brothers and his sister sided with their mother, and she very nearly succeeded in having her way; at one point May even returned her ring. But somehow the engaged couple survived their ordeal, and were finally married in Edinburgh on 2 December 1862 from the house of May's brother, Robert. May was delicate and had been ill – tuberculosis was suspected, prompting James to include among his presents to his bride the prosaic gift of a respirator. The wedding was very quiet. Her father being dead, May was given away by Robert, as head of the Purvis family, but not one of the Gwynnes or Andersons was present. Implacable to the end, James's formidable old mother never forgave him for what he had done.

If marriage held little promise of emotional fulfilment either for May or for James, it was nevertheless a liberating experience for both of them. May soon recovered her health, much relieved by her escape from the disapproving Purvises and the resentful Mrs Gwynne. James, too, was glad to be free from his mother's domination. The firm was doing well, even if James's younger brothers, John and Henry, felt that they should be given more influence and that their engineering products could be improved. James sold the Strand site to Jacob Astor in 1867 for a large profit and bought cramped new premises in Holborn, whereupon Mrs Gwynne backed John and Henry with a £7,000 loan to buy land at Hammersmith, where they set up in direct competition. Gwynne & Co.'s pumps had won international recognition at the two Great Exhibitions, but henceforth the bulk of the massive new orders from the Netherlands and East Anglia were won by the rival Hammersmith partnership. James, however, had not lost his touch. He diversified successfully into a wide range of activities, from mechanized sheepshears to private electric lighting plants and the transmission of telegrams (the "Gwynnegram"), and bought property near the Royal Courts of Justice in the Strand. Like many other industrialists, he also embarked on the typical life of a successful English businessman-turned-gentleman, buying a London house in Harley Street and a country mansion, Abinger Hall, near Dorking in Surrey.

In mid-Victorian England the roles of a married couple were well delineated. Outward appearances were all-important – the manner of horse-drawn carriage in which the wife travelled, how she dressed, how her hair was arranged, who were her dressmakers and her milliners, whom she "received" and by whom she was invited. A lady was supposed to be delicate and, in her youth – with the assistance of whalebone stays – wasp-waisted, her physical appetites unmentioned (or better still non-existent), her complexion protected by parasols, her hands by gloves, and her fragile self shielded by her servants and her husband from the practical cares of living. In her own sphere she had unfettered command. She planned the entertaining and was expected to organize a large staff of manservants, cooks and maids, to which several more attendants would be added after the arrival of children.

In all other matters wives deferred to their husbands, who took sole responsibility for financial decisions and were considered to be the autho-rized experts on questions of politics and morality, which they discussed over port and cigars after dinner, once the ladies had departed. Regular churchgoing and Christian ritual played a central part in domestic life. The Gwynnes, for example, had their family pew in their local church; James conducted daily morning prayers after breakfast for family and staff, and said grace before and after meals.

As the years went by James bought and sold more than one country house before acquiring the two neighbouring East Sussex manors of Folkington Place and Wootton in 1876, five years after Violet's birth. Only a mile apart, the two houses were completely different from each other. Folkington, set in a large park right at the foot of the South Downs, close to Eastbourne, was large and solid, built in grey flint only twenty years or so before the Gwynnes arrived. Wootton, originally a red-brick Jacobean farmhouse, had been added to over the centuries and was redolent with history, a rambling series of intermingling archways, forecourts, barns and cottages.

With country life becoming more appealing and the family growing larger, James gradually started to find the day-to-day management of his engineering business irksome. Though he would not admit it even to him-self, the success of his brothers made a mockery of his refusal to listen to them when they had been in the firm, and he looked forward to the day when his sons might take over. Meanwhile, he turned increasingly to real estate investment, at which he was patient, astute and fortunate enough to be operating at a time of rising prosperity fuelled by the development of the railways. The era marked the height of Victorian self-confidence. The British Empire stretched right round the world, from Canada to South Africa, from India to Australia. Free trade and industrial domination had made the country the world's workshop, banker and shipper, bringing nearly thirty years of uninterrupted economic expansion during James's formative years from 1845 to 1873. Competition from other countries became tougher in the mid- and late-1870s, but growth continued, if more spasmodically, for the rest of the century. Political reform and great public works combined to give the impression of a new Rome, bringing unprecedented health and wealth at home, and a peaceful world order abroad. Against such a favourable background, it would have been hard for a much less able man than James to go wrong in real estate.

The rise of the middle classes was to some extent at the expense of the upper classes, and James's will identifies land and houses bought from neighbouring estates of the Duke of Devonshire, Lord Sackville and Lord Gage. He acquired as much of the property around Folkington as he could, until by the end of his life it might be said that "the hunt could run all day without ever leaving Squire Gwynne's boundaries." Bearded, tall and heavy, with steely light blue eyes behind gold-rimmed spectacles, James Gwynne grew insensibly into the role of the landowner, becoming ever more authoritarian and heavy-hearted. Of their nine children, two boys, Ernest and Hubert, died, one of diphtheria and the other of a fever, before they were a year old. Violet, who was born on 23 April 1871, was the fourth of the surviving seven, preceded by Reginald, Evelyn (known as Eva) and Nevile (the author's grandfather), and followed by Rupert, Dorothy and Roland. Violet was such a tiny baby that, at birth, the doctor could hold her in the palm of his hand and her face would have fitted into a teacup.

Folkington lay deep in foxhunting country. When Violet was a girl the downs above the house were unspoilt, a broad grassy ridge inhabited only by birds and other wild creatures, stretching sixty miles parallel with the coast from Eastbourne past Brighton, before curving inland towards Winchester. A short walk would take her to the bottom of the escarpment, and after a steep five-minute scramble to the top of the downs she could look south to the English Channel or northwards for miles over the Sussex Weald. Close by to the west was the Long Man of Wilmington, an ancient chalk figure cut in the grass. Folkington's grounds were enclosed by a wall, and could be entered through either of two lodges from which long beech avenues led to the house. A shorter drive ran to the home farm, and beyond it to the rectory and the little church, beneath which lay Folkington village, then, as now, no more than a handful of simple stone cottages.

The drawing-room and dining-room windows looked on to box hedges and formal flowerbeds in which there grew 145 varieties of roses; there was a tennis court and, past the uncut grass where wild flowers grew, a path led to a door in a wall which opened on to a large kitchen garden. The conservatory, full of sweet-smelling flowers, was attached to the house by a long passage. Further on stood the hothouses, with their subtropical flowers and ferns, and the greenhouses, from which clusters of purple and green grapes were cut each day. Adjoining the west front of the house through a broad entrance gate, above which was carved in stone the Gwynne coat of arms, lay the brick-and-flint stables, with stalls for twenty horses.

The distinctive atmosphere of Folkington enfolded the visitor from the first moment of walking up the broad steps to the heavy front doors. James Gwynne was allergic to any kind of innovation. As an increasingly absentee owner of his engineering business, his resistance to modernization was to lead him to starve his firm of capital, with ultimately disastrous consequences, but at Folkington it produced a strangely welcoming effect. Ironically, given that he had been one of the pioneers of electricity supply in London, there was not even electricity in the house. Nor were there any bathrooms. Morning baths were brought to the bedrooms, of which there were nine (plus a dormitory with six bedrooms for the indoor servants), by housemaids carrying a mat, a hip bath and two cans, the large one of steaming hot water, the smaller one of cold. There were servants everywhere – cooks, a kitchenmaid and a scullerymaid, the odd-job man who pumped the water, the butler and two footmen, three housemaids and two lady's maids; and when the children were young, nurses and governesses as well.

In winter there were blazing log fires in all the bedrooms; no one who remembered the house from those days had any recollection of feeling the cold even in the bitterest weather. The oil-fired lamps gave off a soft light and a pleasant, if slightly cloying, aroma. In the library James was assembling what was to be one of the finest collections of bound books in Sussex. Despite its heavy Victorian furnishings, the big drawing-room, with its Canaletto paintings of Venice and its grand piano, had a relaxing informality about it which immediately put people at ease. In this room, with its deep, comfortable sofas and chairs, dances, plays and concerts were put on each year at Christmas. The programmes, handwritten in brown ink, introduced one-act dramas containing parts for ten or twelve people so as to include guests as well as family. The concerts, which were sometimes also staged at Easter, were carefully designed to show off the talents of everyone in the household who could sing or play an instrument, with pieces for the piano and the violin and popular ditties, plantation songs and glees. The evening would end with "a reading by Miss Kate Purvis"– May's unmarried sister and everybody's favourite aunt, who was the family's star actress and lived permanently at Folkington – followed always by "God Save the Queen".

# II

## *I Can Never Marry Lord Gage*

THE SETTING IN which James and May brought up Violet haunted the imagination of the Gwynne children throughout their lives; some could never break away, and those who did, or who fell foul of James's ungovernable temper and were driven out, felt a recurrent nostalgia for Folkington. Taught the violin by Mr Liebert, a French *émigré*, and the piano by May, Violet soon showed such precocious signs of talent[1] that May took her at the age of seven for an audition with a concert pianist who occasionally gave advanced tuition to especially promising pupils. The meeting got off to a disheartening start: glaring at the tiny figure of Violet, he said crushingly, "I do not teach children." After much pleading by May, however, he grudgingly agreed to hear a short Mozart piece on the piano. As Violet played he listened in an intent silence, which continued for what seemed to May an unconscionably long time after Violet had finished. When eventually he spoke, his tone of voice had changed dramatically. "I apologize," he said. "I did not realize. Please send her to me." From that day forward, to the intense jealousy of her older sister Eva, Violet was set apart from the rest of the family, becoming the centre of attention and learning at an early age that she could nearly always get her own way through willpower and the exercise of a childlike magnetism.

Violet's younger sister, Dorothy, kept a diary from 1889 for over forty years. Although she rarely travelled from Folkington, it is an invaluable record, its reams of descriptions of banal happenings interspersed with revealing nuggets of detail and flashes of psychological insight, the whole combining to supply much of the historical framework within which the story of Violet's emotional and musical life can be reconstructed. The first

1 Osbert Sitwell, who devoted a chapter to Violet in his autobiographical *Noble Essences*, and who was attracted to the idea of associating two geniuses, recounts a story of Sarah Bernhardt dandling Violet on her knee after a charity performance at St James's Hall. It is quite possible: May and Sarah Bernhardt had many acquaintances in common.

entries start when Violet is about to enter a glittering adult world which, being still a child, Dorothy can only observe from a distance. Dorothy was very plain and there is a somewhat bitter poignancy in her comments on "Bobo's" attractive appearance – Bobo was Violet's family nickname – and on her father's favouritism, which allowed all Violet's waywardness to go unrebuked, while the younger sister's own little transgressions drew the full weight of his disapproval. In these early years, the diary is filled out with letters and programmes of events – fêtes, plays in Eastbourne and family concerts – either pushed between the pages or meticulously glued in. Several of the concert programmes record Violet singing duets with her mother and playing the violin.

The rest of Dorothy's diary entries are largely devoted to shooting parties and hunting. On his seventh birthday each of Violet's brothers was given his own gun and taught to shoot by the keeper. With the exception of Violet, all the children learned to ride and the boys took up hunting with as much enthusiasm as they did shooting, if not more. There were horses everywhere – horses for carriages, farm horses for heavy work, thorough-breds for hunting and point-to-points. Nevile, Rupert and Dorothy were famous locally for their reckless courage cross-country, jumping gates, fences and ditches, and always in the forefront of the field. Violet hero-worshipped Rupert, the bravest of her brothers and sisters, but did not share his passion for the hunt. Perhaps the fact that her health was delicate deterred her, or perhaps she was secretly scared; whatever the reason, although she would sometimes go to the meet in a wagonette (a light four-wheeler) or follow the hunt on foot, she never took a horse. More and more she was absorbed by the piano, practising in the drawing-room in the morning after breakfast and in the early afternoon while the others were out roaming the country-side. When the family reassembled for meals, full of sporting chatter, Violet's provoking wit and artful teasing generally had the effect, sooner or later, of deflecting the conversation on to herself.

As his children grew up James became isolated from them to a degree rare even by the stern standards of remote Victorian fatherhood. He loved them, as they loved him, but he could not relax with them or speak freely with them about anything to do with emotions, his frustration at being cut off from them expressing itself in anger, unpredictability and perpetual anxiety that they might go to the bad. In 1876, when Violet was five, her oldest brother Reginald had to be taken away from Eton[2] for his extravagance, but

2 Reginald was then sent to Lancing, near Brighton, as was Nevile. Rupert went to Shrewsbury. Nevile and Rupert were both sent to Cambridge, James no doubt thinking Eton and Oxford a lethal combination.

there was worse to come, for seven years later the exile of James's own brother, George, to Australia was eerily re-enacted when James removed Reginald from Oxford and banished him to Canada for wild overspending at the university. He owed £280 for a pair of shotguns he had given to a casual friend as a wedding present, £200 to his tailor, £15 to his bootmaker, £100 to his shirtmaker, £140 for jewellery, and over £1,600 to moneylenders, with other debts a grand total of £2,480, equivalent today to the astonishing sum of £125,000. Having previously expected Reginald to succeed him in the business, James was now forced to pin his hopes on Nevile. His chief consolation for what was essentially a self-inflicted alienation from his family was his land, and his greatest pleasure was to drive over the downs in his dogcart (a light two-wheeler), proudly surveying the estate on which he had lavished such care, especially the young trees of the copse and woodland he had planted. In the evening, after everyone else had retired for the night, he would doze in his ample winged armchair before eventually dragging himself up to bed.

Happiest in the early morning, May liked to rise at six and go for a ride, from which she would arrive back radiant to sit over breakfast laughing and exchanging animated small talk with Kate and the children, until the sound of heavy footsteps announced the approach of James. Upon entering he would give a frown all round, while everyone got up to say "Good morning, Papa", and have their faces brushed by his beard. As he sat down to his meal, the smiles and conversation died away. May, who suffered deeply from his black moods and unforgiving nature, appeased him, having a horror of angry voices and developing over the years the misleading protective colouring of someone rather childish and fragile, who had to be spared the harder realities of life. "Mother must not be worried" was the family saying. The adolescent Violet instinctively understood, but could not help slightly despising her mother for her inability either to charm her father into a different frame of mind or to stand up to him directly.

Considering her own sound education at Edinburgh High School, May took surprisingly little trouble over her daughters' schooling. The only serious attempt she made was wholly unsuccessful: a mademoiselle was recruited to give French lessons at the family's house in Harley Street, but the children went out on the balcony and refused to pay her any attention. Violet was to regret this later, when, unlike her mother, she was unable to converse with foreign musicians, French being the *lingua franca* of the musical world at the beginning of the twentieth century.

Governesses came and went, most of them kind and friendly souls, if not always chosen for their academic prowess. From these Violet learned to knit and sew, picked up a smattering of history and French, and acquired a rudimentary knowledge of Shakespeare and the classics. Although full of curiosity and highly intelligent, she was capricious except where music was concerned. At the piano she became a different person, following her lessons intently and spending hours in disciplined concentration. The books she read as a child are typical Victorian fare, lovingly inscribed by her governesses – *Read Me a Story* (1878), *Little Anne* (1883) and *Jackanapes* (1884) – but as she grew older James introduced her to Trollope, Dickens and Surtees. That one book given to her in 1887 on her sixteenth birthday was read and re-read by Violet with exceptional interest can be seen from the well-thumbed and page-marked edition in the present author's library. Despite its forbidding title, *Music Study in Germany*, by a twenty-four-year-old American student, Amy Fay, is a fascinating saga, told through graphic letters home, of a musical odyssey in the 1870s through Berlin, Dresden and Weimar, during which Fay met and worked with Liszt, Clara Schumann and other great musicians of the age.

Many years later, at the height of her fame, Violet used to pretend that her talent came from nowhere, a gift from God. This was an ungrateful fantasy. It ignored not only the musicality of her grandmother Cornelia and her piano-playing aunts, but also the fact that from the age of sixteen she was taken by May each year to London, where they spent three or four months together going to concerts and the opera, often attending two musical events in a day. The performances which Violet heard with her mother were of infinitely higher quality than those on which May had had to educate herself during the early years of her marriage, when English audiences, out of touch with what was going on in the rest of Europe, had been addicted to sentimental Palm Court pieces by obscure composers. It was not until Thomas Chappell started the so-called Popular Concerts in his new St James's Hall in Regent Street in the 1850s – which in fact consisted of then unpopular music, such as Beethoven sonatas – that the repertoire at the Crystal Palace concert hall had improved and English musical horizons had opened up. Nevertheless, it was many years before the Royal College of Music was founded (in 1882), with a charter to teach music in schools and ensure that the subject was cultivated as an art.

May was never far from the centre of this revolution in English taste. She had had good reason to be pleased when her husband bought his house in Harley Street. Not yet exclusively the Mecca for doctors which it later became, Harley Street was home to the rich upper-middle classes – businessmen, judges, parliamentarians and Masters of Oxford colleges, as well as the cream of physicians and surgeons. Many of these prided themselves on being patrons of the arts, and the street was famous for its musical evenings. May's neighbour was Wilhelm Ganz who, forty-five years earlier, as a fourteen-year-old had come to England from Mainz with his father. Now a naturalized Englishman – and a socially ambitious one – he was a superb all-round musician. By the 1880s he had established himself as one of London's leading musical impresarios, bringing to England new singers, instrumentalists and composers from all over the world. It was Ganz who, along with Augustus Harris at the Royal Opera House, Covent Garden, was more than anyone responsible for elevating London within the space of a few years into a city that rivalled Leipzig, Berlin and Vienna for musical excellence.

Wilhelm Ganz's friendship with May took her and the young Violet into the heart of the cosmopolitan cultural élite. It was an era when Ganz could remark with justice that more interesting orchestral music could be heard in private houses than in the public concert halls. His soirées in Harley Street were a testing ground for up-and-coming musicians, a meeting place for the like-minded and a platform for his two daughters, Georgina (Georgi) and Adelina, who were learning to sing. At one of his afternoon concerts May met Mathilde Enequist, a Swedish concert singer who was making her way in London, and arranged for her to give lessons to Violet in the drawing-room at Harley Street. May, who had inherited a lovely light soprano voice from her mother Cornelia, shared the lessons with Violet. By 1890 most of May's friends were musicians, many of them professional singers, including the Italian opera stars Giulia and Sofia Ravogli, Jean Lasalle, the French baritone whose portrayal (in Italian) of Hans Sachs in *Die Meistersinger* at Covent Garden in 1889 had brought him fame, and the coloratura soprano Adelina Patti, nearing the end of her career but still universally regarded as the greatest soprano in the world.

Away from James, May's childish submissiveness vanished and she became a mature woman of independent means, who through her love of music and her insight into Violet's unique talent succeeded in developing her own separate social life. James never accompanied them to concerts or the opera; when they needed male companionship, Nevile or Rupert went with them instead. James did, however, tolerate May's inviting musicians frequently to Folkington, so that from the very beginning Violet was brought up in the company of artists who set themselves the most exacting standards. Adelina Patti was much attached to her own castle in Wales, to which she had added a miniature opera house, and Folkington was the only other home in England in which she was willing to stay. She was fascinated by little

Violet both as a character and as a musician, and followed her progress with genuine curiosity.

Violet's first regular piano teacher in London, Herr Winter, was an expatriate German recommended to May by Wilhelm Ganz; in 1887, under his tuition, she learned to read music. Previously Violet, who had a remarkable ear, had relied entirely on memory, and she had to struggle a bit before mastering the technique of reading. The following year she started to study under another *émigré*, Oscar Beringer,[3] who had left Germany at the age of five, when his father had fled with his family to England as a political refugee from the failed revolutions of 1848. Despite living in poverty, the Beringers managed to borrow a piano, on which Oscar was taught by his sister. At the age of thirteen he was a child prodigy, giving thrice-weekly piano recitals at the Crystal Palace, but he was acutely aware of his lack of formal training and when he grew up he set off for Germany for eight years to rectify the omission by studying under the great masters there – Liszt, Carl Tausig, and the Bach exponent Ignaz Moscheles.

When Violet first met Beringer, he had been back in England for seventeen years. Now nearing fifty, he had made a name for himself as a concert pianist and was the country's foremost teacher of the day, having founded his Academy for the Higher Development of Pianoforte Playing in 1873. He started Violet off with *Beringer's Daily Technical Studies* and *Beringer's Celebrated Scale and Arpeggio Manual*. He was strict with her and intolerant of her unstructured method of learning pieces. Seventeen years old, Violet practised with dedication once she got under way, but was sometimes difficult to coax to the daily routine at the piano.

Mischievous, attractive and young for her age, with an almost studied insouciance, Violet continued to rule the roost at home. Her thick black hair, cut with a short fringe in front, fell to her waist, and was pinned back to allow full sight of her small, intelligent face. She held her head at an arresting angle and her eyes seemed at once to engage and to interrogate her interlocutors. Her strong personality and her determination to get her own way were not immediately suggested by her frail appearance, yet to the irritation of both her sisters she could beguile her father into giving her almost anything she wanted. She appeared to be the only one in the family who was impervious to his violent temper, which in any case was never directed at her. Nothing was more infuriating to Dorothy and Eva than to find Violet serene and carefree while the rest of the family was trembling at one of James's unreasonable outbursts, or in a state of suspended anxiety over

3 According to Osbert Sitwell, citing Gordon Woodhouse, Violet was also taught by Benno Schönberger "between 1888 and 1900".

one of his prolonged sulks. This, however, was something of an act, for beneath the surface Violet also yearned for steady warmth and affection from her father.

Violet attended Beringer's Academy in the summers of 1888, 1889 and 1890, and for several years continued as his occasional pupil in his house in Hinde Street, off Manchester Square. His influence on her style was crucial, concentrating as it did on beauty of tone through touch.[4] In words which foreshadowed Violet's subsequent convictions about the art of playing the clavichord, Beringer was to single out Tobias Matthay's *The Act of Touch* as one of only two books published in England to "have seen the light".

Like Wilhelm Ganz, Beringer, too, had musical daughters of roughly the same age as Violet. Violet was soon to discover how different their upbringing was from hers. Mrs Beringer had come from English colonial stock, her father an officer in the Indian Army. She had a powerful character and unconventional ideas, pursuing a career as a playwright and theatrical producer and allowing her daughters to appear on the stage. One night she took Violet to see her younger daughter starring as Little Lord Fauntleroy. After the play they went backstage, where Violet examined in silent fascination – and stored up in her mind for the future – the apparatus of costumes, props and greasepaint that went into the creation of a stage personality.

Dorothy's diary conveys a clear impression of the intensity and the range of the musical life that May arranged for Violet. The years while Violet was growing up coincided with a golden age for opera. Under Augustus Harris's direction, Covent Garden began to vary the monotonous diet of Italian opera which had been its fare for decades and signed up the greatest singers in the world for leading roles in the works of Gounod, Bizet, Wagner and others. The Opera House became an elegant meeting place, full of glamour, an essential feature of the season for the socially ambitious, a place to be seen at and in which to attract attention. As the curtain rose, the stalls were a swathe of dark shadows and shimmering light, the men's black evening

4 Beringer had five rules for touch and tone-production:
1. Avoid all stiffness in the joints, fingers, wrists, elbows and shoulders.
2. Avoid over-practice of any one particular movement, especially those affecting the weak finger muscles (it was the neglect of this precaution that led to the injuring, and in some cases the permanent laming, of the hand, which was so prevalent among pianists a few years ago).
3. Discontinue pressure immediately after tone-production; continued pressure means unnecessary fatigue.
4. Use the whole weight of the arm for big tone-production.
5. Make use of a rolling motion of the elbow for throwing weight from one side of the hand to the other, or even from finger to finger.

dress set off by their white jewel-studded shirts and their ladies' elegant pale silk gowns, diamond tiaras, sapphire brooches and ruby necklaces.

At Covent Garden May and Violet steeped themselves in *Carmen, Faust,* and *Rigoletto,* going twice in the same season to see the new diva Nellie Melba as Marguerite, and twice again as Gilda. Their tastes were advanced. Violet admired Wagner, who was too strong meat and too novel for the more social of London's opera goers. With her mother she would go two nights in succession to performances of *Siegfried, Die Meistersinger* and *Lohengrin,* starstruck by Jean Lasalle, and even more so by the Wagner virtuoso Jean de Reszke. Violet, with her astonishing ear and memory for music, could, on returning from Covent Garden or St James's Hall, reproduce on the piano with total accuracy any passage that had caught her imagination.

If Violet's academic education was sporadic, there was nothing narrow in her cultural or social upbringing. Music, of course, predominated, but she was also introduced by May to the visual arts and the theatre, and in 1891, shortly before her twentieth birthday, she was presented at Court.[5] This ritual, which continued in London until 1958, marked both the assertion of upper-class connections and also the step from childhood – where an eighteen-year-old would still have been taking some of her meals in the nursery and her hair would have been worn loose with a band – into the adult world. Within a period of a few weeks of "coming out" Violet was deemed to have grown up. She was given her own lady's maid and was taken by May to M. Jean Stehr's salon in Oxford Street, where the proprietor made a study of Violet's face before cutting, crimping and twisting her thick hair, layer by layer, into a chignon (no doubt May noticed that the salon also offered tinting in private rooms "in the utmost secrecy").

Violet attended the Queen's first "Drawing Room", as it was known, of the London Season, arriving in a crush of carriages and curious sightseers at Buckingham Palace in the last week of March with a large group of other girls, all dressed in virginal white and accompanied by their mothers. Violet's dress, made by the couturier Madame Hodgson, was of white satin, draped with embroidered chiffon and caught up at the shoulder with bunches of white hothouse violets. Her train of rich white lace, lined with satin and chiffon, fell away from her neck to stretch out at least twenty feet behind her. In her right hand she carried a bouquet, also of white violets. May's dress, in the fashionable colour of the '91 Season, was in plum silk with purple tints. Once inside the Palace, there was a lot of undignified pushing and shoving to get near the front of the line, hand in the invitation

5 A debutante could only be presented by a matron who had herself been presented. It was not difficult for rich mothers to find suitable volunteers.

card and have one's name announced, for it was well known that Queen Victoria, by then almost a recluse, would only be present for the first half-hour of the proceedings. Afterwards Violet gave a formal tea with cucumber sandwiches and champagne. This tea party after being presented at Court was the one occasion in the Season when the guests were supposed to arrive before the hostess, who would make her way at an unpredictable hour from the Queen's Drawing-Room via two or three stops at the houses of friends and relations, showing to best advantage her Court dress and letting down her train to be admired.

James had been difficult about Violet's clothes, alternately haranguing May to keep the expenses under control and encouraging her to spare nothing that might contribute to his daughter's success. In the end the huge scale of the operation was like the assembling of a marriage trousseau. Required by social custom to change four times a day, Violet now possessed morning gowns and tea-gowns (less formal and, being looser at the waist, less restricting), gowns for afternoon carriage rides in Hyde Park and reception gowns for dinners and balls, not to mention capes, evening cloaks, hats, gloves, shoes and parasols.

After the presentation there followed an uninterrupted round of At Homes, musical soirées and balls until the end of July. Heavily chaperoned, the girls were watched over carefully to see that they only came into contact with "suitable" men. At such events, girls without brothers might for the first time be properly meeting a man of their own age. The purpose behind this social round was unambiguous: it was a marriage market, and the object of the exercise was to find a glorious match, preferably with someone rich, handsome and noble. The less glamorous girls and their mothers would gladly dispense with the looks and the title to settle for the security of a husband with enough money to keep them with a modicum of comfort. Anything – *anything* – was better than being left "on the shelf".

The Season of '91 was not considered one of the most brilliant, but it was obligatory to have been at Mrs Clarence Watson's June dance in Gloucester Square, where the rooms had been covered in flowers, with banks of geraniums, roses and ferns spraying out from the openings of fireplaces, drifting from the tops of mantelpieces and interlacing all the way up her wrought iron staircase; or to Mr George Paget's At Home at Hanover Square, where Herr Wurm's orchestra had been brought over from Vienna to rival the other fashionable "Blue Hungarian Band" which was playing at several parties; or to the novelist Miss Hugh Bell's party, to which most of the "*monde artistique*" were invited and where Violet was delighted, and just a little surprised, to see Mrs Beringer and her eldest daughter.

In between the parties Violet managed to find time for some serious music. She was introduced to the work of the Spanish pianist and composer Isaac Albéniz and his two compatriots, Tivadár Nachez and Enrique Fernandez Arbós, at a series of concerts organized by Albéniz at St James's Hall. In June she returned to St James's Hall to hear another Spaniard, Pablo de Sarasate, at that time the most famous violinist in the world, playing the Beethoven Violin Concerto. Violet's friend Giulia Ravogli was singing Ortrud in *Lohengrin* at Covent Garden with the de Reszke brothers, Jean and the younger Édouard, a bass. For some of the male "debs' delights" Violet's musical sophistication was daunting; to others it turned her into a more desirable challenge.

Immediately the Season was over Violet and Dorothy went to the Netherlands to see their In'tveld and Purvis relations in The Hague and Leiden. Their aunt, Annie Vijgh, hired an extra piano to enable Violet to continue practising, and arranged soirées to which local friends were invited to hear her play. The two sisters made a trip to Apeldam, visiting museums and the studio of Hendrik Mesdag, the Dutch collector and marine painter. Then they moved on to the Hôtel de Promenade at Scheveningen – a sort of Dutch Brighton, with its bathing machines and its quaint way of lining up rows of chairs at the water's edge for the hotel guests.

On her return to England, despite the absorbing interest of her musical advancement, Violet found herself growing restless. The restrictions of a Victorian household were becoming increasingly suffocating. Notwithstanding all her mother had done for her, they were not close to each other, nor had the passing of time done anything to bridge the gap between her and her father. She was, too, growing up in other ways. In 1892 she could not hide from herself that Wilhelm Ganz's daughter Adelina (named after her godmother, Adelina Patti) was exhibiting a more than ordinary affection for her. When Adelina and Violet were together, Dorothy felt uncomfortably excluded. But Violet was also wary, and something inside her warned her to keep the controlling upper hand in the relationship.

Ganz had been following Violet's musical progress since childhood. His interest was as much professional as avuncular and, as her talent matured, he encouraged her to contemplate a full-time musical career. For Violet, however, the growing ambition to play in public as a professional was confronted by the insuperable obstacle of parental disapproval. At the end of the nineteenth century it was almost unheard of for the unmarried daughter of a landowner – an ex-debutante, at that, who had been presented at Court – to take an artistic pursuit seriously, let alone to earn a living from it. To play occasionally in public as a gifted amateur, as Violet did in July 1893, in a supporting role to Oscar Beringer, was acceptable. A paid career on the stage was not. For once, James Gwynne said no to Violet. He would not, as a matter of principle contemplate the idea of letting his daughter achieve her aim. She must do what other attractive young ladies with prospects did, and find a husband.

Objectively speaking, Cornelia's and May's wonderful looks had not come down to Violet – "she had no features," as it was said in the family. Contemporary photographs show a hypnotic gaze with a highly charged expressiveness and a mouth which, on careful inspection, is resolute, humorous but at the same time rather stern in repose. She could switch her smile and her charm on and off, and her melodious voice could carry hard undertones. Yet her vivacious personality captivated anyone on whom she turned her full attention, and she knew how to make the most of her slender figure, sinuous grace of movement and compelling black eyes. She conveyed the illusion of beauty rather than the reality, but men seemed to be drawn to her all the more on this account. Nothing seemed more natural than that she should have her pick of eligible bachelors.

There is a letter in Violet's papers – a paradigm of its type – from a young man signing himself William T. Laisun asking whether, even though he would be away for four or five years, Violet could care for him enough "to be my wife at the end of that time. We are both young now and of course I know you will see many fellows before I come back. I do not wish to bind you in any way, but only to know if you can give me any hope." She received a number of such proposals, which she had no difficulty turning down, until the most suitable of marriages offered itself in 1893 in the person of Lord Gage, the owner of Firle Place, a large estate about ten miles from Folkington. The Gages were an old Sussex family who had built Firle in the 1480s and had enlarged and adapted it into a magnificent house in 1750. Henry, the fifth Viscount Gage, who was very musical, fell in love with Violet soon after she came out. He had been a regular visitor to Folkington, exchanging invitations to shoot and joining Gwynne family outings to the opera and the theatre. Slightly lame, he was slim and gentle and, although he was seventeen years older than Violet, in her parents' eyes the proposed match was ideal.

Violet had already half accepted him when she suddenly became desperate and begged her mother to help her escape. It was not so much that she did not feel a sufficient attachment to Henry Gage; she now abhorred the very thought of a conventional marriage. Her alarm dated from the moment when May had explained the facts of life to her. The shock of hearing what might be in store made her resolve never to undergo what her mother had so graphically described. Violet's change of heart came as a bitter blow to May who, frantic with dismay, did everything in her power to prevent the rupture. As a last resort Violet appealed to her father, who overruled May, saying that no daughter of his would ever be forced into marrying against her will – she would have his full support in breaking off the engagement. The letter Violet wrote to Lord Gage no longer survives, but the reply she received, sent by hand, was kind and dignified, and the two families remained friends.

Firle, Lewes, Sussex September 24th
Dear Miss Violet,
Your letter has been a great disappointment to me but hard as it is, it is far better than any thought that I had hurried you into a promise, that you were not quite certain of caring enough for me. Indeed if I thought for a moment that I had changed your life and not made you happy, this would be far worse than it is now. I think you good and true. God bless you.

Yours ever sincerely,
GAGE

# III

## *An Extraordinary Marriage*

BARRED FROM A PROFESSIONAL career, appalled at the prospect of a "normal" marriage, and still trapped within the confines of Victorian family life, Violet was forced to rethink her future. She was not prepared even to consider submitting to the stock role of an unmarried daughter in a wealthy family – unable to have guests without permission, confined to the house routine, living off a meagre allowance from her parents until middle age, then given a small sitting room of her own in return for nursing them in their dotage, before finally being expelled by the heir – in Violet's case presumably the oldest of her brothers to survive the wrath of her father. She had only to see the life of Aunt Kate or to visualize the fate of Dorothy to know that this was a destiny that she would do anything to avoid.

It was also frustrating for Violet to see that her female acquaintances from abroad suffered far less restriction than she and were not prevented by their parents from appearing in public. There was Adelina Ganz's sister, Georgi; Blanche Marchesi, daughter of the famous Parisian teacher, Mathilde Marchesi; Marchesi's still more illustrious pupil, and Adelina Patti's heiress apparent, Nellie Melba; and there were May's young friends Julia and Sophie Ravogli. When the Ravoglis came to stay, chaperoned by their mother, who spoke only Italian, it made Violet envious to realize that, for all their modesty and charm at Folkington, once they stepped on to the stage at Covent Garden the two sisters would be drowned in the adulation of the audience.

These were all singers, drawn to London as the new operatic centre. And now that British audiences were so much more knowledgeable than before, up-and-coming instrumentalists from all over the world also saw London as potentially the most elegant and sophisticated of European musical capitals. Foreign artists flocked to London, many of them string players from Spain, which was enjoying a period of exceptional musical attainment. Among these was a contemporary of Violet, Nettie Carpenter, an American violinist who had trained at the Conservatoire in Paris and was the only pupil of Sarasate. The two women soon became fast friends. Sarasate had been idolized by Violet since she had gone to one of his concerts two years previously and he was now at the peak of his career, having made his name throughout Europe, Russia and America for the purity, charm and passion of his playing. He had a huge repertoire, though it was the solos he had composed for himself that most drew the public to his performances. In 1892 Nettie took Violet to meet him privately. For two hours they played together. Afterwards they talked. Violet came away more than ever starry-eyed; and more than ever determined that one day the concert-going public should speak of her and Sarasate in the same breath.

Nettie knew everybody who was anybody in musical circles, and introduced Violet to all her brilliant group of fellow soloists, among whom the strongest single influence at the time was the charismatic Isaac Albéniz. Albéniz had thrown up his influential position as a teacher at the Conservatoire in Madrid to come to London, where he became an impresario and gave piano recitals, which often included his own evocative Spanish compositions. The liveliest and most extrovert of his coterie was Fernandez Arbós, who had arrived in London in 1891, having left his job as violin professor to the Queen of Spain, and had been conscripted by Albéniz into performing in a series of concerts at St James's Hall in London.

Nettie Carpenter often spoke to Violet of other musicians she had played with abroad – of Agustín Rubio, a cellist from the Queen of Spain's entourage, and Pablo Casals, the infant prodigy cellist from Catalonia. When Rubio, and later Casals, came to England, Violet felt she already knew them from Nettie's vivid descriptions. An adopted member of the Spanish crowd in London was the French singer, Guétary, as rumbustious and flamboyant a character as Arbós; both of them played regularly with Nettie and were to figure prominently in Violet's musical life. Nettie had no financial help from her family and was struggling to make a living. However much her talent was recognized – she had played several times at St James's Hall and at private evenings to enthusiastic audiences – male violinists achieved many more bookings than she could. Violet helped her tactfully, paying for her railway tickets and giving her small sums of money.

Persuasively as Violet explained to her father her vocation to play in public, James remained resolutely opposed. For Violet to perform on the stage was, in his eyes, practically tantamount to her being a loose woman. Ideas of female independence were gaining ground, but such topics as the "New Woman", currently in vogue, were only mentioned in hushed voices in the Gwynne household. If, a decade earlier, Ethel Smyth, the first notable woman composer in England, had forced her family to release her to study music in Leipzig, she had succeeded only by making life at home intolerable, refusing to go out or speak to anyone, and spending most of the day locked in her room (her brother remembered listening with delight from the back landing while her father kicked at her bedroom door). Such confrontational methods were not for Violet. The scenes which would follow any revolt would have required a physical and mental strength beyond even her will, for she had seen from James's treatment of Reginald how dangerous it was to cross him. There was, too, mounting tension between her father and Nevile, the next son in line, who had entered Gwynne & Co. and was theoretically training to manage the business for James, but was experiencing difficulty in collecting his niggardly salary from his father, let alone in being allowed to take any decisions. Nevile's money problems were all the more distressing because he was engaged to Bluebelle Wake, whose father, an admiral, had died young and whose own finances were no stronger than Nevile's; the way matters stood, it was questionable whether they could afford to get married. Violet was determined to get her way somehow, but she had no wish to be cast out, to become a struggling, impoverished musician like Nettie Carpenter. Her route to freedom must take a novel and imaginative form.

Violet's brother Rupert, only fourteen months her junior, was a gregarious young man. As a Cambridge undergraduate he had many friends, among them the shy Gordon Woodhouse, who, like Rupert, was going through the motions of studying history at Pembroke College (Nevile had also been at Pembroke five years ahead of Rupert, taking a degree in engineering). Gordon came from a wealthy Herefordshire family who had first set up as wine merchants in Liverpool and had for centuries owned vineyards in Sicily, from which they produced the Woodhouse marsala. He was an only son, with two older sisters, both unmarried and, according to Violet, notably plain and dull. His father having died when he was fifteen, he lived quietly with his sisters and his mother at Burghill, a large Georgian house near Hereford with parkland stretching to the foot of the Black Mountains. Gordon's tastes were rural; he was fond of hunting and a keen shot. Short and verging on the plump, with a broad and good-natured face, he had no pretensions to looks. He was cheerful, generous and the despair of his supervisor at Cambridge, who eventually had him sent down for repeatedly failing his exams. He worshipped Rupert, who was dashing, clever and, with his deep-set penetrating Gwynne eyes, attractive to women – all the things Gordon Woodhouse was not.

* * *

In the late summer of 1894, immediately after leaving Cambridge, Rupert
and Gordon held a house party together. Gordon's mother and two sisters
were away on their annual September holiday, leaving the house in
Herefordshire free, and since Gordon knew no personable young ladies
Rupert took charge of the guest list, asking his father to allow Violet to join
them. Permission was granted on condition that Violet was chaperoned
by her governess and accompanied by her lady's maid. For Violet it was a
party which was to echo through the years, for here she met Bill Barrington,
Maxwell Labouchère and Gordon Woodhouse – three men who were
subsequently to feature so prominently in her emotional life. And it was in
Gordon Woodhouse, the most improbable and least fashionable of the
three, that she found what she wanted.

Gordon was innocent of women, and in truth was not greatly interested
in them. The average debutante would scarcely have noticed him, but his
very ordinariness, his improbability as a suitor, were precisely the attributes
Violet was seeking. She saw his kind and sensitive side beneath his undergraduate manner, and she became determined to win him. Once she had
made up her mind she was unstoppable. Gordon was swept off his feet.
Within weeks he had proposed and Violet had accepted.

By becoming engaged to Gordon Woodhouse at the age of twenty-three,
Violet found the solution to all her problems. Her family had no inkling of
anything out of the ordinary. In July they had got Eva off their hands,
married to Charles Isaacson, an apparently well-to-do bachelor, half French,
and little younger than Eva's mother May. That had been a relief, for Eva
was not in the best of health. Then, only two weeks later, Nevile and
Bluebelle were finally married. To Violet's parents, therefore, her engagement to a man of means and good family, a friend of Rupert's recently down
from Cambridge, appeared as natural as it was desirable, especially after the
Lord Gage fiasco. On 7 November 1894 Violet wrote to her father:

> My Darling Papa,
> I am writing to tell you that Gordon asked me to marry him last
> night and I have accepted him, and I hope you will not mind,
> darling Papa. He is such a nice boy, and I think you would like him
> very much if you knew him better, but of course he is shy with you,
> and does not say much. I think I should be very happy with him,
> and I think he is very fond of me! Please do not read this letter to
> anyone but dearest Mother for I quite know it is a silly one but of

course it is rather difficult to write. I am quite sure you would like Gordon more if you knew him better. I like him more and more every time I see him. Eva says she has asked you to come up tomorrow. I don't expect you will be able to, but how delightful if you could, and darling Mother too. You know it is not that I do not love all of you most of all, but I could be with you so often, could I not, and it would be hardly like leaving home.

Now I don't think I can say any more but how much I love you both, and that whatever happens, I shall always be your most loving little daughter. Violet.

On the same day Gordon wrote to James Gwynne, expressing regret at having asked Violet's hand in marriage before obtaining her father's consent. Violet's parents evidently went to London on 8 November, where James had a man-to-man talk with Gordon, at the rather grand house of Eva and Charlie. They talked mainly about money and Violet's happiness. James's diary entry for that date shows how much easier he found it to communicate his affection for Violet to his diary than to her:

Saw J. Gordon Woodhouse at 37 Leinster Gardens, Eva's house today, in the dining room, after lunch, re his letter. Had an agreeable talk with him, told him I only wished for the happiness of my daughter Violet, that she had several offers, but had refused them and said she did not intend to marry anyone. He said he now had £4000 a year, and at his mother's death he would have £2000 a year more, with the house, land and farms – that he dearly loved Violet and had done so for some time past. His mother did not know yet, but he had written to her, and he promised to go and see her at the end of this week – she had always longed for his happiness and wanted him to get someone to make him happy. I said if he would bring his mother with him and come to see us at Folkington that we might make her acquaintance we should be very glad to see her and I should not like my daughter to be or go where she was not welcomed. I also said at my own wife's death Violet would have £500 or £600 a year settled on her, but until her death I would allow pin money, and I hoped he would buy or hire a house in Sussex, where we would be able to see a great deal of them, as we could not bear to have all our children taken away from us. He appeared happy and so did darling Violet. We came back to Folkington by the 3.27 train, the little brougham bringing us to

Victoria. Adelina Ganz came to see us off bringing a bunch of violets for us. I do pray the dear young people may be very happy. God bless them both.

Gordon's mother was torn between sadness at losing her son and a longing not just for his happiness but also for a loving relationship with Violet and the Gwynne family. Three of her letters from this period survive, the first written to Violet after learning from Gordon of his engagement:

*10 November, 1894.*
My Dear Violet
You must think that I have been neglectful in not writing before – from Gordon's letter I did not understand that he had had your father's consent to your engagement. Most heartily I do wish you every happiness and a long life with him, and I hope we may be mother and daughter in heart and mind.

My only son's choice must be very dear to me, you can hardly judge of all I am feeling. Your mother may. If I am not able to rejoice you must remember all I am losing out of my home – but when I see his happiness it will I hope take away all selfish sadness. I hear your kind mother wishes me to come to Folkington. I need hardly say how I long to see you and know you all. If well and the weather fit I should like to come with Gordon – but you must let me know what you wish because I could come later on.

With much love for yourself and your mother ever believe me
Yrs Affectionately                                    E.L. Woodhouse

The second letter from Mrs. Woodhouse is to Violet's mother, who had invited her in the most cordial terms to stay at Folkington:

*13 November 1894*
. . . I hope you will not mind my keeping to your first invitation and coming with Gordon on Thursday, for I fear if I did not it would be a long time before I should be able as neither of my daughters will be able to leave home and I should dread the journey alone, besides I do so wish to know Violet. You know and care for my son for your loving letters have made me long ago feel you appreciated him. I am not so fortunate and wish that we should meet and love each other as soon as we can, so will you forgive me for deciding to come on Thursday, and please do not make the least change in any of your plans, you must in no way treat me as a stranger. I shall be tired and

very ready to go to bed perhaps, as is often the case after a long journey, in common politeness.

If I and Gordon come alone I shall bring no maid. Now I must add how much I feel all your warm affectionate messages and how I trust we shall be united in affection as we shall be in interest in our two loved children. With love to all your family circle, believe me,

Yrs. affectionately                                              E.L. Woodhouse

Mrs Woodhouse's third letter reveals that, although she had made a friend in May Gwynne, she sensed that she had not done so in Violet. Nor had she. Violet's image of herself in the future as a combination of society hostess and artistic genius made for an uncomfortable relationship with Gordon's staid and pious mother. Violet even fancied that she was engaged to be married a little beneath her – if not beneath her sisters,[1] neither of whom did the debutante Season – but the truth was that she was able to summon up so little interest in the Woodhouses that she was genuinely surprised when, many years later, she learned how old and distinguished was Gordon's family.

*20th November*
My Dear Mrs. Gwynne.
You will like to know that I arrived safely here last evening after a pleasant journey. Gordon saw me in the train at Paddington. I was rather dismayed to find myself closed up with one gentleman knowing that as a rule they object to old ladies. However he turned out to be a most agreeable companion and I got a good deal of information about a society that you are also probably interested in "Travellers' Aid". What I heard may be of use to girls from our village who go unprotected to situations at a distance.

The book you lent helped to while away the time so that the journey did not seem long. It was piteous to see the floods in the Thames Valley and the rain again this morning will continue the damage. Dear Mrs. Gwynne I must thank you for the love you showed me. I was more touched by it that I can show. I know I was very undemonstrative and very often wished I could have shown

---

1 Dorothy never married. Eva's marriage to Charles Isaacson (which, like Violet's, was unconsummated) became a source of embarrassment when Charles's finances, which were not as robust as they had at first appeared, were undermined by Eva's desperate attempts to keep up with Violet.

how much I felt and how I longed for the love of your sweet flower. I do hope she will understand me better when she knows me more. I am quite sure I shall appreciate her . . . and with much love to each and all your family party, believe me, dear Mrs. Gwynne. Yours affectionately                                      Elinor Woodhouse

Unknown to her parents, let alone to Mrs Woodhouse, who innocently looked forward to grandchildren, Violet intended from the outset that her marriage with Gordon should be in name only. She had reached a critical point, for she was determined to find her freedom without controversy, and also without submitting to the unwanted embraces of a man. The way she had explained her position to Gordon was that she definitely did not want children. She sensed – might it have been an inference from something Rupert had said? – that Gordon, too, might well be content with a Platonic relationship. Admittedly, Gordon was unmusical, and on the surface the couple had little in common save their liking for the countryside. But he had money, an understated sense of humour, an interest in history, and the kind, affectionate, undemanding nature she was looking for in a permanent companion. Much more importantly, he seemed to lack the physical appetites she most feared.

In later years members of the family and close friends were given to understand that Gordon could never have been a husband in the full sense of the word; an unfortunate hunting accident was hinted at. A more revealing picture emerges, however, from three contemporary letters from Christabel Marshal, who was subsequently to write music criticism under the name of "Christopher St John" and to become a playwright, suffragette and campaigner for women's rights. Acutely sensitive about her cleft palate and heavy build, "Chris", as she signed herself, had the previous year started reading Classics at Oxford. After seeing Ellen Terry at the Theatre Royal in Bristol as Lucy Ashton in *Ravenswood* (a play based on Scott's *The Bride of Lammermoor*), Chris had bombarded the actress with love letters for four years, though she had received only occasional replies. When she met Violet in the Beringers' drawing-room, she instantly transferred her infatuation, as she was prone to do, and it is clear from her first letter, with its sapphic images, that her encounter with Violet had pitched her into the throes of another simmering, unresolved passion.

21 Great College Street Westminster
*May 9th 1895*
My Sweet Violet,
Your note of farewell welcomed me home that day. I could almost

feel your presence in the room as I read it and then could not feel sad. *Now* the blank is so terrible. At every turn I long for you.

Mrs. Ward has grown more and more fidgeting and the husband will compliment me which is so dreadful – still I may be able to bear it if other things are beautiful. I know you will try and let me go to concerts and operas with you sometimes ... and that will be a spring of immortality. I am going to Handel tomorrow night with a ticket I have had given to me, but I almost dread it without you. I feel like a fire when you are by my side.

The Greek testament with its moon-beauty of silver, and sprigged Bay leaves, is my lover, and comforts me. Every day it grows into my heart, and is as difficult to ship off as an idea – it can never be taken away from me.

I am going to write a little note to Gordon soon. Meanwhile my love to him.
                                                                    Your Chris

Even at this early stage in her life, Violet knew how to turn such feelings to her advantage. She had recently written to Chris putting an end to the intimacy of their relationship, but Chris was still lovesick and would do whatever Violet wanted. It might, Violet reasoned, be helpful from several standpoints if Gordon were to be alerted to his fate by another woman; apart from anything, it might clarify Gordon's own inclinations. Adelina would not do; she was too obviously close to Violet. Chris was more outspoken and at the same time more deniable. What better envoy for the delicate message Violet wished to convey?

In the second surviving letter, written just before the wedding, Chris warns Gordon, at first opaquely, then in increasingly direct terms, that his future with Violet can never be straightforward. Re-reading the letter now, a hundred years later, one is struck by its insidiously intrusive tone, as if Chris's private agenda is less to explain to Gordon than to disconcert him and, under the guise of forecasting a happy marriage, to sow the seeds of doubt as to whether he and Violet should be married at all. If that was what Chris secretly hoped, she was too late. Two days earlier, on 25 July , Gordon had put £10,000 of railway preference stocks, with an average coupon of just over 4 per cent, into a marriage settlement for Violet, with his cousin Arthur Woodhouse and Rupert Gwynne as trustees. The settlement specified that Violet had to go through with the marriage within six months if she was to collect the income, and that on her death the whole would revert to Gordon: about children it was silent.

21 Great College Street,
Westminster
*July 27th 1895*

Gordon dear – Today I felt I knew you better than ever before and I cannot resist writing to you about a few things which have been in my heart a long time. I want you to believe that as far as any woman can do I enter into your wonderful love for Violet – and that I can grasp something of what you feel about marrying her. She must always be more or less unaccountable. Genius can never be analysed or accounted for. Because of this I know you may have a difficult time when you are married. But I believe you will be strong enough to face the perplexity of it and not try as most men would to simplify it. You know what the child is to me – how the fire of her mind has kindled a light in my life which can never be put out. So I can talk to you unreservedly about her. I feel in a hundred ways now that she loves you – but not a bit as most women love men – she is always telling me new things she has found in your nature and her eyes blaze over them. There is no fear at all for either of you on the score of appreciation. But Gordon, (forgive me if I am wrong), I can't help seeing that the sweet child sees none of those things in marriage which most women take as a matter of course. Today I thought you understood that when you asked me to come to Taplow [where the couple were to stay after their wedding] on Friday. I love you for it. It argues an unselfishness which to me is extraordinary. Violet is so unconscious and original. She thinks it the most natural thing in the world for me to come – but I, because I have suffered a great deal in my life – am quick to see that an ordinary man would be annoyed. Gordon dear – you are not ordinary – I know it and I have finer instincts perhaps than you would believe. So you will be able to conquer the difficulties of our little brilliant Violet determining that the marriage shall not mean more to her than a close and familiar friendship. You will be patient. And you will be happy. This may all be a mistake, but I could not resist opening my heart to you. I am young but I have gone through a great deal. I have been face to face with terrible things. I hope they have not killed the child in me, only given me a keener insight into the troubles of other people's lives. You must always trust me, and tell me if you are troubled, Gordon. Forgive me if I have stirred up any vague unrest in your heart, which was not there before. You will know I only wrote out of a boundless desire that you should feel there was one person in the world who could enter into your life just now.

On the day of the wedding Chris wrote Gordon a last letter:

21 Great College Street Westminster
*July 31st 1895*
Dear – I thought I would put my letter to Violet inside a little note to you so as not to startle her at first. You know how I am with you both – and how I appreciate the noble unselfishness you showed all the time we were together today. I know your difficulties. Gordon, you have to enter into a position which a common man could not bear. Our little child with her fantastic soul must give you pain unconsciously by her own shrinking from what most natures take as they do their breakfast. I feel so poor and weak but I am with you and all that I have is yours.                    Yours always Chris

Whatever Chris's motives, the meaning of her letters is plain: there are other forms of love, and I have the distressing duty to tell you that, marriage or no marriage, Violet does not want you in her bed. We know nothing of Gordon's response and Chris seems to have reckoned without the possibility, intuitively grasped by Violet, that Gordon was no more eager to share Violet's bed than she his. What we do know is that from the moment they were engaged he became Violet's adoring companion, and that throughout his life he never gave the smallest indication of any resentment of his situation. It was Nevile's wife Bluebelle who best summed up the situation. Many years later, she told the author with wonderment how often it happened that even those who on first acquaintance were indifferent to Violet ended up in thrall to her – it was almost, said Bluebelle, as if she cast spells.

# IV

*Gordon Knew They Would Seldom Be Alone*

O N 30 JULY 1895 Gordon and Violet were married in London in the
family church of St Andrew's, Wells Street, not far from Harley
Street. Dorothy, an awkward eighteen at the time, "may not have looked her
best in a huge white hat with lovely sort of red and green *crêpe de Chine*", in
the words of Nevile Gwynne's daughter, Kit Ayling.[1] Roland, the youngest
member of the family, now twelve, was a page, a pretty boy, his fair hair kept
by his mother in long curls: for the ceremony he was taken out of the skirts
he generally wore – until the age of thirteen – and put into satin knicker-
bockers. Violet was given away by her father, while Rupert, of course, was
Gordon's best man.

Even if her clothes were unflattering, still the day was made for Dorothy
by Gordon's thoughtfulness and personal generosity:

> . . . Gordon dear has given me the most perfectly exquisite present
> I have ever seen almost, it is a diamond pendant and can be made
> into a brooch, it is in a sweet pale blue velvet case, and also a dear
> little gold charm to wear in a pale blue satin case. Bobo didn't want
> any rice thrown, so we didn't throw any. I wore bronze shoes and
> stockings, and white suede gloves.

The difference in standing between the two families was established
with brutal clarity from the moment that Violet changed out of her wedding dress into her going-away outfit, looking, as Dorothy noted, ". . .
quite charming . . . wearing a dress of white muslin trimmed with white
lace and pink silk". Mrs Woodhouse and her two daughters spent the
day after the wedding with Violet's sister Eva and her husband Charlie.

1 Kit Ayling's unpublished memoirs of her father's family are a rich, if sometimes ill-
documented, fund of reminiscence, history and anecdote, tinged with resentment against
her grandfather James and her uncle Roland, and not unduly favourable to Violet. Kit's
beauty and youth gave rise to occasional rivalry with Violet.

Violet's parents, however, together with Rupert, Dorothy, Roland and Adelina Ganz, joined the honeymoon couple at Skindles Hotel, Taplow, in Buckinghamshire. After lunch they all sailed up and down the Thames "in a boat worked by electricity", then took a picnic tea on the riverbank before returning to the hotel, where a fly was waiting to take the Gwynnes to the station. Violet and Gordon escorted them to the platform and asked Dorothy to spend the night with them, but her parents would not allow it. Dorothy was crestfallen, the more so because Adelina Ganz was staying on. It was a long summer evening and Violet and Gordon were elated at the success of the celebrations. After a late supper they sat outside on the veranda with Adelina, watching a display of fireworks which lit up the Thames and laughing and reminiscing until long past midnight.

Gordon had realized before the wedding that he would rarely have Violet to himself. After all, it was he who had invited Chris to Taplow, though unlike Adelina she had in the end thought it best not to come. Now, as the bridal pair moved on to Holland, they parted company temporarily with Adelina but were joined by Violet's aunts Kate and Tina, who did not consider it out of place to choose this time of year to pay their annual visit to their sister Anne Vijgh in Leiden. In Violet's eyes marriage to Gordon had changed very little, except to give her social and financial independence from her parents. She caused a mild stir at the Hotel Garni in Scheveningen by signing the registration book in her maiden name. Nor did she see the need to suppress the self-centred side of her character. A letter inserted in Dorothy's diary at the entry for 12 August 1895 shows her at her most spoiled:

> . . . I had a very sad accident. I must tell you that Gordon had bought a railway rug just before starting for Holland, and he spread it over one of the chairs last night, and I sat down on it in my beautiful dress and when I got up it was all covered over with patches of green, from the horrid rug, and I never noticed anything till Aunt Tina, with the usual Purvis short sight, said "Oh, Violet, what beautiful green embroidery you have on your dress!" And I discovered it was all stained. You may imagine how angry I was with Gordon, and he is going to take it into The Hague tomorrow, and if he can't get it cleaned, he will get me a new one just like it. It is so horrid, for now I have no evening dress with me, to wear at the Opera at Dresden . . .

Gordon took the honeymoon in his stride. He enjoyed making himself useful, organizing a box at the opera house in Dresden, ordering a piano for Violet at the hotel, meeting her Dutch relations (and getting them to send round a hip bath for her), arranging tickets and in general seeing to Violet's every need. He was in a particularly sunny mood when he wrote to Dorothy:

> We are so well and are having such a time. I have seen all the Dutch cousins and everybody and we have chosen a piano which came today . . . You would hardly recognise Violet she looks so well and bewitching, at present at 11 a.m. she is sitting by me fast asleep in a comfortable chair in her pink tea gown and her hair streaming down her back and a bag of sweets in her lap in fact a regular pose and as the people pass by the front windows they gaze at her in awe and wonder and then walk silently on. I hope you are enjoying yourself at Ascot, I wonder if you miss us all, does anyone pinch and tease you? Oh we are enjoying ourselves. Aunt Kate has just come in to pay us a morning call and found V asleep . . . I hate the meals here for we have lunch at 12 and dinner at 5.30 and in neither case are we ready at all. Was it not funny there is only one bath in the hotel, but V and I get it first and keep it for a long time and keep everybody else waiting, but now Uncle has sent us up one from his house so we are better off. V's room is rather small (you know how she likes a small one) so she has to take hers in my room. We have a charming sitting room looking over the sea and opening straight onto the parade.

It was as much a tour as a honeymoon. Scheveningen was within a few miles of Violet's uncles and aunts in The Hague and Leiden, and now it was time to visit Germany, which she had come to think of almost as her spiritual home. They went first to Dresden, where Adelina rejoined them, armed with introductions for Violet, then on to the Wagner Festival in Bayreuth, and finally to Leipzig and Berlin, where again the Ganzes had arranged for her to meet musicians and others whom they thought might interest her. When the Channel ferry brought the three of them back to Dover, Violet and Gordon had been abroad for six weeks.

In London Gordon had taken 6 Upper Brook Street, a large Georgian house in the fashionable centre of town near Hyde Park, with stables for six in a mews at the back. The house was large enough both for entertaining and for accommodating Violet's favourite brother Rupert, who was reading for the Bar and, like all James's sons, was too short of cash to afford his own flat. The square drawing-room, which occupied most of the first floor, was on a grand scale and of exceptional elegance and originality, with a ceiling of advanced Pompeian taste designed by the eighteenth-century architect Samuel Wyatt, incorporating marbled panels and small painted or plaster relief figures of winged griffins and Graces. On the marble fireplace similar figures on pedestals held up bowls of fruit and flowers. Violet had ambitious plans to use it also as a music room, to which she would invite people for matinées and soirées, followed by teas or buffet suppers. She had inherited all the musical friends and connections which her mother had originally made, to which she had added many new ones of her own. May herself, however, was no longer much to be seen in the artistic world into which she had introduced her daughter. James had virtually retired to the country, and without the stimulus of Violet's presence the once frequent visits by musicians to Folkington dried up. It was almost as though it had been May's mission in life to launch Violet on her way and, once this had been accomplished, to fade into the background.

Gordon was a man who to a large extent lived through others. At Cambridge he had lived through his friends, now he lived through Violet. The year before his engagement he had accepted the position of Deputy Lieutenant of Herefordshire, but after his marriage he cut down the performance of his duties to the bare minimum, Violet having made it clear that she had no intention of playing the role of the Deputy Lieutenant's dutiful wife. Her influence affected every aspect of Gordon's existence. As soon as she returned from the honeymoon she had him change his surname by deed poll to Gordon Woodhouse, so that she became Violet Gordon Woodhouse and he – though nobody could ever get it right – became officially Gordon Gordon-Woodhouse, with a hyphen.

In the autumn of 1895 Gordon took a lease on Wootton Manor, the property James Gwynne had bought, with nearby Folkington, in 1876. This arrangement was convenient for everybody. James would be spared the expense of repairs; Violet would be near her family; and Gordon would have a much needed refuge from London, for he chafed at having to put in long stretches there because of Violet's musical career. He was only truly at ease in the countryside, to which he escaped for a day's shooting whenever he could. Dorothy was irked at the sight of Gordon letting his life revolve around her sister, and her diaries, full of fond accounts of his visits to Wootton, paint a misleading picture of what she had assumed was a saddened man, bravely tolerating a subservient position. What coloured Dorothy's views and led her judgement astray was the fact that she herself was secretly rather in love with Gordon: she could never bring herself to accept that he actually preferred the modest supporting part of a man married to a woman more remarkable than himself; a man charged with shielding Violet from the boring everyday demands of the ordinary world and for whom it was enough just to hold a secure place in her affections.

Once he had shed an initial reserve, Gordon was a man of high spirits, an electrifying dancer[2] with an unexpected grace and firmness of command in the waltz. Dorothy's description of their Christmas fancy dress party at Folkington in 1895 shows Violet sulking and Gordon having a tremendous time in a setting which was a far cry from the sophistication of their London existence:

> We cleared the drawing room, and at about 7.15 we had dinner; I dressed underneath but put on a silk blouse for dinner. We dressed after; we powdered our hairs, Mother, Adelina, Sibyl, Blue and I; there was not much rouge, so I used beetroot and it looked quite nice; we wore patches. I wore white satin; I do like powdered hair so much. The dance was supposed to begin at nine, but it didn't start till after nine thirty . . . . It was worth something to watch some of the couples. Mrs. Waller had a fall in the first dance . . . Gordon appeared very soon after it began, looking quite charming in his [hunting] pink, the men all wore their pinks; I danced twice with Mr. Wilde, twice with Mr. Maitland, a barn dance and a polka with Gordon, he is just like an India rubber ball, I simply love dancing with him, it is a different feeling to anyone I have ever danced with; Mr. Maitland took me into supper, he is so dull and heavy, but Gordon sat on the other side. Bobo appeared during the ninth dance, and was a regular wet blanket, I really can't think why she came, she danced No 13 with Gordon, and unfortunately Roley [Roland] knocked her cheek with his elbow and she went upstairs and almost immediately took her departure, taking Gordon too of course, it was such a pity she came.

In Upper Brook Street, however, Gordon was a different man. Dorothy had been staying with them just before Christmas, when it seemed to her that Violet spent less time with her husband than with "Boy", as Rupert was known:

> Gordon wants to have a day in the country, so I am going to stay

---

2 Dorothy, who rarely had enough opportunity to indulge her own love of dancing, was sometimes reduced to waltzing alone in her room.

here with Bobo as otherwise he could not go, I am very sorry to miss Father's and Mother's wedding day, but I am sorry for poor Gordon, I hate to see him leading the life he is doing all day, he sits in a big arm chair in front of the fire, and smokes and reads, it must be very bad for him at his age to lead such an indoor listless life, and the poor boy loves the country so; then Boy seems to take his place in many ways and Gordon is so wonderfully sweet, he never seems to resent it, it is so bad for a young man to live in London and have nothing to do.

Wootton was Violet's first opportunity to create a home in the country. Although twenty years later it was to be converted and enlarged by Rupert into a sizeable country house, it was as an unrenovated farmhouse that Violet and Gordon took it on. Its ancient entrance door faced due east towards the downs, which loomed over the nearby trees and roofs of Folkington. Wootton was like a tiny village, there were so many outhouses and cottages, loosely linked by courtyards and paths leading through arched passages. The rectangular main building, rebuilt on Saxon foundations in the seventeenth century, was on three floors, with a gabled front and two large rooms on either side. In a forecourt a few yards from the door stood the remains of a medieval private chapel dedicated to Saint Giles. The cobbled stableyard was flanked by large barns, used to house carriages. From the top floor you could see over the downs to the English Channel at Pevensey Bay, where William the Conqueror had landed in 1066, and to the north lay the fields and deep wooded countryside leading to Hailsham. The nearest shopping town was Eastbourne, four miles away on the coast, then one of the most fashionable resorts in England.

Gordon was in Herefordshire on official duty when the building work at Wootton was due to start, but Violet was unconcerned – she knew how to get others in her family to do the dull practical tasks for her. She was far more interested in trying her hand at furnishing and decoration.

*Saturday.* My own Darling Gordon,
Thank you very much for your own delightful letter. It was most good of you to write so soon, and I was surprised to hear from you by the first post.

How delightful if the house comes off all right. You ask who had better be left to see after it till you come back. Don't you think if you quite decide on it, the drains and roof could be attended to first, and of course there need not be the least hurry about decorations, papers, paintings or anything else, till you come back, when we could do all that ourselves. Certainly I should think the drains with the roof, would take quite a month, and for that you might ask Nevile or Boy, or Eva and Charlie to have a look. Any of these would do for them, I should think, and you could tell them nothing else need be done till you come back. Don't you think this a good plan, as then nobody need interfere in the least with all the nice part and I suppose the drains and roof would be better looked after by a sort of practical person who knows about things of that sort, than people like you and me, and there cannot be any scope for artistic taste in their arrangement and repairing!! Now I really think this quite a businesslike letter so far. Oh! sweet Gordon, I do miss you so much.

Most of the themes and colours which pervaded Violet's later houses originated at Wootton. The rooms were richly panelled, with dark mahogany or early chinoiserie furniture. In antique shops in country towns she found seventeenth-century oak chests, refectory tables and a set of chairs made with hand-cured Russian leather fixed to the frame with tiny brass studs, the heaviness of the oak softened by being interspersed with lighter eighteenth-century pieces. Her carpets, chair-covers and curtains contained hints of red and ochre, which fused with smoky blues and greys to produce a warm, enticing atmosphere. Her pictures, like the fabrics which she draped over her tables and musical instruments, repeated the same autumnal tones. It was said of the Dutch settlers in Indonesia that, unlike the English in India, who looked at the country with the imagination of a writer, they saw their Eastern possessions with the eye of a painter. Violet's houses had the aura of Renaissance interiors; it is perhaps not too far-fetched to detect in them the In'tveld strain in her ancestry.

Much as she was enjoying her new role as mistress of the household, despatching Gordon to the auction rooms, choosing domestic staff and experimenting with designs and fabrics, Violet was by no means distracted from her music. She practised every day without fail for two hours after breakfast and an hour and a half after lunch, or longer if a new piece or a point of technique required it. She still took occasional lessons from Beringer and was becoming a complete performer, but she was not yet quite certain of her final métier. Her training on the piano had followed the classical German school and her repertoire was typical of the period – Brahms, Chopin, Mendelssohn, Beethoven, Tchaikovsky – but she had an exploring spirit and was restless within traditional confines. She played modern composers such as Fauré; she perceived the depths in Mozart that her contemporaries, misled by his light charm into thinking him superficial, astonishingly overlooked; she saw the pure architectural quality of Bach behind the pompous orchestral manner in which he was then invariably performed; and recently she had been reading with interest about the pre-classical, early music concerts and lecture-recitals which Arnold Dolmetsch[3] had been giving in private houses or in his borrowed studio in Fitzroy Street.

A century ago instruments such as the viola d'amore, the harpsichord and the spinet were seen mainly in museums, while the works of early composers were hardly ever played on the instruments for which they had been written. Arnold Dolmetsch's study of the history of performance practice and his re-creation and playing of original instruments were giving him a reputation as a revolutionary. His ambition was to break the mould, reviving sixteenth- and seventeenth-century music and placing it in its historical context, purged of later romantic accretions. His most influential supporter was Bernard Shaw, the outspoken columnist of the *World*, not yet known as a playwright, but already given to outrageous paradox. Thirsting for new initiatives and dissatisfied with the conventional repertoire, Shaw had been the first music critic to recognize in Dolmetsch's ideas a possible catalyst for change. Shaw's view – that, by looking into the past, audiences would become more open to modern music – might seem idiosyncratic, but others shared it, including Fuller Maitland,[4] the powerful critic of *The Times*.

By the mid 1890s, Dolmetsch's performances were starting to catch on in artistic circles. Poets, writers and painters were excited as much by the fasci-nating details emerging from his research into musical history as by the gentle, pure sound of his instruments. Some, to be sure, went mainly for the show. Barely five feet tall, dark and volatile, with burning eyes and a Vandyke beard, he wore silver-buckled shoes and a velvet suit with lace ruffles. His family, who also affected period dress, were talented instrumentalists and went with him everywhere. To play Elizabethan music he had not merely reinvented Elizabethan instruments, he had reinvented an Elizabethan family

3 Born in France, Dolmetsch came to London in 1883 at the age of twenty-five to study the violin at the Royal College of Music. Almost immediately he began his researches in the British Museum into ancient and forgotten music, especially Elizabethan music. In his spare time he scoured junk shops searching for early instruments, and in 1890 he decided to devote his life to the "authentic interpretation of early music on the instru-ments for which it was written". He obtained and restored a spinet; then a Kirckman double-manual harpsichord; then a set of Italian virginals; and for several decades he continued to expand the range of instruments which he restored, built and played.
4 Fuller Maitland, for twenty-two years (1889-1911) music critic of *The Times*, was one of England's foremost music scholars, as well as being a talented harpsichordist and pianist.

to play them, and placed the whole event on stage as a theatrical display.

For a while Violet's interest had been academic, but when she went to her first Dolmetsch concert in 1896, the sound of early music played on his instruments came as a revelation, showing her possibilities which were to change the whole direction of her artistic life. She immediately arranged to take lessons with him, and after that went to his house regularly, first in Keppel Street, then in Bayley Street (both in Bloomsbury), quickly mastering the harpsichord, the clavichord, the virginals and the spinet. She also extended her repertoire to include works by Corelli and Domenico Scarlatti and by early English composers such as John Dowland, Purcell and Matthew Locke. Dolmetsch confirmed all her instincts about Bach (whose works were still being discovered and whose reputation had not yet approached the pinnacle which it later came to occupy), finding that his music was transformed when played in authentic period style.

Before each of his concerts Dolmetsch would circulate printed notices preparing his audiences for the results of his recent finds. Violet followed his researches avidly, keeping herself up to date with his discoveries and his transcriptions of neglected or misinterpreted compositions. With the exception of Sir George Grove, the originator and editor of *Grove's Dictionary of Music and Musicians,* the musical establishment initially regarded Dolmetsch as little more than a curiosity, and Violet and Blanche Marchesi were almost the only practising musicians who attended his early concerts. There Violet met an unfamilar crowd – the painters Edward Burne-Jones, William Rothenstein, Roger Fry and Walter Crane, the novelist George Moore, the actress Mrs Patrick Campbell and, of course, George Bernard Shaw, who, as one of the original discoverers of Dolmetsch, had not missed any of his concerts between 1893 and 1895.

Soon Violet became important to Dolmetsch both as a client for his instruments, since he was chronically short of money, and as an exponent of his ideas. In 1899 she ordered a harpsichord[5] from him and offered him her London drawing room for a winter concert, on the condition that he would sell the tickets from his own house. A printed programme survives, advertising tickets for sale at 10/6d from Mr Arnold Dolmetsch, 7 Bayley Street,

5 This was Violet's first harpsichord, originally made by Thomas Culliford in the workshop of Longman and Broderip in 1785. According to Mabel Dolmetsch, initially Arnold's assistant and later his wife, it "ingeniously evolved through the adaptation of an ancient single-manual instrument into one with two keyboards, and manifold tonal effects". Arnold's name was inscribed in his handwriting upon a corner of the wrest-plank, something he did "only at the urgent request of a few privileged customers such as Violet Gordon Woodhouse". In 1991 the present owner set about restoring it to its original single-manual condition with the intention of retaining the Dolmetsch keyboards.

Bedford Square, and inviting people to:

A PROGRAMME OF MUSIC
To be performed at MR ARNOLD DOLMETSCH'S
Concert, being the last of a winter series, to
be given at 6, Upper Brook Street, by
kind permission of Mrs Gordon
Woodhouse, on Thursday
evening, 14th Decem-
ber, 1899, at 8.30
o'clock.

Although this was to be a public concert, Violet prepared as if for a private occasion. A small library, planned as Gordon's smoking-room, led off her drawing-room. By letting down a thick green velvet curtain in front of the archway, Violet turned the library into a retiring chamber, from which the Dolmetsch family emerged in Elizabethan costume onto a raised dais where the harpsichords stood. There being no electricity in the house, the drawing-room was lit by two statues holding oil lamps in the niches on either side of the double doors, and by pale violet-coloured wax candles set on the green-striped walls in flat brass sconces. Since no paintings could compete with the beautiful ceiling, Violet had hung the room with silhouettes on glass and engravings in low tones of brown, grey and black. The dark, polished boards of the uncarpeted floor gleamed in the candlelight, and high piles of cushions haphazardly filled the window seats.

During the day Gordon had arranged the flowers – ferns, roses and lilies – brought up from the hothouses at Wootton. The guests were invited for half-past seven, an hour before the concert, and were offered cheese croutons, sandwiches, ice creams and white wine, the idea, not altogether successful, being to avoid an unseemly later rush for the buffet. Violet's room could seat fifty and the audience was allowed to overflow on to the landing and the staircase. The concert was a success, raising well over £30 for Dolmetsch, equivalent to some £1,500 today.

Violet played the Thomas Culliford harpsichord which Dolmetsch had adapted for her earlier in the year, and he had brought with him two more harpsichords for himself and his second wife, Elodie, whom he had married in 1897. The first part of the concert consisted of pieces by Locke, Handel and Telemann; the second part was devoted to Mozart and Bach. Violet played a Handel chaconne and accompanied an aria from the same composer's *Sosarme*, then with Dolmetsch and Elodie played the Concerto in C Major for three harpsichords by Bach, the "orchestra" being a string quintet of two violins, viola, cello and violone.

By 1899, Dolmetsch's obsessional approach, and the support of his growing army of admirers, had severely dented the indifference of the musical establishment. The cognoscenti were now divided into two camps: those who agreed with him that early compositions should be played on the instruments for which they had been written; and those who believed in "Progress", that quintessentially Victorian notion wherein the piano was held to represent a higher civilization by the mere fact of being both more modern and more advanced than most other instruments. Dolmetsch's opponents were infuriated by his claim that the piano was a degenerate version of the clavichord, while his habit of ridiculing Progress, citing Bach as evidence that there had been no improvement in the last 150 years, was held to be beyond the pale and musically decadent. Shaw was much satisfied with this turn of events – at last he had in Dolmetsch the innovator and controversial figure for whom he had long hoped.

Violet was still principally known to audiences as a pianist, but by 1899, under the influence of Dolmetsch, she had allowed the harpsichord to gain at least an equal place in her affections. Her early attempts on the clavichord had also made a deep impression on her. She was beginning to feel that her true vocation might be the performance on these older instruments of the music of composers up to the time of Mozart. Although her playing of the whole range of keyboard instruments was by now up to the best professional standards – and she was determined to drive herself higher still, to the levels of a Busoni or an Anton Rubinstein – her audiences were private. Violet preferred it like that. She wanted the best of both worlds: the gracious lifestyle of the gifted amateur; and the skill, and ultimately the acclaim, of the international virtuoso. The harpsichord and, to an even greater extent, the clavichord, had for her the special attraction of being designed for stately chambers, rather than the concert hall; and she had found in Bach, Domenico Scarlatti and Mozart composers of consummate genius, to whom she knew it was worth dedicating the rest of her career.

Dorothy's diary records that Violet again appeared with Dolmetsch in a chamber concert on 28 November 1900, with Nettie Carpenter on the violin, Agustín Rubio on the cello and Harrison Brookbank singing – evidently she was trying to bring her Spanish (and "honorary Spanish") friends round to Dolmetsch's virtues. After that, however, though Violet eventually became the supreme exponent of his musical ideas, she and Dolmetsch rarely played together in public. Both had a liking for being centre stage; moreover, she was liable to be upset by his violent temper and domineering personality, which were perhaps too reminiscent of her father. Her musical tastes were the more catholic and the range of her repertoire was incomparably wider. She had no time for Dolmetsch's dogmatic zealotry, which led him to understate the debt he owed to other scholars, in particular Ernst Pauer,[6] and to dismiss all music after Mozart as "noise". Even stylistically they drew apart, for Violet increasingly found his tempo rubato[7] too heavy, but although they now went their separate ways they stayed in close and friendly contact. Violet became one of the best customers for his instruments, and they wrote to each other frequently on musical questions.

The years immediately following Violet's marriage had bustled with activity. Apart from setting up Wootton and Upper Brook Street, learning to play new instruments, discovering early music and refining her piano technique, Violet also transformed her appearance. Able for the first time to buy whatever she wanted, she quickly developed a style of her own. Most of her clothes were made at the Bond Street shop of Lady Warwick, who, to the consternation of the old-fashioned, had taken to trade, the title "Countess of Warwick", inscribed in large gold letters beneath the bow window of her establishment announcing that the owner's nobility was not so much a guilty secret as a business asset. In Old Burlington Street Violet also patronized Lady Warwick's competitor "Madame Lucile", owned by Lady Duff Gordon. There she ordered the latest fashionable outfit, a walking costume, consisting of a tight-fitting bolero with a matching narrow skirt gathered to fall wider and longer at the back. Violet's subtly coloured, high-collared blouses were finished in intricate detail, with piped edges, panels and layers of lace or narrow folds of muslin cut on the cross. Within a few years she had accumulated a vast wardrobe, which Dorothy observed with mixed awe and envy:

> *3 May 1899* Bobo showed me some lovely clothes of hers, I never saw anyone with such a quantity, then she brought out of her cupboard a very pretty dressing gown which she proceeded to put on to show me. I asked her if it had been very expensive, "O no", she said "about five guineas!"

If Violet liked to buy clothes, and to acquire them as presents, she equally liked giving them away, for impulsive generosity was one of her more endearing qualities. Dorothy was often on the receiving end:

> *8 July 1900* . . . In the afternoon Ella Pollock[8] and I went to Bobo's

6 Pauer (1826-1905), a copy of whose *Old English Composers for the Virginals and Harpsichord* Violet owned from 1919, was an Austrian pianist and an eminent teacher and scholar, who spent most of his career in England.
7 Flexibility of tempo within a phrase of music.

room and she showed us some of her lovely clothes, what exquisite ones she has, her taste is wonderful . . . Bobo gave me such a lovely opera cloak of hers tonight, it is what I wanted more than anything, as my old blue one is hardly fit to wear and has got so shabby, and this came like an answer to a wish; it is a pale sort of heliotrope, long and has sleeves, it is much trimmed with chiffon and fits me fine, it is so nice to have a decent cloak, I like long cloaks infinitely better than capes. She first gave me a brocade cape, and then much to my joy she gave me this instead. She also gave me a little red dressing jacket, and a little bit of brown lace for a collar.

More than anything, Violet paid attention to her accessories – her gloves, belts and shoes, her velvet-lined hats rimmed in silk and banded in satins; and her parasols, some so finely embroidered that on dark backgrounds the patterns appeared like pale transfers. In summer, cream silk shades, stitched with blue- or red-flowered borders and a spray of coloured dots, opened from their slim bamboo shafts, which had satin bows threaded through their handles, allowing a glimpse of a silk lining of the palest blue. There were other parasols for darker dresses – white appliqué lacework on black silk, or plain shot silk in blue and ochre – the shafts of ebony, the knobs and handles tipped with mother-of-pearl, silver, china or ivory. Instead of bows, silken tassels or plaited braids were threaded through the handles to fall gracefully down the wrist.

Violet also started to collect jewellery and costume jewellery. Her earrings would hang an inch or two below her lobes, often two or three pearl baubles held by fine-meshed gold chains, or layers of many-coloured enamel panels in oblong shapes cascading down from her ears. She once found a pair, almost too heavy for her ears, which had orange glass goldfish floating in tiny water-filled glass bowls. Her hair, which had previously been set close to her head, was arranged each morning in a series of wide, softly folded curls, creating a flattering frame to her face. Dressing for the day, even with her lady's maid to help, became a lengthy and elaborate process.

While Gordon's prim relations were shocked by Violet's extravagance, Dorothy and the other Gwynnes watched with alternating amusement and dismay.

*19th September, 1899,* Lunch and then Bobo played some lovely

8 Ella Pollock, a highly strung musical friend of Violet, became helplessly infatuated with Rupert. When she tried to burst into his bedroom, May and Aunt Kate had to summon her mother by telegram. She had a nervous breakdown, from which, happily, she recovered completely.

> lovely waltzes . . . Just as they were going, Father began to laugh at
> Bobo with all her ornaments and chains and said she never would
> put on ornaments of any kind before she was married. Bobo said she
> had none to wear . . .
>
> *June 1st 1900* Father came back from the station and said "Bobo's
> face was just a mass of powder and paint, you could see it a long way
> off it was so thick". He has such a hatred of powder or anything put
> on the face. He was quite disgusted at the spectacle.

Violet's concern for her clothes and adornments may have seemed self-
indulgent to her family, but, consciously or subconsciously, much of it was
preparation for her career as a performer. She knew where her destiny lay,
and already sensed the need to put across to her listeners an image in which
personality, style and musical expression would combine to maximum effect.
She was turning herself into a jewel, one which would be all the more
precious for lying just out of reach.

Apart from her own instruments, and those belonging to Dolmetsch,
there were very few privately owned, working harpsichords or clavichords in
the London of the day, so that Violet was obliged to give most of her
drawing-room performances on the piano. The soirées of the fashionable
were haunted by talent-hunters. It was at Georgi Ganz's concert in
Viscountess Helmsley's Pont Street house that Violet had first been noticed
by Alfred Schultz-Curtius, an impresario best known for his annual Wagner
Concert Season at the Princes Gallery in Piccadilly. A little later, in
1900, she was wooed by another important figure from Germany, Edwin
Bechstein, who had recently arrived in London to oversee the building of
the Bechstein Hall in Wigmore Street, and was pursuing an aggressive
publicity campaign. It was not only Violet's playing abilities which impressed Schultz-Curtius and Bechstein, but also her mesmeric appearance, in
which, as hard-headed businessmen, they recognized the commercial potential. Both men energetically set out to persuade her to perform in public.

By the summer of 1899, with four years of marriage behind her, Violet's
musical evenings had achieved a kind of cult status. People begged shamelessly for invitations to her parties. She held court in Upper Brook Street
from Easter until the end of July, and again in the late autumn until
Christmas. During the traditional holiday periods she filled Wootton
with neighbours and with visitors from London. Yet even as the adulation
grew and her musical powers approached fulfilment, her private life
was assuming a form that was to be the cause of scandal, and of prurient
speculation, until the day she died.

# V

## A King Among Men

H EIR TO A VISCOUNTCY and descended from a distinguished family
of judges who, in 1722, had inherited Beckett, a large estate near
Shrivenham in Oxfordshire, the Honourable William Shute Barrington[1]
was the eldest of three brothers and three sisters, all close in age, glamorous-
looking and, by every account, devoted to each other. Delicate as a child and
thought to be vulnerable to tuberculosis, he had been educated privately in
Switzerland. He was no scholar, and his relations were fond of telling, with
affection, the story of his return: asked whether he had learned French, Bill
replied that he knew two words, "*oui*" and "*non*", but was not sure which was
"yes" and which was "no". At Trinity Hall College, Cambridge, he devoted
most of his time to cricket and athletics, avoiding any attempt at gaining a
degree. He had first met Violet and the rest of the Gwynnes in 1892 at the
age of nineteen, when he had gone with Henry Gage to shoot at
Folkington, and he had come to know Gordon at university through their
shared friendship with Violet's brother Rupert.

Bill was tall and fair, with golden hair, blue eyes, and classically handsome
features. Kit Ayling likens him in his youth to the hero of a popular novel by
Ouida, "*bel à faire peur*". To Dorothy, fascinated by his looks and his elegant,
often all-black, clothes, he seemed irresistibly charming, "a king among
men". He had considerable presence, bearing himself well, moving effort-
lessly and holding people's eyes with a steady gaze. In character he was
gentle, sensitive and artistic, and was a good amateur watercolourist and
architectural historian. He radiated relaxed confidence, and had about him
the air of a man at ease with himself.

As to what happened to bring scandal into Violet's marriage, the story

---

1 Bill Barrington's father was the tenth Viscount Barrington. One of the family's more
illustrious ancestors was the lawyer, antiquary, naturalist and musician the Hon. Daines
Barrington (1727–1800), who tested the child prodigy Mozart's ability to sight read on his
first visit to England in 1764.

which, many years later, she told her confidante, Winifred Blow, was a simple one. Gordon, worried that Violet might find her life dull alone with him in the country, invited his amusing friend Bill Barrington, whom she already knew slightly, to stay and entertain her. Bill duly arrived at Wootton, but on the third day told Gordon that something terrible had happened – he had fallen in love with Violet and he had to leave immediately. "No, no," said Gordon, "wait. We must consult Violet." Violet joined them, and when the situation had been explained to her, she gave her verdict: of course Bill must stay. And that, according to Violet, was both the end of the matter and its beginning.

Violet's version of events was, however, a good deal too neat and innocent to be taken at its face value. Bill was probably too honourable, and certainly too indecisive, to have set about trying to seduce a close friend's wife unless she had given him some encouragement. After four years of living with Gordon, Violet was in an emotional void. Fond as she was of him, the lack of physical passion or spiritual communication between them was beginning to cause her bouts of edginess and depression, and had left her with a nagging sense of incompleteness. Through her interpretations of Chopin, Beethoven and Tchaikovsky she had formed a distant vision of stirring places – ecstasy, fear, surrender, joy – places, however, which she had been able to visit only in her imagination. She had been the object of Christabel Marshal's infatuation, and had perhaps herself felt drawn towards Adelina Ganz, but real love between man and woman, the sole type of erotic adventure which, a hundred years ago, could be experienced without shame, had eluded her.

When Gordon, dimly aware of the reasons for his wife's moodiness, looked for ways to raise her morale, it would have been Violet who proposed inviting Bill to stay. She found him overwhelmingly attractive, and had done so since his original visits to Folkington some years earlier – and again at the house party in Herefordshire where she had first met Gordon – but she had put him to the back of her mind, presuming that he, like Lord Gage, would want children and a normal marriage. Now her perspective had changed, and when Bill arrived at Wootton Violet turned her bewitching powers on to him. All that we know of her character suggests that, as she sensed that he was falling under her spell, the realization would have come upon her that she might be able to possess him emotionally, while keeping her options open about sexual relations at some future time. In that case, a whole world of fulfilment lay before her, if only she could grasp it.

Having completed her conquest with surprising speed, she must next have turned her attention to the question of how to tackle Gordon.

Throughout her life Violet preferred to transmit difficult messages through others, and she will have persuaded Bill to break the news to her husband (that part, of her story, at least, was entirely believable). Everything now would depend upon the nature of Gordon's response. When he reacted hesitantly, Violet, realizing that her moment had come, took charge. As for Gordon, once he knew where Violet stood, he felt a sense of relief at what all three doubtless saw as a civilized "understanding". She would no longer be bored, and Gordon would never be faced with what he secretly dreaded, a humiliating separation. There was no reason why he should not remain just as friendly with Bill as before, with their shared interests in games and country sports. From Gordon's point of view, their love for Violet might even make the friendship closer.

At first Bill rationed his visits to Wootton to a few days each month, carefully chosen to coincide with the absence of Violet's parents from nearby Folkington. His service as a part-time officer in the Militia[2] also regularly took him away for several weeks at a time. Even Dorothy was not immediately suspicious, although shortly after Bill's confession to Gordon she noticed something out of the ordinary in the way Violet spoke of him. Dorothy had walked over from Folkington to Wootton, where Bill was staying.

> *May 25th 1899*
> People have such strange ideas nowadays. I was talking to Bobo this morning and we began speaking about Mr. Barrington, I said I thought he was good looking. Bobo said "Oh no, not good looking but quite beautiful, and in the right style too, just like a beautiful animal." Why like an animal I wonder; have people to be like animals to be beautiful?

In August 1899, with the London Season over, Violet, Gordon and Bill set off in a horse-drawn caravan for a holiday in the New Forest, taking with them only Violet's lady's maid, Dulciette Summers. Bohemian expeditions of this sort were very much the fashion of the day, and for the occasion Violet had a new set of clothes made for her at Lady Warwick's. Dorothy was unimpressed by the practical arrangements – "how they are going to cook, live and wash nobody knows" – but for once she underestimated Gordon, who had no intention of letting hardship spoil Violet's outing. Gordon organized the food with the help of the cook at Wootton, filling hampers with home-made preserves, cakes, tarts and pies, and boxes of tomatoes, cherries, raspberries,

2 The Militia was a reserve army of volunteers who signed up for six years to be trained in camps and sent on field manoeuvres, ready for deployment (generally at home) in an emergency.

early plums, apricots and red gooseberries. The cook made a cordial from lemon and lime juice, spices and sugar; from Fortnum & Mason in Piccadilly Gordon ordered cheeses, honey-cured American ham, foie gras, smoked salmon, candied fruit and Belgian chocolates; and he raided his cellars for burgundies, white Loire wines and his own best marsalas.

They travelled to Lyndhurst, in Hampshire, by train. Arriving at the station they went to St Michael's Church to see Lord Leighton's frescoes there, recently completed; then Bill and Gordon called in at the New Forest Hunt kennels before picking up the horse and caravan. Bill took charge of the driving, allowing Gordon and Violet to take turns with the reins as they drove past Maltwood Castle and on to the tiny village of Cadenham. The New Forest, a twenty-five-mile-wide tract of ancient oak, beech and chestnut woodland, sheltering rare butterflies and wild flowers, was, then, dark, untamed and full of mystery. Just beneath the soil lay shells, bones and fossils. On one of their walks they came across a snake-catcher, an old man who lived in a cone-shaped hut built on a frame of fir poles, with a hole at the top to serve as a chimney, and a door, just two and a half feet high, woven of gorse. After five days of primitive living, however, the romance of the holiday began to pall, and Violet was quite relieved when Bill took them back to Lyndhurst, where they lunched and had luxurious baths before returning to Wootton.

By 1900 the trio had become so inseparable that the Gwynnes were beginning to feel uneasy and to talk among themselves about the relationship. Dorothy's diaries were full of it:

> *16th March 1900* Gordon and Mr. Barrington are at Wootton, of course he's there, they wouldn't be down if he couldn't be there.

> *19th March 1900* Rupert went away by the 3.40 train. Gordon went up with him. Bobo and Mr. Barrington went by the 5.57. Father is annoyed about Gordon not waiting to go up with them!!!

> *11th April 1900* Gordon to lunch – Bobo and Mr. Barrington down to Wootton this evening. I wonder how long he will be able to stay for it always seems to depend on his staying how long Bobo and Gordon remain there.

Dorothy was right: Violet could hardly tear herself away from Bill. His absence made her feel anxious, at times almost panicky. Knowing he had been weak as a child, she fretted constantly about his health, and begged him for safety's sake not to go out alone on his boat. Whether it was hypochondria or nervous strain that caused the painful attacks of laryngitis to which she had now become prone is hard to say – her letters leave the impression that she frequently used her ailments as an excuse to appeal to Bill to hurry back to her side. She was particularly concerned about his attachment to the Militia, which not only kept him away but threatened danger because of an unexpected turn of events in the Boer War.

In September 1899 a hastily assembled Cabinet, hotfoot from grouse moor and golf links, had seized on a trumped-up crisis to send troops to South Africa. The pretext was the support of the unenfranchised British immigrants who had flocked to the Rand, in the southern Transvaal, in pursuit of gold, but the real objective was to crush Boer independence in the two Afrikaner republics, the Transvaal and the Orange Free State, and to assert the supremacy of Britain in a minerals-rich part of the world. Despite the anticipation of an easy victory by Britain's professional army over a motley collection of farmers serving as part-time soldiers, the war had in fact started worse than anyone believed possible, with a string of heavy reverses for the Imperial forces. Bill, a captain in the Oxfordshire Light Infantry, could not, as a Reservist, be sent on active service abroad against his will, but reinforcements were needed in South Africa, and the mood in the country was jingoistic. "Khaki fever" had broken out, infecting the fashion for everything from clothes to writing paper, and Violet was terrified that Bill's battalion might volunteer in a fit of ultra-patriotism.

Violet's fears, although never realized in the event, were by no means groundless. By December 1899 there had been several serious defeats, notably at Magersfontein and Colenso, and three British garrisons had been cut off and besieged, the largest a division-strength force of 12,000 men at Ladysmith in Natal. General Sir Redvers Buller, who had been sent to command the British forces against the Boers, and who was thus in charge of the rescue operations, had cabled to London asking for men who could ride and shoot as proficiently as the enemy; the Government's response had been to order the formation of an "Imperial Yeomanry" drawn from the hunting and shooting classes. In February 1900 the tide of war began to turn, as Buller changed tactics, avoiding set-piece battles and deploying artillery and small-arms fire as cover for troops attacking in broken formation, using the natural shelter of rocks and slopes. On 28 February Ladysmith was relieved. Dorothy was in London with Violet when the news arrived:

> *1st March 1900* . . . Suddenly in the middle of supper the band played God Save the Queen. The people were on their feet in a moment & singing, shouting it out with all their hearts. One man at a table next to us with a fine voice literally made the room echo;

then cheers rang out & everyone was holding up their glasses drinking the Queen's health. More cheers loud & strong for Buller & up went all the glasses again; it quite thrilled me, it was all so spontaneous & natural. I would not miss being in London tonight for anything; Bobo & I came back here in the fourwheeler; the boys walked to see some fun . . . the streets were full of cheering crowds. Got into bed about 1.50 a.m.; I combed Bobo's hair for her; Summers [Violet's lady's maid] was in bed. Tonight is one not to be forgotten; it shows how the people feel the war, & how it has really touched them; we did enjoy our evening jaunt.

Somewhat uncharacteristically, even Violet had caught the khaki fever and was knitting socks for soldiers at a leisurely pace.

*2 March 1900*

The papers are full of the enthusiasm of the country. Yesterday the City must have been a marvellous sight. The auctioneer at Covent Garden market yesterday, after singing God Save the Queen, pelted his audience with cabbages and farm produce!!! Everyone was carried away. Last night we noticed nearly all the cabmen had flags on their whips; these are stirring times; Lord Dundonald[3] was the first to reach Ladysmith; and Buller followed: what the feelings of the people must have been to know they were free once more. Gordon at the beginning of breakfast made a remark about "corns". Bobo threw down her knife & fork, said she could not take a morsel more & sat by the fire & read the papers!!! After breakfast went out in the Victoria [a light four-wheeled carriage with a folding hood] with Bobo. We went to Goss, the chemist, Marshall & Snelgrove, London Shoe Company, Barbellion, where we had some chocolate to drink: I did not want to have anything but Bobo was quite faint & said she would not have any unless I did, so I had to. It was very delicious.

. . . read a little then Bobo came in & we talked and knitted until tea time – Bobo karki [*sic*] coloured socks for the soldiers; I think the war will be over before the socks are done!! I taught her the heel that I do.

Bill spent much of the spring and summer of 1900 in barracks at Gosport or Portsmouth, where Violet wrote to him two or three times a week.

3 This was not in fact true – Colonel the Earl of Dundonald was miles back on the veldt, with a young war correspondent who later claimed to have been with the first troops into Ladysmith, Winston Churchill.

*8 May 1900 Tuesday*

. . . Mr. Bill's letters are real treasures full of Jewels from his spirit. I thank Mr. Bill, I am well, well, how could I be else, with his love wrapped round me, like the golden sunshine. My very Dear, all this golden happy life, which is living in you so much, believe me I keep much of it in my Spirit; it takes care of me, Body and Soul, whilst you are gone away, this secret, beautiful, sweet life, which no dull eye of the world has ever looked on to spoil – Neither Parting, nor even Death itself can alter my love for my darling Mr. Bill, except, perhaps, to make it still more spiritual – But he knows this so well, all these things I have said! Now for all our newses. Did you have a delightful Sea amusement on Sunday, I hope so – I wish you did not have so much dull, tiresome work. Still, you are let loose after 4 months Militia, this will not be so bad . . . I am working very steady now. I was so happy to have such a beloved letter from my dear Mr. Bill, & God Bless him for it, for himself, for me & for always, V.

Violet was now obsessed by Bill, who had become, for her, the source of everything that made life worth living.

*16 June 1900 – Friday evening 7.30*

I begin my letter to you now, my so dear Mr. Bill. Tomorrow I go to spend all the day in the country, if fine. Last night, as I was ready to rehearse with Arbós and Rubio, very much tired and dragged out of bed for it, I saw on my plate at dinner, a letter from my fairy Prince! It was lying unopened on my lap, all the time of dinner and all through the so long hard work after, giving me such pleasure, like holding his hand! Then when everyone was away, very late or very early, about one o'clock, I read your dear letter, which gave me much much fresh life just like coming out all in green leaves for the summer. Blessed Mr. Bill, you have such a beloved soul, and your love waters my Tree of Life, and keeps it so well. All I may ever do in my life of good, even in art, is made much greater in every way by this wonderful Tree of Life which has grown up from all this happiness and love, which we have for each other and for every lovely and delightful thing in the world, whose roots are planted so deep in nature, and whose branches are growing so high, that we no longer can say where begins us, and where comes nature, the Earth and the Sky, and our Tree has all the happy birds of Fairyland building their nests in it, our thoughts with wings, whose flights are boundless, and who yet return to sleep and wake again in our Tree of Life and

Love – Ah! Mr. Bill, what happy memories we have dwelling within us. I have been ill these several days, but now today am better . . .

Except the Rehearsal last night, I have not touched the piano since Tuesday morning. This is something dreadful, but I find to feel really ill inside is so abominable, I do not like to do it again, all the more as Mr. Bill lays some store by my funny little life . . . I must say goodnight to Mr. Bill in a hurry, no time to read over, and find any mistakes – I shall now have to work so very much, till Monday week is over and then . . . I have had 3 letters from papers and magazines asking for an illustrated interview, in the last 3 days, I who have already had them with Lord Mayors, the Pr. of Wales, Mr T. Sloan (I do not know who is this last gentleman!) Mme Melba, Miss Marie Tempest, Lady Warwick, etc.! Now I must go.

Many blessings for Mr. Bill, please God to take much and great care of his dear and precious life.

After eighteen months of intermittent living together, Violet, Gordon and Bill finally decided to make the arrangement between them permanent. At this point Gordon felt that he ought to make some explanation to his mother. It was better that she should hear of their communal plans from him rather than from possibly uncharitable rumour. Moreover, he owed a visit to his family in Herefordshire. But when he reached Burghill the atmosphere was claustrophobic, and wholly inauspicious for a tête-à-tête. Bored and dispirited, he hated every minute of his stay and could not bring himself to broach the subject of his marriage. Violet wrote to Bill:

21 August 1900. Gordon writes me that he finds his family quite abominable & is *very dull* & there is hardly enough to bring away from the gardens to make this horrible sacrifice worth his while.

Gordon returned to find Violet in a restless frame of mind – the London house was too large and insufficiently modernized; the Gwynne family was too much on top of them in the country; Wootton was very expensive to rent, since all the capital cost fell on Gordon, while the improvements made to it were to the benefit of Violet's father, who excused himself from either spending his own money on the house, or giving it to Violet, on the pretext that he preferred to leave her money in his will. In any event, feeling it right in their new circumstances to withdraw a little from Folkington, Violet and Gordon repaired temporarily to Cobbe Place, a few miles away on Lord Gage's Firle estate, while they looked for somewhere else to live. Gordon took charge of the practical details.

Wootton Sussex.
*September 13 1900*
My Dear Bill – I have been over today to Lewes and seen Ld Gage's
agents and have I believe fixed up everything with them, and
provided he gives his consent to us hiring the house, Cobbe Place,
from Mrs. Ingram for a period of one year we shall be able to go in
on the 1st October next. The Agent was just able to break with the
other people on a small technical law matter so let us have it. Violet
tells me you expect to hear tomorrow whether you will be disbanded
or go into winter quarters. I hope the former and I expect you will
get free by October. You did not miss any shooting last Thursday as
we walked the whole morning for 2 brace of birds . . . your creation
of sweet peas, convolvulus etc. in your garden is coming out and the
convolvulus are very pretty and the peas will be out in another day
or two. Your clematis is out, a most rotten flower I don't think you
will like it at all. I forgot to say the house has to be taken furnished
to start on, but I think that is a good thing as we can then find out
what we want. Nothing more has been arranged about buying the
place but that can be gone into later and Gage is away at present.
From Gordon.

Gordon seemed less troubled by Violet being in love with another man
than by the long periods of inactivity in London to which he was
condemned by her music, for by 1900 her artistic life was even fuller than
her emotional life, as she experimented with an unprecedented range of
styles, periods and instruments – Spanish music, Mozart, Bach and the early
composers, the classical and romantic repertoire, the piano, the harpsichord
and the clavichord. While Violet learned, practised, rehearsed and performed, Gordon languished. In October she wrote to Bill that he was
spending his time "grumbling and sleeping on his sofa in the smoking room,
surrounded by quantities of bulbs in paper parcels. He has changed his
country attire for something still older and worse to look at. He is going
back tomorrow with great satisfaction." Not that Gordon was an energetic
man at the best of times. Even in the country he was liable to relapse into
idleness, and Violet had to coax him out for a daily walk on the downs by
promising to play bagatelle with him.

Gordon's mother, meanwhile, was not entirely naive, nor altogether
cut off from reality. Her suspicions had been pricked, and on 28 November
she paid a visit to London, where she stayed with Violet and Gordon in
Upper Brook Street. Gordon had gone to Christie's to look for antiques,

and while Violet was practising, Dorothy, who had come over from Eva's for lunch, took the opportunity to sit and talk privately with Mrs Woodhouse. The talk was a long one. There was much on Dorothy's mind, and she felt that the events which were troubling the Gwynnes should not any longer be kept from Gordon's mother. Only two days before Dorothy and Nevile had witnessed a curious incident after one of Violet's musical evenings.

> *November 26th 1900* . . . it was nearly 12.30, at last they were all gone but Nev. and Mr B. He was going to drop Nev. at Neville Street. Bobo was sitting on his knee, their arms around each other's waists, and Nev. couldn't get him to move. At last, at about 12.40 they went downstairs; then I had to go and talk over the evening with Bobo in her room . . . then Gordon came & they talked on & they had some supper . . .

On 30 November Gordon and his mother took the train to Folkington with Dorothy. It was a sombre journey. Gordon fell asleep, while his mother kept looking at him with a sad expression on her face; the observant Dorothy saw her eyes continually wandering to where he was sitting. As well as hurt and anxiety, his mother felt an unaccustomed anger at what she had heard from Dorothy. Gordon was not to know it, but on her return to Burghill she determined privately that for so long as Violet was alive, he should never inherit her fortune.

Violet's last Christmas at Wootton was a jolly affair, with both Gordon and Bill in high spirits. Dorothy recorded in her diary a speech by Bill in which he took for granted that he was now a permanent member of the family:

> *Christmas Day 1900* We got a very warm welcome from Bobo and Gordon, the latter kissed us in turn under a great bunch of mistletoe hung up in the hall . . .
>
> Father and Bobo sat at the head of the table and Gordon at the foot . . . Mr. B. next to Bobo . . . And many were the toasts. Mr. B. made a charming speech hoping we should all be together for many years to come etc. Then came the crackers galore, and a huge cake all iced with almond paste and the icing all festooned with violets, quite lovely. Then we had fun with the crackers. Mr. B. had a helmet of silver paper which fitted close to his head. He looked splendid in it like a knight you see in old pictures. I had some weird things – a heavy black moustache and a pair of knickerbockers!!

Once Violet had made up her mind to move house, she acted quickly. Within a month of Christmas she had found new places to live both in the country and in London. Southover Grange, an Elizabethan house built in French stone from Caen, stood on the very edge of Lewes, ten miles from Folkington, close to the familiar South Downs. The house had historical associations, having at one time been owned by John Evelyn, the seventeenth-century diarist and man of learning. Its front looked on to a quiet lane nudging into the lowest slopes of the town, while at the back a walled garden of some two acres reached almost to Lewes station. Visitors who came by train could reach the house by a short walk through a door in the wall, skirting a kitchen garden and a water garden planted around a narrow stream, then passing by hedges and chestnut trees until they reached the lawn, in the centre of which a huge mulberry tree spread its shade over a heavy wooden seat. Beyond the lawn lay the flagstoned terrace and the French windows of the drawing-room. With a large reception room and an equally large music room, both panelled, the house suited Violet perfectly. It even still had its original Elizabethan staircase and chimneypieces. On 22 January 1901 she sent Bill an elated telegram, "SOUTHOVER IS YOURS. VIOLET", to which Gordon added good-humouredly, "AND MINE. GORDON". It was, after all, he who would be writing the cheque.

Violet's new London house, 9 Park Place off St James's, was also architecturally interesting. It was by far the most impressive house in the street, set back sixteen feet from the others and possessing a Doric porch, a basement and four storeys, including a garret. Inside the wide entrance hall the staircase rose round an open well. On either side were two large drawing-rooms, one of which had a Louis XVI fireplace; another similar fireplace adorned the master bedroom on the first floor. Equally convenient for musical entertainment as Upper Brook Street had been, and if anything even more chic, the house had been exquisitely decorated by its fashionable former owner. It had electric lighting instead of oil lamps, which appealed to Violet's sense that she was living at the beginning of the modern age. Four days after Queen Victoria's death, itself symbolic of the passing of an era, Violet wrote again to Bill:

*January 26th 1901 Upper Brook Street*
After Mr. Bill's letter this morning, I sit down at once to give him the news. I guessed you would be very busy now, with the poor Queen's death which is so sad a thing, but one cannot help feeling that it is so suitable a thing for her to die at the very start of this new Century.

She so absolutely belonged to the old one, and was such a bulwark of it, and she could have had nothing in common with this one.

Now for Southover Grange – Gordon is going to pay seven thousand pounds for it and it is ours from March 25th. Then the agent thinks that there will be no difficulty to get rid of this [i.e. the house in Upper Brook Street], and some peoples have already been over it, and Mrs. Darter says all are delighted with it. I have only been houses hunting once, but with the wonderful lucks we seem to have of seeing what we like at once, instead of looking for *years*, like other people, we have found a perfectly charming house, with much fewer rooms than this, but quite fascinating ones, a bedroom for me as big as this one, in which I now write – a small dining room, entirely panelled in real old oak, electric light, etc. etc. Now I do not know, everything is in air still, but Gordon and Boy are both enraptured!! The name is No. 9. Park Place, St. James' – Perhaps you know it! It belonged to a Mr. Ben Guinness[4], rich Lady Charles Beresford's young man, who has certainly done it up with enormous taste, nothing need be altered if we got it.

. . . You wrote me a letter which was such a pleasure this morning. Do you know what I am doing? Thanking God all day and night that you are in England. I dare not to complain at not being with my so darling Mr. Bill, when so many blessings and happinesses are flying round our heads. Now I look always forward to seeing him again soon, and then when he is disbanded!! Our year! We shall let the London house, if we ever possess it! And go, Oh how many thousand Leagues from the world, straight into our own happy, simple, beautiful life – Mr. Bill will go and make his visits, and come back again to his home, for I am not sure if he must quite forget the world and all that is in it!

. . . the Hound is making loud snorings, I hope he will not continue with them all night – He does not even wake himself up with them!!!! There is only one being whom I allow to make such a music in my presence, with his beautiful nose, but he asks no permissions – alas! I have heard none of this musics for so long! Bless my Mr. Bill.

Violet was accustomed to being in control both of her emotions and of her relationships, but with Bill all semblance of that control evaporated. She

4 Benjamin Guinness had served in the Royal Navy and was now a rich banker. His friend Mina Beresford was the wife of an admiral, Lord Charles Beresford.

missed him dreadfully when he was away, and had to struggle with herself not to complain at his absences.

*February 16th 1901*
Dear Mr. Bill, with his explanation. I am his, and where I live is his, to come and to go when he pleases, with or without reason. Now, suppose we settle matters so Mr. Bill comes here Wednesday. Then he goes to his sister on Thursday, and comes back either Saturday or Monday, then we will go to Cobbe Tuesday. I should love to have him here on the Sunday, at my musics, if he is back, and I think he would not be bored. Blanchie [Blanche Tollemache] will be here etc. It is Gordon's birthday and I must entertain him all the day, I promised I would. I have already been out with him this morning, and called on Arbós at his studio, done shoppings etc. Tonight, he, Boy and I are going to the play. I have given him a very nice new dressing gown, he is rather pleased, but I can see he thinks he will have to pay for it! Blanchie sent him a beautiful jug with Leech's pictures in silhouettes all over it, I should like it myself. What a fun when Mr. Bill comes here on Wednesday, does my good sir know that he has been away already longer than ever before.

It is clear that Violet was free of any feelings of guilt about her husband, who appears in her letters as a comfortable and comforting figure, a friend and confidant who could not conceivably be wounded by anything she might choose to do. Indeed, there was little for her to feel guilty about. Far from rejecting Gordon's love, she accepted it, and in her own way returned it, on terms which were quite independent from those governing her affair of the heart with Bill.

Gordon had, of course, known from the outset that his marriage would be chaste, but although Violet quite often discreetly shared a bed with Bill they never embarrassed Gordon by sharing a bedroom. Besides, even for Bill Violet's love was more spiritual than physical. The affair was to be childless, and it is not impossible, given her horror of the thought of marital sex with Lord Gage, her romantic friendships with Adelina Ganz and Christabel Marshal, and her lifelong habit of combining ice with fire and intimacy with distance, that even at the height of their erotic passion her relationship with Bill was not fully consummated. In any event, whatever its nature, it seems not to have struck Gordon as posing a threat to him. On the contrary, a remarkable letter he wrote testifies not only to the protective nature of his friendship with Bill, but also to his acceptance that Bill's relationship with Violet was the key to her happiness, and therefore to his own.

*1 March 1901* Dear Bill, V. tells me you are bad with cold & in the doctor's hands. Mind you take great care of yourself & remain under him until you are really quite well for it will not do for Bill to get seriously ill . . . mind you get well for it would be most inconvenient for me to have to go with you to Switzerland during our first year at Southover, but of course I should have to look after you. Cannot you come here and be nursed on "sick leave". You old cock I think Southover would agree with you. Gordon

March and April were hectic months. Violet's last day at Upper Brook Street found her dreaming about Bill and, as always, leaving the hard work to Gordon.

*April 1st 1901 Upper Brook Street*
The last Sunday spent by either of us in this house. Think of all the happy Ghost Sundays rising up all around me! But we shall take the happy reality away with us, is it not so? & Darling Mr. Bill what parting can matter, when we are close to one another? Brook St. unspoiled will always be our kingdom, & will stay in our dreams forever happy . . . Gordon came back Friday night from Southover and Cobbe, everything was going on quite well. The Wootton furniture all arriving. The little Eastbourne man will charge £97.16.7 for green papering and painting all the house except the hall, dining room, library and drawing room. Gordon says this is cheap as all the basement is included . . . I must confess to you that the room of all others I should like to have for our sitting room is the dear little library, we could make it something marvellous you and I with our toys etc.

With their affair now nearing the end of a second idyllic year, Violet sought ways to bind Bill to her more closely. Her music was not a strong enough tie – indeed, he was more or less indifferent to it. What she needed was for him to think of where she lived as his home, not merely as a place to visit. It was for this reason, among others, that she had left Upper Brook Street, which for all its many happy associations with Bill was essentially the house of her marriage. To mark her new life, she wanted new houses with Bill's possessions in them.

*April 13th 1901.*
. . . Of course send your things to Southover such fun to receive Mr. Bill's luggages there, in his bedroom . . . Gordon is full of works and so busy and happy trotting about in some clothes stranger than

even his usual ones, unreprimanded by me, because he is so useful, which is taking advantage to the utmost. Caravan shoes full of holes, and a coat with ten gaps in it, stockings and shirt to match. He and Dulciette, in fact, go about dressed like a pair of scoundrels . . . I send you kisses, very many . . . I pray to God to let my soul be always with Mr. Bill's soul and how can I ever feel lonely again so long as my soul is worthy to take care of yours which is so beautiful and beloved.

Throughout the move to Southover, Violet discussed with Bill in minute detail the layout of the rooms, the interior decoration and the furniture, just as she had once discussed Wootton with Gordon. The oak pieces fitted well into the new house, but since the drawing-room lacked a centrepiece Gordon gave her a magnificent antique cabinet of seventeenth-century Dutch inlay marquetry; within its door were sixteen drawers, in which Violet kept her Japanese dolls, tiny pieces of bric-a-brac, and presents from Gordon, Bill and Adelina. She liked dark polished floorboards overlaid with antique Turkish carpets, carelessly thrown one over the other to cover any signs of wear. The walls in the hallway above the oak panelling were painted in deep saffron; for the small sitting room she chose an Arts and Crafts wallpaper from Liberty's, a design of brambles with pale grey-green leaves and maroon berries.

Letting Bill know of progress with the house, Violet later in the month wrote a little mischievously to him about Gordon.

. . . There is another excitement that is bursting to get out of the bag, I am having your floor all stopped and polished. The men are to do it tomorrow beginning at 6 a.m. Such a fun for Gordon, sleeping in his room, won't he be angry, he does not know, so it will wake him up with a surprise. Now if you do not like your polished floor you can have your carpet put down but I think very much that it will be charming . . . I put all the china out with Adelina yesterday, and I am going to put Mr. Bill's Christos in its place as I think he will like it.

In the absence of children, Violet's menagerie was to become something of an extended family. Her favourites were her dogs – at first a Highland terrier, later several Pekinese (for which in her old age she was to develop an inordinate affection); but her taste was catholic, and she shared with Bill a fondness for almost every animal, from ponies and donkeys to lambs, pigs and birds. Bill sent her two tame starlings, which she hung in a cage in her bedroom opposite her blackbird, Obadiah. Of another bird Violet wrote,

"Titus is now one of the greatest joys in my life, and is really quite tame, though he will not let me think so yet! I may only touch his foot through the bars, nothing else." The pets seem to have fulfilled the desired purpose – "I am pleased Mr. Bill is happy and satisfied to pass some of his life . . . with all this outlandish family of peoples, pigs, birds . . ."

Interior decoration and animals were, however, essentially trivia, and Violet knew it. When Bill left the Militia, he would have to find a more substantial occupation or he would grow bored. The idea of asking him to take care of the garden proved to be an inspired one, for the task released in him a creative talent which one day would result in a master-piece, and which otherwise might have lain dormant for ever. He had already shown a great interest in plants and herbaceous borders at Wootton, but it was not until he came to Southover that he gained his first experience of garden design. Initially there was a touch of competition between him and Gordon, who had his own border, but soon the gardens were Bill's domain alone.

As a watercolourist and architectural historian, Bill was fascinated by the interplay of water, trees, plants and open spaces, of light and shade, of differ-ent heights and colours. He read gardening books from cover to cover and took the *Garden*, the weekly magazine run by the Irishman William Robinson, who also lived in Sussex, and who was the father of the naturalist school of garden designers. Robinson, the author of the influential *The English Flower Garden*, had, as much as anyone, been responsible for the move in England away from the architectural formalism of the French, Italian and Elizabethan styles of garden to what is today thought of as the typically English style, in which classicism takes second place to nature, and areas of wild flowers, woodland and water are mingled with lawns and garden plants. From Southover, Bill wrote to Robinson, and they began to exchange visits and ideas. Nothing could have given Violet more pleasure than to watch Bill's growing mastery. She needed to be proud of him and to look up to him; and in the garden not only was he an artist, he was indisputably in charge.

Hitherto, because of Bill's frequent absences and the seeming normality of Violet's marriage, their love affair had been private enough to be concealed from the outside world, other than the close family. But in the summer of 1901, when his Militia service came to an end, he came to live at Southover and it was no longer possible for anyone to misinterpret the nature of Violet's domestic arrangements.

*21st July 1901* Went to spend the day with Bobo . . . Gordon was there with an umbrella and he took us to Southover . . . Oh it is so beautiful in the garden!! An old stone terrace and old high walls, mossy paths, it is ideal and the house inside is so lovely, furnished of course in perfect taste. The hall perhaps the most beautiful because of the old oak panelling. Mr. B. is there, he lives with B and G now. Blanche Tollemache, Rubio and Adelina left this a.m. Bobo was in such charming humour.

Dorothy, usually dispassionate about family matters except where they affected her own interest, continued to be swayed by her feelings for Gordon and misread the *ménage à trois*, seeing in it a tragedy for him. May was equally unhappy. She had longed for a brilliant match for Violet, and for grandchildren. Now she found herself faced with a childless marriage and a looming scandal involving a penniless aristocrat and a compliant husband. Dorothy captured her mother's anxiety.

*3rd August 1901* Mother had a bad night worrying about Bobo and Mr. B. It is no good fretting now, we must grasp it and look it in the face, nothing will do now but accept it! I am very sorry!!

# VI

*More Daughter than Pupil*

SHORTLY AFTER VIOLET HAD become interested in early music for the harpsichord and clavichord, she came under a new musical influence. Born in 1856, Agustín Rubio was a Spanish cellist with formidable gifts as a performer and composer, and an even greater talent for teaching. Edmund van der Straeten, in his *History of the Violoncello*, published in 1915, describes him as the possessor of "a brilliant technique of left hand and bow, combined with a fine tone . . . he employs [the pizzicato] in solos of his own composition as an accompaniment to sustained melody, treating it much like a guitar, or mandolin, and changing from accompaniment into melody with extraordinary rapidity". The story has it that in 1891 Rubio, having gone with Albéniz and Arbós to hear the fifteen-year-old Casals play in Barcelona's Café La Pajarera, had given the young Catalan lessons. Rubio had been so impressed by the quality of Casals's playing that he became convinced that he had found his own musical heir, in whose hands he could safely leave the future of the cello in Spain.

Many of Rubio's friends were leaving Spain in the early 1890s to seek more cosmopolitan arenas, and shortly before Violet's marriage he too left the Spanish Court to make London his home. There he became the guiding spirit for the growing number of his compatriots who were enriching the British musical scene with their exuberant talent and their own original compositions. His bushy black beard, which in time grew white, gave him a biblical appearance, accentuated by his dark clothes and his black felt hat. There were fire and power in his deep brown eyes, and an almost palpable simplicity, sincerity and goodness in his nature. A Roman Catholic, and a profoundly religious person, Rubio lived as though bound by vows of poverty in two shabby little rooms in Fulham, a much loved father confessor in *émigré* musical circles. It was hard to think of him in worldly terms, and Osbert Sitwell was doing no more than voicing the universally held opinion when he described him in one of his essays as a close approximation to a saint.

Although Rubio learned to express himself colourfully in English, his use of the language remained a strange and idiosyncratic concoction. He utterly neglected his own personal comfort, thinking only of music and of his friends. To keep him going financially was a hopeless cause, for, as Violet used to say, no sooner did one give him money than he immediately gave it away to someone even poorer. Nonetheless, judging by the grateful cards he sent her over the years, Violet did help him frequently:

> Dearest Violet, you are a stravagant daughter!!!! and I have too little mouth to thank you properly! anyhow I wish you very happy Xmas and New Year and I hope to meet you some times before I disappear! thanking you again and again with much love Rubio.

To Rubio, Violet was indeed more a treasured daughter than a pupil. He poured out his gratitude and affection for her in fractured English:

> My dearest daughter Violet,
> Many thanks for your kindness: as a father I must tell you that you was rather EXTRAVAGANT! anyhow, and for your satisfaction, that was in a opportune moment, and you help me splendidly. God bless you! I wish you every possible happiness in the coming year, in which you must tell everyone how Bach and Mozart SHOULD BE DONE. Hearty greetings for all, from your loving father A. Rubio.

Although she had encountered him occasionally with Nettie Carpenter soon after his arrival in England, it was not until 1898 that Violet came to know Rubio well. He had spent much of 1897 touring Europe and America with Adelina Patti. On his return, hearing Violet play with Arbós in his studio, he recognized in her one of those rare artists, like Pablo Casals, through whom he could hand down to future generations his understanding of the great masters. The rapport between them was instant. Violet was an eager and responsive disciple, in whom he saw infinite possibilities. It was a matter of complete indifference to him which instrument she played: for him interpretation was all important, and he would work with her for hours on a single phrase. When she practised, he would sit by her with a rapt expression on his face, alternately praising her, urging her to fresh efforts and submitting the way in which she had formulated some passage to unsparing criticism. The slightest deviation from the ideal he had conceived of how she should play, say, a Bach prelude or fugue would drive him to fury. But with Rubio her imperious character retreated, and however fierce he became she remained invariably gentle and humble.

Violet's earliest known public concert with Rubio was in April 1899 at the Curtius Club in the Princes Galleries in Piccadilly. She played on the piano Beethoven's Sonata in A and Chopin's Polonaise Brillante in C Major, in both cases with Rubio on the cello, and then gave a solo performance of Grieg's Sonata in E, which the music critic of the *Standard* found "a very artistic reading. . . winning a hearty recall". From then on Rubio attended almost all her soirées, often bringing with him his and Nettie Carpenter's mutual friends Guétary and Arbós. Their style of composition, like that of their mentor Albéniz, was inspired by the infectious rhythms, harmonies, and turns of phrase of Spanish vernacular music, and struck a resonant chord in Violet's temperament, leading her to introduce contemporary Spanish work into her repertoire for the first time. Dorothy's diary gives the flavour of one of her concerts, in which the programme combined dance music composed by Violet's Spanish friends with more conventional pieces:

*February 21st 1900.* Bobo and Arbós played the most exquisite Spanish dances. They gave an encore. Bobo had a real success. When the concert was over Schultz-Curtius gave a supper party at Princes restaurant . . . Bobo and I came home in the brougham. She was most excited and quite delighted with the success she had made and all the pretty things that had been said to her; she said she was a born public player as directly she had an audience all her nervousness went . . . Adelina [Ganz] turned over for Bobo in the trio, and Rubio in the Sonata; he and Arbós thought a lot of Bobo's playing.

Next day, Dorothy rushed out to see the reviews. The Gwynnes particularly wanted to know what Fuller Maitland had written, knowing his predilection for disparaging notices – knowing, too, that his opinion counted for more than that of any other critic.

*February 22nd 1900*
At breakfast we went out for *The Times* to see what Fuller Maitland had said about Bobo last night. When it came it was handed to me to find as knowing *The Times* so well I had the pleasure of reading out this splendid critique. It is really delightful and doubly so coming from Fuller Maitland for he is really so unpleasant as a rule. I never read such praise. Bobo was delighted of course.

What Fuller Maitland had written was indeed complimentary:

The charming little concert last night . . . brought forward Mrs Gordon Woodhouse . . . a pianist of rare skill, finished technique, and musical intelligence, and above all possessed of the invaluable quality called temperament. As a player of concerted music she was heard to special advantage in Saint-Saëns's delicious trio in F, op. 18, in which she was associated with Señor Arbós and Señor Rubio, and in which she maintained such a justice of balance between her own part and those of the strings as is by no means common among professional players. Her solos were Brahms's rhapsody in G minor and Chopin's impromptu in F sharp, both of which were played with distinction, great beauty of touch and entire sympathy . . .

So perfectly attuned was Violet to the rhythms of Rubio's and Arbós's playing that it seemed natural to attribute the trio's appearance together to their supposedly shared "Spanish blood". A reviewer described their summer concert at the St James's Hall in 1900 as

> the most interesting of the year . . . the association of these three artists, all of Spanish birth, in Señor Arbós's "Spanish Pieces" for the violin, violoncello and piano was productive of a surprising performance – one, indeed, which was the feature of the afternoon. The work is singularly attractive . . . It consists of a "Habanera" and a "Seguidilla" written with great talent and knowledge of effect, and full of dash and spirit. The performance was worthy of the work. Mrs Gordon Woodhouse's . . . playing is remarkable, delicate yet powerful, sympathetic and strong. It is not disparaging to her talents, however, to say that her personality is the secret of the fascination of her playing. In concerted music she is very sympathetic and unselfish; she gave everything required to the pianoforte part in the Schumann trio, and yet never overpowered the strings.

The legend of Violet's Spanish origins was catching. Reviewing one of their performances at the Curtius Club, the critic of the *Daily News* referred to Violet, Arbós and Rubio playing with "all the spirit and abandon of genuine Spanish gypsies". Violet did nothing to discourage the myth. Like so much else about her, her "Spanishness" was, of course, a theatrical attribute, acquired with an eye to her audience. It was also a subtle way of deflecting speculation about the origins of her Romany looks and faintly olive complexion.

Violet now enjoyed a status in musical circles that was almost unique. Strictly speaking, she remained an amateur, in that she was unpaid and not under contract to any agent or impresario, but the quality of her playing was recognized as ranking her alongside the best professional musicians.

Schultz-Curtius acted as her *de facto* agent, sometimes arranging concerts devoted to her alone.

*March 9th 1900* The Curtius Concert Club
On Wednesday night, it was Mrs Gordon Woodhouse's evening; and the gathering was particularly brilliant.

Mrs Gordon Woodhouse is an amateur only in name. She is in reality one of those gifted musical natures absolutely dominated by the artistic sense. And of how few artists can this be said? When she plays the piano, it is evident that Mrs Gordon Woodhouse is not so much concerned with the mere execution of the piece as with the actual interpretation of the composer's idea. To an ample command of technique the player adds a certain charm and quaintness in her playing which are a result of her own temperament. Her performance has, therefore, always a spice of originality in it, which, while in no way affecting the accuracy of her reading, gives to her rendering a something of spontaneity and unconventionality which is most welcome.

This was seen as much in her Brahms "Rhapsodie" as in her Chopin "Impromptu", although the latter piece seemed far more to evoke her sympathy. Perhaps her musicianly qualities were on the whole more conspicuously exhibited in her playing of the Fauré Sonata.

Violet celebrated her twenty-ninth birthday with Dorothy and some of her closest musical friends, including Rubio, Guétary and Adelina Ganz.

*April 23rd 1900.* Bobo is having a little musical party which consists of Adelina, Miss Woodford, Sheila Chichester, Rubio, Curtius, Braham Tollemache [Denis's uncle]. We had tea in the square Drawing Room. Rubio and Guétary came very late. A lovely birthday cake. After, Bobo played the harpsichord with Rubio on his cello. Then she played, still on the harpsichord, and Guétary sang. Then he sang Basque songs and Rubio accompanied him on the cello . . . Bobo had such lovely flowers sent to her, among others a big bouquet of red roses from Bechstein.[1] Guétary made such fun of them. English roses made in Germany.

That Violet's two homes were open houses to performers from all over

---

1 Early that summer Edwin Bechstein arranged for Violet to be photographed by Fellows Wilson to promote Bechstein pianos, and promised to give her a concert grand with a value, according to Violet, of 300 guineas.

the world was a feature of considerable importance in the musical culture of England at the turn of the century, a time when English society hostesses, with rare exceptions, generally confined their hospitality to people from their own backgrounds. A few rich businessmen and a handful of famous players or opera singers were admitted to society drawing-rooms, but for most foreign musicians London could seem lonely and unwelcoming.

Before meeting Violet, such artists as Arbós, Busoni, Delius,[2] Schultz-Curtius and others would congregate in small foreign restaurants, like Gambinus's or, most popular of all, the Meschine family's Pagani's in Great Portland Street, where they would sit grumbling for hours over coffee. The British Sunday was for them unbearably dreary, so strictly observed that apart from the parade for the fashionable in Hyde Park after church, and impromptu religious addresses at Speakers' Corner, the city ground to a standstill, the silence occasionally broken by the sudden jarring notes of a street organ. "All my ideas of a Sunday afternoon in London were surpassed today," wrote Ferrucio Busoni to his Swedish wife in Berlin. "It would be impossible to imagine anything so empty, gloomy, lonely, dead and paralysing as the reality." For these exiles, therefore, Violet's musical afternoons and evenings were a godsend and especially her Sunday concerts – a shocking innovation, made the more outrageous by the noisy polyglot jokes, play-acting, dressing up, late nights and sheer high spirits of her unconventional artistic friends.

Although Busoni was in the end to become famous not only as a performer but also as a composer, teacher and musical theorist, it was as a pianist that he had swept all before him in 1899 in England. With his Corsican temperament, his mane of thick black hair and his mesmerizing eyes, he matched the Victorian image of the archetypal Latin artistic genius, touring the country to packed audiences and admiring reviews for his recitals of Beethoven, Chopin and Liszt. Between concerts he was often entertained in London by his German acquaintances, the Matesdorfs, who played host to a wide circle of expatriate musicians. In the spring of 1900 he had asked Mrs Matesdorf to introduce him properly to Violet, whom

2 The composer Frederick Delius, who had been born in Bradford of German parents, lived mostly abroad, but had arrived in London at the end of 1898 hoping to get his opera, *Koanga*, performed. He had a list of contacts, including Schultz-Curtius, a Mrs Joshua, well known as a patron of the arts, and Violet. Pale, aesthetic and monk-like in appearance, he had a waspish tongue. Shortly after his arrival he wrote to Jelka Rosen (his future wife) in France that Mrs Joshua was "a pretentious, stupid woman spouting morals, philosophy and political economy in one breath – no artist and arrogant as hell. I came to loggerheads with her over Nietzsche." But he took to Violet immediately, describing her as "nice, artistic and unpretentious".

he had barely met before. He had heard a great deal about her from many quarters – from the Ganzes, from Beringer, from their shared Spanish composer-performer friends, from Schultz-Curtius, and from the dynamic Edwin Bechstein, who hoped to capture both Busoni and Violet as customers – and now he wanted to use the opportunity of one of his relatively rare appearances in England to get to know her better and to play with her in the Matesdorfs' drawing-room. If Bill had been musical, history would no doubt have been left a more interesting description of the evening, but all we have, tantalizingly, is Violet's note to him of Saturday 12 May 1900: "A party last night given by a woman who was once a pianist, I believe, now fat and married to a very rich German in Mount Street. There was so beautiful music, lots of artists – another pianist as well as me, a very celebrated man called Busoni, then Arbós, Blanche Marchesi, some of the singers from the opera . . ."

Busoni was notoriously critical of other pianists, speaking of them sometimes with respect but hardly ever with admiration. He believed a performer at the highest level must possess intelligence, culture and a comprehensive training in music, literature and human nature, as well as character, flawless technique, and an almost impossibly demanding list of other qualities. In the international music fraternity his approval was held to be the ultimate accolade. That night Violet must have met his exacting standards, for he spoke of her afterwards on several occasions as "one of the greatest living keyboard artists".

Her contemporaries from this period unfortunately left no more than an overall impression of her playing method and style, scarcely ever going into refinements or technicalities. It is clear from reviews of her performances that the power and strength of her playing belied her fragile appearance. Rubio's influence had been quickly absorbed; after just twelve months of intensive tuition Violet had progressed from talented musician to superb and original interpretative artist, with a rare ability to penetrate the musical intentions of a composer. Rubio had taken her beyond the accuracy, technique and sensitive touch of her German teachers to a new depth of understanding. He encouraged her – drove her – to express her music not only through the intellect and the hands, but also through all the metaphors and nuances of emotion. It was typical of him to suggest of the adagio of a sonata by Mozart that it reflected the feelings of a young man in love with opera singers: from then on, whenever she played that passage, Violet always had in mind the singing of Jean de Reszke, who had made such a an impression on her as a sixteen-year-old.

Greatly as she revelled in her success, the strain sometimes told on her of simultaneously having to live up to her artistic reputation, entertain on a grand scale, decorate and furnish her houses, keep Gordon happy, and conduct her semi-secret romance with Bill. Nor can we entirely rule out the possibility that she allowed the love of Adelina Ganz, known to Bill and Gordon as "That Woman", to be rewarded with something more physical than merely returned affection – though, if so, the reticence of the era would have ensured that the affair was kept utterly clandestine. Amid all this activity, Violet needed to exercise considerable self-discipline to keep in practice. Writing to Bill in May, she complained that in a forthcoming concert she had to play both harpsichord and clavichord: "I fear this will mean few holidays till it is over . . . my fingers are so stiff and cross and I have no time to practise this week . . ."

Her versatility at this stage of her career was extraordinary. If she saw as her true vocation the playing of early music on the clavichord and harpsichord in elegant chambers, she was nevertheless able to switch at will to performing the piano works of the romantic composers in large concert halls. The frequent changes of technique required by her wide repertoire and the variety of her instruments demanded arduous practice sessions. "My concert is on June 25th," she wrote to Bill, ". . . I must be working so very hard beforehand, this is really a very big Concert, and a hall holding 1500 people to be filled! . . . I ought not to be much away till it is done . . . 7$\frac{1}{2}$ hours practice yesterday, 5$\frac{1}{2}$ today . . ."

Her hard work paid off handsomely. At the age of twenty-nine she had come to be regarded as on a par with the greatest pianists in the world.

*27 June 1900* – Wednesday morning 8.30 o'clock
Good morning Mr Bill, I write this early, as since the Concert I have so much attentions from peoples, I have all the day to be running about . . . I must tell you that it was a very great success, much the best I have ever made, and the Hall was very full. There were heaps of splendid notices in the papers, but Mr B. did not see them. I shall send them, but Arbós has them at the moment – all except this, from *The Times*. There were many pianists there, and 2 of them told Rubio and Arbós, that Fuller Maitland, *The Times* critic, the only *really* respected one, said all the time every pianist, even d'Albert and Paderewski, who wants to play Schubert well, must go and learn from Mrs Woodhouse!! And he said he had never heard anyone touch the piano like I did since Rubinstein died. I could not resist telling this to Mr Bill, not from vanity, but he must know all my newses! I had many letters, about 28 yesterday, and 14

this morning, but no rude ones !!

With her letter Violet enclosed Fuller Maitland's review from *The Times:*
. . . Mrs Gordon Woodhouse, an amateur pianist whose finish, taste
and musicianship many a professional musician might well envy, has
the special gift for playing concerted music, and with Señores Arbós
and Rubio she gave a capital performance of Schumann's lovely
trio in F, op. 80; Beethoven's sonata in A, op. 69, was also played
with the violoncellist . . . Mrs Woodhouse's solos were Brahms'
rhapsodie in G minor and Schubert's impromptu in B flat; both
were exquisitely played, for whether decision or delicacy be required,
the player has either at command, and her tone and touch are always
beautiful.

This concert was attended by Christabel Marshal, who had finished her
degree at Oxford and was now working as secretary to Lady Randolph
Churchill and her son, Winston. In 1899 she had fallen in love with Ellen
Terry's daughter, Edith Craig, with whom she had settled into an all but
married relationship which was to last fifty years. Christabel was not, of
course, an altogether impartial observer of Violet's playing, but she had a
well-developed ear and later became a serious music critic. Immediately
after the performance she wrote to Violet.

> 4 Whitehall Court *June 25th 1900*
> Darling Violet
> I can't tell you how much I enjoyed your concert. I thought you
> played the Brahms & Schubert magnificently – with such *grip* as
> well as fascination in yourself. Also in the Beethoven with Rubio
> you quite took my breath away. I have always thought you wonder-
> ful but I did not quite realise how fast you could run towards
> mastery of the piano. I limp so slowly towards it in my line that
> I can't understand how in a year you have got so far. I hope it
> isn't wrong of me to have liked the Spanish dances better than
> anything. No other 3 people could play like that, and your three
> faces all different shades of exquisite yellow marble completed it.
> These things do matter. Your looking the whole time like a Tanagra
> statuette gave me as much joy as your playing.
> On Thursday I hope to send you a copy of "The Crimson
> Weed"[3] – but will you like a darling order it from a library as well –
> just to help it on its sale. Bless you. Ever your Chris.

3 Christabel Marshal's novel, published in New York in 1901.

It had been perceptive of Christabel to refer to Violet's appearance. Her style and her clothes, on which she had lavished so much attention, allied to her magical playing, tended to produce a hypnotic effect upon her audiences. She had a new dress for each performance – pale grey silks, cream and mottled brown satins trimmed with lace or velvet. At the piano she sat motionless, her features reflecting a combination of intelligence and extreme sensitivity. When she played a piece of music, her listeners often had the impression that they were hearing it executed, for the first time, in perfect sympathy with the intentions of the composer.

On 19 November, with several more public concerts looming, Violet lamented to Bill her lack of practice and the clash between her social life and her music:

> I am working very hard, a concert on the 28th, another on December 2nd, and another on the 3rd, a big one in St. James's Hall. I am not fit to play in one of them; so out of practice. With all these things, I was too busy to go to Lady Charles [Beresford] the other night!! . . . There are 10 people coming to dinner tonight, & a rehearsal, & I must go & work.

At the end of the year Violet received a rare bad notice. Dorothy, with the merest hint of *Schadenfreude*, recorded the reaction at Folkington:

> *4th December 1900.* After breakfast read *The Times*, they don't say at all nice things about Bobo's playing. They say "Papillons" was spasmodic and exaggerated in its phrasing and not well played. The *Daily Telegraph* ignore her altogether. I expect she will be very cross today. I am so glad the papers praise Giulia [Ravogli] tremendously, she has such a lovely voice. Though Father and Mother don't say much about it, I can see they are much chagrined at the adverse criticism in the papers about Bobo; Father says he hopes it will be a lesson to her not to stick herself forward too prominently again.

In the past Violet might have been furious, but by this time she was more self-confident. Rubio's opinion was what mattered most to her, and her account to Bill was positively triumphant:

> *December 5th 1900*
> I write one word . . . that I played very well last night and Rubio thinks it was "superb"!, though the newspapers each said very horrid things about me, still that does not really matter does it. They

always do not like things played differently from other people . . .
Have ordered several more pairs of spectacles!! I wonder if I shall
ever wear them. They are of course only for reading music.

Violet's family thought that she was being spoiled by success. Dorothy
refers unsympathetically in her diary to a threat by Violet never to play at
the Ganzes again because Adelina's sister Georgi was not respectful enough:
". . . I am sorry Bobo is so put out, she has such an amount of admiration
and spoiling it is enough to turn anyone's head and she resents it if everyone
does not lie down and prostrate themselves at her feet. It is such a pity the
little thing has got like that . . ." In her irritation Dorothy apparently overlooked that it was not exactly recently that Violet had "got like that": she
had been self-centred and high-handed ever since she had been singled out
from her sisters as a child prodigy twenty years earlier.

For all her dedication and hard work, at the beginning of 1901 Violet
found, for the first time in her life, that her music was taking second place to
her emotions, as is clear from a letter to Bill.

> *April 21st 1901*
> . . . Schultz-Curtius has been here, offering for me to play at one of
> his opening concerts at Bechstein Hall. June 8th or June 22nd – I
> wonder!! So long since I played and truly my mind and soul and
> heart are with Southover, the sun, gardens, birds and Mr Bill, my
> beloved sunshine of life – I suppose I must play this summer, as our
> year is retreating further into the distance. I have freedom of Park
> Place for you, a little latch key, but I will bring it when I come . . .

Two months later she wrote to Bill again in the same vein:

> *June 18th 1901*
> . . . Meantime I am sick with fear about my concerts, and I do wish
> they were over, I think I have lost my nerve for playing in public;
> I cannot sleep with fright . . . and isn't it dull for me to be working
> so hard in a hot, shiny city, when, thank God, you are alive, my
> darling Mr Bill and we have our souls, bodies, spirits and garden to
> put them in our Garden of Eden, made so by our love . . .

Violet's schedule was punishing, but she overcame her exhaustion by
sheer willpower. Moreover, normal rules hardly applied to her, and now,
without shedding any of the emotional or artistic commitments which had
occupied the first six years of her marriage, she was about to strike off in a
completely new and even more startling direction.

# VII

## *Ménage à Cinq*

THE GWYNNES WERE still trying to come to terms with the truth about Bill when, disconcertingly, another figure appeared in Violet's ambit. Since first meeting Violet at Rupert's and Gordon's famous house party in 1894, Max Labouchère had paid occasional visits to Folkington and Wootton. Now, in the autumn of 1901, he was becoming a permanent fixture at Southover. A tall man with a big nose, a quizzical smile and – until Violet made him shave it off – a moustache, he was a voracious reader and collector of literary and historical miscellanea, naturally indolent, but intellectually energetic and having a lawyer's gift for lucid exposition. Dorothy was frightened of his devastating wit, confiding to her diary that he was so brilliant that she hardly dared open her mouth in front of him. He brought to Violet a cosmopolitan sophistication inherited from his family, rich Dutch Huguenots who had intermarried with the Barings and who had extensive merchant banking connections in Holland and in England.

Max opened new worlds to Violet. Looking back in later years, she used to say that in everything but music it was he who had educated her. His detached, amused manner was strongly reminiscent of his uncle Henry,[1] who had a unique gift for deflating opponents in the House of Commons without making enemies of them, and who, after Oscar Wilde's disgrace in 1894, had had no challenger for the reputation of being the most entertaining conversationalist in London. A particularly disarming characteristic

1 Henry Labouchère's career spanned Eton, Cambridge, a spell in Mexico with a circus lady in an Indian camp, ownership and management of a theatre, the diplomatic service from Washington to St. Petersburg, editorship of an investigative journal and twenty-five years as a radical Liberal MP. He it was who "did not mind Gladstone's always having the ace of trumps up his sleeve, but objected to his pretending that Providence had put it there". Gambler, philosopher, barrister, philanderer and admirer of all things American, his championship of Home Rule for Ireland and of the Afrikaner cause in the Boer War ran counter to the jingoistic sentiment prevailing in 1901 and made him temporarily "the most unpopular man in England".

which Max had inherited from his uncle was his reluctance to take himself seriously. At Oriel College, Oxford, he had taken a Third in Modern History, the then fashionable degree for the undergraduate with a first-class mind and little appetite for work. After Oxford he was called to the Bar, had started to win some briefs, and was in 1902 living the life of a man about town with his friend and fellow-barrister, Rupert Gwynne, when he found himself falling in love with Violet. Uncle Henry, himself a formidable orator and a good judge of such matters, believed that Max would have made an outstanding advocate if he had persevered; that, however, would have meant assuming responsibility, which Max was prepared to go to considerable lengths to avoid.

Max, who had a deadly eye for humbug, recognized in Violet someone equally sceptical of conventional wisdom. He could always make her laugh, and she was happy to spend hour after hour with him, assimilating his knowledge and matching herself against his quick intelligence. Max, in turn, was charmed by her directness and fascinated by her unattainability. He liked her wit, her sense of fun and her bold, down-to-earth, sometimes risqué conversation, and was attracted by her lack of those self-consciously feminine mannerisms which irritated him in other society women (her coy letters to Bill, which reflect her sense of insecurity with him, give no idea of her forthright style with everybody else of either sex). Although he was not himself musically educated, he shared her then unfashionable love of Mozart, and his most deeply hidden sensibilities were touched by her playing. He took care, however, to lock his feelings away behind a mocking, ironical exterior.

Dorothy could not yet cope with the idea of Bill living with Violet and Gordon, let alone the new presence of Max. She accepted invitations to Park Place and Southover throughout the Season of 1902, gripped, as a spectator, by Violet's unfolding drama, but at the same time unsettled by her own first tragic experience of love and rejection. It was an experience that was to rob Dorothy of the happiness she had previously found in her familiar world of books, horses and walks on the downs, and to leave her "always yearning and dreaming of that other world of love, from which I have been shut out and where I never asked to be taken", as she wrote in an agonized entry in her diary.

The cause of Dorothy's turmoil was the louche charm of a distant cousin, Jimmie Gwynne. A married officer in a Welsh regiment, Jimmie had taken part in the Siege of Peking in 1900, an event which had stirred the imagination of the whole world, as the foreign legations were temporarily besieged by the violently xenophobic and reactionary Chinese sect known as the

"Boxers" (from their own title, "Fists of Righteous Harmony"). When he returned to England in 1902, Jimmie had tales to tell of intrigue, battle, pillage and rebellion in far-off China, tales which he could safely embellish at Folkington. Dorothy, beguiled, had been encouraged by him, only to be cruelly dropped after a few months marked by incidents of an unknown nature, which she first recorded in her diary but later scored out irretrievably. Jimmie flattered James by tracing the Gwynnes' ancestry to Welsh princes, and brought with him from the Forbidden City furs, jewels and two Pekinese dogs given to him – or so he said – by Prince Kung, the former Foreign Minister to the Manchu Empress Dowager of China, as a reward for having rescued him from the Boxers. One day Jimmie disappeared from Folkington, deserting Dorothy for ever and bequeathing the Pekinese to Bluebelle and to Violet; from hers, Violet bred a long line of offspring.

Engrossed in her own infatuation, Dorothy failed at first to understand the full implications of Max's frequent appearances at Park Place and Southover. She was more alert to the allure of his debutante cousin ("Miss Labouchère is a dangerous lady," she wrote), who came out in 1902 and was liable to sit up into the small hours talking with Rupert ("he will be her next victim," Dorothy forecast). With the awakening of her own senses, Dorothy began, too, to look at Bill and Violet in a new light. Her sister's ability to attract and hold men increasingly excited Dorothy's jealousy, while her own feelings for Bill oscillated between oversensitivity – "Mr Bill and Mr Labouchère came to tea . . . I know Mr Bill dislikes me" – and fantasy – "I had such a nice dream about Mr Barrington last night."

Longing to have more time alone with Violet, Bill could be cool towards Dorothy when she got in the way, but he was also well aware – and if he forgot, Violet reminded him – that he must expend a certain amount of charm on her for Violet's sake, however plain she was, and however annoying he might find her. When he chose, as he did with other women too often for Violet's liking, Bill could turn on a devastating flirtatiousness, which would win over Dorothy immediately. Her diary for 2 May 1902 records her fixing roses on to her evening gown as she dresses for one of Violet's concerts, which was to be followed by a ball at the Goldsmiths' Hall:

> I went down when I was ready with a quaking heart to see if Bobo approved of me. She was in her room with Mr. B. and they both said my dress was charming so I returned upstairs with a light heart again. It is the first time anyone has given me flowers for a dance and I think it is very kind. Mr. B. says he didn't send me the flowers . . . of course I knew he did.

Mr. Bill was so charming to me he danced lots of times with me. We couldn't get round on the waltz for the crowd was far too great but we had two most perfect polkas. He dances and looks so graceful. He *is* distinguished-looking. He seemed greatly taken with Miss Mayhew. I wish I were pretty like she and am always at my worst with him for I am rather frightened of him and very shy and awkward.

Adelina Ganz was just as much to be seen at Park Place and Southover as Bill, Max and Gordon. Not only was Violet immensely attractive to women, she needed their constant company. Through them she found relief from the unsympathetic and unyielding masculine side of human nature, exemplified by her father. At the same time she often brought out in women the submissiveness she despised in her mother, by exploiting the affection that she aroused in them and virtually turning them into acolytes. Adelina was one of her few female admirers to preserve the status of an equal. Dorothy was bewildered by the relationship, on which, rightly or wrongly, she put a completely innocent interpretation. The day after the Goldsmiths' Hall ball, thrown into confusion by Violet's glamorous way of life and by the emotional charge of the household, Dorothy confided to her diary in her bedroom at the top of the house in Park Place: "Adelina is with Bobo. I get so tired of her and jealous, yes, jealous. Today she was dressed in a lovely hat that Bobo had given her."

Violet's intermittent coldness, from which Dorothy had suffered over and over again during their childhood, was a weapon which she used to deadly effect whenever she felt she had not been shown the deference that she believed was her due. She could create a frightening atmosphere of disapproval, reducing those around her to a state of misery. Three weeks after Dorothy's fit of jealousy over Adelina there was a frosty encounter between the sisters at Southover:

*24 May 1902*

I did not enjoy my day at Southover at all. Bobo was so disagreeable to me. Bobo didn't welcome me with any hug but coldness; soon after the others arrived we had lunch. Adelina was there. I never go to Bobo's but what she is there. I am sick of seeing her, she is so very much at home and I am made to feel such a passing guest; she was very rude to me at lunch; it was all about the day I didn't travel down with Bobo in the train. Lunch was so dull and heavy, no one seemed at their ease. After lunch Bobo took the hen party over the house. Mr. B. joined us. Father, Boy and Gordon bought a cricket bat for the servants at home. Lord Gage and

Mr. Peel [Lord Gage's father-in-law] came to tea.

As if Bill and Max and Adelina were not enough, yet another complication had appeared on the horizon in the person of the Hon. Denis Tollemache, a tall, handsome and dashing seventeen-year-old just down from Winchester. This time music was the connection. Denis's aunt Blanche was one of the earliest musical friends of Violet's mother May; his uncle Wilbraham Tollemache, known as "Braham", was an organist and composer[2] who embarrassed the Tollemache family by the extravagance of his admiration for Violet's talent. Denis had been taken to hear Violet play at the age of eight. It was a case of love at first sight, and now, as Denis reached manhood, his childish infatuation was turning into a deepening passion which was to last his whole life. Less subtle than Max, Denis wore his heart on his sleeve – his open nature would have made it impossible for him to behave in any other way – and Violet, secure in his adoration, succumbed rather too often to the temptation to take his feelings for granted. He, for his part, found her fragile appearance, her quicksilver movements, her provocative gaiety, her changes of mood, completely irresistible. He prided himself that he was the only one of her men genuinely capable of appreciating her musicality.

Denis was a younger son in an old, long ennobled Suffolk family. His looks were Italianate, with dark, almost swarthy, skin, black hair, and brown eyes framed by strong brows and cheekbones; later, as a cavalry officer (he rose to command the 7th Hussars), he was to grow a flowing military moustache. He was a man of uncomplicated thoughts, impulsive emotions and steadfast enthusiasms. Violet apart, he devoted himself to the army, his family estates and his grandfather's eccentric young second wife, affectionately known to him as "G.M." (short for Grandma). In 1902 Denis's father died, and his mother's remarriage the following year virtually ended his contact with her. When his grandfather died in 1904, leaving "G.M." with a life interest in his Suffolk estate, she and Denis more or less adopted each other as honorary mother and son.

The first mention of Denis in Dorothy's diary comes towards the end of 1901, when a visit late at night to Violet's house in Park Place draws a couple of exclamation marks: "November 1901. I was sitting in Bobo's room when a ring came at the door – Summers went down and it was Denis

2 His Sonata in A Minor for Violoncello and Pianoforte published in 1905 by the Vincent Music Company, is dedicated "To his friend Señor Rubio". On 2 July 1906 a concert was held at the Aeolian Hall of W.J. Tollemache compositions and songs, with Nettie Carpenter on the violin and Winifred Christie on the piano.

Tollemache come to pay a call at 11.20 p.m.!! Bobo went down but I went up to bed."

Unknown to Dorothy, the purpose of Denis's call had been to declare his love. His military ambitions had taken him straight from school into the 7th Hussars and, after a period of training, he was due to be posted to South Africa. For Britain, the course of the Boer War had changed for the better early in 1900, and in fact Denis arrived in South Africa, where he was to spend two years with his regiment, just after the signing of the Treaty of Vereeniging in May 1902, which ended the fighting and re-established British supremacy in the Afrikaner provinces. When he called on Violet in November 1901, however, all this lay in the future. The new weaponry of the late nineteenth century had made it a particularly dangerous war, which by the time it was over had cost the lives of 22,000 British, Imperial or colonial servicemen. Denis wanted Violet to know that he might not survive, but that if he did he would return to court her with all the persuasion at his command.

Violet could only succeed in keeping all her admirers in train if Gordon and Bill were prepared to co-operate. This proved far easier than she might reasonably have expected. Gordon's feelings for her had never wavered. Though their marriage was now seven years old, he was still spoiling her, terrified that she might grow bored if he failed to meet her every demand. Her life was full, yet however much affection and attention she received, she always craved more. And now that she had collected four male devotees, none of whom ever criticized her and each of whom responded to different aspects of her nature, the extraordinary plan was beginning to form in her mind that Max and Denis, as well as Bill, should eventually come to live with her and Gordon. Perhaps they could, together, give her the proof that she was uniquely lovable which had eluded her in her youth, partly because of the tense atmosphere generated by her father, and partly because her own precocious talent had led to her being deprived of a normal Victorian childhood and adolescence.

She did not have to resort to any elaborate manoeuvring. The notion that he could, or should, set limits upon her behaviour did not cross Gordon's mind, any more than did the concern that his position as a complaisant husband might attract ridicule. He wanted only that Violet should be happy, and that his friendship with Bill should be unaffected – nothing else mattered to him. Having cheerfully fitted Bill into his marriage, Gordon was now equally willing to make sure that Max, and later Denis, should feel at home. He himself was content to retire into the background and play the role in which he felt most at ease, sheltering Violet from domestic chores, paying the bills, organizing the kitchen and making the household run smoothly.

As for Bill, he too welcomed the arrival of Max and Denis. He was confident enough in his relationship with Violet not to have any anxieties about it. Relaxed and English to the core, Bill had little in common with the intensity of Dolmetsch, the bohemianism of Rubio, or the flamboyance of the rest of Violet's foreign entourage. Max and Denis made a refreshing contrast to these exotic artists, coming from backgrounds similar to his own and sharing his outdoor interests. Rather than sitting at home pretending to be interested in obscure composers, Bill could take the new additions to the household off to watch Sussex in the county cricket championship, where their Oxford and Cambridge contemporaries, C.B. Fry and Prince Ranjitsinhji, regularly headed the English first-class batting averages. His feelings towards Denis, as a young brother officer, were those of a kindly and protective uncle; Max, meanwhile, could provide the intellectual stimulus which Bill knew Violet needed. All in all, to have these two as comrades in arms would be thoroughly agreeable. By dividing between them the task of dancing attendance on Violet, Bill would be allowed greater opportunity for long country house weekends. Moreover, he and Violet were both perhaps naive enough to believe that the outside world would be less likely to suspect the degree of their own intimacy if he was only one of a crowd living in her house.

Violet's deepest feelings were certainly reserved for Bill. Fond as she was of the others, they were essentially there to indulge and entertain her, to worship at her feet and to provide an extra reason for Bill not to stray. Now that he had left the Militia, he was able to be with Violet practically all the time, but he also had increased freedom to travel. As the eldest son of a landed aristocrat who had not yet come into his estates, he found himself in a traditional vacuum, which he filled in the traditional manner – with sport. Bill had learned to ride, shoot and fish around the Beckett estate when he was a small boy, and on coming of age he had been given Medlar Cottage, close to Beckett House, to use as his hunting and shooting box. He went regularly to the cottage, sometimes with friends, sometimes just to be alone. And since he was well liked, and it was not yet universally appreciated that he was actually living with Violet and Gordon, he was in great demand as an eligible bachelor at country house parties all over England and Scotland, where he was able to spend his time doing what he liked best.

Bill's popularity was a source of anxiety to Violet. She was not alone in finding him attractive; indeed, his beauty was such common currency that he was made the barely disguised hero of a contemporary novel by Fox Russell, *The Honourable Bill*. Coating his prose in the sentimentalism of the day, the author describes how his protagonist's "athletic frame and sunburnt face conveyed an idea of self-reliance and strength, which was in the highest degree comforting. . . at once so gentle and so masterful". A man of honour who had been in the army "eking out his pay with the small pittance he received from his brother", he was "passionately fond of fox-hunting, with no fancy for town pleasures". The climax of the book, when lack of confidence prevents him from proposing to the woman he loves, even offers a stereotype of the emotional indecision which marked the real Honourable Bill.

The Boer War drew to its conclusion in the late spring of 1902, while Denis was still en route for Cape Town. After the early disasters, the final success was a tremendous relief, masking from the public eye the unpleasant facts of war, including the insanitary, disease-ridden refugee camps in which, before the intrepid reformer Miss Emily Hobhouse went out to investigate them and press for change, too many Afrikaner and black non-combatants had been interned and died. When Field Marshal Lord Kitchener announced the signing of the peace treaty, Britain erupted into celebration. Articles in popular journals advised "people who are wise as well as patriotic" to secure plenty of decorative flags in good time, recommending "Union Jacks with medallion portraits of the King and Queen at 1s 11¹/₂d the dozen".

On 2 June Dorothy took a train and was met at Lewes station by Gordon. From above the town there came the constant sound of guns going off on the downs. Dorothy's delight in victory was heightened by Bill's absence from Southover: "We found Bobo in her sitting room; she looks very thin and pale but her throat is better. Mr B. is away *Oh such a relief*." After lunch the party walked into the centre of Lewes, where flags were draped from every house, to buy their own decorations for Southover. The bamboo rods with gilt tops, which were meant to hold the two huge flags they bought, were so long that Gordon could not get them into the house and had to stand in the lane and feed them up to Violet through the bedroom window. Dorothy was full of chauvinistic sentiment, but Max poked fun at the absurdity of toasting a war which had achieved so little at such high cost. Admittedly, his uncle had finally sided with the pro-war faction, but Henry Labouchère was a politician, while Max was free to be as outspoken as he wished.

In the same year in which Violet started to put her grand design for living into effect, Lady Barrington fell seriously ill. In October 1902 Bill received a letter from his father, which he forwarded to Violet, saying that his mother had been diagnosed as having cancer, and had only fifteen to eighteen months left to her. Violet knew what pain his mother's suffering would cause Bill, and reconciled herself to the fact that his place would increasingly

Violet as a small child.
Already there is a hint of wilfulness and resolution in her face.

Violet's grandmother, Cornelia In'tveld –
a legendary beauty but with a secret
in her background.

May Gwynne,
Violet's mother,
seven years after
her marriage.

James and May Gwynne, Violet's parents. Their marriage was violently opposed by the Gwynne family.

Violet, aged one year.

Violet and her brother Nevile, who struck his father in 1902 and was secretly disinherited.

Violet at sixteen.

James Gwynne – tyrannical, rich and morose, he speculated profitably in real estate.

Violet's youngest brother Roland, who was dressed in skirts until he was thirteen. He grew up to be an incorrigible intriguer.

Violet's sister Dorothy – an awkward girl who observed and noted in her diary details of Violet's extraordinary life.

Gordon Woodhouse and Violet's brother Rupert at Cambridge in 1893.
Rupert unexpectedly inherited all the Gwynne estates.

Violet and her elder sister, Eva,
who was intensely jealous of Violet's success.

James Gwynne, Violet's father, with two of his sons,
Roland and Rupert.

Folkington Manor, Sussex, where Violet spent her childhood.

Oscar Beringer, the German *émigré*, who taught Violet at his Academy
for Advanced Piano Tuition in London.

Arnold Dolmetsch, scholar and zealot, who changed the course of Violet's career in 1894 by introducing her to early music and the harpsichord (*1925, National Portrait Gallery*).

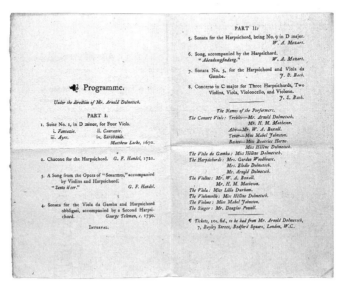

Violet held a concert in her house in Upper Brooke Street with Arnold Dolmetsch and his "Elizabethan family" in 1899.

Violet's husband, Gordon
Woodhouse. The marriage
was to remain unconsummated.

Maxwell Labouchère, barrister,
wit and man about town. His death
in the First World War deprived
Violet of her intellectual mentor.

The Hon. Bill Barrington –
the love of Violet's life.

The Hon. Denis Tollemache –
a dashing cavalry officer who
was under Violet's spell from
his school days until his death
in 1942.

Bill Barrington, top right, next to his father, Lord Barrington, with
his three brothers. The Barringtons were a close-knit family, who
resented the fact that Violet's hold over Bill prevented him from
creating a family of his own.

Captain Barrington, second left at the front, with the militia band of the Oxford
and Buckinghamshire Light Infantry in 1900.

Three snapshots of Violet, found in Bill's possessions after his death and probably taken around 1903, in her early thirties.

Violet before her marriage. Suspicions about her ancestry were deflected
by a false trail suggesting "Spanish origins".

be in London so long as his mother was alive. For once it was Violet who would have to adapt, which would mean spending less time at Southover. Meanwhile she did her best to distract him with letters full of chat about everyday events:

Southover Grange, *November 12th 1902*
Dearest
... I am going to write you a homely letter, just of our little Southover doings. About what you are thinking I cannot speak, it is too near, my beloved, for a pen and therefore too near me too, though the love I bear you is so great and so close that, believe me, my so dear one, I am carrying your trouble with every step and with every breath and alas! that I cannot lift one corner of it off your heart. But I shall try not to make it any heavier by being selfish of your love ...

That pony dealer called to see Gordon and he had actually nearly bought one of those dear little stumpy ponies, quite by himself, without either of us to urge him on! He took the little blue cart and tried it out, harness and all. It fits beautifully. He is going to present it to either you or me!

Dorothy, recording Lady Barrington's illness in her diary, was unable to resist a dig at the way Violet gave Bill priority over Gordon: "We were to have gone to Southover yesterday but Mr Barrington's mother is very ill and he has to remain in London and of course Bobo couldn't leave him in town alone. Oh No she must stay in Park Place and see he is comfortable there!"

Violet kept constantly in touch with Bill. Wherever he went, he was followed by loving letters written in violet-coloured ink, marked with her own distinctive  (ϕ)  and pushed into mauve bordered envelopes. The brief period  when he had been a distraction to her work was over – now he was an inspiration. On the anniversary of their earliest days together, Violet wrote him a note from the heart:

*Midsummer's Day 1903,* 9 Park Place, London
My Darling and beloved Bill,
Today is one of those times when I remember very much that wonderful summer when you and I were treading that magic path so full of golden sun and glory, along which you have walked with me for these four happy years, and for which blessing how can I ever find words or deeds to be grateful one little quarter to God or to you? I am working very hard now and very well thank you I hope you are also. Good evening, Mr Bill, my beloved.

Throughout the rest of 1903 she kept him informed of every detail of her daily existence. Cars had first been allowed on public roads, with a 12-mph speed limit, in 1896, but by 1903, when the King became an enthusiast, the limit had been raised to 20 mph and driving began to catch on. In September, while Bill was shooting at Scruton Hall in Yorkshire, Violet wrote that she had been "in a racing motor, a Panhard . . . to Newhaven and back in half an hour . . . very exciting, like a perpetual switch-back. I had a hood and many veils". On the primitive unmetalled roads of the time cars threw up choking clouds of dust, affording Violet a welcome opportunity for dramatic dressing.

There was, self-evidently, a narcissistic streak in Violet, which she had the good grace to acknowledge and which Gordon, Max and Rupert (Denis was still in South Africa) flattered exorbitantly. "They are all very nice and do what I wish, and it is like looking at your own reflection in a spoon, or something of that sort, all the time." A few days later she wrote to Bill again, having learned from Max that his highly eccentric father,[3] who liked to move from house to house, decorating and restoring them in the hope of selling them at a profit, was thinking of renting Cobbe Place as a base for speculative operations in Sussex. "I think Max rather dreads it for us . . . I cannot imagine what they would find to do in the neighbourhood, can you?"

The experiment of having her men together at Southover was working well. Max, like Bill, contributed modestly to the household expenses. Their days were fully occupied with outdoor activities or in preparing hospitality for visitors, leaving Violet free to practise as long and as intensively as she wanted. Gordon worked on the orchard, while Bill was making good progress with the garden. One day, when Bill was away, William Robinson came over, and Dorothy noted in her diary Bill's pleasure when she passed on to him Robinson's enthusiastic comments about his design plans and, in particular, about his water garden and his rare plants. There was hunting or cubbing on the South Downs with Rupert, Dorothy and Roland, and the men all rode in the Eastbourne Hunt point-to-point each year, for which James Gwynne was Steward – Rupert, who was by far the best rider, won the event several times. Rupert often invited them over to shoot duck or pigeons at Folkington, and Violet's former fiancé, Henry Gage, would from time to time ask them to shoot at Firle: apart from Rupert, however, Violet

3 Arthur Labouchère liked horses. He was asked to withdraw from his father's bank, Williams Deacon & Co., when he showed more interest in trying to drive a four-in-hand to the office than in getting to know the firm's business. In winter he regularly took his pack of hounds to Biarritz. Sixty-two when his wife died, he next married a girl forty-three years his junior. Max was his second son and third of four children.

did not see as much of her family as before. Her father was driving her brothers to despair with his meanness and was in the midst of a particularly bitter series of quarrels with Nevile. For someone of Violet's temperament, who could not abide family arguments, Folkington was becoming a less congenial place to visit.

Although in name Managing Director of Gwynne & Co., Nevile had been given no decision-making powers. He had advised his father either to modernize the factory or to close it, since it was being consistently outclassed by the rival Gwynne firm at Hammersmith, but James had contemptuously ignored him. James's autocratic decision to sell the old Purvis rice plantations in Java at a knock-down price had also been taken without Nevile's agreement and against his judgement (and was to prove a costly mistake for May and Aunt Kate). For years Nevile had bowed to his father's will, but latterly he had been unable to contain himself. Eighteen months earlier there had been a dreadful row, which had culminated in a hand-to-hand struggle in which he had thrown James to the ground. When May had tried to intervene, James had committed an unforgivable sin, in Victorian eyes, by striking her. That night, 17 February 1902, James had written a codicil to his will: "It is my will and desire that my second son Nevile Gwynne shall be excluded from any participation in any portion of my property I may die possessed of owing to the disgraceful way in which he treated me this evening. He raised his hand and struck me in a most undutiful and improper manner. I leave him and his family £500 and no more."

Now, in August 1903, James and Nevile were still unreconciled, and it had become impossible for them to work together any longer. James incorporated the codicil into his will and, after yet another row, Nevile finally resigned, or was effectively dismissed, from his father's firm. Despite James's great acumen, it proved to have been Nevile who had been right in their disagreements over business policy. The following year Gwynne & Co. had to be merged into James's brothers' more successful firm, whereupon Nevile joined his uncle as a partner. The breach was deep, forcing Nevile, Bluebelle and their young children to move away to Hertfordshire and to cut their links with Folkington.

Violet was to a large extent insulated from family disputes by her own very full life at Southover. In the evenings she would play for neighbours or visitors from London. After dinner, if they were on their own, the members of the ménage would read aloud to each other (Denis, when he got back to England, proved to have the best voice). Bill would stretch out on the huge bearskin in front of the fire in the drawing-room and fall asleep, his head resting on the bear's head. Violet snatched every possible opportunity to be alone with him, often slipping up to London to see him. Their relationship was now unmistakably physical. A postscript to an otherwise nondescript letter from Violet about the garden implies that they were in the habit of falling into each other's arms whenever they had a moment together: "Do not you think we are very clever in making 'home' *directly* together wherever we find ourselves; for example, the smoking room in Park Place yesterday!!!!"

Sunday nights were reserved for formal musical occasions for up to fifty people. Rubio – his ticket, like Nettie Carpenter's, paid for by Violet – would arrive by train from London, accompanied by Arbós or Guétary. Violet also played privately for distinguished visitors. The sculptor Auguste Rodin was brought by William Rothenstein to hear her play Mozart in Park Place, and Bernard Shaw brought Ellen Terry there to listen to an after-tea performance of baroque music. When he was in England Sarasate would come as often as he could, bringing with him one of his two Stradivarius violins.[4] Violet was eager to promote the compositions of her Spanish friends. In the summer of 1903 she held a public concert in the drawing room at Southover, where pieces by Arbós, Guétary and Sarasate were included in an otherwise conventional programme of piano works by Tchaikovsky, Brahms and Beethoven. Arbós, the most musically ambitious, stole the show with his Spanish Trios, in which he was accompanied by Violet on the piano, Nettie Carpenter on the violin and Rubio on the cello.

Having played with him for more than ten years, Violet was disappointed when Arbós concluded that, financially, his career would prosper better abroad, though she understood his reasons. Late in 1903 he left England to take up the post of conductor of the Madrid Symphony Orchestra, with which he toured the world, returning to England only intermittently. Bill was in Scotland when Arbós left; a sentimental Spanish farewell dinner, with speeches and musical talk, was no competition for the grouse moor.

*September 26th 1903* Southover Grange
Dearest Mr Bill
. . . Arbós's dinner was a rather sad affair. He was very sorry at leaving and so was everybody else. He sent you some messages. I am glad to find that he has £2,600 for the six months now waiting for him in the bank and, as well as this, he has all his expenses paid in travelling, etc., and 15 shillings a day as well. He can also make a great deal more in extra concerts. The last man made £5,000 each time so Arbós will be a rich person after a little time.

4 Made in 1713 and 1724 by Antonio Stradivari (?1644–1737) at the height of his craftsmanship.

Meanwhile Lady Barrington's slow dying was becoming harder and harder for Bill to watch. Violet had a horror of suffering which led her in later years to blot out any mention of pain and illness, but for Bill's sake she was able to summon up words of comfort. On 4 November she wrote: "It is so dreadful for you to have to look, and be able to do nothing to help her in her pain." Next day she wrote again:

*November 5th 1903*, Southover Grange
My Darling Mr Bill,
I am writing among all the roaring of these bothering bonfires. All this sham joy, when my dearest is in such trouble, is hard to bear . . . I feel it almost to be rude and intrusive to talk much about all your sadness when I am so far out of it, but Beloved, my heart is with you always and God bless you every minute of the day and night. How proud you must be to have so brave a Mother. I wish if God will give us a courage to face the great change and terrible darkness with such an unflinching and splendid spirit. This is something which will live in her children's hearts, all through life, is not it, my sweetheart, the memory of this brave spirit. Good night, good night, blessed Mr Bill.

By now the end was, at long last, in sight:

Hotel Albemarle, Piccadilly
Best Beloved,
We know that God will bless her and take all her pains away, and this is how he has answered your prayers, my dear one, and it must be the best way, though through so solemn and awful a gate. Thank you for writing to me when you did and at such a moment. I do wish I could put my arms around you and hide your dear head on my heart, while we would whisper to God how we should make better our lives that we may not be dismayed when we must look on the awful gate of eternity.

Lady Barrington finally died on 16 November, taking with her the last reason for Violet to cloak her relationship with Bill in the few remaining shreds of convention. From that time onward, interrupted only by family commitments, sporting excursions or Denis's army career, she and her four men lived quite openly together until, one by one, death separated them from each other.

In 1904 Denis returned from South Africa. The next two years were ones which Violet afterwards looked back on as among the most contented of her life. If many people were shocked, and if the more malicious gossips put it around that she was virtually running a male harem, she was cocooned in the courtly protection of her men, to whom she gave, and from whom she received, unquestioning loyalty. Her supreme musical powers gave her a confidence which amounted to imperviousness to the criticism of ordinary people. There were no humdrum constraints at Southover; Violet did what she wanted, how she wanted, with whom she wanted. The atmosphere there, though relaxed, hummed with purpose, while the variety of the guests' ages and nationalities, combined with the *frisson* of suspected impropriety in the hosts, gave their gatherings a spice not to be found in other English country houses.

By now Violet had almost given up the piano in favour of the harpsichord. She was, however, tempted back to it one last time by Nettie Carpenter. On 23 February 1905 Violet returned to Bechstein Hall with Nettie to hear, for the third time in a month, the young Russian-born cellist, Boris Hambourg. He and his two elder brothers – Mark, a pianist, and Jan, a violinist – had acquired a remarkable popular following. Since the start of her friendship with Rubio, Violet felt a particular affinity with the cello; now, inspired by Hambourg's broad, clear phrasing and beauty of tone, she responded in a rash moment to Nettie's suggestion that the three of them should play together during the Eastbourne season. On 4 March, in what proved to be Violet's final public performance on the piano,[5] she returned to her old repertoire with a concert in the Town Hall at Eastbourne. She opened with Tchaikovsky's Trio, with Nettie on the violin and Boris Hambourg on the cello, and followed with solos by Brahms and Beethoven – Ballade and Contre Danse. Although neither the reviewers nor the members of Eastbourne's fashionable music-going set noticed any falling off in her performance, Violet herself was not happy with it. Her technique was by now so attuned to the harpsichord that she had found practising for the piano stretched the muscles in her fingers and left her hands shaking. Her perfectionism told her that she had not quite met the standards she demanded of herself, and had it not been for the pleasure of helping Nettie and Boris Hambourg in their careers, she would have regretted having agreed to play.

5 A month later Wanda Landowska, who was to be Violet's most serious rival as a harpsichordist, made her first appearance in England at two recitals at Queen's Hall, reviewed favourably by Christabel Marshal in *The Lady* on 20 and 27 April. In the first, Landowska played Bach on the piano and Handel and Couperin on the harpsichord: in the second, she traced the development of the waltz from Byrd and Morley to Chopin, using two harpsichords, an eighteenth-century square piano and a modern grand piano.

Southover was now as much the centre of Violet's musical life as Park Place. There was, of course, the London Season, as well as excursions to Manchester and elsewhere, wherever the best performances were to be heard, but she did much of her practising at Southover and, in addition to her Sunday salon, she often held special events there. She had kept in touch with Arbós since his departure, and in the spring of 1905 she staged a play-through of his comic opera, *El Centro de la Tierra*, in the music room. Violet had asked a large number of guests, though she left to Gordon the planning of the entertainment. To suggest the illusion of the opera house it was necessary to cut off the singers from the audience, so a curtain was put up and two maids detailed to hold it back or let it go at appropriate moments. The piano was masked behind a Japanese painted lacquer screen. A liveried servant, well rehearsed, was to come forward during the performance and unroll a placard on which was written in bold letters that part of the plot which needed explaining.

Risking the weather, Gordon had three tables for supper, each seating eight, placed outside on the terrace and three more indoors. On the lower branches of the trees close to the house hung oil lanterns with red glass panels, giving off a subdued light. Plants were set on pedestals, their flowers and leaves tumbling down on to the flagstones. In the centre of the tables sprays of lily of the valley encircled brass candlesticks, on the shades of which Bill had sketched characters from the opera in green and orange crayon. The menu was written in violet ink on cream cards: hot consommé, with croutons spread with foie gras; fried fillets of Dover sole with cold horseradish cream sauce in hollowed-out cherry tomatoes; cold poached quails stuffed with grapes and served with cubes of herb aspic; saddle of mutton with a filling of puréed young turnips, accompanied by a hot mousse of green peas with a cream sauce; raspberry ice cream with a puréed strawberry sauce; tiny cheese soufflés served hot; and, finally, muscat grapes, purple and green figs, white peaches and nectarines from the greenhouses. With the meal Gordon served hock, red burgundy, champagne and a wine cup for the young.

The evening was a success. The spirited opera, combining the Moorish and gypsy elements in Spanish music, moved the precocious Arthur Waley, then a sixteen-year-old schoolboy at Rugby, to write a thank-you letter to Violet in which, rather pompously, he expressed the hope that "the powers that be will make something of it". For Waley, whose translations of oriental literature were to earn him an international reputation as a scholar, the event was a stepping stone in his musical initiation; it was, too, the start of his enduring friendship with Violet.

That same year, 1905, Max's mother died and he dutifully went to France to see his father, who spent much of his time in Pau hunting with his friend Henry Ridgeway, the Master of the Pau foxhounds. Max was unable to persuade Bill and Gordon to bring Violet to join him in what had become one of Europe's most anglophile resorts. Pau had possessed an English community since 1814, when, in the final battle of the Peninsular War, the Duke of Wellington had beaten Napoleon's Marshal Soult twenty miles away at Orthez, six weeks before the Emperor's abdication and exile to Elba. So chic was the town in Edwardian times, its position, on the edge of the Pyrenees in south-western France as perfect as its climate, that the names of the *haut monde* of Europe filled the registers of its luxurious hotels, the Hôtel de France and the Hôtel Gassion. King Alfonso XIII of Spain visited the town for his health; King Edward VII went there to play on the first golf course to be laid out on the Continent. To the Labouchères, Pau was home from home, and they are remembered in the area to this day as "les Labouchère d'Orthez". Through his father Max knew all of local society; nevertheless, he was in love – and without Violet he was lonely. He wrote a bantering letter from his hotel, scolding Gordon, Bill and Violet in turn (Denis was away soldiering again), but still genuinely a little put out at the lack of correspondence, especially from Violet:

> . . . A whole week and no sign of a letter. *Nous sommes trahis!*
>
> Excuse these gentle reminders to the brotherhood from an absent brother's feelings on a blank Friday. How goes it with the Arbós concerts? Have they (that mysterious "they" behind all such enterprises) yet baited the Bechstein Hall with a live Princess? Do your Sunday evenings still gaily scandalise the non-conformist conscience? Oh! I feel much too far away . . . four letters a month and three people the other end! That oughtn't to be difficult ought it?
>
> Love to you all from Maxwell.

To outsiders, especially those who thought of Violet as little better than a high-class courtesan, it was puzzling that her men were on such good terms with each other and were not more jealous. Could they conceivably be – inexpressible thought, only ten years after Oscar Wilde's imprisonment – a nest of homosexuals? Surely not. They were too clearly besotted with Violet, and there was never even the breath of a suspicion of that sort, although in retrospect some people saw something ambiguous about Gordon's masculinity. Could it be that she granted her favours to each of them by turn? Yet that was equally implausible, for had that been the case, they would have to have been superhuman not to have quarrelled with each other. The truth was that, like it or not, privately each of the other three accepted Bill as her real husband. Denis certainly had periods of misery over the yawning gap between his passionate love for Violet and her cooler affection for him; and to a lesser extent Max suffered in the same manner. Although for the time being she kept both Max and Denis at bay, at least where a physical relationship was concerned, she had the gift of making each one of her men feel uniquely important when she was alone with him, as she often contrived to be. In their different ways Denis and Max were free spirits, and after the liberating air of Southover the prospect of a normal marriage with demanding children and a conventional wife was hard for either of them to contemplate. That all four men enjoyed each other's company, as Violet had foreseen, was a considerable help in dispelling any tensions and keeping the atmosphere harmonious.

It was also in 1905 that Violet lost one of the closest in her circle with the marriage of Rupert. It was Rupert who had introduced Gordon to Bill at Cambridge, and who had brought both of them together with Violet. Violet loved having him around, for his charm was the equal of Bill's, and he was even more high-spirited. He had been living with Violet and Gordon in London at Park Place and he was, of course, their neighbour at Folkington; now Bill and Gordon were to be ushers at his glamorous wedding to the Hon. Stella Ridley, a twenty-year-old orphan from a well-connected Conservative political family. By any standards, Violet should have been delighted for him. Marriage, however, has a way of being catching, and Violet felt some anxiety that Bill might follow Rupert's example – after all, with her, Bill had no standing in law and, it seemed, no prospect of children. There had even been some talk between them that he and Gordon might exchange places, but the public scandal of a divorce, together with Bill's lack of money, ruled out that idea.

Violet's intuitive alarm about Bill's state of mind was well founded. Now thirty-two, he was growing restless; without the Militia he felt ineffective and motiveless, despite his success in gardening and garden design. Although he invariably came across as a man at ease with himself, to have to rely so much on Gordon financially was bad for his self-esteem. Yet he could not afford to buy his own farm, and his patronizing, sanctimonious new stepmother, whom Lord Barrington had married only five months after the death of Bill's mother, was already beginning to get through the dwindling remains of his father's wealth at an alarming rate. Bill went away for long spells to Medlar Cottage. The spectre of losing him altogether sank Violet into a depression, made worse by the continuous whirl of her social life and her gruelling hours of practice. In the autumn of 1906 she suffered a crisis which brought on thoughts of withdrawing from society:

*October 6th 1906*, Park Place, London

Dearest Bill . . . and now I must tell you the result of all this solitary meditating is that I have a strong thought of taking a cottage in Folkington village, in fact imitating you the other way round! But not for the same reasons! There is a large cottage which I do not think you have ever seen near to the downs and near where the laundry is now. I think it has three bedrooms and three downstairs rooms. This would hold poor Kiddy [Bill's pet name for Violet], Dulciette and Suzanne and also the puppet [Violet's Highland terrier]. Here I could go and be all alone away from the great cruel London. I could walk about the downs. My family can look after me if I am ill, and there is a churchyard where I should not be ashamed to ask to be put in if I happen to go away. Dear Mr Bill, I have been this burden to all our once so happy and blessed little circle. Here I shall hide my unhappy little head until I can hold it straight again. I am so tired, I do not think I can stay here always and not be so sentimental. There are many practical reasons. Doctor Lancaster says my throat is not well at all and London is so bad for it. Now do not think on sad things, darling Mr. Bill. You are never to blame in one scrap, in fact no-one is . . . I send you all my heart on this sheet of paper. V.

The crisis was soon over. Bill could no more live without Violet than she without him. If he needed an activity by which to regain his self-respect, Violet would find it for him, Gordon would discreetly pay, and Max and Denis would co-operate. Collectively, they decided to put Southover on the market and look for a place where Bill could try his hand at farming, preferably nearer his home ground in Oxfordshire.

*6 December 1906*

. . . I hope you get this tonight, I hope so and then it might sleep quite close to you where I sometimes rest my head, and used to very often do, in such a peace and great love . . . someone made an offer of £5,000 for Southover the day before yesterday but that is too little I think.

Southover was swiftly sold and, with Medlar Cottage as their base, the "brotherhood", as Max had called it, searched for a year for another "jewel", this time one which would have with it some land. By the end of 1907 they had found what they were looking for.

# VIII

*Golden Years Before the War*

A PROPERTY AS ROMANTIC as Southover, Armscote House, near Stratford-upon-Avon in Warwickshire, with its farm and the potential for another beautiful garden, was exactly what Bill sought. Standing on the edge of the ancient hamlet of Armscote, close to the borders with both Gloucestershire and Oxfordshire, it possessed the character of an unspoilt Tudor farmhouse. Outbuildings added over the centuries rambled amiably around the main building, with its double-gabled front in Cotswold stone. A lane passed by the entrance door, which was protected from the gaze of the curious by several yards of sheltered walled garden in which was set an iron gate. Carriages and cars entered through an archway cut into the centre of a long, low, thatched barn and leading to a yard enclosed, on three sides, by stables and open farm buildings, and on the fourth by the east wall of the house. By a grass field outside the yard gold lettering on a black board proclaimed that George Fox, founder of the Society of Friends, the Quakers, had once been arrested – it must have been some 250 years earlier – while holding a meeting there.

The other men shared Bill's enthusiasm. "Tomorrow you will know about the house – how exciting", he wrote to Violet. "I don't believe *you* want it but we do. The water difficulty will probably be easily overcome by making a well in the field opposite or somehow." In his eagerness he wrote again from Melrose in Scotland, where he had gone to fish. His letter, full of endearments to "Kiddy", with her "little black head" and the ring on her finger "that was once mine", shows that their relationship was now restored to all its former tenderness:

*November 24 1907,* Melrose
My dearest Heart – Here we are at our day and not one small short line from you just to remind me that it is Sunday evening. Unkind! It's different me not writing to Kiddy 'cause my letters dull, dull, dull as

97

blazes with nothing that interests her only the same old tale no fish [i.e. no salmon], no water, fish dying of disease . . . but *all* Kiddy's news is full to overflowing with the things I want to and long to hear and when there is no other news there is that most beloved of all news that comes fresh from Kiddy's heart and this is still the first Sunday for a long time that I have had no reminder that there is one little black head and devoted heart waiting for me at home with out-stretched arms and a ring that was once mine on her finger . . . I wonder if you have gone down to the farm for another look round today, it is rather an undertaking: you are just as pleased with it I hope. Have you mentally furnished and arranged all the rooms? . . . I can picture the house when finished but I always put in whole made trees, it wants an old sycamore or 2, or elms. I am longing to come back and cherish that little black head and take Kiddy's little face in my great big hands and just kiss her eyes full of love for *me* and only me. Why? Only God can answer that, bye bye little half, bye bye little heart, bye bye till we meet again. God bless my little half and little heart. The big half sais [sic] his prayer for the little half and puts a kiss just there for her.

By 1908 they were installed at Armscote. The property was in a dilapidated state and, remembering the problems she had encountered in modernizing Wootton and Southover, Violet had been hesitant about it at first, fearing that they might have taken on too much. Her caution was soon justified. The chimneys defied all attempts to stop them driving smoke back into the rooms, and on further investigation the "water difficulty" proved virtually insuperable. It was not for nothing that Armscote had been called Pool House before they bought it and changed its name. Tucked against one side of the house was a dewpond, which turned out to be the only source of water, and by no means a reliable one. As the shortage became desperate, Violet importuned the village's oldest inhabitants for information about ancient springs and brought in diviners, who scoured the grounds with willow wands, discovering six long-forgotten well shafts. She was assured that there was water at 200 feet – only to find that the liquid each well produced was brackish. Finally, an artesian well was driven down to the "greensand" (a type of sandstone) to keep the salt out. Nevertheless, the charm of Armscote offered rich compensation for its practical short-comings. Violet restored a wooden-beamed spinning barn that stood near the west side of the house and made it into her music room, linked by a passage to the low-ceilinged, panelled sitting-room, where the life of the house gathered around the sixteenth-century fireplace, which was as wide, though not nearly as elegant, as the fireplaces at Southover.

From the back door the garden stretched an acre or so to another lane, on the border of which stood The Red House, an Elizabethan building of the same period as Armscote (and belonging to the property), built of stone and faced with red brick. Violet could not make up her mind whether to call it a cottage or a house – it seemed too big to be one and not quite big enough to be the other. Here Denis made the gesture of setting up an establishment for himself, a hundred yards from the others. With a private income of £800 a year, not including his army pay, he could afford to maintain a façade of independence in a way that Max and Bill could not. He had his own London house in Moore Street, Chelsea, and, to keep up the appearance of living separately, he even ordered blue embossed Red House writing paper. These arrangements were as much a matter of chivalry as of pride – he wanted to do what he could to protect Violet's reputation. There was, however, a price to pay. Denis's relationship with Violet was inevitably less intimate than that of Max, who was with her the whole time. The others simply treated the Red House as an annexe, appropriating Denis's spare bedrooms whenever there was an overspill of guests from the main house. The neighbours were not convinced by the semblances of separateness, and to this day Armscote is known locally as "The Abode of Love".

With her propensity for intense enthusiasms, Warwickshire was now held by Violet to be the most poetic county in England. It was, of course, Shakespeare's county, and Violet threw herself into his life and works, befriending Oliver Baker, the grey-bearded, scholarly artist, antiquary and Shakespeare scholar, who had an encyclopaedic knowledge of the history of the countryside and became Violet's guide to the poet's early years. Other new friendships followed. There were Graham and Kathleen Rees-Mogg at their Elizabethan house in Clifford Chambers, a village a few miles to the north-west, where it is said that Shakespeare spent the last night of his life carousing; the poet Francis Brett Young, who also wrote novels about the West Midlands; and the Flower family, whose fortunes had been founded on brewing and who were much involved in the administrative life of Stratford-upon-Avon.

A more controversial acquaintance who lived near by was Marie Corelli, the ambitious and bestselling author, then with twenty-one novels behind her, whose age no one knew, whose photograph, now that she had reached dumpy middle age, she would no longer allow anyone to take, and whose parentage she invented (her real name was Mary, or "Minnie", Mackay). Her gushing books, full of semi-digested science and religion achieved almost hysterical popularity and, attracted surprising admirers, from Oscar

Wilde and Swinburne to Gladstone. Before taking up writing she had had pretensions as a pianist, having shown a precocious talent for the instrument as a child. Impatient of daily practice, she had preferred to invent her own music, "a spiritual thing unfettered by rules". When Violet was eleven "Signorina Marie Corelli" had given a concert in the drawing-room of a house in Harley Street a few yards from the Gwynnes. She had asked that the audience sit in perfect silence while she uplifted them with fifteen of her own "Spontaneous Improvisations".

Marie Corelli had moved to Stratford in 1900 with her lifelong companion Bertha Vyver. She had installed a harpsichord, a piano and a harp, and could often be found seated at one of her instruments when guests arrived, waiting expectantly to be revisited by her muse. She was extremely unpopular locally. Edgar Flower, who had quarrelled with her over the siting of the new Shakespeare Library,[1] publicly declared that he would give £1,000 to get her out of town. Many of her London friends, however, remained loyal, including Max's uncle, who had helped her cause with some belligerent journalism of his own when she had counter-attacked her critics after receiving bad reviews. As a twenty-year-old Violet had once sent Marie Corelli an admiring letter, having met her through Nettie Carpenter, but she was now embarrassed at the memory and took to claiming that the only reason she had liked *Ardath* was because of its chapter on Sarasate.[2]

The other big house in Armscote village, Ladle Farm, was a grace-and-favour dwelling lived in rent-free by the local land agent, Henry Stanton, and his wife, Mary. Mary Stanton was far more broadly educated and better informed than might have been expected of a vicar's daughter, having travelled widely with her sister in the Far East before her marriage. Tall and grey-haired – she was about fifty when she first met Violet – she was highly intelligent, artistic and knowledgeable about music. She had almost nothing in common with her husband, a straightforward fellow who spent his days working in the open while Mary read indoors. When the *ménage* arrived, she was bowled over by Violet, falling so completely under her spell that she gave up her home and her husband and went to live at Armscote. What, exactly, was her position there was hard to define, beyond saying that she did anything and everything Violet asked of her, whether running errands, answering the telephone, shopping (except for the food, which was Gordon's province), helping to organize Violet's professional appointments,

1 While Mayor of Stratford, Edgar Flower's son Archibald had raised money for a Shakespeare Library from the American philanthropist Andrew Carnegie.
2 In 1898 Corelli attended all Sarasate's concerts in St James's Hall. She devoted a chapter of *Ardath*, "The Wizard of the Bow", to a description of one of these concerts.

or arranging invitations and transport for weekends. Some might have seen this as an ignominious role, but that was not how it felt either to Mary or to Violet's circle.

For Bill, one of their new acquaintances counted above all the rest. In 1906, shortly before the Woodhouse entourage arrived at Armscote, Lawrence Johnston had come to live at Hidcote Bartrim, some four miles away. Born in 1871, he had been up at Cambridge just after Bill and on coming down had fought in South Africa in the Boer War. Hidcote was a gift from his rich American mother, a small stone house with some cottages and outbuildings, and 280 acres of land, on a high windy spot on the edge of the Cotswolds, which she had chosen on account of his weak lungs. Not that there was anything else frail about him. Fair, blue-eyed and dressed with meticulous military neatness, he loved working out of doors; and owned his own pack of dachshunds.

Johnston had partitioned off eleven acres of his farm in which to begin a garden at Hidcote just as Bill was laying out the garden at Armscote. Thorough in everything he did, Johnston had studied architecture before formulating his geometrical ground-plan, which enabled him to play with perspective through a carefully graded series of enclosures on different levels opening into each other. (Fifteen years later, under the influence of Norah Lindsay, that "most inspired and elusive" of all English gardeners, as the horticulturalist Jane Brown has described her, each enclosure was to be given its own dramatic character, ranging from formal to almost wild.)

Bill's experiments at Southover and his own well-developed ideas on colour tones, balance and design led to exchanges with Johnston which were to play a major part in the creation of the magnificent gardens of Armscote, Hidcote and Nether Lypiatt. Bill believed, along with Robinson's famous collaborator, Gertrude Jekyll (who wrote for Robinson's new magazine, *Gardening Illustrated*), that a garden should give the illusion of having been there for ever; its relationship to the surrounding fields, hills and buildings should have a naturalness born of scrupulous attention to detail. Paths, terraces and low walls should enjoy the same consideration as borders, with lavender falling over edges, and rock plants, thyme, snapdragons, hollyhocks, lupins, pinks and valerian growing out of cracks and crevices. Orchards and avenues, far from being independent of the main garden, should flow out of it, with casually mown paths and spring and summer flowers underplanted in the long grass. Although Johnston was too reticent for Violet's taste, she appreciated his professionalism and included him in her life for Bill's sake. It was a necessary concession. No one at Armscote felt restricted in asking to the house whomever they wanted; if, however, Violet did not approve of someone it was pointless even for Bill to continue issuing invitations.

When Violet went out to dinner, or to the theatre, or on an expedition of some kind, she took her men with her. It appealed to her sense of style; moreover, it was fun. She liked to amuse them and to be amused by them, to charm and to be charmed, to be spoilt by them with treats and presents. Bluebelle Gwynne recalled a typical day in London when, after practising at Park Place until mid-morning, Violet summoned her maid to bring her cape, hat, parasol, gloves and hand-stitched walking shoes and sailed off to Fortnum & Mason with four men in train. Shop assistants swarmed round her. On being asked what they could do for her, she answered with a laugh that that depended on how generous her friends were feeling that morning – according to Bluebelle, Denis bought the most. When, back at Park Place, Violet had finished unwrapping their purchases, she saw that she had been given far more than she wanted, and for the next few days showered presents on her visitors.

Although Violet did not know it, her extravagance was obliging Gordon to live increasingly beyond his means. On top of the upkeep of two houses – and their inhabitants – and the cost of entertaining, he had been paying out for heavy dressmakers' bills from the honeymoon onwards. The rot had begun to set in with the 1905 Season, when women's clothes reached a high point in luxury and expense. Gordon had survived with relative ease the rich brocades, fine velvets and lustrous satins of the late 1890s, but the Edwardian fashion for elaborate lace and hand embroidery had turned the business of buying clothes for spoiled women into a rich man's sport. Finely sewn clusters of flowers, leaves and medallions made Violet's evening gowns seem, from a distance, a mass of glittering silver, gold and moonlit sequins. She seldom ordered one of a kind, but duplicated her garments several times over, employing subtle variations of material and design. Gordon swallowed hard, settled the accounts and said nothing, sure that something would turn up long before the situation grew alarming – perhaps his mother's death, or that of Violet's father, would provide the capital they needed. There was, after all, plenty of money in the background.

Violet's social life did not always run as smoothly as her domestic life. Her *ménage* flouted every tenet of contemporary decorum. The tone of high society had become less stiff with Edward VII's accession, but discretion was still demanded in any alliance outside marriage. Some would not receive Violet, others refused even to speak to her. Among the more broad-minded, the sheer number of her followers could be awkward for the would-be hostess – Dorothy records Violet "coming over with her tail". Dorothy's own attitude, except where Gordon was concerned, had by now become that of an amused but faintly scandalized observer.

> *6 August 1908.* This is an extraordinary house. I mean the inmates.
> V. with all these men, Maxwell, Bill and Denis, and seeing her
> behaviour with them all. There is only one place for her and that is
> Ladakh in India, "The women's paradise". Gordon of course is
> *servant* and bottlewasher to the whole party. It is passing strange,
> and where will it end?

Nowhere was the disapproval stronger than among the new Lady
Barrington's set. Charlotte Barrington, Bill's stepmother, was a snob, with a
partiality for Continental grandees. The most recent tenant of Beckett, the
Barrington family seat in Oxfordshire, had been a bedridden arms manufac-
turer, a Mr Whitehead, whose daughter had married an Austrian count
called Hoyos and whose granddaughter had married the son of the "Iron
Chancellor", Count Otto von Bismarck, the founder of modern Germany.
During Mr Whitehead's tenancy the house had been packed with Prussian
and Austrian nobility, but on his death in 1906 the estate had reverted to
Bill's father. Charlotte Barrington had set about redecorating it, making
bathrooms, installing central heating and improving the electric lighting. To
recoup some of the cost the Barringtons let the house again to new tenants,
with whom Bill's stepmother, in what he called "her usual unpleasant way",
interfered abominably, even refusing them permission to hold a ball there.

From his vantage point at Medlar Cottage beside the end of the lime
avenue in the park, Bill kept track of all that went on at Beckett. His father's
estate was being badly neglected. The local tenants of the farms and cottages
complained to him of leaking roofs and dangerously decaying trees, while
the tenants of the big house seethed at Lady Barrington's condescending
arrogance. Bill was furious at the declining state of his heritage. Charlotte
Barrington, for her part, made no secret of her disdain for his relationship
with Violet, whom she refused to acknowledge. She was, however, intensely
anxious to accumulate more information, which she could then use to turn
her husband against Bill. In August 1908, hearing that the "Woodhouse
Circus" was at Medlar Cottage for the weekend (Armscote being full of
workmen, and therefore uninhabitable), she hit on the plan of persuading
her cronies, the Hoyoses, to do some reconnaissance on her behalf. Dorothy,
who was not party to all the background of the situation, captures the
flavour of their unsuccessful spying mission in her diary.

> *August 14th 1908.* We were going for an expedition after lunch, but
> Bill had a wire to say some women call Hoyos were coming to see

him, and O how rude they were when they did come! But I run on too fast, after lunch I went to sit out in the park under the trees with my book. Tea was late for these visitors of Bill's; it was in the dining room. The party consisted of a married lady, Reventlow [married to the Danish Count Reventlow] or some such name, and her two sisters Hoyos by name; and the husband, a very nice man, the only civil one of the party. I suppose they didn't like V. or had heard about her, or something, anyhow their frigidity was icy; and they treated her as if she were not fit to speak to. I was dancing with fury inside, but it was rather funny too, as the two sisters were so frightened of being left with us for a moment, and rushed away to sit and wait at the Barrington Arms; there is humour even in rudeness, truly! When they had gone (I am sure they were no gladder to go than I was to get rid of them!) I went for a good walk by the farms and in the park. Denis came this evening. V. didn't feel well, with a sore throat.

Violet's move to Armscote coincided with the start of what was to be a close musical collaboration and an immensely important friendship. Ethel Smyth was a dramatic woman of exceptional intelligence, a rebel, a crusader in the cause of feminism, a vigorous and racy writer, and the first woman to persuade the sceptical musical worlds of Germany and England to treat with seriousness compositions other than by a man. Her path and Violet's had crossed briefly before, but now, at the beginning of 1908, circumstances threw them together. Ethel had been trying, to no avail, to win backing for her opera *The Wreckers* – later considered her masterpiece. Several musical patrons offered their houses for play-throughs, to which they invited impresarios, music directors and potential sponsors. Violet met Ethel Smyth again at one of these occasions, arranged in London by the Princesse de Polignac,[3] generally known as Winnie, who had used her influence in Paris to promote a number of composers, including Fauré, Debussy and Ravel. Winnie's ability to recognize genius was not restricted to music, and she had also drawn into her orbit avant-garde painters, including Monet and Picasso, as well as the writers Marcel Proust, Cocteau and Colette. Although not entirely convinced by Ethel's romantic, richly

3 Born Miss Singer, Winnaretta de Polignac was a talented musician and painter and the heiress to a vast American fortune derived from the family sewing-machine business. Following her affectionate marriage of convenience (she was a lesbian, he wanted the money) to Prince Edmond de Polignac in 1894, she created Paris's leading artistic salon.

coloured music, Winnie had recently had an affair with her, and so was happy to do what she could to promote *The Wreckers*, with its interesting libretto by Henry Brewster.[4] Ethel had high hopes that, with Winnie's help, Covent Garden might at last stage the opera.

To announce the performance in 1908 of a new operatic work that was not written by Puccini was the surest guarantee of empty seats at the opera house. Moreover, this was a man's world, and even Winnie could have achieved little for Ethel without Violet's energetic support. The vitality and direct appeal to the emotions of *The Wreckers* had so impressed Violet that many years later she remarked of the play-through at Winnie's, in which Ethel played the piano and sang some of the parts, that "rough sketch as it was, her solo performance gave me a better idea of all that was in the work than any complete performance in the theatre". Violet therefore consulted a Spanish friend, Gomez, a member of the London Symphony Orchestra, and with his help managed to persuade the celebrated conductor Artur Nikisch[5] to insert into one of the LSO's forthcoming programmes the prelude to the second act of *The Wreckers*, entitled "On the Cliffs of Cornwall". The concert, on 2 May 1908, marked the first public performance in England of any part of *The Wreckers*, and emboldened Ethel to bear the inevitable financial loss of staging the first two acts of the opera (without sets or costumes) at Queen's Hall on 28 May with the same orchestra, again conducted by Nikisch. With typical generosity, Blanche Marchesi offered to sing the lead role without payment, and to supply most of the chorus from among her own singing pupils. These two public performances did much to increase Ethel's reputation, while she felt that through Nikisch's "divine" conducting, which made her music sound exactly as she had meant it, "she had put her foot firmly on the ladder at last".

At the time, Ethel had been recovering from the death of Henry Brewster and from her passionate affair with Winnie. She had been wholly unsuited to Winnie, being both too old – she was fifty – and too carelessly and unfashionably attired in heavy tweed suits and baggy dresses. The romance had whirled from love to rejection to hate before settling into a calmer affection, so that when Ethel met Violet she was more than ready to adopt a new object of admiration. In her memoirs, *A Fresh Start*, she records how in 1908:

> a friendship which I knew was going to be one of the chief joys of
> my life took deep root. I had met Violet Gordon Woodhouse, that

4 Henry Brewster, the only man to whom Ethel was ever romantically attached, died before *The Wreckers* had a complete public hearing.

5 Nikisch had recently been dismissed from the post of Director of Music at the Leipzig Theatre for overspending his budget.

supreme harpsichordist, before Harry's death, but it was not until 1908 that I began to see a great deal of her, often staying with her in her very beautiful stone mullioned house near Stratford-on-Avon. For the first time since Pauline Heathcote's death, I knew the close, loving alliance with one of my own breed . . . the artistic instinct of Violet Woodhouse, though more conspicuous in music, was equally potent and infallible in other fields, and there was surely never a more ideal companion for an artist.

Ethel Smyth's infatuations – successively with the German aristocrat Elisabeth von Herzogenberg, with one of Queen Victoria's ladies-in-waiting, Lady Ponsonby, and with the exiled French Empress Eugénie – were legendary. Once she had succumbed the experience was all-consuming and she incorporated her *grandes passions* into her creative life, finding in them a source of inspiration. In Violet's case, that inspiration came easily, since the two women shared a single-minded devotion to music and their friendship drew them both deeper into their work. To the end of her life Ethel saw Violet in the most lyrical light, describing her as "by the Grace of God such a musician as one seldom meets" and as the possessor of a "natural kinship with beauty in every form – art, literature, or nature".

In the summer of 1908, Ethel settled in at Armscote for a three-week-stay, bringing with her a mountain of work. Violet even gave up the music room to her, allowing the composer's ink bottles and paste pots to take over, and putting up with a good deal of "piano thumping" (Violet had by now come to abhor the sound of the piano, especially when it was played in the forceful style adopted by many performers of the day under the impression that they were following the methods of Liszt).

Known for her harrying manner, Ethel's invigorating personality and unfeminine appearance made her something of an acquired taste for men – Graf Seerbach of the Dresden Opera House once said that if he were ever to catch sight of her in the street he would leap into the nearest cab, drive to the station and take the next train out of town. She was, however, too self-absorbed to be more than mildly aware that her visit might cause discord between Violet and her "superhusbands", as Ethel's friends privately described them. Gordon at least made her feel welcome. His sense of humour appealed to her and he promised to send her a parcel of her favourite brazil nuts every Christmas. Denis either saw or pretended to see her qualities; he even lent her his house in Moore Street whenever she needed a London base, though no doubt he did this less out of affection for Ethel than in the hope of pleasing Violet. Bill and Max, however, were distinctly unenthusiastic. The slight discomfort in the atmosphere caused by her visit was matched by physical discomfort. The greensand into which the artesian well had been sunk had started to silt up the pipes, reducing the water pressure to such an extent that after a while the household became grateful for enough drops to make a small cup of tea. Ethel joked with Gordon that Armscote had opened her eyes to the reason why the Elizabethans considered baths unhealthy.

The more Delius saw of Violet the more he liked her. He contacted her whenever he was in England and in the summer of 1908 invited her to the Albert Hall to hear his symphonic poem the *Mass of Life*. To his wife Jelka, who had stayed behind in France, he wrote that the piece was splendidly played by the London Symphony Orchestra and admirably conducted by Arbós – "first class" – and that Violet was looking "as pretty and artistic as ever". Delius introduced Violet to Thomas Beecham, who as a conductor had been chiefly responsible for introducing Delius's work to the public, and who was then on the threshold of a parallel career as an impresario of opera and ballet. What he had done for Frederick Delius he could surely do for Ethel Smyth, and Violet now set her heart on interesting Beecham in Ethel's work.

In the weeks after her stay, the friendship between Violet and Ethel intensified. They plotted and schemed together, and went to as many of Beecham's concerts as they could. They agreed that they had never heard orchestral music played so perfectly in England, and they did not shrink from telling him so. But he was a hard nut to crack. His acute money troubles, caused by his estrangement from his father, the possessor of a large fortune made from patent medicines, had caused him to cultivate the art of elusiveness – to confuse his creditors he kept three addresses. His avoidance of Ethel was deliberate. In June 1908, a month after hearing *The Wreckers* at Queen's Hall, he wrote to Delius, "I really think it is the most idiotic and miserable rubbish I have ever heard." On this occasion Beecham was not, perhaps, being entirely objective. He was annoyed with Nikisch for having inserted Ethel's opera into the London Symphony Orchestra's programme at the expense of a work by Delius, who had been cut out at the last moment.

Eventually, however, Violet did succeed in introducing Ethel to Beecham, who, like many before him, succumbed to her fixity of purpose and agreed to conduct *The Wreckers* the following year. The production became a titanic battlefield. Ethel wrote to Delius in 1909: "I have fearful fights with Mr Beecham, who Mrs Woodhouse and I love . . . !" Finally, however, Ethel's musicality won over Beecham's initial distaste, and towards the end of his life he was to write that hers was "one of the three or four English operas of real musical merit and vitality written during the last forty years".

Ethel liked to think that there was a romantic element in Violet's feelings for her – as there certainly was in hers for Violet. In Violet's library, which still exists, there is a copy of a life and translation of Sappho, the Greek lyric poetess from the island of Lesbos who was born in the early part of the seventh century BC. The book was a gift, and bears on its flyleaf, in Ethel's handwriting, the inscription: "Violet from Ethel – 'Hey nonny no' epoch November 1909 – 'I love delicacy, and for me love has the sun's splendour and beauty' (Motto written by Sappho on purpose for V.G.W.)." Ethel and Violet both knew that Sappho was, supremely, the poet of love between women; they almost certainly also knew that "Hey nonny no" was an old Elizabethan expression used as a coy substitute for explicit sexual language. Ethel used the words as the title of one of her finest works, a choral piece[6] which she wrote during the first part of her relationship with Violet.

That gift of Sappho's poems and the inscription in it, taken together with Ethel's reference to Violet in her memoirs as "one of my own breed", could easily be interpreted as claiming Violet for a sister lesbian; that, however, would be both too literal and too modern an interpretation. For Ethel, music and music-making expressed and generated an extreme erotic intensity, and Violet was her musical soulmate. How much of this erotic charge was reciprocated by Violet is something that cannot be known for certain; but it seems more in Violet's nature to have found in the performance of music, with its own high passion and release of creative tension, an end in itself. Beside, when the way in which Ethel writes about Violet is compared with her raving about Elisabeth von Herzogenberg, it is almost impossible to gain the impression that Violet and she were ever lovers in a physical sense.

Whether or not Violet felt anything more than ordinary affection for Ethel, her relations with Bill were certainly "improper", as counsel used to put it in the divorce cases which, in those days, filled the columns even of *The Times* and the *Daily Telegraph*. Less than twelve months after the beginning of her friendship with Ethel, Violet had written Bill a note which she suggested he destroy:

9 Park Place, London, *1909 January 23rd Saturday*
My Dearest, Thank you very much for sending the wire. I was so

---

6 Described by Kathleen Dale, the composer, as "an audacious blend of primitiveness and modernity, a dare-devil of a roister's song . . . the musical atmosphere of utter abandon . . .". It was not published until 1911, when it became very popular among the suffragettes.

glad to hear you were safe back, tho' sorry that you had a poor day. How cold the weather is. I almost expected that hunting would not be happening. I have very little news to give you . . . I am going to a party at Mrs Hunter's . . . And you? Did you enjoy the balls very much? Did you dance every dance? Now my heart I must stop. I send you hug upon hug, – Did you see in the papers that a most compromising piece of evidence in the Atherton case was that Mr Stirling's handkerchief was *found under Mrs Atherton's pillow*! I wonder if our housemaids read the papers, don't you. You had better burn this.                              Your Your Your K.

Later in the summer of that year, seeing Violet so caught up with Ethel, Bill had thought it safe to accept an invitation to fish in Norway, but when the time came Violet bitterly regretted letting him go. It was the familiar story. Bill had so often set off to stay with a brother or sister and been summoned back by a telegram twenty-four hours after his arrival, on the pretext that Violet was suffering from one of her sore throats. He nearly always answered the call. This time, however, Violet (or rather Gordon, whose task it was actually to sign and dispatch the telegrams) had difficulty reaching him. Bill's reply made favourable mention of Adelina Ganz, who in retrospect seemed to him to be a considerable improvement on Ethel.

GLUDT JEPSTED MELDALEN TRONDHEIM
*August 1909*
My Darling Heart,
What does Gordon's telegram mean, I have written 3 or 4 times, I am not sure which, but posts go from here three days a week and they take a good long time . . . I start back on the 26th, arrive good-ness knows when, about the 2nd of September, and shall come straight to the farm as quick as possible. Wasn't that a splendid picture of Adelina in the Mirror with her papa's Golden Wedding . . . Everyone has come in and as there is only one room it is jolly hard to think what one is writing . . . I hope I won't find my sweet-heart too dreadfully thin but anyhow she will be more happy and no nasty trips to Norway hanging over her head to make her worry & when she is happy she will find it better to get well & strong, I do want her so much. It is too late to reply to your telegram. Now, my Darling heart, I must end, you may get two by this post. God Bless you and beloved one take care of yourself for me My Prayer.

It was only the members of Violet's inner circle who knew of the waves of anxiety which swept over her whenever Bill was away. To the outside world she invariably appeared relaxed and in control with her men. Even Dorothy, well as she knew Violet's heart, and much as she had the opportunity to observe her at close quarters, did not suspect that she might be lacking in confidence when it came to her relationship with Bill.

At Folkington, meanwhile, a great deal was going on beneath a superficially calm surface. As James Gwynne aged into his late seventies, Rupert, from his base at Wootton, where he had gone to live with his wife, came increasingly to personify the future of the place. He had a weak heart, and perhaps this gave him only a short lease of life, but it was impossible to detect this from his flirtations and infidelities, from the dash of his riding, or from the energy with which he now embarked upon a political career. In 1910 he was elected the – Conservative – Member of Parliament for Eastbourne, helped by his wife Stella's influence in the party. Roland still lived at Folkington, and was May's closest confidant; he was, however, beginning to acquire a reputation as a snake in the grass: it would be much to his own advantage if Nevile remained disinherited by James in favour of Rupert, who had no sons. Dorothy also lived at Folkington, observing everything, though her intuition into the private calculations of the characters in this saga was less acute than Roland's. The absent Nevile was under the impression that, over the years, he and his father had become reconciled, but was this wishful thinking? The situation was murky. It was far from clear who, if anybody, knew James's intentions other than James himself.

As Violet's sister, Dorothy was above criticism, and was always welcome at Armscote. The men had learned to treat her with affectionate banter. In the summer of 1910 she received a three-in-one letter inviting her to stay. Bill began: "My Dear Dorothy . . . I haven't seen your beaming countenance for some time, bring a Kodak and add largely to your collection of wild flowers. Bring a saddle and a habit . . ." Max added a note mocking her hypochondria: "Dear Dorothy . . . Life here is far more refined than at Medlar Cottage . . . Of course there is no local doctor . . . Denis will be put at your absolute disposal. I send you my love Maxwell." And finally Violet:

> I think it would be nice if you could come next week, and stay a month. The weather is beautiful, there are two nice hot bathrooms, and a nice open motor, so you see how many attractions there are, not to mention that Maxwell is here, and we will try to get Denis if you are unable to do without him! There will also be room for your maid. Now mind you come or I shall be very angry. Answer me in London as I intend to go there for a day or two.

Dorothy came and went. This time, however, there was nothing in her diary about the emotional atmosphere at Armscote, no doubt because the chief talking point during her visit was Violet's involvement in the women's suffrage movement. The issue of the emancipation of women was one of the central controversies of the early part of the twentieth century. Women were becoming more outspoken and assertive. They demanded the right to be taken seriously as professionals, whether as barristers or doctors or teachers; they demanded undergraduate places at Oxford and Cambridge; and above all they demanded the vote, for which they were prepared to risk ridicule, gaol, and sometimes even their lives.[7]

Violet's adoption of the cause was mainly due to Ethel. Like many female contemporaries who had made their way successfully in a man's world, Ethel had had little reason at first to focus on the need for a campaign for women's votes and had been inclined to dismiss it. A chance conversation with an Austrian friend had persuaded her otherwise, however, and after she had met Emmeline Pankhurst, the charismatic champion of the suffragettes, Ethel could talk of little else. Tough and determined, Mrs Pankhurst, who, with her daughter Christabel, had founded the Women's Social and Political Union in 1903, had emerged as a leader at a time when a succession of bills promising to enfranchise women were being defeated in Parliament. Under her guidance, the suffragettes became increasingly militant, chaining themselves to railings and damaging property in protest at the Government's continued failure to give women the vote.

Mrs Pankhurst greeted Ethel coolly at first. She considered that, as a well-known figure, Ethel should have set an example by joining the movement when it had first been formed, and it was not until she gave up music temporarily, to devote two years to the cause, that Mrs Pankhurst became convinced of her commitment. Ethel sailed into the fray, throwing a stone at a cabinet minister's window with the objective – successful, as it turned out – of being imprisoned. In spite of "dreading the iron door being slammed and the key turned" during her confinement, the ensuing few weeks in London's Holloway gaol passed like a happy dream for Ethel, since she was put in a cell next to Mrs Pankhurst, the woman she now idolized. When Thomas Beecham visited her there he found her conducting her militant song "The March of the Women" with a toothbrush through the bars of her cell to the massed voices of her sister inmates in the courtyard below.

Violet lacked the stomach for the rough-and-tumble of street politics,

7 The most drastic protest was that of Emily Davison, who died after throwing herself under the King's horse during the 1913 Derby. Many other suffragettes went on hunger strikes in prison.

with its danger of violence and arrest. She did, however, lend her name to the suffragettes, arranging with Christopher St John (as Christabel Marshal now called herself) for Mrs Pankhurst to speak in Park Place to a meeting of potentially sympathetic women, including her sister-in-law Bluebelle and a group of feminist friends – Winnie de Polignac, Edith Craig and the singer Mabel Batten with her lover, Radclyffe Hall. But Violet was motivated more by loyalty to Ethel and Chris than by personal conviction. Music, art, literature, nature, friendship – these were the real stuff of her life, with which no social theory or political movement could hope to compete.

In September 1910, after eight years' absence, the last five of them in America, Dolmetsch made a brief and unexpected reappearance. He was only in London for three weeks, and Violet went to hear him play in the hall at Clifford's Inn. After the concert they dined together. Dolmetsch was on his way to France to seek employment with one of the three Paris harpsichord manufacturers (he finally settled on Gaveau), but he planned annual return visits to England and Violet asked him to play in public with her again when he was next back in London. Earlier in the year she had ordered, for $60, an octavina spinet from Chickering, the Boston firm where Dolmetsch had been working under contract. Now she loyally got him off to a good start in his new job at Gaveau by ordering a harpsichord and a specially designed clavichord, a smaller model which could be easily ferried between Armscote and Park Place. Once Dolmetsch had made this compact instrument, Violet had a shelf built in her car to hold it. Far from complaining about its lack of authenticity, Dolmetsch was delighted with it, proclaiming that four octaves and a tone were sufficient for most baroque music. Curiously, his wife Mabel recalled in her memoirs that in the end he found the smaller instrument kept in tune better than the larger ones.

Whether because time and fashion had moved on, or because his novelty had worn off, Dolmetsch was now more liable to encounter mockery than before. Mabel, who was his third wife, successfully produced four new potential "Elizabethan" children for him. His academic standing was undoubted, but as a performer he had become something of a caricature of himself. The Cambridge don and man of letters, A.C. Benson, who was the epitome of civilized learning and came from a family with a well-developed sense of the ridiculous (his brother, E.F. Benson, was the author of the famous Mapp and Lucia comic novels), went to a Dolmetsch lecture recital at the university. His diary entry portrays a weird zealot surrounded by an audience of relentless seriousness.

We went to the Dolmetsch concert of ancient music in the hall . . . the place was crowded with odd and faded undergraduates – from King's [College, Cambridge]. The dais full of strange, brightly painted harpsichords. Dolmetsch, a man of sixty, a mass of grizzled hair, looking as if he had been unwashed for ten days, pointed beard, low collar: Mme. D. dressed like a Medici picture, and a tall grim lady in a blue shawl, who sat gloomily in the background. D. spoke in a very strong German accent. "I have known D. for 30 years" said [a friend] "& he used to speak quite good English; his accent has grown on him – he finds it a success".

Dolmetsch showed his lutes and viols and talked on. "The old people used to make music for themselves, in a room just such as this – now we pay to hear *noise*, we do not hear music, it is noise we hear! What I am going to play to you is awfully beautiful – awfully simple, but really quite beyond the reach of the modern people". He described the instruments . . . Then some odd tinkling things were played on virginals and lute – sounds as if one had shaken up a cage of mice and canaries together . . . There were just one or two lovely things – a duet for two viols – a recorder solo – but the rest was very barbarous, I thought. But the whole thing interested me – the strange pose, the unreal air of the whole; & yet the uncertainty that these odd creatures really lived in their absurd art – a curious mixture of admiration and despair, with a strong desire to giggle. It was all so real & yet so fanatical, as D. glared over his recorder . . . We went away after Part 1 – the absurdity being uppermost. The collection of people, listening with grotesque earnestness to these very odd sounds – the deliberate antiquity of it all, the sweeping aside all progress of the art – it interested me as a revival of what the old world called music – & the sense that they probably found the same emotion in it as we find in the new music. It is all a symbol, of course; but few people there understood that! They thought it was the thing itself which was beautiful . . .

Not everyone saw the Dolmetsches in an ironical light. Ezra Pound, the American-born modernist poet widely credited with much of the responsibility for the twentieth-century revolution in poetry, viewed his mock-Elizabethan display less as an affectation than as a renewal of the musician's art. As music critic of *The New Age*[8] he wrote:

8 An influential political and literary weekly magazine, edited from 1907 to 1922 by the Fabian and advocate of Social Credit, A.R. Orage.

I have seen the God Pan . . . the older journalists tell me it is "cold mutton", that Mr. Dolmetsch was heard of 15 years ago. That is a tendency that I have before remarked in a civilisation which rests upon journalism, and which has only sporadic care for the arts. His topical interest is over . . . I have seen broken down spinets in swank drawing rooms. I have heard harpsichords played in Parisian concerts, and they sounded like the scratching of multitudinous hens, and I did not wonder [that] pianos had superseded them.

. . . So I had two sets of adventure. First, I perceived a sound which is undoubtedly derived from the Gods, and then I found myself in a reconstructed century – in a century of music, back before Mozart or Purcell, listening to clear music, to tones clear as brown amber. And this music came indifferently out of the harpsichord or the clavichord or out of the virginals or out of odd shaped viols, or whatever they may be. There were two small girls playing upon them with an exquisite precision; with a precision quite unlike anything I have ever heard from a London orchestra . . . Mr. Dolmetsch was, let us say, enamoured of ancient music. He found it misunderstood . . . He found the beauty was untranslatable with modern instruments; he has repaired and has entirely remade "ancient instruments".

As Violet came of age musically, her interest in scholarship grew. In France the study and performance of early music played on original instruments was dominated by the Polish-born Wanda Landowska who, as a theorist, often clashed with Dolmetsch and, as an interpreter, differed in several stylistic respects from Violet. Violet was by now a consummate clavichordist, and was becoming interested in the use of that instrument by J.S. Bach. Landowska, who at this stage of her career earned her living and her reputation exclusively from the harpsichord, was sceptical; she believed that Bach did not even possess a clavichord.

In 1911 Violet entered into a correspondence on the question with Dolmetsch, who replied with a tendentious attack on Landowska (Appendix I), in which he asserted that Bach possessed several clavichords and used them frequently. The basis for Dolmetsch's polemic rested partly on the question of whether a sound worthy of Bach's genius could be extracted from the clavichord. In Violet's hands it certainly could, since she was equally at home on both clavichord and harpsichord. Landowska, however, disliked the clavichord, a fact which Dolmetsch used casuistically against her to suggest that it was because her technique was inadequate that she disagreed with his argument. Dissatisfied with Dolmetsch's analysis, Violet sought a second opinion from the Professor of Sacred Music at St Patrick's College, Maynooth, near Dublin, who took the view that Landowska had the better of this particular debate (Appendix II).

Sheltered though Violet had generally been from politics, the intense social unrest of 1911 now impinged on her through its effect on Denis. For a century since the French Revolution, liberal and leftist ideas had been gaining ground throughout Europe. In England, these had largely been absorbed into the system through social and electoral reform. Nevertheless, the industrialization of the big cities had made for harsh working conditions and vast pools of new wealth concentrated in the hands of relatively few shareholders – a potentially explosive combination, exacerbated by class distinctions, and one which the extreme left was ready to exploit. Contemptuous or despairing of the parliamentary process, Marxist revolutionaries preached violence and "direct action" on the street. Many of the unions had been heavily penetrated by militants, and within the Socialist "Second International" (an organization of International Socialist groups which was effective from 1889 to 1914) England ranked with Germany, and above Russia, as the two countries which were judged most ripe for the overthrow of capitalism and established systems of government. The crisis was acute enough to keep Denis away from Armscote on emergency duty with his regiment for most of 1911. Strikes and lockouts were erupting throughout the country, and the army was on permanent stand-by. The ugly language of class warfare made its first appearance; the threat of chaos and a general strike was in the air. Nothing, not even the suffragette movement, had prepared people for the anger and hatred which spread out across the country, the echoes reaching as far as Armscote to disturb the peacefulness which Violet regarded as her birthright.

In the course of the previous year, disruptions among several groups of workers had culminated, in November, in a sympathy strike by miners in South Wales. Violence and looting at Tonypandy, in the Rhondda Valley, had proved too much for the local police to control, and Winston Churchill, as Home Secretary in H.H. Asquith's Liberal Government, had responded by sending 300 extra police from London to the Rhondda, who kept the peace sometimes by rather over-zealous use of the truncheon. The summer of 1911 saw renewed strike action by seamen, firemen and dockworkers, while another brutal dispute was settled only just in time for the Government to countermand the dispatch of 20,000 soldiers to London. In August soldiers fired on port workers in Liverpool, killing two men; four more strikers were shot and killed at Llanelli in Wales when troops fired on a crowd attacking a train. That same month Asquith met the railway unions in the House of Commons, but failed to avert a strike and handed over the negotiations to the Chancellor of the Exchequer, David Lloyd George, a Welshman and a charismatic man of the people. For a while England seemed on the brink of anarchy. Denis wrote to Violet from his barracks at Hounslow, on the western outskirts of London, liverish from inaction, feeling unloved by her and not at all relishing the idea of going into action against the rioters:

AUGUST 17th 1911
My Darling V.
Here I am back again at Hounslow, confined to barracks and waiting to go on strike duty! . . . They have recalled all men from furlough and are preparing for a big thing – to protect the railways if things are serious – It simply is appalling being kept here – It will make me ill if it goes on many days. There is literally nothing that one can do but sit in a chair or walk around the dusty barracks square. I think I would rather go out and fight rioters – though I don't feel very brave about that job! Also my next sight of you seems so precarious – that blessed chance of really getting a few consecutive days, which I am so longing for – and my time is getting so short. It will be a terrible wrench to my inclinations when I do get free – duty pushing me to the G.M. who wants me, and my heart drawing me to you, who don't want me . . . I can't even go to the White City to get your flowers . . . Well, it's past dinner time, and I'm not changed yet, I must say goodnight, and send all my love to you.

Yr. Own Denis.

A note from Violet playfully asking Denis for protection was enough to put him in better spirits.

MONDAY AUG 21st 1911. Cavalry Barracks. Hounslow.
My own beloved little Queen,
What a DARLING you are to write and cheer me up. I can't tell you how much I appreciate it, and how I adore you. It certainly is a wretched thing to be shut up here – since last Wednesday and I getting such a liver! And we have had nothing to do, but just be "ready". They have been telephoning different things a dozen times a day. At midnight they said we could disband, and I began to prepare to go away again. Then they said we must wait until the ruffians' "demonstration" in Hyde Park was over. Then that things were not "favourable", so we must have a squadron ready to move at once – My squadron is ready, but nothing has happened. We all feel

so cross that we shall be very fierce if we do get at a mob that throws stones at us . . . Of course the Government have had a bad scare, and now want to be on the safe side. It is greatly due to their weakness in letting the mob have their own way at Tonypandy, in Wales, early in the year. They thought they would be allowed to ill-treat and intimidate the peaceful ones as much as they like . . . I will certainly ride as hard as I can to Moreton in the Marsh to guard you, if you want it – if the regiment won't follow I'll come without them . . . My chance of seeing you soon is getting so desperate, because I must go to Helmingham when I get away, and I MUST stay a few days because the G.M. is so nice to me . . . so I fear I may not get to you, O bewitching One, until about Sept 1st . . . I've heard a *very* funny story but I think I won't commit to paper (as Bill wouldn't like it). I'll tell you in private if you like. Goodbye my darling little one. A thousand thanks.
From yr own Denis.

To Violet, Denis's references to riots and civil disorder were but distant rumbles of thunder, and she showed little enough interest in his army career. He, however, was as obsessed by her as ever, perhaps more so. From the moment when, as a child, he had first met her, he had not looked at another woman. When, in September 1911, he learned that he was to be sent to India with his regiment, he was desperately upset, not so much at leaving Violet as at how little she seemed to mind him going. Knowing his addiction to romantic adventure stories, she gave him a book by the French novelist Pierre Loti, in which she wrote an affectionate inscription, and included in the package a pair of socks she had just finished knitting. "It was dear of you to work so hard and finish me those *lovely* socks. You know how well I shall treasure them," he wrote pathetically from the ship on 21 October. But her letter saying goodbye was far too short, and he begged her to write often, to tell him anything of "home chat" even if it might make him jealous of Max.

It doesn't matter having "nothing to say". Write me a little of your fun and gaiety with Maxwell – *I also* like to laugh and be happy – I assure you, if I have the chance. I do beseech you to try to think a little kindly of me – I have had so much misery with nothing but love in my heart, and longing for better things. It was a perfect Godsend that you were nice to me my very last day – for the previous week I was almost in despair – and felt that I could not come back any more to England which was homeless to me. But my last day, and your sweet goodbye gave me new hope and I *do* believe that underneath you spare a little affection for poor me, who loves you with all my heart. If only you would manage to tell me so, (if it is true), when you write, just think what a state of ecstasy you would raise me to – Is it very hard for you? I don't mind going away for a bit, if I have anything left in my life to look forward to, and your affection and true friendship, my darling little one, is my only goal towards which I am pining. Do forgive me for all the troubles I have unwillingly caused you and love me again.

Denis had good reason to envy Max. Not only did he have the knack of making Violet laugh, sometimes at the army's expense, which made Denis feel vulnerable, but he lived with her constantly and was permitted frivolous escapades with other women. Denis, of course, wanted nobody but Violet, and it seemed unfair that his own unswerving loyalty should be less well rewarded than Max's apparent fickleness. There had been a telling example not long before Denis had sailed for India, when Max had started a new flirtation. Major Pirie, a British officer serving in Egypt, had a beautiful half-French wife called Valérie. Since the Egyptian hot season was unsuitable for women, Valérie spent the summers in Henley-on-Thames, where the Piries had a house. Valérie was strongly attracted to Max, and in his detached way he was not uninterested in her. Violet, however, was as self-confident about Max as she was nervous about Bill, and allowed him the freedom to visit Valérie as often as he pleased. Violet's tactic was to starve Max of letters, knowing this would bring him hurrying back to Armscote. When Max stayed away with the Piries for a long weekend, he left Violet in no doubt where his real affections lay.

Copse Hill, Greys, Henley-on-Thames, *Friday*
Beloved Tookees,
You shall have no chance of complaining that I do not write – so regular are my letters that you will soon find them monotonous. I have just finished my solitary breakfast in the garden. The major went to London before it was light – is he considerate? Yes and No – and Madame has lazy habits, even when she has not a cold. Yesterday was devoted partly to gardening, but chiefly to the accouchement of the Pirie pig, who under our constant and careful supervision presented unto the day seven healthy porkers. The way things reproduce themselves here is surprising, if I stayed here a week I should feel anxious even for my tobacco pouch. I am sure a pair of boots could not be trusted to spend 24 hours in each other's

company . . . tomorrow is fixed for the river expedition to Reading . . . I see that the 7th [Hussars] got defeated in the final. Now that it is over Denis can have a good tuck into soup and pudding. I am sorry his fasting had no reward. It is a great pity that you do not like me well enough to write occasionally. But it is a severe test of the affections, and they are like strawberries, they lose their flavour when forced. Still I promise to draw no over bold inferences, should you send me a line to say that your cough has been driven out of paradise. I love you more each day, and if I stayed over Monday, I were like to have eaten away my tail. Please give Pansy a jackdaw, Bill a quart of cream, and Gordon plenty of work for his stomach's sake. All my love I give to you sweet Pet that you are – Maxwell.

Another letter from Max, this time written en route to Italy, shows that, for all Denis's jealousy and Max's insouciance, the relationship between each of the two men and Violet was remarkably similar – the same loneliness without her, the same joy over a brief note from her. Max's letter does, however, contain oblique sensual hints which are not to be found in any of Denis's surviving letters.

Darling Tookees,
How charming of you to send that bright ray to dispel the dark shadow that fell across our parting.[9] Oh! My Tookees, it was mean of providence to play you such a trick: but if such incidents are always to bring me such a dear letter from you, then I cannot meet enough funerals . . . Next came dinner at the restaurant you know of, where great friends change dainty morsels from plate to plate: alas! never a bit changed I . . . but oh Tookees, what time little Christians are tucked in their beds, I felt very sad . . . And now Tookissima, it is time here for goodnight – Sleep very well – Thy very name is a caress, and the memory of the sweet and subtle fire makes the breath come quick. My beloved, with thy coat upon my back, thy waistcoat round my rybbes, thy chain upon my hum! hum! hum! Thy image in my heart, can I forget thee, tell me – Yes or No? . . . Maxwell.

Violet set about incorporating Valérie into her own life, and planned a visit to Sicily with her. The expedition fell through, however, when Max had

9 Being superstitious, Violet had been upset by meeting a funeral cortège just before Max's voyage – traditionally a sinister warning.

to explain the ground rules: Valérie must pay her own expenses, and concede to Violet the best seats in trains and the best rooms in hotels. Nevertheless, the two women remained friends, and Max was to become even closer to Valérie after her husband's death at the beginning of the Great War.

In 1911 the thirty-eight-year-old English composer Ralph Vaughan Williams had published a small book on English folk song. The sentimental parlour songs and ballads which the Edwardians and their Victorian parents had so enjoyed were, to Vaughan Williams, musically weak, designed only for relaxation. In this they seemed quite different from true folk music, which stemmed from authentic experience and expressed itself in forthright musical language. Violet had observed, when playing pieces from the Fitzwilliam Virginal Book,[10] the manner in which Elizabethan and Stuart music had evolved from folk tunes. She found the gap between folk music and early music – with its freedom of rhythm and suppleness of phrasing – notably smaller than that between folk music and classical or romantic music (folk themes had been used by, among other composers, Haydn, Beethoven, Tchaikovsky and Brahms, but in changed form, harnessed to an essentially incompatible style). She saw immediately from Vaughan Williams's *Fantasia on a Theme of Thomas Tallis*, which she had heard conducted by Beecham at Queen's Hall in 1910, that he had made the same connection.

The idea of an English folk-song revival, which would also be a renewal of English music, appealed to Violet's artistic instincts. Contemporary poets and writers such as Housman, Kipling and Hardy had also incorporated a rural culture into their work, producing masterpieces in which the English language, rid of literary mannerisms, was refreshed. Moreover, Violet failed to see why Bartók and Grieg should be permitted by musical sophisticates to display their folk-song badge, while Vaughan Williams should attract condescension for doing the same in an English context. For several years, Vaughan Williams and his collaborators, Cecil Sharp[11] and George Butterworth,[12] had been combing the country conducting research into cataloguing folk song, though their efforts were too late to save all that

10 An amateur performer's manuscript collection made in the early years of the seventeenth century, given by Lord Fitzwilliam to the Fitzwilliam Library, Cambridge.
11 Cecil Sharp (1859–1924) dedicated his life to the collection, publication and performance of folk song and folk dance in England, and more than anybody was responsible for the salvaging of this national heritage.
12 George Butterworth (b. 1885), composer, was killed in action on the Somme in 1916. He worked with Sharp and Vaughan Williams in the movement for the revival of English folk song and dance, and some of his compositions – such as songs and settings of poems from Housman's *A Shropshire Lad* – reflect the folk-song influence.

should have been saved, not least because since 1860, with the flight of the rural population to the towns, the traditions of folk song and narrative had been rapidly declining. As Violet came to appreciate the scope of their achievement, she was both stimulated and impressed. The experiences of her formative years, when she had been immersed in the Sussex country-side, led her to believe that the loss of this heritage risked depriving the new urban world of its soul, while her musical intelligence told her that here was a treasure house which might supply inspiration to any creative composer.

As luck would have it, Cecil Sharp heard Violet play some folk music in April 1912, shortly before Vaughan Williams was due to come to Stratford. He wrote to her immediately, asking if he might introduce Vaughan Williams to her. The letter could not have come at a better time: she was longing to meet the composer, not merely to play music but also to explore English folk song more profoundly, now that it had started to form a regular part of her repertoire.

*DRAGONFIELD UXBRIDGE 7 April 1912.*
Dear Mrs Woodhouse,
I hope you were not overtired after your exertions of yesterday. If it is any satisfaction to you to know it I can assure you that your playing was by many people considered *the* feature of the evening. As for me despite some natural anxiety last night I enjoyed every note you played. Perhaps I liked "The Little Raven" and "As I walked out" better than any of them − they seemed to suit my mood − but all were beautiful. I want you to let me bring Vaughan Williams & Butterworth to see you some day and ask you to be kind enough to play to them. You know it is a mania with me to try and make use of everybody who can help the movement in which I am so interested, and above all I want to convince the younger musicians of the artis-tic possibilities of our folk-songs, and no one can doubt them when *you* play them. [illegible] made me tingle last night − don't show this to your husband or he will laugh at me! − and I have known and loved the tune for years! We must arrange a perfect little concert at Stratford in August. Coming just at the end of all the hurly burly of the session it will be especially welcome to us all. Much as I love dancing I love music more.

Again many thanks
Yours sincerely,
Cecil Sharp

I felt like an elephant on the piano last night after your first group of tunes!

During the autumn of 1912 Vaughan Williams, Sharp and Violet assembled a programme for an afternoon concert to be held in Stratford on 24 April the following year. They planned the date to coincide with the time at which Vaughan Williams was due to take up the position of musical director at the Memorial Theatre in Stratford for a month , where he was to arrange and conduct entr'acte music for some of the Shakespeare plays. The concert consisted mainly of English folk tunes collected by Cecil Sharp and arranged by Violet for the harpsichord, as well as a number of early English pieces, in one of which she played the virginals. Unbeknown to Violet, Vaughan Williams hated the harpsichord. That he nevertheless arranged a *Folk Song Fantasia* for harpsichord and flute[13] especially for her to play in this concert was, according to his wife, "a great tribute to the personal charm of Mrs. GW". From 1913 onwards Violet regularly inserted Vaughan Williams's arrangements – such as those of the songs "Through Bushes and Briars" and "The Dark Eyed Sailor" – into her programmes.

Violet and Vaughan Williams enjoyed each other's company, though they never became close friends. Not by any means prudish himself, he viewed her household with a tolerant twinkle in his eye, and once remarked casually to the distinguished modern harpsichordist Ruth Dyson, "Oh yes, Mrs Gordon Woodhouse – had four husbands and slept with them all at once!" Of course, Vaughan Williams had no first-hand knowledge of Violet's private life, but his remark indicates that if she had ever thought that the principle of safety in numbers would protect her reputation, then her plan had certainly backfired.

One project of Vaughan Williams, which in the event never came to fruition, was to write the music for a new ballet for the Ballets Russes. Violet had not yet herself come to know Sergei Diaghilev, the Russian impresario, but she had been stunned by his meteoric descent, at the instigation of Beecham, on the London scene in 1911, 1912 and 1913, in which the verve, colour and audacity of his productions had made all other ballet performances seem by comparison too pale and timid to be worth watching.

Diaghilev's genius permeated all aspects of his ballets. He swept away the jaded tradition of romantic, fairy-tale evocations of distant lands and bygone eras to reinterpret the past from his own contemporary perspective. Unlike other impresarios, he conceived and commissioned every aspect of the production, the story line, the music, the design and the choreography. He

13 Played in the Stratford concert by the French flautist Louis Fleury.

had ruthless energy and willpower, and would only use artists who collaborated wholeheartedly with his vision. When he found that Michel Fokine, the chief choreographer to the Ballets Russes, was not radical enough, he trained Fokine's pupil, Vaslav Nijinsky, to supplant him. Diaghilev and Nijinsky became lovers, and together they broke the over-tight embrace in which music and dance had formerly been clasped, to form a looser relationship, in which the dancer danced with spontaneity and abandon. If Violet was transfixed by Nijinsky's portrait, half-human, half-elf in *Le spectre de la rose* in 1911 (a Ballets Russes piece performed to music by Carl-Maria von Weber), his choreography and dancing in Debussy's *L'après-midi d'un faune* the following year completely overwhelmed her. Taking inspiration from Greek bas reliefs and vase paintings, Nijinsky had choreographed for himself a sequence of walks, runs, and angular arm poses in profile, a kind of two-dimensional movement that cut across and away from the music with total freedom. An entirely new style of ballet had emerged.

Ethel Smyth's two-year crusade in the cause of the suffragettes deprived her of the opportunity to share Violet's enthusiasm for Diaghilev, but by 1913 her campaign was over and she was ready to return to music. Her forays into politics, together with continued frustration in her professional career, had convinced her that "men are curs" and that women are the possessors of deeper resources than even she had previously discovered. Shortly after her release from the cause she sent Violet the first part of her autobiography, *Impressions that Remained* (the full edition was published in 1919). Ethel had almost as remarkable a gift for writing as for composing, and Violet wrote back to her admiringly:

> *29 November 1913,*
> Darling Ethel,
> Your book is quite enthralling and entrancing. Your wonderful critical sense. I can only say that, as more than half of people's depths are unseen, like icebergs, and not to be expressed, or revealed by any words, I can dimly apprehend but I do, I do, what you are.

Now, however, circumstances were again to separate Ethel and Violet. An inveterate traveller, Ethel went to Vienna to hear a concert of her own music and then travelled on to Ireland. Then, in December she set off for Egypt, where she stayed in a remote hotel twenty-five miles outside Alexandria, which had been suggested to her by Ronald Storrs, the Oriental Secretary at the British Agency in Cairo. She wanted to be alone to work on her new opera, *The Bosun's Mate*.

At the end of the year Denis returned from India and Violet and her four men were once more reunited. As the spring of 1914 turned to summer Denis took them all to Helmingham during his leave. "The party will be a large one if you don't mind", he wrote to G.M., "I'll give you the list – V. and Gordon, Bill Barrington and Max Labouchère, and Mr. and Mrs. George Crawley".[14] They went on to visit Bluebelle and Nevile and their four children in Hertfordshire. Kit, the eldest, by this time almost grown up and much in awe of Violet, was desperate to hear the famous Italian tenor, Enrico Caruso, sing in Puccini's *Madam Butterfly* at Covent Garden. To her great joy Violet offered to have her to stay overnight in London and to take her to it.

The murder of the Archduke Franz Ferdinand at Sarajevo on 28 June, which within weeks would set off a chain reaction leading to world war, caused hardly a ripple of interest in London. Far more exciting was the Russian season at Covent Garden. Beecham had brought the Russian Opera to London for the first time the previous season, and was now once more in close collaboration with Diaghilev. Together they planned (with the backing of Beecham's father, with whom he had been reconciled) to make the summer season of 1914 something that London had never known before. There were to be eight operas, including a short cycle of German opera in which the brilliant new soprano Claire Dux would take a leading role in Mozart's *Die Zauberflöte*. In the Russian productions, their star bass, Feodor Chaliapine, would take on five great roles, culminating in that of Boris in Mussorgsky's *Boris Godunov*. As for the ballet, there were to be half a dozen new ones, including one all-English production of *Dylan*, by the composer Joseph Holbrooke. Diaghilev and Nijinsky had quarrelled, leaving the field open for Fokine to enchant London with Ravel's *Daphnis and Chloë*, while Stravinsky's *Rite of Spring*, whose insistent, throbbing music and savage choreography by Nijinsky had so shocked Paris in 1913, was to make its first appearance in England.

Kit Gwynne duly arrived in Park Place for her treat at the opera, to find her aunt in Slavic mood, her mind full of Chaliapine and Diaghilev. Violet snubbed Kit's adolescent taste, dismissing Puccini as superficial – "Yes, there are some pretty things in *Butterfly* – for instance the love duet and the music when she is waiting for Pinkerton to come back to her" – and sitting down at the harpsichord she played the main themes from the opera, bringing them casually out of her infallible musical memory. But Violet stayed at home that evening, and it was Gordon who was deputed to take Kit to hear Caruso at Covent Garden.

London's musical and artistic season in the summer of 1914 was the most glorious that anyone could remember. The city glittered and sparkled

14  George Crawley was a designer and architect.

in the glow of post-Edwardian opulence. The long country-house week-ends, the rich and extravagant entertainments and the elaborate social rituals of the drawing-rooms of Mayfair seemed as permanent as nature itself. The waltz from Strauss's *Rosenkavalier* was the backdrop to every ball or dance. Artists from Diaghilev's company might as often be seen at the dinner tables of *grandes dames* such as Mrs Alice Keppel, Margot Asquith, Lady Howard de Walden or Lady Ripon – as at those of the writers and artists of Bloomsbury. There were new plays by Shaw, Harley Granville-Barker and Arnold Bennett. The theatrical designer Norman Wilkinson caught the mood of the day by conjuring up a retinue of fairies painted in solid gold for Titania in a production of *A Midsummer Night's Dream*. Linking all these different worlds were the rich American hostess Emerald Cunard and the eccentric, flame-haired aristocrat Lady Ottoline Morrell . The brightest new stars of the social and artistic scenes were the eighteen-year-old Lady Diana Manners (later better known by her married name, as Lady Diana Cooper) and the twenty-one-year-old Osbert Sitwell.

As the Season of 1914 drew to a close, society dispersed for the end of the summer. Ascot, Wimbledon, Henley and the Eton and Harrow cricket match at Lord's were over. There was no sense of impending doom in the air. The grouse moors were about to beckon Bill and the rest of the shooting classes; then there would be partridges, pheasants and hunting. Violet would return to the garden and the music room at Armscote – already she was planning visits, expeditions and invitations. But all at once her idyllic life was shattered, and this time there was nothing she could do about it.

# IX

## To the Trenches

THE FIRST WORLD WAR was fired by a linked series of rapidly igniting fuses. Bosnia, to which independent Serbia laid claim, had been annexed by Austria. When the heir to the Austro-Hungarian throne, Archduke Franz Ferdinand, was assassinated by a Serb nationalist in the Bosnian capital Sarajevo, Austria made humiliating demands on Serbia, including the dismissal of all "anti-Austrian" officers and high officials in Serbian military and state organizations. The Serbs were willing to give way on almost every point, but Austria, encouraged by her ally Germany, was bent on war: jealous of the British Empire and in the grip of the Prussian military machine, Germany, which had only been united under that name since 1871, was looking for a pretext to oust the Slavic influence and establish a Teutonic hegemony in the Balkans. This would be a prelude to winning a wider conflict and gaining for Germany an empire and "a place in the sun". When Serbia's concessions were rejected, Russia, ever alert for a chance to exploit troubles in the Balkans so as to gain access to the Mediterranean, mobilized to defend its Slavic ally.

These ominous diplomatic manoeuvres drew in France, which was bound to Russia by a mutual defence alliance and which thirsted to restore its military honour by revenging its defeat at the hands of Bismarck's Prussia in 1870. Nevertheless, even up to the last minute war might have been avoided. Serbia, Russia, and France were all prepared to accept whatever compromises were necessary to pacify Austria-Hungary, as was Britain, which was trying to act as peacemaker. But by now Germany had taken charge. The army staff had a long-standing and fully worked-out plan to destroy France as a military power by striking towards Paris through Belgium, whose neutrality was guaranteed by Britain. Afterwards Germany would turn on Russia, and finally (or so the more belligerent geopolitical thinkers urged) on Britain.

Events spun bewilderingly out of control. On 1 August Germany declared war on Russia, and on 3 August on France. On 4 August German troops invaded Belgium, whose neutrality was guaranteed by Britain. Britain's ultimatum to Germany, that a state of war would exist between them if Belgian territory were violated, expired at 11.00 pm that day and when the hour passed without a German withdrawal, the King, in Council, declared war. Neither the Dominions nor the Colonies were consulted, but within days their Governor-Generals and Viceroys had followed suit. The Kaiser ignored the desperate appeals of his cousins, Tsar Nicholas II and King George V, while his Chancellor, von Bethmann-Hollweg, described the agreement on Belgium's neutrality as "a scrap of paper" and freely admitted in his speech in the Reichstag on the day of the invasion that Germany had broken international law.

At first, few suspected that the war would be fought other than by standing armies and navies. Wild optimism ruled in Paris and Berlin, and people in Britain believed the war would be over by Christmas, expecting France and Russia, with a little help from the British Army, to defeat or hold Germany and Austria-Hungary in the field, while the Royal Navy's supremacy would enable it to maintain a blockade in the North Sea. But British confidence was built on insecure foundations: despite its industrial power and its empire, the country's armed forces were smaller than Germany's, and lagged behind in many areas of warfare – submarines, aircraft, artillery, hand grenades, machine-guns, wireless telephony, motorized transport, even binoculars. The Regular Army divisions of the British Expeditionary Force, which crossed the Channel early in August, were embarrassingly few, and where should they be sent? At the urgent request of the French, they went to Mons, just inside the Belgian border with France, 130 miles north-east of Paris, to take up a position on the left of the French Army, which was by then retreating before the massive German onslaught.

Modern combat came as an appalling shock to soldiers brought up on rifle fire and glorious cavalry charges with drawn swords. Before September was out, reports of the carnage and exhaustion of troops facing high-explosive and machine-gun fire were filtering back home, and the need for massive reinforcements was beginning to become clear. Lord Kitchener, appointed Secretary of State for War on 5 August, was among the first to realize that battles between professional armies were no longer the defining characteristic of war, and that what lay before the country was a prolonged engagement of the whole nation and the empire. This was to be, as it has ever since been called, the Great War.

Violet knew that Denis, as a Regular soldier, would go into battle, but when Bill was called up as a Reservist and Max began to talk of volunteering her private world collapsed. If Max went, she would have only Gordon left, for he had been declared unfit for active service. The first to depart was Denis, albeit to an unexpected and unexciting destination. On returning from India, he had started a two-year foreign-language course at the Military Staff College at Camberley in Surrey, hoping to further his career by qualifying as an overseas military attaché. When war broke out, however, he was despatched to Edinburgh as a staff officer attached to home defence. His letters express his frustration at finding himself far away from his glamorous regiment, by then in action out in France. Some weeks after the war had started, he wrote to his step-grandmother, G.M.:

> *Tuesday October 1 1914* . . . No. G.M. dear, I have not been "training Cavalry". I am a General Staff Officer to the Lowland Division, which is composed of Infantry and Artillery . . . As you know, I am a cavalry soldier who has always been accustomed to work with fully trained Cavalry, and the best in the world – all these confreres of "My own arm" have been engaged in earnest in their real work, which I have studied and prepared for. While here am I, as a result of going to the Staff College to advance my prospects, relegated to a territorial Division [i.e. of the Territorial Force, the Regular Army's principal reserve] defending the coast of Fife . . . Of course I am eternally hoping and expecting to be transferred, as the need out there grows greater – but I can't bear the thought of waiting months, until this Div.n goes out in its turn, and then of being still with a terr.1 Div.n – not first rate and above all not cavalry.

With the fashionable military ardour of the time, Denis pulled every string he could in order to get himself moved to a cavalry unit at the front. Two years before the first appearance of the tank, horses still represented, in theory, an army's chief source of mobility. Having obtained all his professional training with the cavalry, and having no first-hand experience of battle, Denis utterly underestimated the impotence of horsemen against artillery, barbedwire, trenches and machine-guns.

> I really do not care a bit about the "Staff" compared with the supreme necessity of getting out to the front, with regular cavalry – where my instincts and training belong. This is THE great war of the century, the equal, if not more, of the Napoleonic wars. I have worked hard at my profession to fit myself for this, & to take my proper part in it. If I am not allowed to do this, I do not feel that I shall care to go on soldiering. How should I feel afterwards, as a Staff "expert" lecturing to others on War? . . . I simply would not accept such a position.

Well, I still expect that I shall get a chance in time – but it is very hard to hear of new cavalry brigades and Divisions being formed, and still to get no place within them but to remain out of sight & mind, marooned in Scotland.

While Denis fretted in Scotland, Bill rejoined his old Militia regiment, the Oxfordshire and Buckinghamshire Light Infantry, which had been stationed at Portsmouth for training. It was a tremendous blow to Violet when he was passed fit and refused to appeal on grounds of health. She visited him whenever she could, but opportunities to see him were all too rare.

As the first casualty lists of the retreat from Mons began to appear in the newspapers, Violet became distraught, her only solace being the occasional return of her men on leave, when she managed to disguise her anxiety and remind them of the happiness which lay in store for them once the war was over. Of a visit to Folkington by Denis and Violet early in the war, Dorothy records how Violet was "in such a charming humour and so deliciously clothed. Denis is very gay and quite as devoted to V. as ever!!" But another diary entry comes closer to the truth about Violet's real state of mind.

*October 21st 1914*
V. came down to lunch and tea. Poor child Oh my heart simply aches for her. It's terrible to see a soul in torture. You feel almost ashamed to see it; as if it were too sacred for other eyes. Oh God what women have to suffer.

Violet now went over regularly to Folkington, thoughtlessly showing all Denis's love letters to her sister, who still yearned for romance in her own life. There is jealousy and sadness in Dorothy, as well as sympathy, when she contrasts her own loneliness with the love Violet attracted so naturally.

*October 31st 1914*
V. came down for the day. What a truly beautiful love D's is. Why do some people get love like that. His love at its most perfect 'cos there is no self in it. It made me feel lonelier and sadder than ever when I read his letters and yet almost reverent before something so wonderful.

Despite the swaying fortunes and the uneasy equilibrium of the first few months of war, the illusion had persisted that it would soon be over. As 1914 drew to an end, however, and as the opposing sides dug in, eventually creating a line of trenches that ran from the Swiss border to the Channel coast, these hopes were being replaced by far more sombre expectations. Max, who, at forty-one, might easily have excused himself on the grounds of age, was among the first to volunteer. Violet's youngest brother Roland, aged thirty-two, also joined up, but Nevile was clearly too old at forty-six and was in any case turned down on medical grounds. Rupert, the same age as Max, was exempt by reason of being a Member of Parliament, though he, too, could never have passed a fitness test, as his health had been undermined in youth by rheumatic fever, which had weakened his heart. A man's reasons for not being in uniform were crucial in those days, when volunteering for the front was seen as the touchstone of patriotic courage, and white feathers were handed out in the street or sent anonymously to those whose resolution had apparently failed them.

Shortly before Christmas Violet's father, who had been in declining health for almost a year, took a turn for the worse. Violet wrote consolingly to the stricken Dorothy from the hotel, close to Bill's training quarters. Of late, with her own men away, Violet had been seeing more of James, who was becoming mellower with the approach of death. But her chief preoccupations remained elsewhere, with Bill's forthcoming leave and Denis's latest military bulletin. Denis's news had been all bad – heavy losses in France and a shortage of high-explosive shells for the artillery.

> *December 19th, 1914.* South Pier Hotel, Southsea
> Darling Dorothy,
> I am so sorry that Darling Papa is worse again. I sent a wire, or am sending one now. And, my dearest, I fear you are depressed and sad & I can do nothing for you. Do write & tell me how you are, if you feel inclined to & everything about you.
> O, Dorothy, just think dear Bill is expecting to have a short leave next week, for 3 whole days! From Tuesday next, till Saturday! Isn't it *wonderful*? After nearly five months. He is very busy today so I shall not be able to see him till this evening at his fort, as he cannot leave it today all day long. And Denis hopes to have a week's leave from 10th to 17th. I must try to bring him down to see you. Bill, of course, wants to rush straight to Armscote for his tiny leave. I am thinking a great deal about you, my dearest, & wish you could be happy. I hear from Denis today that our casualties have been over 5000 this last week or two. And we have lost 50 officers and 1500 men through the Indians bolting. Isn't it *awful*! Also we are short now of lyddite [a high-explosive compound used in shells], which seems wrong . . .
> Your loving Violet.

On 20 January 1915, Max joined up, following Bill with a commission in the Oxford and Bucks at Portsmouth. Violet began to feel as though the whole architecture of her life was falling apart, for in March, having lingered on for a few months, James Gwynne died. Although he had been deeply in love with May when they married, she had never returned his affection in equal measure, nor had they become close companions. After the birth of Roland in 1882 they had no longer shared a bedroom, and he had become progressively more introspective after he had given up the day-to-day running of his engineering business. Secretive, withdrawn and dictatorial, he had banished Reginald, sacked Nevile and left Roland to be brought up as a mother's boy, while he regarded Dorothy as "difficult" and Eva as having married beneath her. It was not surprising that his children, other than Rupert and Violet, felt distant from him, and that the atmosphere at Folkington had grown heavy, the more so when, a few years before she died, May's mind started to cloud over and her gaiety became increasingly intermittent.

James's will had been lodged with his solicitor. The executors and trustees were Rupert, Roland, Gordon and his old merchant banker friend, Herbert Twining, but the contents were secret, and the family awaited the outcome of the reading with differing expectations. Despite being the eldest son, Reginald had few hopes. Now married and living in Saskatchewan, he had returned occasionally to England, where James had cold-shouldered him and advised him to declare himself bankrupt.[1] In Canada he was a man of stature, a general in the Canadian Army, but at Folkington he was a non-person, a not uncommon fate for disgraced or rejected relations in unforgiving post-Victorian England.

As the second son, Nevile had greater reason for optimism. He was convinced that by the end of his father's life he had completely repaired their earlier rift, which dated back to their physical tussle in 1902 and his enforced departure from the family firm in 1903. Rupert had repeatedly assured Bluebelle that he would not abuse his own favoured position at Wootton to take advantage of her husband. Since James was certain to want to hold his assets together for future generations of Gwynnes, Nevile expected to take Reginald's place and to be left virtually the entire Folkington estate. As for Violet, she believed that her father had promised her a decent legacy at the time when he had declined to give Wootton to her and Gordon. In any event, some act of posthumous generosity seemed her natural due. Was she not James's favourite child? And as the family's accredited genius, was she not obliged to lead an expensive lifestyle? That, at least, was how Violet saw it.

1 In 1894 James had proposed offering a 20 per cent settlement of £500 to Reginald's creditors, but had been told by the moneylenders' solicitors that this would be unacceptable. The remaining alternatives for Reginald were to stay abroad, to face imprisonment for contempt of court, or officially to become bankrupt.

The will was read by the solicitor to Nevile and Rupert in the Folkington library. Angry voices could be heard and Eva, Violet and May exchanged uneasy glances outside. Suddenly the door opened and Nevile appeared, his face unnaturally white. Beneath the appearance of reconciliation, James's resentment had never healed – or perhaps had healed on his deathbed, too late for him to add a codicil. The will was dated 1903. James had cut Nevile completely out of his large inheritance, leaving everything in trust for Rupert and his male heirs, if any, failing whom the estate would pass in trust to Roland and his male heirs. Even Nevile's son John, James's only grandson (and the author's father), was not mentioned in the complex hierarchy of potential male legatees. Violet burst into tears and flung her arms round Nevile. The tears were also for herself, for she too had been left nothing, though initially the brothers were too preoccupied with the main drama to remember clearly what, if anything, the will said about her. She was mortified and, for the first time in her life, seriously worried about money. The previous year she and Gordon had moved from Park Place to Ovington Square in Chelsea so as to reduce their expenditure. From her new house she wrote anxiously, though without recrimination, to Roland.

*9th April 1915*  37 Ovington Square, London S.W.
This is only for your private ear, please!

    Dearest Roland, Thank you for your letter. I do miss Bill. Would you, my dear boy, mind telling me how affairs are! I hate to appear mercenary! But you told me that I had been left, you thought £450 a year. Rupert told Gordon only £250! and now Gordon tells me that I have not been mentioned at all in the Will, that he can see, & I understand from a very unpleasant letter which Gordon received from Rupert this morning, written thro' a *typewriter*! that I only have an allowance thro' mother, & as she pleases! I suppose it is the same for all the daughters; but it makes me a little hurt, as I have been told not a word! Would you mind, therefore, telling me what you know? I do not want the shadow of money to ever stand between me and those I love. And I do not love darling papa one atom the less, whatever might happen, & this I feel sure you understand. But we are no more rich, in fact poor, and if I have been left very little, or perhaps nothing, I cannot understand what I have done to deserve it, but I must further reduce my expenses! if I can! What I dislike most about our means being so straightened [*sic*] is that it costs so much to go to Portsmouth to see Bill, & I do hate seeing him so seldom . . .Yours, dear Roland, V.

It took several readings and consultations with lawyers before the members of the family were able to grasp the full implications of James's will, so tortuously had it been worded in his obsessive intent to control the direction of his fortune for generations to come. Cutting through some 7,500 words of dense, unpunctuated clauses and sub-clauses, its essence was that May would receive a life interest in his estate, after which would come Rupert, followed by class after class of hypothetical male heirs, and then class after class of potential female heiresses. A codicil, dated 24 October 1914, specifically excluded Reginald, but Nevile and his family were excluded by silence. Dorothy was left a life interest in the Folkington Home Farm house, and Roland was left a life interest in farmland and property known as the Michelham Estate. The provisions about the heirlooms were so detailed as to contain instructions for their insurance, while future heirs or heiresses were required to change their names to Gwynne or else forfeit their inheritance "as if the person so entitled were dead". In all, the estate was valued at £233,492, equivalent to some £12 million today.

There was dark talk in Nevile's family that Rupert must have had some understanding with James about the will – how else could he have afforded to marry and fight a parliamentary seat? – and that he and Roland had conspired to prevent Nevile being reinstated. Rupert was no longer on speaking terms with Nevile, and for a time there was even a chill in his relations with Violet, who felt that Nevile had been treated abominably and that she herself had been robbed of her promised, and now badly needed, inheritance. The episode left an aftertaste of betrayal, vengeance and intrigue.

Soon, however, Violet had other things to think about. Max received an early transfer to France. This was a further turn of the screw for Denis, whose jealousy of Max's ability to amuse Violet was now replaced by more admiring envy of his opportunity to prove his courage. Denis wrote ironically to Violet:

> Yes it is odd, as you say, that Maxwell is the one who is now a soldier at the Front, he who used to affect the radical ignorant belittling of our army. I'm glad to hear he looks so hearty and well on it, and seems to take so well to those strange habits. I feel sure that he will become a Brigadier before long, and the thought of it makes me laugh – but I hope he will anyhow and I certainly think far more of him than I ever did before, tho' I can well believe that you found him looking more natural when he had got his suit of civvies on. Has he grown a moustache again, like he used to have years ago, before you made him shave it off?

With three of Violet's men away in the army Armscote had become a lonely place. Servants and labourers were increasingly hard to find, as men

of military age volunteered. Moreover, Gordon was feeling financially insecure now that Violet's expectation of a legacy had been disappointed, and
they therefore reluctantly decided to make Ovington Square their home
base. Occasionally, at weekends, they would take staff from London to
Armscote, but otherwise they left it to be looked after by one old servant
and a part-time gardener, supervision taking the form of regular visits from
Gordon.

Throughout this time, Violet had been doing her best to salvage what
she could of her artistic life. Cultural activities in England were less drastically affected by the war than might have been expected. Initially, music
institutions throughout the country closed down, considering it unpatriotic
to provide entertainment during a national crisis, but soon there was at
least a partial recovery. Thomas Beecham persuaded the Hallé Society in
Manchester and the Royal Philharmonic Society in London to set an
example by producing a new repertoire (German music was banned, and the
programmes were filled with French, Russian, English and Italian works).
Musicians living abroad began to return. The Deliuses came back from Grez
with their French cook and were lent a house near Watford by Beecham;
Isidore de Lara, a figure of shadowy romance and once a popular composer of
ballads and light opera, arrived from Paris to set up weekly War Emergency
Concerts in aid of the many musicians who had lost their livelihoods.
Fortuitously, Dolmetsch had settled in Hampstead in north London only
weeks before war broke out, having left the Gaveau factory earlier in 1914.

Amid a wave of popular sympathy for "gallant little Belgium" numerous
grateful Belgian artists escaped to London following the German invasion
of their country. Within months Belgian actors staged three plays at the
Criterion Theatre, portraying bourgeois life in Brussels; and Dolmetsch's pet
institution, the Art Workers Guild, gave Belgian musicians honorary
membership for the duration of their exile. Some artistic events carried on
as though nothing had changed. The annual Promenade concerts established twenty years earlier by Henry Wood continued without interruption
at Queen's Hall. Shakespeare's 350th birthday anniversary and the tercentenary of his death were celebrated with an orgy of plays and Elizabethan
music. Public lectures abounded: in February 1915 Rudyard Kipling gave a
speech at the Mansion House on the importance of military bands, praising
their melody and rhythm; a month later the controversial painter and art
critic Roger Fry, who had introduced French Post-Impressionist painting to
London with exhibitions at the Grafton Galleries in 1910 and 1912, lectured
at the Art Workers Guild to an unruly audience, many of whom cried out
"indecent" at the sight of Matisse's paintings.

Some years previously, Christabel Marshal had obtained a position as music critic of *The Lady*, Britain's first women's weekly magazine, where she produced reviews of a quality so high that Ethel Smyth was driven to complain bitterly about the "undiluted all-maleism" of the daily press, which deprived a wider readership of Chris's "first-line female intelligence". Her reviews of Violet's wartime performances, initialled simply "C.M.", are so warm that it is hard sometimes to be sure whether it is the critic, the erstwhile admirer or the feminist speaking. Of one of Isidore de Lara's early War Emergency Concerts she wrote:

> Far and away the best of these was given on 4 March 1915 at Steinway Hall. English music of the past was exquisitely played on the harpsichord by Mrs. Gordon Woodhouse, who has no rival on this instrument. Through her skill we were made to be proud of the wealth of inspiration, the happy joyful creativeness of sixteenth-century English composers. Afterwards Ethel Smyth's imaginative songs and fine string quartet made up the second half of the programme.

Now self-employed, Dolmetsch was working hard to complete the text of his definitive book on the interpretation of seventeenth- and eighteenth-century music. Short of money and eager to put his ideas into practice, he was glad to have the opportunity to play some works by Bach with Violet at a "Bach-Beethoven-Brahms Festival" at Queen's Hall in April, with the London Symphony Orchestra under the Belgian conductor Henri Verbrugghen. For Bach's Concerto for Two Harpsichords they used Gaveau instruments, of which Dolmetsch had made one for himself and the other for Violet. The *Daily Telegraph* praised Violet handsomely, noting her "beautiful balance of tone", but the critics were signally unimpressed by Dolmetsch's attempts at authenticity in the Concerto for Two Violins. They were even more severe about his solo part in the Brandenburg Concerto No. 1 on the violino piccolo, in which the small instrument's thin, silvery tones were all but inaudible, making a comic contrast with the richness of the LSO's strings.

Chris, who had become friendly with Denis's music-loving aunts Grace and Blanche Tollemache, missed the Dolmetsch concert. Writing to Grace in June she remarked wistfully that she hardly saw Violet any longer and that the war was having a deadening impact on her own hopes of literary recognition:

> *8 June 1915* . . . I have seen Blanchie within the last month. We talked of nothing but the war. Barren talk it must be. I haven't seen V. for ages. She doesn't trouble about me. I heard her play at an 'Emergency' concert but not at the Queen's Hall. I heard she was

splendid with Dolmetsch. I feel as if I should never write again (I don't count grinding out words for *The Lady* as writing). When you have two books held up it is very hard to produce anything & war has a sad effect on the imagination. It is really the triumph of the commonplace and the material. Ideas are dragged out to justify slaughter ... I had a medal blessed for Denis before he left & always pray for him.

The patriotic poetry of Rupert Brooke made a deep impression on Violet ("If I should die, think only this of me: / That there's some corner of a foreign field / That is for ever England ..."); and like many others she had been moved to tears by Laurence Binyon's poem "For the Fallen"[2] when it appeared in *The Times* in September 1914. But there was a strong resistance to false sentiment in her, fostered by Max, and she was likely to be receptive to something more brutally candid if and when the time was ripe for such writing. Already Max had encouraged her to move on from the nineteenth-century poets so beloved of her father – Byron, Tennyson and Arnold – to the less mannered poetry of Walter de la Mare, Rudyard Kipling and Thomas Hardy. Hardy had been one of the few poets to have written honestly about the Boer War, and in Kipling's *Barrack Room Ballads* and *Five Nations* she admired a voice which spoke without sentimentality for the ordinary man.

The new poets discarded period themes and archaic diction, and instead addressed their subject matter in vernacular imagery. The most up-to-date of them, known as the "Georgians", had as their publisher and mentor Edward Marsh, a scholar, civil servant and collector of contemporary art, who edited the five volumes of *Georgian Poetry* that appeared between 1912 and 1922. Had it not been for the even more revolutionary works of T.S. Eliot and Ezra Pound, who attacked the *Georgian Poetry* series, and the shocking later war poetry of Wilfred Owen and others, the Georgians would probably be regarded as having marked the decisive break between academic poetry and twentieth-century modernism. Violet read their work avidly, though not from any desire to be thought fashionable, for her taste in poetry was entirely personal to herself, and wide enough to accommodate everything from Ezra Pound to the Elizabethans.

It was in 1915 that another woman fell under Violet's spell. The thirty-

2 The poem includes the lines "They shall grow not old, as we that are left grow old:/ Age shall not weary them, nor the years condemn. / At the going down of the sun and in the morning / We will remember them", which are still read out during ceremonies and church services all over Britain on Remembrance Sunday.

year-old Marguerite Radclyffe Hall had produced a few slim volumes of poetry when, in 1910, she had come with her lover, Mabel Batten, to Violet's suffragette meeting in Park Place. Her notorious book *The Well of Loneliness*, the first overtly lesbian novel in English, was not published until 1928, but she had already made a modest name for herself in 1912 with a book of Housmanesque poems entitled *Songs of Three Counties*. Marguerite was rich, independent and beautiful in a masculine way, with high cheekbones and an aquiline nose. She dressed in severe grey suits, though not yet in the men's pinstripes she would later affect. As a child, she had been so talented a child pianist that the celebrated German conductor Artur Nikisch had urged her (without success) to come to Leipzig to be his pupil. Her method of composing a ballad was first to find a poetic rhythm by singing out the refrain, and then to invite other composers to improve on the music she had written. Neglected and lonely in childhood, she fell in love in 1907, aged 20, with the much older Mabel Batten, an Edwardian *grande dame* of Bohemian tastes who had been the foremost amateur lieder singer of her day. If Mabel was the mother figure in the relationship, it was nevertheless Marguerite who assumed the dominating role, first distancing Mabel emotionally from her husband, and then setting up house with her in Cadogan Square after his death.

By the beginning of the war Marguerite (or John as she now called herself) was being unfaithful with another married woman. She had tired of Mabel, and felt trapped in the affair. What was worse, Mabel had recently become a permanent invalid as a result of a car crash. In the winter of 1914 Marguerite began to look to Violet for sympathy, guessing that she would be more accessible now that Bill, Denis and Max were away, and hoping that she would soon be bored with being left to her own devices with Gordon and the quiet Mary Stanton. Throughout her life, Marguerite took satisfaction in dislodging women from their husbands, and the prospect of supplanting not only a husband but also three quasi-husbands was a real challenge. But perhaps not an insurmountable one: Marguerite knew Christabel Marshal, and had heard tell of Adelina Ganz.

Fascinated by Violet, Marguerite started visiting her regularly at the house in Ovington Square. As her hopes of forming a relationship rose she dedicated to Violet (in words similar to the dedication to Mabel Batten of some earlier poems at the height of that affair) her new volume of poetry, *The Forgotten Island*, which was published in the spring of 1915. The fifty-three stanzas, set in a mythical Greek landscape, contain an erotic appeal to a woman whose eyes are "deep as the pools of a forest, soft with the brown and gold of the autumn", and whose body is "slim as the delicate cypress".

As Radclyffe Hall's biographer puts it, "the poet reaches a fever-pitch of desire, but requital eludes her and she recedes, waiting, chiding and lonely." Printed at the beginning of *The Forgotten Island* is the inscription:

> Dedicated to Mrs. Gordon Woodhouse.
> My dear Friend, Please accept these few poems, which I dedicate to you. I have written them down just as they came to me, and such as they are I now offer them. Perhaps they may find favour with you, perhaps no. In any case they must plead their own cause. M.

Marguerite, who died in 1943, did not keep a diary, and how far she was able to take her infatuation with Violet cannot now be discovered. Probably Violet responded as she seems previously to have done to Christabel Marshal, allowing Marguerite to come very close but withdrawing when the mood became too charged with erotic tension: the answer to whether Violet ever had a physical affair with another woman might perhaps have been found somewhere in Chris's voluminous collection of letters, had they not been burnt after her death. In any event, Violet and Marguerite clearly remained on quite intimate terms after Marguerite's infatuation had passed, for Violet lent her a set of treble virginals in 1919.

Until the summer of 1915, the war had left Violet in a state of mind that was more a consequence of loneliness than of personal anxiety or of the terror that she might see the name of one of her lovers in the casualty lists that filled the newspapers. But as the year wore on, life in Britain became increasingly uncomfortable, and the dangers rather nearer to home. The first Zeppelin bombing raids, which began in June, did little to frighten most Londoners (though Dolmetsch was much disconcerted by them), since the bombs were primitive and the raids infrequent. But it became harder to travel round the city after dark for the streetlamps were painted dark blue, so that seeing at night came to depend largely on the moon. Evening entertainment began to be abandoned in favour of daytime amusements, and charity concerts – for which Violet was in constant demand – took the place of social musical soirées.

The war news, too, was more threatening. Max had already gone out to France, and in July Denis finally reached the Western Front with the 4th Dragoon Guards. His earliest surviving letter home, dated August 1915, reveals his regiment minding the horses in reserve behind the lines, or reduced to digging trenches. Fresh to the battle zone, Denis has still not grasped that cavalry will have no part to play in what is to become a war of barbed wire, howitzers, shrapnel and machine-guns fought over a landscape of cratered mud. About to encounter a new phase of the war, marked by suicidal British and French infantry attacks against well-entrenched

German positions, all he longs for is a great attack. Meanwhile, he blames the Government for the shortage of guns and shells and for "the painfully obvious crying need of more trained men and horses".

Supplies in the battle zone were generally scarce, and Gordon took considerable trouble over supplementing Denis's and Max's equipment and rations with precisely the right kind of clothes, food, tobacco and small luxuries. Financially, Violet was now entirely dependent on Gordon, but without her other men, and above all Bill, she could not help finding her husband dull. It suited them both that he got away quite often to see that things were in order at Armscote, and he seldom intruded on her life in London except when he was needed for shopping expeditions or to make himself hospitable to her guests. Marguerite, of course, was a diverting consolation, but for Violet no woman could entirely compensate for the lack of male company, and nobody of either sex could make up for the absence of Bill.

One visitor who strained even Gordon's tolerance was Dolmetsch, who struck him as affected and humourless. Gordon did, however, put up with him for Violet's sake, and looked after him benignly at supper on his occasional appearances at Ovington Square. The outbreak of war had put an end to most of Dolmetsch's commissions to build instruments, but his book *The Interpretation of the Music of the XVII and XVIII Centuries*, published in December 1915, set the seal on his academic reputation. A month before it came out he gave Violet a copy, in which he generously inscribed: "To Violet Woodhouse. You have loved the old masters of music. Their innermost secrets are now revealed. Had it been for you alone, their discovery would have made me happy."

Ezra Pound, who had been impatiently awaiting Dolmetsch's book, found that it more than met his expectations. In revolt against romanticism, Pound wrote verse in which the sound of the words and the disposition of lines on the page created a kind of musical score. By breaking up his verse visually, he also produced something analogous to the way in which Cubist painters like Braque and Picasso fractured and reassembled their images (Pound was the undisputed leader of the poetic movement known as "Imagism"). As a music critic he agreed strongly with Violet's and Rubio's emphasis on the importance of interpretation and phrasing, and as a poet he created his effects by intense concentration on small clusters of words, as in Greek lyric fragments or Chinese poems. Now he found corroboration of his theories of the affinity between music and poetry in Dolmetsch's book. That work is a mine of information about rhythm, pause and ornamentation in early music, features which are vital to expression but which cannot be understood from conventional musical notation, just as the cadences of a line of poetry cannot be deduced from its metrical structure.

Meanwhile, out in France, Denis finally awoke to the reality of modern warfare. By now, a number of cavalry officers had transferred to the infantry, where they filled the gaps caused by heavy casualties in battle. In February 1916, Denis, too, left the Dragoon Guards to join the 1st Battalion of the Northamptonshire Regiment as second-in-command. It was to be a terrible year, starting with the titanic struggle between the German and French Armies for Verdun, in the Meuse district south of the Ardennes, and cul-minating in the late summer with the series of attacks in which British and, to a lesser extent, French troops tried to draw off pressure from Verdun by a frontal assault on the German positions further to the north and west, around the River Somme. Denis's new battalion was to be engaged throughout most of this terrible battle, but he received his first four months of blooding in infantry command north of the Somme, at Loos, not far from Arras.

The front line near Loos was dominated by the Double Crassier, two parallel slagheaps 100 yards apart, each 800 yards long and 80 feet high, with the "Valley of Death", as the British troops christened it, lying between them. The British held three-fifths of the northern heap and one-third of the southern, the Germans occupying the rest. The troops on both sides had cut stairways in the slag to the crests and had dug trenches along the tops, giving them vantage points from which to fire down on the Valley of Death and on the enemy trenches in the plain below. On the Double Crassier itself, there were constant skirmishes with grenades. At the closest point between the two sides, where the trenches were only thirty yards apart, the opposing troops could actually speak to each other, keeping their heads beneath the parapet. Mines created vast craters, for which both sides competed to seize as shelter or for grenade-launching sites. For a soldier to put his head up twice in the same place above the parapet or crater rim was to invite a sniper's bullet. In April the battalion suffered its first gas attack; the men could see little through the green-tinted eyepieces of their clumsy gas masks, but the enemy were reluctant to advance into their own poisonous fumes.

Denis was soon steeped in all the minutiae of infantry tactics, and by the time the Battle of the Somme began on 1 July 1916 he was fully equipped for command. The German positions along the eighteen-mile front had been made almost impregnable by an extensive system of trenches, deep dugouts, thick belts of barbed wire, and formidable redoubts commanding the tactical strongpoints. Denis was spared the opening slaughter, in which the British lost 57,000 men, nearly 20,000 of them killed, in the first few hours of their attack, without gaining more than a handful of their objectives. His battalion was sent by train to the battle zone on 6 July and marched immediately to the front, passing countless ammunition columns and artillery batteries, coming under enemy shellfire and meeting streams of ambulances and walking wounded returning from the forward lines.

As they moved up, the British troops were baffled by the complexities of both armies' trench systems. Denis's Northamptonshires were soon occupying a captured German trench system, a part of which, separated from the British-held sector by barricades, was still occupied by the enemy. On 20 July a "surprise" assault on a trench junction was anticipated by the Germans and met with heavy machine-gun fire and grenades. On 22 July a midnight attack on an enemy position north-east of the village of Pozières started in chaos, with hardly a company reaching its assembly position on time due to overcrowding in the maze of trenches. German machine-gunners and bombers hidden in shell holes caused havoc among the advancing Northamptonshires, and by dawn on 23 July this attack, too, had failed. Recoiling to the British front line, the survivors came under heavy artillery fire. By the time it was relieved next day, Denis's battalion had lost 268 officers and men killed, wounded or missing, more than a quarter of its strength.

This ghastly series of actions, about which Denis himself never spoke a word for the rest of his life, is covered in graphic detail by one of his subalterns, Lieutenant Preston White, in letters to his mother at home, in which he records "an undying remembrance of the dim light as dawn began to break, the jostling mass of men with fixed bayonets, the continual rap-rap-rap of machine guns overhead, the wounded and dying men brought down the trench". The letters show occasional glimpses of Denis "directing things with a purple cloud of language floating around him" or "sitting on top of a parapet, cool as ice", or gently chiding White for his clumsy rescue under fire of a badly wounded man – "Don't stand the poor fellow on his head". A brief rest followed before the battalion, made up to strength by reinforcements, went into the front line again, this time near High Wood, towards the eastern end of the British sector. On 14 August Denis, who had gone forward to reconnoitre, was hit by a shell fragment. His wound was not serious, but it was enough to put him out of action for a few days and perhaps also to save his life, for between 15 and 21 August, in a series of actions, often involving hand-to-hand fighting, his battalion incurred 374 more casualties.

No sooner was he released from hospital than Denis rejoined his battalion in the front line. On 9 September another violently contested attack, in divisional strength, was launched, this time against High Wood, in which the Northamptonshires suffered 140 casualties, although the division as a whole did succeed in taking some of its objectives. For a brief period the battalion was now split up, each of its companies being used to plug gaps in other units depleted by losses. At the end of September they regrouped, handed over to their reliefs, and marched out of the line, to take no further part in the Battle of the Somme. In two months the 1st Northamptonshires had lost some 800 men out of a nominal strength of 1,000. On 16 October 1916, upon the promotion of his commanding officer, Lieutenant-Colonel Bethell, a man of exceptional inspirational ability, Denis took over command of the battalion. In the words of the regimental history, "Major Tollemache was known to all who had served under him in the Somme battle as an officer of remarkable intrepidity and coolness under fire."

When the Battle of the Somme finally spluttered out on 18 November, the British and Dominion casualties numbered over 400,000, of whom some 100,000 had been killed. They had advanced six miles, but were still three miles short of their first day's objective. The French had lost about 50,000 men killed, out of total casualties of over 200,000; the Germans over 150,000 out of a total which varying estimates give as being between 473,000 and 680,000. Of those who survived, great numbers had been mutilated or psychologically broken by the stress of battle. So dreadful, however, was the carnage that no figures can be more than an approximation.

Bill had sailed from England for the Persian Gulf on 11 December 1915, and disembarked at Basra on 8 January 1916. Having seen first Max and then Denis leave for France in the spring and summer of that year, Violet could not bring herself to go to Portsmouth and wave goodbye to him. He had been sent to a new unit, the 2/1st Battalion of the Oxford and Bucks, one of a number of drafts sent out to reinforce a combined British and Indian Army expedition which had occupied Southern Mesopotamia (now Iraq) in November 1914, with the objective of safeguarding Britain's oil supplies from Persia (the threat came from the Turks, who were the ruling power in Mesopotamia and who had joined the war on the German side earlier that month). The conditions Bill encountered were appalling. In the rainy season mud brought all wheeled transport to a halt. The glare, the dust and the heat were oppressive. Sickness was rife and supplies were short. It was impossible to escape the flies, most of them disease-bearing, which swarmed over everything. A fellow-officer, Edmund Candler, left this account of them:

> The flies in the tents, dug-outs and trenches, unless seen, were unbelievable. To describe them is to hazard one's reputation for truth. You could not eat without swallowing flies. You waved your spoon of porridge in the air to shake them off; you put your biscuit and bully

beef in your pocket, and surreptitiously conveyed them in closed fist to your mouth, but you swallowed flies all the same. They settled in clouds on everything. When you wrote you could not see the end of your pen . . . The Mesopotamian variety is indistinguishable from the English horse-fly except that many of them, one in twenty perhaps, will bite . . . at night the flies will disappear, and the mosquitoes and sandflies relieve them, completing the vicious circle. Mosquitoes are local . . . the sandfly is another and more insidious plague. A net with a mesh wide enough to exclude him is suffocating, and he will keep one awake at night with a hose of thin acid playing on one's face. He is also the transmitter of a microbe which will lay you out by the heels for three days with a virulent fever . . .

Towards the end of 1915, shortly before Bill's arrival, the 6th Indian Division under Major-General Townshend had pushed northwards up the River Tigris, ambitiously hoping to take Baghdad from the opposing Turkish forces. Blocked by the enemy some eighteen miles short of the city, Townshend had retired to Kut al-Amara on the north bank of the Tigris, desperately short of food and most other supplies. On 7 December the Turks had closed the ring, and a long siege began. From then on, the relief of Kut became the overriding aim of the expeditionary army, which was then commanded by Lieutenant-General Sir Fenton Aylmer.

The battalion spent a week in training marches around Basra before being dispatched to join the relief force. Bill's first task was to lead this column of 850 men on its march up the Shatt-al-Arab, the waterway formed by the junction of the Tigris and the Euphrates. The logistical organization was abysmal and from the beginning nothing went right. The men, not yet fully fit, struggled forward with only a mug of tea and a couple of biscuits in their stomachs. Downpours drenched everyone's kit and the ground soon became a quagmire. The tents and food went missing, and the transport never arrived. Sickness broke out, and by the second day, 17 January, the battalion's medical officer was already evacuating the worst cases by hospital boat back to Basra. Bill wired to headquarters for rations, but was ordered to advance two days' march to obtain supplies at Qurna, fifty miles north of Basra. Three days later the column lost its way and floundered in a bog. After a fourteen-mile march they collapsed exhausted into Qurna in cascading rain, which alternated with bouts of sleet and burning sun.

On the 25th they set off again through hip-deep streams, repeatedly losing their transport carts in mud up to the axles. The plight of the men was even worse than that of the officers, but for Bill, with his weak constitution, the strain at the age of forty-two made heavy demands on his determination. He first saw action in March, as second-in-command of the battalion to Major Carter in an attack on the Dujaila Redoubt, a strong Turkish position eight miles east of Kut, which was the key to the investment of the town. For this battle, the culmination of the second attempt to relieve the town, General Aylmer had deployed over 20,000 fighting men, supported by cavalry and 68 guns, against the Turks' well-fortified positions on both banks of the River Tigris. At 7 pm on 6 March, Bill's battalion, numbering 29 officers and 406 other ranks, formed up in pitch darkness, crossed the river, and promptly lost its way in a maze of Turkish trenches. Some of the attackers found the Redoubt unoccupied, and for a few hours the relief of General Townshend seemed possible, but confusion and delay allowed the Turks to regroup and on 8 March the assault was finally called off. General Aylmer withdrew and was summarily replaced.

The final attempt to raise the siege took place early in April. This time Bill and his troops were in the third line. In front of them several attacks were launched, with extremely heavy casualties, and on the morning of 7 April Bill took over command of the battalion from Major Carter, who had been wounded. He found the rest of the battalion in hastily dug trenches 400 yards from the enemy lines. The first night was spent searching for wounded, many of whom drowned in the flood waters of the marsh. The British front line was plainly visible from Bill's position, beyond it a long row of green canvas buckets marking the dead. Yet again the attack petered out, and on the night of the 9th the battalion retired to a reserve position. On 22 April a Turkish counter-attack beat back the relieving force, removing Kut's last hope of rescue, and on 29 April 1916 General Townshend surrendered his emaciated garrison of 12,000 troops. His men were sent on a "death march" to Syria; treated abominably by their captors, a third of them died en route or during their long captivity.

In the Middle East the collapse of Kut – coming as it did after the previous year's catastrophe at Gallipoli, where a large force of British, Australian and New Zealand troops had been pinned down by the Turks on the heights overlooking the Dardanelles and ultimately forced to withdraw – was taken as a sign that the hitherto all-conquering British Imperial Army was not invincible. At home in Britain, a thin, watered-down version of events was all that the public learned of this phase of the Mesopotamian campaign.

For the time being, Bill rested with his battallion, awaiting events – perhaps there would be reinforcements, and then an autumn offensive to capture Baghdad. The climate, the food and the flies had undermined his health, however, and on 27 July he contracted dysentery and began a seven-week spell in hospital. Defeat, illness and a sense that the campaign in which he was engaged was irrelevant to the main theatre of war were an affront to his pride, but he was out of immediate danger and there was a reliable postal service to England. Throughout the burning summer he corresponded regularly with Violet.

In London, Violet had much to concern her. She was worried about Bill's illness; she had read with mounting horror the casualty lists of the Battle of the Somme, in daily fear of seeing Denis's name among the dead or missing; it could only be a matter of time before Max found himself in some hazardous action; and in September she learned from Roland that he was to be sent to France. Violet wrote to him from Ovington Square on 28 September, May's birthday, a fortnight after he had left England for France, her letter encapsulating her current preoccupations. Apparently Roland had confessed to her his dread of facing the enemy guns, and her first aim was to reassure him that he would come out alive; but the letter also talks of rumours of a truce in Mesopotamia (which might allow Bill to return), and reveals that she was resorting to spiritualism, and that Gordon was sending weekly parcels to Denis on the Somme, the sector to which Roland himself was heading.

> Darling Roland . . . I have heard a time or two from dear Mother, & it is her birthday, & how we wish her a lovely one next year, with her beloved Roland back. Do you remember seeing a Mrs. Duncan here once, who comes to give me massage? Well, she is a clairvoyante[3] & a very good woman & I gave her the dear little note which you wrote to me to hold & she told me she felt *very confident* about you & your safe return, & she has seen you, which makes it perhaps easier to feel. I am very fond of her, & she has often helped me very much. She does nothing of this sort for money . . . I had a letter from dear Denis this morning, & he says "Of course I shall do *anything I can* for Roland if he comes to our Brigade" & again "Would I not be nice to any brother of you, indeed I will be if I get a chance". He went up to the thick of the fighting on Monday last & I pray God he will be kept safe . . . If you want any foods or other things sent out, Gordon would do it for you with pleasure – He sends Denis out things every week, just a few oddments. If

3 By 1916 spiritualism was extremely popular among bereaved and anxious relatives – mainly women – trying to extract hope and meaning from the senseless massacres on the Western Front.

other people contribute towards the Mess, one feels one must also. But I expect you are at a Base & perhaps in Billets – Perhaps at Etaples?[4] – But you must not say. If dear Denis's Brigade or Div. comes out safe from this present push, I believe their share in it is supposed to be over.

Now I have nothing else to tell you I think – we had letters from beloved Bill last week after you left – He was expecting heavy fighting out there in Autumn, but perhaps you are right – There is all this gossip about Gen. Townshend being home & the Turks trying to make peace, but I cannot believe this . . . I can say anything to you in my letters, but of course you have to be more careful poor dear. By the way, I hear you ought not to put "France" only B.E.7. which I think better to write in full. The Post Office issued a notice to that effect some time ago. I do not know if this applies to the Base, but it does to the Troops in front I know & they scratched out "France" on one of my letters & I have never put it since.

Now darling Roland, keep up your heart. I know it must be horrid . . . I feel I know you very well, & remember that you are protected. I often feel that darling Aunt Bunnie [Kate] who knows you & loves you, & knows & always knew all the nasty things about us & loved us just the same, is able to help & is helping & protecting *you*.

God bless you darling Roland
& keep you safe
your loving V.

Always tell me *anything*. You are quite safe. I will never repeat what you wish me not to. *Bless you*."

The following month, Violet was preparing for an important concert with Rubio and Blanche Marchesi, arranged by the superlative viola soloist Lionel Tertis, who had initiated his own series of "one hour" concerts at the Steinway Hall. She wrote on 24 October to Denis's aunt Grace, a letter in which, among other news, she touched incidentally on her own attitude to war work. There was at the time a good deal of moral pressure put on women of leisure to undertake practical tasks to help the war effort, but Violet had no intention of doing anything of the sort. She was quite certain that she could do more good by concentrating on making beautiful music.

---

4 Etaples is on the coast, fifteen miles south of Boulogne and twenty miles north of the mouth of the Somme, a staging post equidistant at fifty miles from the killing fields of Flanders and Picardy.

Dearest Gracie –

. . . I am delighted at your letter which I have just got. I am here, so whenever you come to London I shall be ready to play to *you*. They have been trying to make me make papier mâché baths etc for the wounded, but when I went to look yesterday, the fumes made me feel very ill, & I felt a strange disgust, so I am going to wriggle out of this. I may have to do some other sort of work, but I shall have some time to practise. We are going to play the Golden Sonata by Purcell on Nov 7th at Steinway Hall. It is truly & literally divine, sumptuous, glorious. Hawkins says in 1776 "Its repute is still so great that there are still some people living who cannot speak of it without rapture, who heard it when Purcell was alive & his works were played". I was very pleased with your *lovely* verses. I never know if I can make things to music. It comes suddenly. I shall keep them with me in case. Do you know that Denis has been made a Lieut. Col. Very fine at 32 years old I think. He was looking aged & very tired & can one wonder – Dear Bill has been ill again in that climate – I must suddenly stop. Much love from V.

On 16 November Christabel Marshal reviewed the concert in *The Lady:*

The chief feature of a programme of rare interest was a beautiful performance of Purcell's Golden Sonata, in which Mrs. Gordon Woodhouse's art as a harpsichordist was very valuable. Agustín Rubio, Lionel Tertis and Desirée Defaüw took the string parts and showed admirable discretion in tuning their instruments to the tone of the harpsichord. Madame Marchesi sang songs to the harpsichord accompaniment of Mrs. Woodhouse. Mrs. Woodhouse's solos of 16th and 17th century music were played with that vitality which distinguishes her interpretations. Those who have heard this artiste will never be guilty of thinking that the piano has superseded the harpsichord.

The onset of winter at last brought Violet some respite from the worst of her anxieties. Denis had somehow survived the disastrous strategy of the British Commander-in-Chief, General Sir Douglas Haig, of attack regardless of the cost in lives; with luck neither he nor Max would see heavy fighting until the weather improved and the ground hardened next year. Bill had not been promoted and he experienced the minor indignity of relegation to command of a company – but the good news was that his health was mending and that he was to be posted to India. Overjoyed for herself, but reading

Bill's chagrin correctly between the lines of his telegram, Violet wrote to Roland in March 1917: "I have just heard that a wire has arrived for me from darling Bill. STARTING INDIA IMMEDIATELY VERY FIT BUT NOT REQUIRED FEB 21st. I *am* so relieved, but I do hope beloved Bill is not very much hurt in his heart at being moved? It sounds rather as if he were".

# X

## Death, Capture, Return

THE NEW YEAR OF 1917 brought revived hopes to Britain. Universal conscription for men between the ages of eighteen and forty had been introduced, bringing to an end the sense of injustice which attended voluntary enlistment and relieving the army of the need to hurry wounded or shell-shocked men back to the front before their recovery was complete. The Prime Minister, Asquith, had been toppled from his post in December, his languid amateur administration giving way to the infectious, if devious, energy of David Lloyd George at the head of the coalition government. The war production lines were flowing, and the country as a whole had come to feel a sense of purpose, of a "nation in arms". The Secretary of State for War, Lord Kitchener, had drowned when HMS *Hampshire*, in which he was travelling to Russia, had struck a mine off the Orkneys in June 1916, and the conduct of the war was now in the hands of a slimmed-down War Cabinet and of General Sir Douglas Haig, commanding the British Expeditionary Force in the field, and General Sir William Robertson, Chief of the Imperial General Staff, at home. The military commanders exuded confidence. Haig, in particular, was convinced that it required only one more major Allied offensive to break Germany's morale.

Yet behind the scenes there was a good deal of tension. The military "brass hats" mistrusted the politicians, whom they suspected, with good reason, of lacking the stomach for the murderous stalemate of attack and counter-attack on the Western Front and of wanting instead a cheap diversion in Italy or the Balkans. This mistrust was fully reciprocated by Lloyd George, who was maddened by the obstinacy of the army chiefs and detested their strategy of attrition – the willingness to accept massive casualties provided that the enemy's casualties were even more unsustainable. In the last analysis, however, Haig nearly always got his way. The sheer scale and self-perpetuating momentum of the Allied war machines, together with the imperative need to co-operate with the French Army, which bore the brunt of the fighting on the Western Front, determined the outcome of every disagreement.

Domestic life was not all plain sailing either. There is a tendency to look back on wartime as a period during which human weakness is suspended, to be replaced by selfless idealism. But Gordon found that his meat deliveries were being waylaid in the streets by parties of well-dressed women who had taken to accosting the butcher girls (the boys having been sent to the front), putting token money in their baskets and decamping with joints of meat which they subsequently divided among themselves. He tried taking Violet to the Savoy Hotel instead, but the menu there was meatless and costs had rocketed. By March 1917 food prices had risen more than 90 per cent since July 1914, while Gordon's income had remained, at best, static. Millions of tons of shipping had been lost to German U-boats, and at one point Britain had only three to four weeks' supply of food in stock.

As the casualty lists grew longer, Violet's soirées and Sunday afternoon concerts became increasingly crowded. Officers on leave flocked to her house, cadging invitations from friends of friends and finding in her playing a refuge from the horrors of the trenches. Their numbers were swelled by the lonely or bereaved relations of men at the front, seeking solace from the fears and sadness which haunted them, and by others for whom Violet's circle represented a rare oasis of civilization. To accommodate some of those she had had to turn away, in April 1917 she gave a public concert at her house in Ovington Square for the benefit of Blanche Marchesi's War-Work Fund. The drawing-room was packed. Behind the chairs and in the doorway, men in uniform stood motionless, rapt, silent.

Violet badly missed Bill, and pleaded with everyone she knew who had the slightest influence to use it to get him back. It was small consolation to her that in India he would at least be safe, as she waited in vain for reassurance that his desire for their reunion matched hers. The truth was that Bill was enjoying his independence. The wide avenues, elegant colonnades and pillared clubs of Bangalore, the capital of Mysore State in southern India, where the officers lived in palatial bungalows with walled rose gardens and verandahs covered in purple bougainvillaea, made the town the most agreeable place in the Empire for a sports-loving soldier. Revelling in the regimental polo, cricket and pig-sticking, and fascinated by the town, in its setting three thousand feet up in the hill country, with its dancing girls and its snake-charmers in the precincts of the Bull Temple, Bill made no effort to hasten home. Violet's anxiety was made worse by her fears for Denis and Max, who were still in the trenches. The two men did their best to shield her from the unspeakable details of life at the front, but they could not conceal the unprecedented scale of death and destruction.

Roland, too, was out in Flanders, that open and largely featureless region straddling northern France and south-western Belgium, which lends itself so well to battle, since vast armies and quantities of equipment can readily be manoeuvred there when the ground is firm. Here Germany had chosen first to strike at France; and here now, holding the left of the Allied line, more than a million British troops and their German enemy endlessly exchanged shellfire, observed each other from higher ground or undermined each other from tunnels, emerging from their trenches to make sudden, violent raids upon each other, or, sometimes, to advance slowly to their death for pathetic gains of a few hundred yards.

What exactly happened to Roland in Flanders is an unsolved mystery. In September 1914, a month after war had broken out, he had enlisted in the Sussex Yeomanry, which spent the next two years in Brighton and Canterbury, first on horses and later on bicycles, "guarding the coast". In 1916 he was sent anonymously a white feather, the symbol of cowardice. Whether to clear himself of this ignominy or because as their commanding officer he had no choice, in September 1916 he took a draft of 150 men to France to reinforce a battalion of the Queen's (East Surrey) Regiment. He saw action almost immediately on the Somme, and was then moved north to Flanders where, in February 1917, he won the DSO for "conspicuous gallantry and judgement" in leading a highly successful daylight raid on the enemy trenches.

Writing in April to congratulate him and at the same time to thank him for a birthday present, Violet told him that she felt "tremendously proud". Yet apart from his mother and Violet, for whom Roland was always their darling little son and brother, the rest of the family mistrusted him. It was not so much that they suspected he was homosexual in the days when homosexuality was illegal and a matter of shame – that had nothing to do with courage, and might easily have been ignored or denied. But he was known to be scheming and dishonourable, to a degree that induced most of the Gwynnes to disbelieve that he was capable of having conducted himself bravely in battle. On his return to England after being wounded in August 1917, Roland was clearly a broken man, from which his family, or most of them, drew the conclusion that he had finally shown his true colours and that his DSO must somehow have been the result either of a mistake or of deceit.

There is, however, another, more plausible, explanation. Most of the family disliked Roland because they thought he had behaved deviously over their father's will, and they were confirmed in their prejudices by his later moral disintegration. They overlooked that to lead a daylight raid across no man's land left very little room for ambiguity about a man's conduct. In all probability what destroyed him was the cumulative effect of terror – first when he was exposed to shellfire on the Somme, then when he had to force himself to keep his nerve beyond his natural limitations for an hour and a half during the raid, and finally in August when, during the Third Battle of Ypres, he was wounded painfully in the knee and left out in no man's land until he could be brought in by stretcher-bearers. Among the Gwynnes, Violet and May alone understood that courage in a frightened man is greater than courage in a fearless one. Towards the end of June 1917 Violet had written to Roland again, her letter revealing by implication how badly he was already showing the strain in the period between his decoration and his subsequent wounding:

> My darling little Roland,
> I have just got your touching little letter . . . Never mind *what* you say to me – I am proud that you tell me everything & indeed I do like to know, even tho' it is so awful. If only I could share just a scrap with you, but I can only sit still & feel for you all . . . Mrs. Duncan is coming this afternoon, & we shall think so much of you. It does seem cruel & quite wrong that you should be left in [the line] so long . . . O Roland Dear, my heart just aches for you. It must be awful to be quite alone too – Please God you will be happy again some day dear. Gen. Bethell is coming to dinner tonight – His Brigade was in the Messines-Wycharte affair [i.e. Wytschaete; the brilliantly successful British capture of the Messines-Wytschaete Ridge, overloooking Ypres, 8–11 June 1917, the prelude to Passchendaele]. I cannot understand why you are not getting leave – This is just a line from my heart. I send you my very dear love –
> God bless darling Roland from his loving V.

Not for Roland the nonchalance of a Max or the reticence of a Denis, those conventional protective devices behind which men hide their fears. But Violet saw through such pretences and her prayers went out for the suffering of all her men. She followed events in the sectors or theatres where they were engaged, through correspondence, through the newspapers and through contacts with senior officers such as Brigadier-General Bethell, Denis's former commander on the Somme. In her April letter to Roland, Violet had written "dear Denis's Div. is now regularly moved into [Lieutenant-General – later Field Marshal – the Earl of] Cavan's Corps. They may have 2 weeks out to retrain etc. – I hope so." The 1st Northamptonshires had in fact spent the spring of 1917 recuperating from the Battle of the Somme.

Now, after an uneasy rest marred by sickness, they headed north to the extreme left flank of the Allied line, near Nieuport on the Belgian coast, ten miles west of Ostend, reaching the sea on 23 June. The sector here consisted of sand, broken by clusters of rushes and high dunes, with mounds and breastworks in place of trenches. The mile-long front was held by two battalions, facing east into the morning sun. Behind them ran the Yser Canal, spanned by three bridges. The position was so patently vulnerable to being cut off that it was known colloquially as the "Death Trap", but it was supposed to be covered by artillery from the rear, and long periods of inaction had lulled the army into using it as a training area for raw young officers.

On 4 July Denis led part of the battalion into the front line, leaving most of the men behind the canal. A few days of quiet, enlivened only by a couple of raids, confirmed their expectations of a peaceful tour. Then, at 6.45 am on 10 July, German heavy artillery, field guns and trench mortars opened up with a tornado of fire. The breastworks were obliterated, the Yser bridges destroyed and all the communicating telephone lines cut. There was little return fire, for the Germans had launched their bombardment at the precise moment when the French and British artillery were exchanging positions. The forward British infantry units, completely isolated, could only dig their comrades buried by shellfire out of the sand and await their fate.

For twelve hours the bombardment continued before troops from the German Marine Division fell abruptly upon Denis's men. The first the officers in the battalion headquarters dugout knew of the infantry assault was when enemy soldiers began throwing grenades down the ventilation shafts. "Lt. Colonel Tollemache at first declined to surrender and wished to fight it out to a finish," records the Regimental History. "Fortunately he broke his revolver, and was unable to carry out his intention, for the position was hopeless, and no other course than surrender was open." Before dusk the Battle of the Dunes was over. Nine soldiers from the battalion swam back to safety across the canal. The rest were killed or captured, among them Denis, who was to spend the last sixteen months of the war as a prisoner in Freiburg.

The few survivors of the battle could give no coherent account of what had happened, and for some time the friends and relatives of those missing were in an agony of doubt. Soon the legend grew that Denis and the other headquarters officers had stood back-to-back, firing their revolvers at the enemy until they had fallen. Max wrote lovingly to Violet:

Darling Tookees
. . . When I read that his regiment had been cut off, I felt that Denis must have died with his men. The account you sent me is

wonderful: his splendid courage and bravery shines forth as the light from some glorious star.

Truly his soul must be in the hand of God – The wonder of it but Oh God! The pity of it. May God keep you. Maxwell

P.S. My thoughts travel back to Armscote, it is only the constant sound of guns a few miles away that breaks the illusion and reminds one of the desolation so near. How close to paradise those Armscote days were – looking back they seem wondrously beautiful. And now oh! Tookees! All our hearts are sad and ache for all our pride in that last wonderful act of self sacrifice.

Desolate at Denis's presumed death, Violet wrote to Grace Tollemache on 28 July. She believed that he had had a premonition of death the evening before the battle.

Dearest Gracie, I have nothing to say. The loss of 23 years of such devotion from a heart of such beauty & spirit as that one, & now the utter, complete blank. He wrote to me on the night before at 9.30, just as serene as possible, but I think he knew he might never go back. He said when he was going over in the Death Trap "I expect I shall be very glad to get back here again". I am sorry that you did not write. He missed your letters & said they were such delightful ones with extracts from old books which he loved. He said with rather a hurt smile "I shall have to write & ask Aunt G. why the devil she does not write to me". He was delighted when you wrote to me & I always told him so when you did. Bless him the darling     V.

It was like having St. George for a lover.
Gen. Archie Montgomery said he minded about him more than any of the others perhaps, *he was such a magnificent soldier gone.*

Proud of Denis's courage and painfully conscious that she had too rarely been generous enough with her love, Violet prepared a memorial mass, to be held at the church of St Martin-in-the-Fields in London. A military band was to play with muffled drums; there would be Denis's favourite hymns, including "The Battle Hymn of the Republic". Violet herself would play "Saforsky's Farewell Lament" by Purcell and John Bull's "Goodnight". No sooner had the invitations been sent out, however, than a different account of the battle began to circulate. Max, on the threshold of his own ordeal in Flanders, wrote again:

Darling Tookees,
I have just received two letters from you. . . . Beloved there does still

seem a ray of hope. Some of the officers must have been taken wounded and please God the dear lad is among them. What you say about St. George is the very truth – gay, passionate, serene and of perfect courage, he has qualities that one looks for in a fine and rare nature. May I have the bright light of his courage before my eyes in my time of trial. I think of you at the window looking onto the green trees and my heart goes out to you. God bless you always.

Max, of course, knew the realities of combat, but even now, there were still a few people in Britain who believed the propaganda image of a war in which every British officer fought courageously to the death and only Germans surrendered. For Denis's two maiden aunts, clinging with misguided patriotism to the first version of events, the confirmation of his capture shattered their heroic illusions. Far from being relieved that Denis had survived, they were ashamed that he had not died with his men. Blanche Tollemache sent Violet a letter full of vitriol, accusing her of ruining her nephew's life, and at the same time implying that Denis had buckled under fire. Incandescent with fury, Violet wrote to "G.M.":

Ovington Square, London. *Thursday.*
Dearest Lady Tollemache, Blanche has written me such a foul letter, practically accusing Denis of being a coward. I think she is quite sorry he is alive. *Five* sheets of low abuse. If she goes about saying these things to Stanhope [a cousin of Denis] etc. I shall strangle her. She tries to make most disgusting mischief between you and me, but darling Lady Tollemache, you will never let her will you? I am sorry she saw darling Denis's card for she comments on it with every mean abuse. I thought it most touching. He was probably almost without food & had been so for 8 days, & never a complaint. She tramples on his honour and spits in his face. However, there is no use talking of this, except that she *must not* write to him like this! Can you not give her the wrong address. She abuses me for sending him things & the only thing which she suggested sending him which was some particularly good soap she has never thought of doing. I will never have her in our house again for what she dares to say about Denis, & she drags up things which happened years ago & tells lies about them. She has made me feel bitter & furious for the first time in my life. She says that dear Bill would have been better than Denis! He, who is as proud as a devoted uncle to him & as fond. I *will not* say any more, but YOU do not resent that Denis has loved me & my home for 21 years? I know you do not, bless you.

I would rejoice for you if he would marry some day, & I pray God he may have the chance, & you know this, & we would perhaps find him someone between us who *would* appreciate his beautiful nature.

Now about the kit. Mr. Lightly came and opened it, & there are many things he wanted; the extra tunic, trousers, cap . . . I sent yesterday a parcel containing what is in the enclosed list, & when Gordon returns tomorrow, he will pack & send off the clothes. This cable has been received from the King of Spain so he did make enquiries, but yours were much more useful . . . Did you send him Froissart? & a book of old French verses, & a R.L. Stevenson? If not shall I send them? There is an Oxford Book of Verse which I gave him & a novel by [George] du Maurier which I also gave him, & a small Hakluyt's Voyages which I think Gracie did, and a book of Bacon's essays. . . . Freiburg is a bad place for the constant Air Raids from the French. I heard that most senior officers are sent after a time to Heidelburg [sic] . . . If one needed it, we could get at Prince Max of Baden [the Kaiser's second cousin; he became Chancellor of Germany in October 1918] surely & I am thankful that there is one nice German in authority . . . Now my love to you. I am beginning to think Blanche & Grace are Devils. But our Denis belongs to the Archangel Michael & St. George, God bless him. From Violet.

Your letter this morning was like blue water, after reading Blanche's. *Thank you for it.*

August 1917 was a turbulent month for Violet. On top of the emotional dramas surrounding Denis came Roland's wounding and then the news that Max had gone into action at Passchendaele. Violet never made up her quarrel with Blanche, and her relationship with Grace became stiffer and less natural. She felt obliged to keep up the flow of information to them, as she was the main recipient of Denis's letters, but henceforth "Dearest Gracie . . . with much love from V" declined to "My Dear Gracie . . . from V". By the end of the month she had word (evidently censored) from Denis to pass on to his aunts:

37 Ovington Square *31 August 1917*
My dear Gracie, Last night I had a letter from Denis, from Freiburg. He was in a place of several storeys "built round a court-yard. There is a narrow entrance from the st. & then it is entirely enclosed. Our rooms look to the court yard, & we cannot see anything at all beyond except a patch of sky. The courtyard is about 50 yards each way & has some plane trees in the middle. For

exercise we can but walk round & round the yard, with high walls all round. They take us to a swimming bath once a week, & for a bit of a walk after the bathe. I enjoy the walk & a blow of fresh air. I hope we shall be able to continue the walk after it has got too cold for bathing, but at present, there is, I believe, no authority for it except to the bath & back. We give our parole not to escape while out. There are no rooms here with less than 3 officers in them, while the bigger ones have 15". He also says "You did not know (no more did I!) that I had the making of a tinker among my many accomplishments". This refers to a tin he had made into a charcoal stove.

Yes, I think I shall definitely be in London in November & December: Roland has had a further operation on his leg & it is still very bad.

It was in the interlude of desperate doubt between the assumption of Denis's death and the news that he was safe, if a prisoner, that Violet had first met Osbert Sitwell, when he had come to one of her Sunday afternoon performances. For the twenty-five-year-old Osbert, well read, widely educated and just entering high society, the war had signalled the break-up of that civilized way of life which he had come so recently to know and enjoy. He was proud of his Sitwell lineage, which stretched back six centuries. As an officer of the Grenadier Guards he had had no choice but to fight, although his preoccupations were literary, musical and aesthetic and he was a pacifist by nature and conviction. Accepted into London's most glamorous drawing-rooms, he relished everything associated with pre-war England, not excluding its snobbery. In 1915 he had been sent out to Flanders in a Reserve battalion and had witnessed the chaos behind the lines during the Battle of Loos, where two of the golden friends of his youth, Julian Grenfell and Ivo Charteris, were killed. (Loos, where Denis, too, had received his baptism of fire, in 1916, is one of those doom-laden names, like Ypres and the Somme, which reverberate throughout the Great War.) Billeted back in Chelsea Barracks with blood poisoning, Osbert planned to establish himself as a symbol of the battle against "the Philistines" and against all those who were engaged in prolonging what he and a few kindred spirits regarded as an inglorious war. Violet had read Osbert's first anti-war poems in *The Times* in May 1916; later that year he had published more poems in his sister Edith's new magazine *Wheels*.

That July of 1917, as Osbert had listened to Violet's playing, he had sensed how badly she was suffering beneath the sparkling surface. When he heard the cause he managed to make contact with King Alfonso of Spain (who, as a neutral, looked after the interests of prisoners of war), through whom he was able to confirm what by then Violet and G.M. had discovered from other sources – that Denis was alive and a prisoner of war. Osbert's energetic concern was a sure path to Violet's friendship. For his part, he was utterly enchanted by her. As he put it in *Noble Essences,* she belonged

> to a nation of her own, to that legendary nation of human genius who form so rare a race . . . We became friends after our very first meeting. This had taken place at her house, in late July 1917, at the south west corner of Ovington Square. Here, in the large finely proportioned room which had once been Bertolozzi's[1] studio, she played . . . I shall never forget the impact of the atmosphere, so unlike any other I had known, – warm, full of gaiety, beauty, and at times a faint luminous sadness: still less is there likely to pass from my memory the shock of the whole new world that her playing revealed. Never, for example, had I realised the greatness of the harpsichord as a vehicle, neither the immensity nor the grandeur its sound possessed. Her surroundings, too, the furnishings of the room with their dark surfaces locked by flame, impressed me by their strangeness.

Osbert Sitwell was only one of many who were transfixed by the atmosphere generated by Violet's music at this particular period of the war. Ronald Storrs had returned from Egypt to serve briefly as Middle Eastern adviser to the Cabinet, before being sent out at the end of 1917 as Military Governor of Jerusalem (and later civil Governor of Judaea). Like his friend T.E. Lawrence "of Arabia", Storrs was one of those rare English figures who recur in the history books, forever intriguing in exotic territories, fluent in non-European languages, and equally at home in Whitehall, in the Senior Common Room of an Oxford or Cambridge college, or in an oriental bazaar. In a letter written at the end of August Violet mentions "a man called Ronald Storrs who has just come back from the East, he was Kitchener's Secretary & Arabic expert in Egypt, & he likes the harpsichord & music for it more than anyone I ever met. He does not mind if I want to have him or not, he comes, & sits in your curtains, & it is simply for the harpsichord; nothing for me . . ."

Within days of Roland's wounding near Ypres, Max was in action in the same sector of the Flanders front. Here, twenty-five miles north of

1 Francesco Bertolozzi (1727–1815), an Italian printmaker who settled and worked in England.

Loos and twenty miles south of the coast at Nieuport, General Haig intended to break the German Army with a last superhuman effort. In the spring of 1917 the French Army, demoralized by the dreadful casualties of the hopeless offensive of General Robert Nivelle, had crumbled into mutiny, and although General Philippe Pétain, Nivelle's replacement, had worked wonders in restoring morale, it was no longer effective for anything other than defensive operations. Nevertheless, while it was vital that the British should take the brunt of the strain on the Western Front, the futility of the Third Battle of Ypres (or Passchendaele, as it came to be called, after the tiny village that was the ultimate British objective) seems in retrospect to have been clear from the outset to almost everyone except Haig.

The battle, in which, with a few brief spells for rest out of the line, Max was engaged almost from the outset, lasted for three and a half months before it finally petered out in the mud of autumn and winter with gains of a few thousand yards and the loss of about 300,000 dead or wounded British and Dominion troops. The true figure will never be known – two memorials at Passchendaele bear the names of 90,000 British Empire soldiers killed in the Ypres Salient whose bodies either were never found or could not be identified. None of Max's letters survive from his time at Ypres, of which Sir Philip Gibbs, the correspondent of *The Times* at the front, wrote:

> All the agonies of war were piled up in those fields of Flanders. There was nothing missing in the list of war's abominations . . . week after week, month after month our masses of men struggled on through that Slough of Despond, capturing ridge after ridge, until the heights of Passchendaele were stormed and won. As a man who knows something of the value of words and who saw many of those battle scenes I say now that nothing that has been written is more than the pale image of the abomination of those battle fields, and that no pen or brush has yet achieved the picture of that Armageddon in which so many of our men perished.

Max's battalion was not involved in the opening battle on 31 July, but on 17 August it moved up to the front and took over a part of the line in the thickly wired Glencorse Wood sector either side of the Menin Road, the main route eastwards out of Ypres itself. The ground was in a terrible state. Heavy rain had fallen with little interruption since 1 August. The weather had come as no surprise to the Meteorological Office, which had been recording similar conditions in the area for over eighty years. Flanders is flat and low-lying, its water table close to the surface, and endless shell-fire had ruptured the land drains and dykes, reducing the battlefield to a vast bog. The trenches hardly existed; where they did, they were hip-deep in liquid mud. The men sheltered in shell holes, or in concrete pillboxes and blown up dugouts captured from the enemy. The unburied dead lay everywhere, the stench of death so all-pervading that it seeped into the soldiers' uniforms.

For eight sleepless days Max was in action with his battalion either at the front or on work details, carrying heavy stores forward for 2,000 yards through gas bombardments. By 23 August the battalion's casualties had been so severe that it needed to borrow men from the King's Shropshire Light Infantry. From midnight to dawn on 24 August the enemy shelled with growing violence. At 4.45 am the battalion was attacked and fell back, but restored its position within hours in the face of savage machine-gun fire. Communications broke down completely, except for messages sent by runners. At 3.00 pm on the 25th, the battalion was relieved and moved to billets behind the line. Of the five captains on the roll on 1 August, one had been promoted to a command elsewhere, and two had been killed; only Max and another remained. Given a few days' leave, Max hastened back to Violet on 30 August.

In the War Cabinet in London, shock at the scale of the loss of life led to bitter exchanges, to which General Robertson responded by urging Haig to tone down the optimistic nature of his despatches. But still Haig persisted with the offensive. The British Army was overlooked by the Germans, who held the Passchendaele Ridge, from which observers could direct a hail of accurate artillery fire. If only that ridge could be seized, surely the way would be open to Ostend and the German submarine bases on the Belgian coast? Unheeding of the "Swamp Map" prepared by the Tank Corps, which showed the terrain to be impassable even to tracked vehicles, and believing only in the sanguine reports of his Chief of Intelligence, General Charteris, Haig pressed on with yet another assault, from which he predicted "decisive results". The attack went in on 2 September, screened by five massive barrages from howitzers and field artillery, and machine-gun fire of unprecedented weight. A second assault took place on 26 September which was answered with twenty-four German counter-attacks. General Charteris wrote:

> The casualties are awful; one cannot dare to think of them . . . I would not have believed that any troops would have faced what the army is facing . . . It is easy enough for us here, with all our information about the Germans, to count the cost coldly, to strike a balance sheet and see what is right to do. But for the men, and even more so for the regimental officers, it must seem a pretty hopeless

outlook. Yet it is not at the front, but in England, that the calamity of casualties affects resolution.

On 4 October, Australian troops spearheaded a third major attack. Like the first two, it succeeded in its immediate objectives, and, this time, the German Army found itself on the brink of defeat. Then the weather came to its rescue. By 12 October the battlefield had become a treeless wilderness of slime and water-filled shell holes, in which all movement was impossible. For a brief spell Max's battalion was taken out of the fighting to refit and recuperate. On 16 October it was in the line again, averaging thirty casualties a day from the constant shelling. Men crowded into pillboxes for protection. Secretly praying not to be sent again into attack, they watched in dread as twenty-one parties of senior staff officers visited them and other front-line units to examine conditions for the next big push. The battle, however, was now effectively over. When the battalion was relieved on 24 October, Max was promoted to major and second-in-command. The battalion stayed at Ypres until Christmas, then withdrew to rest, re-equip and take in reinforcements, in preparation for going back into action further south, in the Somme sector.

In January 1918 Max returned again to England for a fortnight's leave, where he found Violet still pining for Bill. Having been so often near to death he had put aside a little of his flippancy and when, at Violet's prompting, he wrote appealing to Bill to come home from India, his letter combined his customary self-deprecation and mockery with a more serious note of yearning for the idyllic life that they had all once shared.

37 Ovington Square S.W. *January 24th, 1918.*
Dear Old Bill,
Before returning to France next Monday I must write you a line. V. is fairly well, but two years is a long time and it will be a wonderful day when she hears that you are really on your way home – Surely it is time that you had a spell at home after all this absence: you must try and manage it, if ever you get the chance. Yesterday we went to Armscote for the day; it looked like the home of Sleeping Beauty; long grass on the lawns, no one moving, and the house most beautiful inside and out, simply calling us to come back. Please God it will not be very much longer before we are all together again there. I had a very short time to glance at the stock & the land; Gordon will tell you all that is doing in that line, as he is in touch with it. The beasts looked fairly well, considering the rough weather of the last few weeks, and I noticed particularly how the clover was growing on

Parkers Hill field. I understand it is for hay this year, if the labour can be found. Of course many things require attention, but we will give that if we get the chance.

I have been having a fairly easy time in France as second-in-command, but there is a danger of another senior major coming along, which may mean that I have to go back to [command of] a company. I hope not. My lot are just taking over from the French down south. This will be a change after rather a long spell in that dirty Flanders. Getting in and out of the line had become rather an awkward job owing to the great distance and the mud . . .

It is a wonderful rest being in London and such a joy to see V. again. Old Poo [one of Violet's Pekinese] is very ancient, almost blind, but keeps going – he is a wonder.

I have seen the charming coats you have sent V. – also the jewel which is very beautiful. You must hurry up and come and see them being worn. I hear you are tattooed with dragons – and probably look like Topsil's book of beasts. I remember seeing a man in Barnums [the circus], but perhaps you have not indulged quite so extensively in the pictorial business – I suppose you have not had "Merry Christmas" emblazoned on your tail. There is much talk of peace in the air, but we must hang out for proper terms – if we can get them I am prepared to return to civilian life without delay – and I guess you feel the same.

Best of luck and a speedy return,                    Yours ever, Max.

After Ypres, the peacefulness of Armscote and the emotion at being reunited with Violet were overwhelming, and the thought of losing them, perhaps for ever, and returning to battle was nearly too much for Max. He had continued to see Valérie Pirie when on leave; indeed family lore, passed on from Valérie's daughter to Kit Ayling, has it that after Valérie's husband was killed early in the war he had had thoughts of giving up his "irresponsible" ways and marrying her. But in the end, when his moment of truth came, his thoughts were only of Violet. As though he had a foreboding that his time was short, he wrote to her whenever he could, expressing his feelings for her more strongly, and more explicitly, than ever before. The first of his letters on his return to France will have been written from near Boulogne, the closest safe French port to the front.

*31 Jan 1918*. Darling Tookees, I see in the paper that there was a bad Air Raid the night of the day I left. I do hope they did not drop any bombs near Ovington Square. How I wish that I had been there with you that we might have supported one another. I am sure that you will let me know as soon as you have news about Bill, I feel strongly that you will be successful this time, but Rupe will have to keep pushing. We go into the line in a day or two, but so far as I know it is a comparatively quiet spot and very different to Flanders – so St. Francis should have a simple job so far as I am concerned. It seemed vilely cold last night in a sort of oast house, after the comfortable beds I have lain in this last fortnight, but I shall soon get used to that. I came in for a few bombs, at a little town I stayed in the night before. There was a French civilian sharing my room and he called down every sort of curse on the Germans and amused me considerably . . . My Beloved, when I think of you & the wonderful happiness of being with you, this business seems almost unbearable, but I know one must just keep hopping about the cage until somehow the door gets opened – perhaps that will make up for all, when the door is opened – may it be soon.

God bless you Darling Tookees & keep you quite safe. All my love Maxwell.

The next letter, although undated, was almost certainly written on 1 February.

Darling Tookees,
I have got over all right and am going to catch a train about midnight to my new destination, or at least in that direction – for the real hide and seek business will begin the other end . . . I can hardly realise yet that my leave is over, oh Tookees, it was just fourteen days of paradise – for you made it so. All my love sweet pet. God bless you, Maxwell.

On 2 February Max went back into the line on the Somme. His superior officer took over temporary command of the brigade, leaving Max for the first time in command of the battalion.

*February 2nd. 1918.*
Darling Tookees,
We go up this evening. I am sorry to say that the Colonel has to go to act as Brigadier for a month, while the Brigadier is on leave, so I shall have to look after the Battalion. I trust nothing unpleasant will happen during that time. I have two commissions that I wish Gordon would do for me. The first is to change the braces I bought

at Harrods for a longer pair, the present pair are too short for the Colonel and put a painful strain upon his breeches. The other commission is rather a nuisance. It is to get a baton for the Bandmaster. I believe they are usually in ebony, and I want, or rather the Bandmaster wants, the following inscription engraved on the silver end of the ebony wand: W.E. Bond. Bandmaster 5 Oxf. and Bucks Lt. Inf 1916.17.18. Presented by Major M. Labouchère.

I think either Hawkes or Chappell would provide a suitable article.

I still read of air raids in London but they are not doing much damage. A few minutes ago a German plane had a go at the balloon just over our heads. The tenants floated away gracefully in their parachutes, the balloon collapsed, and I hear the German plane was knocked out on the return, so everyone should be content.

If you knew, perhaps you do know, how carefully I have avoided all responsibility through life and how irresponsible I have become, so you can guess that I look forward with great misgiving to the next month. There are so many things to think of and of many of them I am quite ignorant. I almost think you will have to burn a candle for me over this business. I expect to get a letter from you soon, but the post is most erratic down here. All my love – dear pet.

Maxwell.

For a while the sector was quiet. The weather in March was beautiful, and Max wrote again to Violet:

Darling Tookees,
We go up tonight. It is an almost perfect day, with bright, hot sun. What a day for a Sunday walk at Armscote with no bomb-dropping aeroplanes overhead. I expect your Sunday Party is just collecting. I wish I could slip in – perhaps you will play my piece. What beautiful music you do make Tookees. What amazing pleasure and happiness you have brought into our lives. You are truly a wonderful little fellow, and God, how I love you. Maxwell.

In planning the campaign for 1918, Haig had judged correctly that there was a crippling shortage of recruits of military age to replace German casualties. Moreover, the United States had finally joined the war on the Allied side and it could only be a matter of time before American troops and equipment changed the balance of power on the Western Front. On the other hand, Russia had been knocked out of the war, first by catastrophic military defeats and then by Lenin's Bolshevik Revolution, freeing large numbers of German troops to transfer to France and Flanders. Rejecting any idea of a negotiated peace, General Erich Ludendorff, whose power in Germany was second to none, planned as his last desperate throw a massive counter-attack to annihilate the Allies on the Somme, hoping to win the war quickly, before the American troops were ready for battle and Germany was defeated by the hideous arithmetic of attrition.

On 21 March the storm broke. Shortly before 5 am the German guns opened up with a merciless bombardment of high-explosive, gas shells and mortar bombs. At 6.05 am, in anticipation of the inevitable attack to follow, Max ordered his battalion to stand to. At 9.45 am an avalanche of infantry overran the British forward outposts and went on to break the British line at several points. The situation soon became grave. At 11.30 am, its own forward posts having been obliterated by shellfire, Max's battalion met the enemy at close quarters. Hand-to-hand fighting followed before the position was abandoned. The story was the same everywhere along the British line throughout 21 and 22 March, as units, shattered by the bombardment and overwhelmed by weight of numbers, fell back before the German offensive. On the evening of the 22nd the CO of the 5th Oxford and Bucks rejoined the battalion and took over from Max, but by the morning of the 23rd he had been mortally wounded and Max found himself back in command. They again retired under heavy machine-gun fire, fighting all the way. On the 24th the onslaught was renewed and they were driven back once more, always maintaining good order despite dreadful casualties. It was during this terrible period that Max wrote his last letter to Violet.

> Darling Tookees, We are moving every hour day and night. We lost three quarters of the officers and men in the first three days – I am in command of what is left. God knows where we shall be tomorrow. Beloved, the beautiful thought of being together again at Armscote seems rather doubtful just now, yet I pray it may be so, all my love is with you, Darling Tookees and Bill and Gordon. I have lost everything except what I stand up in. Please ask Gordon to send me an Auto Razor, also a tube of Hazeline or Lanoline and a pair of overalls (Mackintosh) from Cordings. Again all my love and God Bless you always,                                                  Maxwell.

On 31 March Max was recommended for the DSO for gallantry. After the briefest of rests, the battalion was back in the line and on 4 April it faced a heavy German bombardment, followed by four waves of infantry attack. In the forced retreat Max was badly wounded, losing a leg, and was left behind to be taken prisoner. He had only needed his luck to last another twenty-four hours, for next day Ludendorff's offensive, utterly exhausted, ground to a halt. On 20 April 1918 Max died of wounds in the tent of a German field hospital. Reporting his posthumous award of the DSO, *The Times* recorded the formulaic citation:

> While commanding his battalion at a time when a retirement was in progress, he showed marked ability and coolness, and it was due to his fine handling of his men that the enemy were checked. His cheerfulness and disregard of danger did much to inspire his men.

Back in England, Violet was distraught when she learned that Max was missing and wounded. She was by turns terrified and optimistic, and kept reminding herself of Denis's unexpected survival. At times she seemed to enter into Max's pain and feel it physically as her own. When the news finally came through neutral Switzerland that he had died, she was ashamed to find herself too drained to grieve, her sensation nothing but dull, shocked emptiness. More than ever she needed the comforting presence of Bill, whose long-delayed return from India brought him back to Armscote in April, just a few days before Max's death was officially confirmed. It was not for another month that he received, forwarded from Bangalore, Max's letter of 24 January appealing to him to come home to Violet. This voice from the grave, imbued with selflessness, wit and unassuming courage, made Max come vividly alive as Bill and Violet read and reread his words together.

With Max gone, Violet felt an unfillable void at the loss of his rich and colourful character. What Rubio had been to her musically, Max had been intellectually, opening new worlds of knowledge and ways of thinking to her, and always in that ironic tone she found so engaging. Unlike Bill and Denis, he had not prepared for war, and as she emerged from her initial numbness the unfairness of his brave death filled her with anger as much as sorrow. It was a long time before she could summon up images of Max as he had been before the war. In the end, however, she learned to do so. Many years later, her friend Isabel Armitage spoke to the author about a dinner party at which Gordon, Bill, Denis and Violet had been reminded by a chance remark of something Max had once said. A fleeting look and a smile passed between the four of them. It was, said Isabel, "a moment wreathed in gold".

On his return from India Bill found Violet politically as well as artistically under the influence of the Sitwells. Shortly after meeting her, Osbert had introduced her to his younger brother Sacheverell (Sachie) and his sister Edith. Displaying none of the patriotism which had gripped the rest of the country, Osbert had bent every effort towards keeping his brother, who was in the army, as far away from the front line as possible. Hitherto Violet's attitude to the war had been conventional. It had disrupted her life and caused her deep anxiety, but she had not questioned its purpose, accepting that German militarism had made it inevitable, and blocking out any suspicion that Bill, Max and Denis might be wasting their courage on a cause which could as well be pursued by negotiation. Even before Max's death Osbert had begun to change the direction of her thinking, leading her to fear and despise the political attitudes which the Sitwells held responsible for more than three years of bloodshed. After the slaughter of Passchendaele, following that on the Somme the year before, she had been unable to accept that the Government could permit the General Staff to launch further offensives without at least spelling out its terms for a truce. She therefore capitulated completely to the Sitwell argument and lent open support to the rather feeble peace movement which ineffectually eddied about in Britain until the end of the war.

Over the last year all three Sitwells had successfully manoeuvred themselves into prominent positions in London's artistic world, writing voluminously and using their extensive social connections to create publicity for Edith's magazine *Wheels*. Through Edward Marsh and Oscar Wilde's literary executor, Robert Ross, Osbert had met Siegfried Sassoon in 1916, and the two had immediately struck up a friendship. Sassoon, an officer in the Royal Welch Fusiliers, had been through the Battle of the Somme, had been decorated with the MC for his almost mad heroics at the front (he had been recommended, unsuccessfully, for the VC), and in the late spring of 1917, while convalescing from a wound, had taken a fateful decision: he would risk a court-martial by openly attacking the conduct of the war.[2] The War Office, horrified, immediately sought ways in which to muzzle him. Accusations of cowardice being, under the circumstances, absurd, the Under-Secretary for War declared Sassoon to be suffering from shell shock and sent him to the Craiglockhart War Hospital for Neurasthenic Officers, near Edinburgh. There he wrote poetry, received friends and corresponded with fellow opponents of the war; there too he met and encouraged a young soldier-poet who idolized him – Wilfrid Owen. Sassoon's poems give a vivid picture of the attitude of the ordinary soldier at the front:

> I'd like to see a Tank come down the stalls,
> Lurching to rag-time tunes, or "Home Sweet Home",

2 Sassoon's protest was read out in the House of Commons on 30 July 1917, and published in *The Times* on the following day: "I am making this statement as an act of wilful defiance of military authority, because I believe that the war is being deliberately prolonged by those who have the power to end it . .".

> And there'd be no more jokes in Music-halls
> To mock the riddled corpses round Bapaume.

Osbert's disillusionment with the war, if less gallant and less symbolic than Sassoon's, was its equal in intensity, and they united to lampoon the generation which seemed so remote from the young men on whom it was inflicting such torment.

Edith Sitwell used *Wheels* not only to provide some of the new war poets with a platform, but also to inveigh against the "Georgians" and their sponsor, Edward Marsh, whose alleged crime was his belief in traditional metre, rhyme and poetic sentiment – derided by the Sitwells as sterile compared with their own advanced ideas. Today it is hard to see the Sitwells' campaign as anything other than an exercise in publicity-seeking. Many of the poets of whom they most approved – such as W.H. Davies and Siegfried Sassoon himself – were published by Marsh, and there was no clear distinction between the two camps.[3] It could certainly not be said that *Wheels* maintained purer standards when it came to modernism and free verse. Edith pursued the cynical but earnest novelist Aldous Huxley, only to receive as a reward for her efforts some jaunty verse of no great quality; much of what she published was traditionalist in form and content; and some of it, like the versifying of Nancy Cunard and Iris Tree, was, at best, mediocre.

The Sitwells were not intellectual heavyweights, nor were they exceptionally talented, but they had a certain style, and possessed determination and energy. It would be too facile to attribute their eminence in aesthetic circles to their standing in society, but it is perhaps not too harsh to say that their influence was transient. In the end what they brought to the scene was wit, colour and panache – a flair for the arts and a gift for transmitting their own enthusiasms rather than a lasting contribution to the artistic legacy. As Violet's friendship with them developed, Ovington Square became a salon, a Mecca for poets, artists, writers and lovers of music. Over the closing months of the war Osbert and Sachie sought consciously to turn her into a cult figure. In *Noble Essences*, the fifth volume of his autobiography, Osbert writes: "Among those whom my brother and I took at various times to hear this great artist play were T.S. Eliot, Bernard van Dieren, W.H. Davies, Wilfred Owen, Aldous Huxley, Arthur Waley, Ezra Pound, Robert Graves, Robert Nichols and Siegfried Sassoon . . ." Some of these, such as Waley and Pound, were, of course, already well known to Violet. Others were new to her, including the poet W.H. Davies, to whom Osbert devoted a chapter of

---

3 Among the leading "realistic" war poets, for example, Marsh also published Robert Nichols and Robert Graves, while Edith Sitwell's main prize was Wilfred Owen.

his autobiography.

In the last two years of the 1914 war, when W.H. Davies used to come to stay with my brother and me from Saturday to Monday in Swan Walk, we always used to conduct him to Ovington Square about four o'clock on Sunday afternoon; one of us, tall and clad in the Brigade of Guards grey great-coat, with brass buttons, striding along on either side of his smaller, but thickset, figure, with its dipping gait. Being a genius herself, Violet Gordon Woodhouse of course identified, on her very first meeting with this other extraordinary and fascinating individual, the same quality, the identical power of seeing beyond the mountain ranges and molehills that hedge us in, that he equally recognised at once in her. Because of this, perhaps, they soon became fast friends, and [Davies would give vivid descriptions] of his visits and of the "rupture", as he pronounced it . . . with [his] Welsh lilt and accentuation, that he had felt when he heard [her play] the harpsichord. One of the results of these visits was that Davies wrote and dedicated to her the beautiful poem with which I end this portrait. He brought it to her with the true words, "A woman like you should live for ever!"

*On Hearing Mrs. Woodhouse Play the Harpsichord*

We poets pride ourselves on what
We feel, and not what we achieve;
The world may call our children fools,
Enough for us that we conceive.
A little wren that loves the grass
Can be as proud as any lark
That tumbles in a cloudless sky,
Up near the sun, till he becomes
The apple of that shining eye.

So, lady, I would never dare
To hear your music ev'ry day;
With those great bursts that send my nerves
In waves to pound my heart away;
And those small notes that run like mice
Bewitched by light; else on those keys –
My tombs of song – you should engrave;
"My music, stronger than his own,
Has made this poet my dumb slave."

No visit to Ovington Square was more poignant than that of Wilfred

Owen, perhaps the greatest war poet in the English language and the inspiration for Benjamin Britten's magnificent *War Requiem*. Until his meeting
with Sassoon at Craiglockhart, Owen's writing had been no more than
promising, in a rather conventional way, but in the course of many long
conversations in their hospital rooms he reached a turning point. From then
on, Owen resolved to write only of his experience of the trenches, fusing the
pity and terror of war into language of simple directness.

> Gas! GAS! Quick, boys! – An ecstasy of fumbling,
>     Fitting the clumsy helmets just in time;
> But someone still was yelling out and stumbling,
>     And flound'ring like a man in fire or lime . . .
> Dim, through the misty panes and thick green light,
>     As under a green sea, I saw him drowning.
>
>     In all my dreams, before my helpless sight,
> He plunges at me, guttering, choking, drowning.
>
> If in some smothering dreams you too could pace
>     Behind the wagon that we flung him in,
> And watch the white eyes writhing in his face,
>     His hanging face, like a devil's sick of sin;
>     If you could hear, at every jolt, the blood
> Come gargling from the froth-corrupted lungs,
>     Obscene as cancer, bitter as the cud
> Of vile, incurable sores on innocent tongues, –
> My friend, you would not tell with such high zest
>     To children ardent for some desperate glory,
> The old Lie – Dulce et decorum est
> Pro patria mori.[4]

Having been passed fit in November 1917, Sassoon returned to the front,
and in July 1918 wrote to Osbert that he must meet his new friend Owen,
who would "do very well as a poet some day". Osbert had, in fact, already
done so; he, too, had taken Owen under his wing and had started to
exchange poems with him. When Sassoon came back on indefinite sick
leave in August, after being wounded again in July, the three poets went
together to see Violet and hear her play. Sixteen months earlier, Owen had
become disoriented, and had been accused of failure of nerve, after several

---

4 "Lovely and befitting it is to die for one's country" – a quotation from the *Odes* of
Horace.

days of continuous exposure to heavy shellfire, in which those about him had been blown to smithereens; he had been invalided home and sent to Craiglockhart. Now he was considered fit for battle and was about to return to the trenches.

For two hours without a break, Violet played Bach, Mozart and early English music to them, her own pain at Max's death still raw enough to enable her to penetrate in some way the state of mind of a man about to re-enter the battle zone. Owen, wrote Osbert, sat "dazed with happiness at the fire and audacity of the player". Afterwards they walked across to the old, walled Chelsea Physic Garden, to which Osbert had a key, and sat in the sun. Owen was "so listlessly happy . . . that he could not bring himself to leave the Garden and go to the station and catch the train". Within weeks, Wilfred Owen was in France once more, determined to prove his bravery, to endure every horror, and to set an example to the young men under his command, whom he thought of as being in his care. In October he was awarded the MC for gallantry. He died on 4 November 1918, a mere seven days before the Armistice was declared, while leading his men as they fought to cross the Sambre Canal under intense enemy fire.

The end of the war came unexpectedly, even though the German forces in France had been retreating steadily since August. The Royal Navy's control of the seas had led to shortages of food and other supplies in Germany, and there came a time when there was no longer any prospect of replacing the army's casualties with fresh troops. Strikes, riots, even mutinies began to break out in German cities. Suddenly Ludendorff lost his nerve. One by one, Germany's allies – Bulgaria, Turkey, Austria-Hungary – capitulated. The Kaiser abdicated and fled to Holland, and at last, on 7 November, German envoys set out for the Allied lines to negotiate a surrender.

The Armistice was signed on 11 November, and at 11 am the sound of victorious guns burst over London. A slow crescendo of distant shouting built to riotous joy and echoed throughout the country. Crowds entering from the suburbs erupted into the centre of London, cheering and shrieking in wild celebration; lorries filled with drunken soldiers chugged down Whitehall. In Oxford Street flag-strewn taxis tottered along, overflowing with passengers waving flags and rattles.From Millbank, beside the Thames in Westminster, fireworks shot into the sky with terrifying clarity as night fell. Violet was overcome with relief that the fighting was over, but she had no sympathy with the rejoicing in the streets, for it seemed so out of keeping with the catastrophe which had preceded it – and with the wonder, grandeur and awfulness of Germany's downfall.

A week after Armistice Day, Violet received a letter from Denis, still in his prisoner-of-war camp, which reveals that she had been writing to him at least twice a week, and suggests that, even as a prisoner, he had been growing more confident in his relationship with her:

Freiburg (Baden) *Monday Nov. 18, 1918.*
Beloved V.
. . . A devil of a lot has happened since I last wrote at end of Oct. I delayed my first November letter, waiting for Armistice, to see what was laid down about return of prisoners. Then when at last we heard that, we of course got into a state of expecting to start for home any day, so that it seemed useless to write, as we were likely to reach home before a letter. As it is, my pet, if you get this at all, it will probably be after you have got me back . . . We do not yet know when we are to go, but we hope within a week – nor do we know in the least how long a journey it will be, or by what route. In fact we know nothing except that the War is finished and that our Gov. is demanding us back, and a dam' good thing too. In fact, my only one, I am confident of eating my Christmas dinner in your bewitching company – for the first time since 1910, but in much happier circum-stances – and that is nice for me to go on with, thank you! Meanwhile there has been this Revolution. They are things that I disapprove of as a rule, but of course there must be exceptions to every rule (you see how broad-minded I am!). I do not know if my mind is as broad as Chaucer's – I certainly appreciate the breadth of his as expressed, for instance, in "The Miller's Tale", & the Reeve's also; (not *tail* as Bill would write it!). No, I have never seen Canterbury Cathedral. It must be magnificent, from your account of it, and I should dearly like to worship in it with you one day – & why not – for all things have now become possible. A few of your September letters are still missing – in the middle – but I've got them complete from 22nd and all the first 8 of Oct. charming and gay as they are, and I love to hear of your watching the sun rise from your bed, and then your delightful amusing accounts of the other Hotel guests. I laughed very much at your ultimatum to the Padre – that if he wanted to hear your Octavina he must come alone to your bedroom! He might have replied "I'd rather have a cup of tea, ma'am" – like that painter and decorator, in an old story of yours, who preferred a glass of beer! Then you tell me of the tiresome woman with white fluffy hair, who lives with a husband and 2 dogs in one small room. How truly domestic, virtuous and beastly. As you

say this must be among the horrors of married life, and I would prefer a smart and chic courtesanship – with nice hot baths and etceteras. Then you tell me that Bill has got a month's leave for his farm, & that is most splendid – as you hoped not to start it until mid Oct, I hope that you were still farming when Armistice was settled, & that Bill (seizing the golden moment) at once got an indefinite extension. In fact, darling, I hope that he is now quite free, that all your troubles are over – that very soon I shall have the intense, the dreamed-of joy of seizing your fairy figure in my arms and hugging you.                          Your own Denis

Denis was back in England before the end of November. During his captivity Violet had kept from him the besmirching of his honour by his aunt Blanche. Now his reputation was fully restored when he received, like Max and Roland, the DSO, an officer's highest award for valour after the Victoria Cross. At last he and Violet were able to laugh together over the episode of the cancelled memorial mass, about which he would tease her for years to come. But Max was gone for ever, and the carefree security of the years before 1914 was never fully to return.

# XI

*Society in Upheaval*

THE AFTERMATH OF WAR brought many changes to Violet's household. Money was very tight now, especially since she had missed out on a legacy from her father; staff wages had soared, and in real terms the value of Gordon's stock-market investments was greatly reduced. Denis had survived the trenches, an experience from which no man, not even one as steady as Denis, returned unscathed; he suffered recurrent nightmares in which he dreamed of being buried alive, but remained a full-time professional soldier, living in his house in Moore Street, two minutes' walk from Ovington Square, where Violet was still the centre of his world. Time did not seem to heal the pain of Max's death. For a while even Violet's relationship with Bill entered a period of crisis.

At the end of the war Violet was forty-seven. Bill, at forty-five, was as strikingly good-looking a man as ever, the more attractive for having matured through experience. He had been very happy in India, where through the army he had found independence, comradeship, sport, and the self-respect which was always slightly diminished while he lived under Gordon's roof. His return to England was unsettling. Society was in upheaval. Income taxes had risen nearly fourfold from 8 per cent to 30 per cent, and socialist ideas had gained ground throughout the country. The Armscote farm, in which he had invested his modest capital, was a shambles. The value of his livestock had dropped by a half, farm wages had doubled, and it was hard to find good agricultural labour. As a gentleman farmer he faced something close to impoverishment.

At some point during his time in India Bill had met another woman, and had even thought of marrying and settling down. There are no letters or diaries: the only trace of the drama that remains is the account of Kit Ayling, gleaned from what she was told by her mother, Bluebelle. Whoever "the other woman" was, Bluebelle told Kit that she would have made a suitable match for Bill. Violet had had an inkling that something was not quite right, but it was not until she learned the full story from Rupert that her suspicions were confirmed. She reacted with passion and energy, enlisting Rupert, Gordon and Denis in turn to remind Bill of his "grave moral obligations" towards her.

As for Bill, he was pulled in conflicting directions, torn between his sense of honour and his affection for Violet on the one hand, and on the other a conviction that this was his last opportunity to break free from a way of life that had brought him happiness, but sometimes of too cloying a kind. He would have liked children, and his sisters pushed him to give up Violet, marry and produce an heir. But to leave her would be a betrayal, for to all intents and purposes he had been her husband; he had even given her his ring before the war, and he knew that she would be lost without him. In matters of emotion Bill was not a decisive man, and he found himself caught in a struggle conducted by people of far more resolute willpower than he himself could summon up. From such a contest there could be only one winner, and once Bill came face to face with Violet, the intensity of her feelings and the strength of her character quickly prevailed.

Although the immediate danger had passed, Violet's victory represented a triumph of determination rather than a return to confident happiness. In the past she had been nervous of her ability to hold Bill; once before she had all but lost him. Now her doubts had been reinforced, and she had to keep close watch on him. She particularly feared his visits to Beckett, where his adoring relations (except for the musical ones – his sister Maude and his niece Lorna) thought Violet a witch, while his stepmother detested both her and Bill equally. "That descending harpy", one of his family called Violet. More generally, she was just "That Dreadful Woman", who was responsible for the fact that he had not married, and for ensuring that his occasional visits home were so fleeting that he rarely even stayed the night.

If Bill's roving eye was manageable through vigilance, Gordon's financial problems were more intractable. He had spelled out his situation to his future father-in-law at the time of his marriage to Violet – he was well off, though by no means rich. For more than twenty years, however, he had been spending more than he could afford and had been forced to eat into his capital; as Violet reverted to her old ways after the war he found himself under severe pressure. Her houses, her lavish hospitality, her present-giving, and her clothes, with which she had indulged herself since the first days of their marriage, were now a serious drain on Gordon's depleted exchequer, and Violet appeared incapable of voluntary retrenchment other than on a token scale.

Clothes were her greatest extravagance. Under the influence of Diaghilev, the French couturier Paul Poiret was designing oriental costumes with bold, bright colours and a narrow line, often broken up with panels or tunics over the top of a skirt. The corset was finally abandoned, and Violet no longer confined herself to high-necked blouses, nor to wide evening skirts in silk or taffeta. Two photographs taken in 1919 show her flamboyantly adopting the new style, dressed in Indian fashion with a silk turban and wide lampshade tunics delicately embroidered, with turquoise, pink and ochre animals, and figures sewn in silver or gold thread.

To Violet clothes were not merely for self-display – they were works of art, and a storehouse of potential presents. She would sit at the desk in her bedroom and write to Bill to describe a Chinese robe or a flowing silk tea-gown that she was wearing for her own sheer pleasure; or she would conduct her nieces to her wardrobes (Rupert's and Nevile's daughters were never well enough dressed in her eyes) and show them her clothes, as if they were a collection of paintings. If she thought a particular article would suit one of them, she would gaily give it away.

Her dressmaker was now Venturette in Beauchamp Place. Venturette, whose real name was Hélène, was a charming Frenchwoman whom Violet had taken up to help design her evening dresses. "They were very picturesque, subtle and original," according to Rupert's daughter, Elizabeth, best known as the cookery writer Elizabeth David

> especially when Aunt V. was dressed up with her extraordinary jewellery, necklaces, bracelets, earrings, all dangling and clanking – but Hélène told me that sewing the dresses was a terrible task, and Aunt V. was so capricious that suddenly she would decide she'd like to have the linings of all the flounces changed from white to red or something of that kind, and nothing would do but that she must have the dress ready for dinner the following evening. Hélène told me that she had sometimes to sit up all night sewing in order to finish a dress for Aunt V. who was not by any means always grateful or pleased.

Second only to the cost of clothes was the cost of Violet's servants – cooks, housemaids and lady's maids – from whom she obtained unswerving devotion. After the war she acquired, through Rupert's wife Stella, a new lady's maid, called Lily Blandford, to replace Dulciette Summers. Dorset born and bred, large and dominating, Lily attended to every detail of Violet's appearance. Hats, muffs, chamois leather gloves, velvet or snake-skin shoes with square heels, brocaded evening slippers with pointed toes, blouses, dresses for morning, afternoon and evening – all were kept in perfect condition by Lily. She was on call most of the day and night, and in moments of calm would be found hand-stitching Violet's silk underclothes, trimming and piping them in satin. Two or three times a day she brushed and rearranged Violet's hair. Without following the twenties cut-bob fashion, Violet nevertheless wore her hair shorter than before and set closer to the head, flat at the top and pinned in layers and curls of chignon either side of her cheekbones. Close though Lily and Violet were, however, their relationship was also formal. When her mistress was going out, Lily would be summoned grandly to help her put on her gloves.

Then there was the tempting new phenomenon of city department stores, like Debenham & Freebody and Marshall & Snelgrove in London, where Violet treated herself to frequent spending sprees, accompanied by Gordon, Bill and Denis, who swept up the bills at the end. For a brief period she discovered Woolworth's, where she was amazed to find that one could buy all sorts of things for 6d – pens, brooches, handkerchiefs and hair-combs. That particular love affair did not last long, however.

As Violet ran through Gordon's fortune, he found that he could no longer bolster his finances by selling shares without running the risk of depleting his capital before he could collect the inheritance he expected from his elderly mother on her death. Yet he could not bring himself to reproach Violet for her spending, any more than for her unpredictable demands. It was not so much that he was weak, though no doubt she was an infinitely stronger character than he; nor that he was blind to her failings. As time passed he came to see through all her pretensions, but he continued to love her just as he always had, never ceasing to be fascinated by her caprices and her firefly darts and fantasies. After nearly twenty-five years of marriage he was no less flattered to have been chosen by her than he had been as a young man, and had he been rich enough there would have been no limit to his spoiling and indulgence. By the end of the war, however, he was not far from financial collapse. Something, he knew, had to be done about it.

Hitherto Violet had played selectively in public where and with whom she wished, setting her sights by the standards of the foremost international virtuosi, but detesting the idea of being "a professional", with its implications of a relentless grind to earn money. Nevertheless, in their reduced circumstances she had to take the plunge, and in 1918 she engaged Ibbs & Tillett as her agents. The agency's management realized that they had a catch in Violet, and advertised her in a special promotional pamphlet:

A recital by Violet Gordon Woodhouse is one of those all too rare opportunities of hearing the Sixteenth century music as it was really intended to be heard. Mrs. Woodhouse is not a revivalist. She plays music that is full of vitality, in the only way in which it can be played, so that its vitality can be appreciated, namely on the instrument for which it was intended.

On the inside of the pamphlet were printed extracts from reviews in *The Times*, the *Daily Telegraph*, *The Lady* and one from the *Pall Mall Gazette* that ran: "Anyone who has not heard Mrs. Gordon Woodhouse play the harpsichord should do penance for missing so good an opportunity. She is a great artist."

The agency informed impresarios that other performers could be booked with Violet – the cellist Beatrice Harrison, who had won the Mendelssohn Prize and who had a reputation for outstanding interpretations of contemporary music; the soprano Dorothy Silk; or the new group of madrigal and folk-song singers, the English Singers, who toured Europe and America promoting English music. Well aware of the drawing power of her appearance, Ibbs & Tillett commissioned a watercolour of Violet from the French painter Charles Dechaume, which portrayed her sitting at the harpsichord, wearing an intricately layered dress and resembling a delicate piece of porcelain.

She was soon much in demand. In her late forties, and practising more intensively than ever before, she was at the zenith of her abilities. Her playing was entirely lacking in sentimentality, her technique was perfect, and the years spent under the guidance of Rubio had given her a deep insight into phrasing. The mainstays of her repertoire were Bach, Scarlatti and Mozart, but she often also featured music by William Byrd, Purcell, François Couperin, Handel and Haydn in her concerts, as well as works by contemporary composers such as Béla Bartók, Francis Poulenc and Vaughan Williams. She would usually end her programme with early English music and arrangements of folk tunes.

Her contract with Ibbs & Tillett also allowed her to be engaged for private concerts, which, to save the embarrassment of having to discuss money, she booked through them. After the war London's hostesses resumed their drawing-room music parties, and as soon as word spread that Violet had become more available she was snapped up to play in private homes – in Sir Philip Sassoon's newly decorated house in Park Lane; in Lord Howard de Walden's house in Belgrave Square (his wife, Margherita, always known as Margot, was very musical); in Lord Glenconner's house in Queen Anne's Gate; in the house, next to the Ritz, of Lord Wimborne, heir to a steel fortune; in Bertha Stoop's house in Hans Place and in her other house outside London on the river at Wandlebrook, both filled with the fabulous collection of Impressionist paintings belonging to her husband, Frank, one of the largest shareholders in Royal Dutch; in the house of Ethel Smyth's sister, Mary Hunter, in Epping Forest; in the Chelsea house of the American hostess and painter Ethel Sands; and in the house of Miriam Joshua, whom Delius had found so intellectually pretentious.

In these beautiful settings, in libraries, reception rooms, halls and galleries, Violet's music was heard at its best. She did not limit herself to a single instrument. One Tuesday at the Glenconners' house in July 1919 she played Scarlatti, Bach, Purcell and John Bull on the harpsichord, Giles Farnaby and Thomas Morel on the virginals and treble virginals, and Bach's Prelude and Fugue in B Flat Major on the clavichord. Lady Randolph Churchill wrote to tell her afterwards that she had brought Dame Nellie Melba to Violet's concert and that they had both been enchanted. "I am CRAZY about Mrs Woodhouse", Melba had written afterwards, underlining "crazy" five times. "I shall never forget the Bach and Scarlatti, too wonderful . . . I wish I knew her, she is too attractive in every way."

The house in Ovington Square, where Violet found time to continue her own musical afternoons and evenings uninterrupted, was as much as ever a magnet for the sensitive and the artistic. Many of the musicians who had fought in the war had returned lost and disillusioned, themselves changed and society turned upside-down. In Violet's company their confidence was restored, and new friendships were made. In December 1918 the Deliuses had written to some Paris-based American friends of theirs, the Clews, reporting that they saw Violet often, and that her milieu was charming. "Poets, musical people – *les jeunes y vont*. She is not young", wrote Jelka Delius to Marie Clews, "and not got up 'young'; but just dressed and to her finger tips in harmony with her delicate dainty instruments and her whole person." Ten days later, on Christmas Day, Delius wrote to Henry Clewses: "There is one really artistic salon – Mrs Woodhouse – a real artist – who plays the harpsichord most beautifully and plays us all the lovely English music of the 15th and 16th centuries – also Bach and Scarlatti."

One night Delius came to dinner with Violet and announced that he had brought with him a harpsichord piece written specially for her. Had his character been different, one might have thought he had composed it out of a sense of black humour, or perhaps from a desire to tease Violet, since she was such a tease herself. There is, however, no hint of anything but respect and affection in his dedication to "the great artist and dear friend Violet Gordon Woodhouse". Perhaps the least idiomatic composition ever written for the harpsichord, its antique flavour is almost drowned by the over-rich chromatic harmony. The chords, which require stretched hands and arpeggios, make no sense without a sustaining pedal – which the harpsichord does not possess – and the purple harmonies jangle each other out of recognition when plucked on the harpsichord as opposed to being struck on the piano. The piece sounds like the piano's revenge upon the harpsichord.

On another of his many visits Delius, by then nearly sixty, introduced Violet to his young acolyte Philip Heseltine, who as a mere schoolboy in 1910 had sought him out, long before Delius's stature as a composer had been recognized. Half sensitive soul, half devil, with a reddish beard, Heseltine had reached an extraordinary stage in his life. His reputation ruined through feuding with influential figures in the music establishment, such as the critics Ernest Newman and Edwin Evans (Heseltine had gone so far as to punch Evans in the Café Royal for criticizing Bartók), he offered his own compositions to a publisher under the pseudonym of "Peter Warlock", convinced that they would otherwise be turned down. He was, however, extremely talented, and hoped that Violet, or one of her rich friends, might back his new musical periodical, the *Sackbut*, which took its name from an early type of trombone.

When, in the spring of 1919, Warlock's songs were published and taken seriously by the reviewers (his true identity was not uncovered until November of that year), he began a process of rejecting his past self in order to create a different and rather frightening persona. Nevertheless, for all his wildness, Violet was impressed by his ability. By playing works by John Bull, William Tisdall and Thomas Morley to him, she had reignited his temporarily dormant interest in Elizabethan music, leading him to haunt the Library of the British Museum, where, from the original manuscripts, he transcribed and edited early English music. Obsessive and thorough, he made of his task a quest for a Holy Grail and, through a combination of scholarship and brilliant insight into the score, he was able to enter the Elizabethan spirit as few others have done. Violet followed his results closely, and would later include in her repertoire a number of his pieces which had been influenced by early English music.

Two months before the war ended Diaghilev had returned to London, after a four-year absence, to present several short ballets at the Coliseum Theatre. Although no longer accompanied by his two stars, Tamara Karsavina, who had been unable to get out of Russia in 1918, and Nijinsky, with whom he had quarrelled, Diaghilev and his troupe were greeted with elation, despite the demeaning circumstance of having to appear on the same programme as circus turns and music-hall acts. With Léonide Massine taking over as the new lead male dancer, the crowds had poured in to see Rimsky-Korsakov's *Sadko*, and Leon Bakst's designs in *The Good-Humoured Ladies* to music adapted by Vincenzo Tommasini from Scarlatti.

Violet did not think much of the pot-pourri of twenty Scarlatti sonatas orchestrated into *The Good-Humoured Ladies*, and when Diaghilev introduced a spinet on stage she was not surprised that the idea backfired, the instrument's slight sound being overwhelmed by the orchestra. Jelka Delius complained of the big, high, dingy theatre and was "not impressed" by the rustic Russian scene in *The Midnight Sun*, with its "rows of red suns with big faces and dark blue background", which was "only one number in a common smoking Music Hall programme". But Diaghilev could never disappoint Osbert and Sachie Sitwell or Lady Ottoline Morrell; starved of his audacious originality during the bleak war years, and little caring that his depleted resources had forced him into keeping such incongruous company, they had taken parties to the Coliseum on every night they could.

By the following year, Diaghilev had returned to his former heights of brilliance. Tamara Karsavina, having recently escaped from Russia by marrying an Englishman in the British Embassy in Petrograd (as St Petersburg had been renamed in 1914), had arrived in London thoroughly out of practice, but none the less prepared to take on the principal role in Diaghilev's new production, *Le Tricorne*. With its music by Manuel de Falla, choreography by Massine and designs by Picasso, the ballet was a sensation. Once again London became entranced by all things Spanish. Soon there were Spanish dancing schools, a wave of enthusiasm for Spanish literature, history, music and architecture, and an exodus of tourists to Spain to see the bullfights and the art of Madrid and Barcelona. To Diaghilev, Violet was, of course, partly Spanish; her sense of rhythm so excited him that he suggested making a ballet from her short composition (now lost) which she called "Queen Elizabeth's Pavan", to be played on four harpsichords[1]. But the dancers would not co-operate; they could not dance to such a fragile sound – remember, they said, how the spinet had been drowned out in *The Good-Humoured Ladies* the year before. Even Violet's new friend Tamara Karsavina, whom Diaghilev had brought to Ovington Square in the summer during the rehearsals for *Le Tricorne*, agreed that this was one of his ideas which could not be made to work.

1 Osbert Sitwell mentions in his essay on Violet that she "had at times composed, but these works, remarkable though several of them were, have vanished, and only one little song, written in 1894, is still in existence". Unfortunately, even this song is now lost.

That same summer of 1919, Diaghilev brought Picasso to Violet's house. The painter had become rich and famous through Cubism, but was now returning to a naturalistic style. Since his marriage to the socially ambitious ballet dancer Olga Khokhlova, Picasso had enjoyed being lionized. He had bought a dinner jacket in Lamb's Conduit Street, and had taken to attending parties wearing expensive suits from Savile Row and shirts from Jermyn Street. Bertha Stoop, who as a friend of Picasso and an authority on modern art had more or less invited herself, and who was coming to think of herself as responsible for ensuring the success of the occasion, was anxious on Violet's behalf. For several days before Picasso's arrival she implored Violet to remove from her walls some pictures which hung in the hallway through which he would have to pass. Violet had bought them for £6 each from the artist, an old gentleman called Wentworth Huysha, who had spent his life studying German mediaeval painting. The pictures, painted on wood in dark encrusted colours, portrayed sailing ships in full rig against flat seas covered with foam-tipped waves; or knights in armour, their horses plumed and canopied in stiff, rich material, while maidens knelt in obeisance, reaching to touch the cloth. They were, remarked Mrs Stoop, anything but avant-garde, and would give Picasso a very poor impression of Violet's taste.

Violet quite liked her Huyshas, although she had really only bought them to help the painter, but Mrs Stoop, warming to her task, gave it as her opinion that when he set eyes on them Picasso might well stalk out of the house in disgust – for all Khokhlova's social aspirations, he remained temperamental, uncompromising and artistically fierce. "Too bad," said Violet, stirred to her most obstinate. In the event, however, Picasso had eyes for nothing else: he went back continually to look at them and finally offered to buy them. Mrs. Stoop mumbled something about Huysha's sense of colour and design, but she had already gone too far. Indeed, her efforts to recover lost ground were probably misplaced, for Picasso was an inveterate teaser. The previous year, in Diaghilev's flat in Paris, he had been found peering at an eighteenth-century court painting which hung above the sofa: asked why he was examining it so carefully, he had replied, "I am studying it in order to learn how *not* to paint."

It was not only Picasso who had a volatile disposition, for Violet herself would have been equally capable, had she been offended, of ruining their meeting. Osbert Sitwell recorded that her moods

were swift, ardent and unpredictable. And there were moments,
I suspect, when she could have set fire to the world with her rage,
just as, at other times, I have seen her make it glow with gaiety and

affection, or make it blaze with great comfortable fires to warm those near her . . . [On occasion,] when her audience . . . confidently expected her to perform for an hour, she would on the contrary, and very probably because she happened to have taken a dislike to someone who had been brought into the room, sit down, give one short piece, and then jump up from her chair and shut the instrument, clavichord or harpsichord, very deliberately and with an air of utter finality (indeed, at these times her face would wear a look of such irredeemable obstinacy that it would take a hardy person, or one who did not know her, to ask her to continue).

In 1919 Violet introduced the clavichord into her public performances for the first time. Much as she believed that the instrument belonged to the chamber and the private music room, the hall at the Art Workers Guild in Queen Square, Bloomsbury, with its dark panelling, provided a comparatively intimate setting and was of a manageable size, having a capacity of about a hundred seats. Moreover, as a professional clavichordist under contract she had some obligation to promote both herself and the clavichord. Though she never became a true scholar in the academic sense, her knowledge of early music and the evolution of musical instruments was extensive. In January 1920 she combined a discreet puff of publicity with a display of her learning in an article for the first issue of *Music and Letters*, a new quarterly edited by Arthur Fox Strangways,[2] in which she discussed early keyboard instruments, including the virginals, the harpsichord, the spinet and the clavichord, with particular reference to the clavichord's role in composition. The article was accompanied by a reproduction of the piece Delius had written for Violet and a photograph, archly described as "inserted at the editor's special request", of Violet playing her eighteenth-century harpsichord, wearing a hatched and flowered black silk gown with wide lace cuffs and lace décolletage.

The clavichord made a remarkable impact when Violet played it in public. After a performance at the hall of the Art Workers Guild, on 17 March 1920 the music critic of the *Observer* wrote:

After the harpsichord came the clavichord – the still small voice of music, with a tone so tiny that the rustling of a lady's skirt or the creaking of a chair might ruin our pleasure in a prelude or fugue of Bach. We had no such distracting noise; everybody present was spellbound by the silvery beauty of the tone, and the really dramatic

2 Strangways, a schoolmaster and music critic, founded and ran the magazine at his own risk to give musicians, rather than critics, the opportunity to discuss their art at length.

power of the playing, and the F minor Prelude and Fugue from Book II of the "48" [i.e. Bach's *The Well-Tempered Klavier*, two sets of twenty-four preludes and twenty-four fugues] made an effect which is assuredly only possible on the instrument for which its creator intended it.

The first ever recordings of the harpsichord, issued by the Gramophone Company under its trademark "His Master's Voice", are of Violet performing in July 1920. For several years after its invention in the late 1880s the gramophone had been considered little more than a toy, and even after such well-known singers as Caruso and Melba had agreed to make recordings, it was some time before instrumentalists came to realize its potential. Initially it was the practice of the recording companies to truncate chamber music and movements from orchestral works drastically, but by 1920 full-length recordings were the norm, and Violet signed a three-year contract with the Gramophone Company for £400 a year to record pieces by Bach, Scarlatti and Couperin, together with some early English folk dances. (Since one of the terms of her contract was that she agreed to be an active propagandist for recorded sound, she later wrote an article for the second issue of the *Gramophone* magazine, which had been founded in 1923 by Compton Mackenzie, extolling the educational possibilities of the invention.) Although there is a great deal of surface noise in these recordings,[3] they give a good idea of the sheer vitality of her playing.

With her recording contract, the money Gordon had settled on her at the time of their marriage, and her fees from professional concerts, Violet's income was now well over £1,000 a year (equivalent to about £30,000 today), enabling her to pay for her own staff and to make a considerable contribution towards the costs of her clothes. For their part, the Gramophone Company launched her in style on her career as a recording artist in September 1920, hiring a reception room in the Piccadilly Hotel, where an invited audience of distinguished musicians and critics listened to a selection of her records. Violet introduced the programme – "very little of the delicate beauty of tone of the old-world instrument has been lost in these reproductions," she said, "neither has it been sentimentalized as so often happens to the human voice when recorded."

The occasion produced extravagant reviews, not only in praise of the technical achievement but also hailing Violet as the greatest living exponent of the harpsichord. The *Daily Telegraph* led the chorus:

3  Reissued by Pavilion Records Ltd on compact disc GEMM CD 9242 in October 1996.

## HARPSICHORD RECORDS. A NEW DEPARTURE.

*September 18 1920.*

That was truly a revelation which took place the other afternoon in a salon of the Piccadilly Hotel. Never more completely nor more triumphantly has Science played the role of handmaid to Art than on this occasion when a company of musicians and critics were invited to hear a number of records lately made by The Gramophone Company of music played on the harpsichord by that distinguished artist, Mrs Violet Gordon Woodhouse; the actual artist of the afternoon was "His Master's Voice", and surely it would be impossible to find an artist more loyal, more faithful, more efficient, or more at ease! Those who have heard Mrs Woodhouse in the flesh have heard one who is well-nigh incomparable as an exponent of old keyboard music; and those who were privileged to hear these reproductions of her playing are unlikely to forget the occasion easily. The programme chosen was one to delight the connoisseur. The famous Fitzwilliam Virginal Book was drawn upon for the first "item" – the seventeenth century "Nobody's Gigge" – and immediately one was in another world, and the clock had been set back three centuries. It was hard to believe that old Farnaby's music [Giles Farnaby, *c.* 1560–1640], so precise, so accurate, so charming, was really issuing from that elegant and rather austere box – mechanically. Following this came three English folk-dances: the undying "Newcastle", the sweet "Heddon of Fawsley" , the vigorous "Step Back". The rhythm of each – all praise to the "original player" – was a pure joy, and the obvious thing to do was to shut one's eyes and enjoy this intriguing illusion. Most of us did. Thereafter we had two Scarlatti sonatas, the familiar but ever lovely "L'Arlequine" of Couperin and "Tambourin" of Rameau, a Gavotte of Purcell, and a Prelude and two Fugues of Bach. The really striking and wonderful thing about this latest achievement of science is not the perfection with which the mere dynamics of the music are reproduced – we have been accustomed to excellence in this direction for a long time now; it is the fidelity to the tone-quality of the original instrument – in this case Mrs Woodhouse's own – to its very physical (one might almost say, spiritual) character. What all this postulates by way of education alone – apart altogether from its sheer aesthetic pleasure – is incalculable. As a scientific consummation it is more than a simple triumph. It is uncanny.

\* \* \*

Like many of her friends, Violet had found her religious beliefs shaken by the war. Brought up in the Church of England, she had never questioned the existence of an afterlife, but had found her Christian faith to be of little comfort over the loss of Max. The war's huge casualties had made alternative religions and various forms of spiritualism very popular and, as she tried to make sense of her aching sadness, Violet began to wonder if it were possible for the dead to communicate with the living. "If only we could know more about the other Side," she wrote to Roland. "I am reading William James's [psychiatrist and writer, brother of the novelist Henry James] letters just now, and although such a great scientist, he seems so much to have the feelings of a continuance and a future life that I feel comforted."

Spiritualism, given respectability after the publication of a book written during the Great War by the distinguished physicist and scientist Sir Oliver Lodge, led many of Violet's friends and acquaintances to participate in seances. Radclyffe Hall had started visiting a medium immediately after Mabel Batten's death from a stroke; Philip Heseltine dabbled in the occult and had read widely on telepathic experiments; Pamela Glenconner spent many hours at the planchette table. Violet sought the company of anyone who might be able to "enlighten" her further about the supernatural, including Bertrand Russell's erstwhile mistress, the Bloomsburyite Lady Ottoline Morrell, whom Violet visited in September 1920 at Garsington Manor, her large house near Oxford. There, in the words of Lady Ottoline's biographer Miranda Seymour, "homely evenings of backgammon, poker and chat were replaced by the feverish shuffling of the tarot pack". Evidently Violet found something of what she was seeking, for she visited Garsington almost exactly a year later.

Soon, however, she was faced with more mundane events, for in the winter of 1920 the post-war economic bubble burst, with devastating effects on the property-owning classes. Under Lloyd George's Liberal/ Conservative coalition government there had been a brief boom, due to pent-up demand for goods after the austerity of the war years. There were, however, fundamental weaknesses in the country's economy. The United States and Germany had in many ways overtaken Britain industrially; the public debt had risen sharply to finance military expenditure; inflation was high; and exports were too dependent on the supply of finished goods to the Empire, at a time when those markets were themselves weak because of collapsed raw material prices. Recession quickly turned into depression, accompanied by renewed trade union unrest.

The Barringtons were even worse affected than Gordon. The combination of increased tax rates, high wages and outdated estate management (Bill bitterly reproached his father with neglecting everything except his own pigeon shooting) had eaten into Lady Barrington's spending money, and she began to press Lord Barrington to sell Beckett to pay off their debts. But the estate was complex. Lord Barrington had only a life interest, and the permission of Bill and the trustees was needed if the estate were to be sold. The value of farmland and large houses had fallen sharply in the slump, so that the timing of the crisis could scarcely have been more awkward. In any event, Bill was not inclined to give his consent.

Bill consulted Rupert, who, as a barrister in the Inner Temple, advised setting up a scheme which would protect the Beckett estate from a new round of death duties when Lord Barrington died, while at the same time reducing the annual tax bill. The scheme would, however, entail Lord Barrington handing over Beckett immediately to Bill and living off an annuity, for which he would have to rely on the generosity and good faith of Bill and the trustees. Bill's father, by this time set in his ways and completely under the thumb of Lady Barrington, refused even to allow his solicitors to attend a conference to discuss Rupert's proposals. He counter-proposed the raiding of the Beckett estate's replanting account to meet his immediate overdraft, and the sale of one of the family's most prized heirlooms, the Diamond Bees (a pair of brooches, each consisting of two large diamonds for the body and a smaller diamond for the head, with gold legs and ruby eyes), to contribute to his unpaid and overdue tax bill. From that point onwards Bill's relations with his father went steadily downhill, deteriorating from affectionate concern to frustration, mutual incomprehension and, finally, anger – all of it recorded in surviving correspondence.

Bill's temper was not improved by his own financial situation, for he too was in debt. Uncertain how best to raise money, he asked his solicitor whether he could use the Armscote livestock as collateral for a loan. The solicitor very sensibly told him to do no such thing – it would ruin Bill's credit and impede his management of the farm. Thus the problems remained unsolved, to cast a pall over Bill's mood throughout the second half of 1921. He contrived to borrow against his own life insurance policy, while his father stumbled on, propped up partly by Lady Barrington liquidating some of the shares in her portfolio (a gesture of which she made very heavy weather), and partly by the sale of whatever could not be proved to be part of the settled estate. Eventually, however, Bill had no choice but to agree to the disposal of Beckett to avert his father's bankruptcy. The property was put up for sale, withdrawn from the market, and then put up for sale again several times between 1922 and 1927. Like Denis, Bill was at heart an old-fashioned landowner and while Violet breathed a silent sigh of relief at this turn of events – how on earth could she have coped if Bill had taken over the running of Beckett? – for Bill the ruin of his father and the impending loss of his birthright was symbolic of the sad ending of an era.

Artistically, Violet carried on to new heights. There was something indefinable about her post-war playing which reached beyond the appreciation of the musically knowledgeable. The Bloomsbury painter and art critic Roger Fry, who owned a Dolmetsch clavichord, wrote Violet an admiring letter after attending the second day of a series of concerts in London celebrating the Bach Festival in 1922. He was painting her portrait at the time, a slight oil sketch of her playing a harpsichord, for which she had, at most, two sittings. The chief interest of his letter lies in his conviction, as a civilized and highly cultured layman, that by comparison with Violet any other performer must seem shallow:

7 Dalmeny Avenue London N7
*February 24th 1922*
Dear Mrs. Woodhouse,
I was at the Aeolian Hall last night and I must tell you of the extraordinary effect of your playing. I thought I knew what you could do and that was wonderful enough but last night I thought you were beyond everything. You seemed to follow Bach into more remote depths of feeling than one had guessed even in him. Delightful as the rest of the concert was I felt with the others that I was only getting at Bach through a veil but you seemed to become his idea absolutely. I want to thank you for a great experience of the most intense and purest delight, and to say that I must hear the A minor Fugue once more some day.

I want to tell you what an immense impression you created in the audience. I talked to many afterwards, much more musical people than I am, and some who had never heard you were quite overcome and all agreed that you MUST be made to play more in public. Surely you could give a series of Harpsichord concerts in the Aeolian Hall. I'm confident they would be a great success. When are you coming to see my pictures and when shall we go on with the portrait? Do come some afternoon next week . . . Your very sincere admirer Roger Fry.

P.S. It's great presumption of me who really am not musical to write like this but I am sure I know when things are absolutely first rate.

The Hungarian composer Béla Bartók, who was just beginning to gain recognition in Europe, but who was less well known in London, made his first post-war visit to Britain at the beginning of 1922, interrupting his tour to spend two nights with Philip Heseltine at his house in Wales. Having made a pilgrimage to see Bartók in Budapest the previous year, Heseltine was convinced that he was "one of the half-dozen finest creative intelligences in the musical world today". His compositions owed much to years of painstaking research and to the rising European interest in national traditions. In parallel with Vaughan Williams, Cecil Sharp, and others, but quite independent of their influence, Bartók and his collaborator, Zoltán Kodály, had travelled for ten years among Romanian and Hungarian country people collecting folk song, until the war put an end to their expeditions. Rebelling against the predominantly German influence upon music in Hungary, Bartók used elements of folk music in his piano compositions to create an original idiom of his own.

Heseltine convinced Bartók that Violet had a unique gift for seeing into vernacular and folk music, evident in her interpretations of Spanish composers like Albéniz and Arbós, of early English music, and of Vaughan Williams. She would be able, said Heseltine, to play Bartók's strange scales and harmonies and peasant dance rhythms in a way which would cast new light on them, even for the composer himself. He wrote to Violet, urging her to play Bartók's pieces on the clavichord for him, adding "he is very anxious to have an opportunity of hearing you play English folk music on the harpsichord before he leaves England." Taking Heseltine at his word, Violet contacted Bartók in Elm Park Gardens in London and invited him to her afternoon concert of seventeenth- and eighteenth-century music at the Aeolian Hall on 21 March, promising to play privately to him afterwards at Ovington Square.

The following year, 1923, was the tercentenary of the death of the sixteenth-century English composer William Byrd. Violet was invited to make a special commemorative recording for His Master's Voice, and that July a twenty-strong committee, which included Vaughan Williams, put on performances of Byrd's music all over London. Violet's slot was at the Aeolian Hall, where she performed with the English Singers and a string sextet from the Royal College of Music. In the same summer she gave a concert at Eton in which she played Bach's Partita in B Flat, items from the Anna Magdalena Notebook (a small collection of keyboard music by Bach, put together for his second wife), a Mozart sonata, pieces by Couperin, Domenico Scarlatti and Purcell, and, as a finale, some anonymous folk dances. The sound of the harpsichord was a novelty not only to the boys but also to one of their masters, John Christie, who would later found the Glyndebourne Opera Festival.

One of the boys who dined with Violet after the concert was Vere Pilkington (subsequently a Chairman of Sotheby's), who had been transfixed by her playing. His enthusiasm so charmed Violet that she invited him to join her, Kit Ayling, and Agustín Rubio at a concert in London before he went up to Oxford. Arriving early to hear Violet play some Mozart before leaving for the concert, Kit found Rubio sitting beside her in rapt contemplation, his stick on the floor. By this time crippled with arthritis, he walked with difficulty, but constantly visited Violet in Ovington Square, "living through her with his beloved Masters whose works, because of his infirmity, he could no longer play". In the taxi on the way back after the concert, Vere Pilkington made some puerile remarks to the effect that "Beethoven was right out of date and terribly dull", whereupon Rubio beat the floor of the taxi with his umbrella and blasted him with a picturesque and scathing tirade, to the point that Kit started to feel sorry for him. Vere left, deflated and stunned, while Rubio rumbled on for some time, despite Violet's efforts to soothe him. She kept on saying "Rubio, I was so afraid you were going to hit him with your umbrella!"

Recognizing in Vere a talent which would enable him to develop into one of the best amateur musicians of his day, Violet tolerated his youthful conceit. When his father gave Vere a harpsichord as a present for his twenty-first birthday, she encouraged him to extend his range to the clavichord and the virginals. He was in fact one of only two followers of Violet who could be described as a pupil, the other being the Australian harpsichordist, Valda Aveling. After Violet's death he wrote to Gordon:

> For nearly thirty years I was under her wonderful spell, & she was the inspiration of all my music-making. I am quite sure that she was the greatest instrumentalist of my generation; & probably the greatest clavichord player there has ever been . . . it is a tragedy that her records were made so long ago that they are only the palest reflection of that great genius.

Although her recording contract and her professional performances permitted Violet to make an increased contribution to the household expenses, the finances of both Gordon and Bill continued to decline, until eventually they were forced to take the decision to give up Ovington Square. Left without a base for entertaining or practising in London they turned to Denis, who made his house in Moore Street available. A typical early-Victorian house, with two small rooms on each floor and a tiny garden, No.

40 was not large enough to accommodate them all simultaneously, so when Violet was in town Gordon and Bill were obliged either to stay at the Travellers' Club, or to remain at Armscote.

The windows of the main room in Denis's house faced the afternoon sun from lunchtime until dusk, and Violet, who was engaged for several concerts in private houses, found the hot summer of 1923 uncomfortably stifling. She had recently performed in one of the six vast reception rooms of Philip Sassoon's house in Park Lane, with its new sepia and gold frescoes by the French artist Jose-Maria Sert, depicting elephants and howdahs, rajas and pavilions, melons and bulrushes. There she played Mozart's Piano Concerto in A Major, with Anthony Bernard conducting the London Chamber Orchestra. As the Season drew to its close, she wrote to Roland at Folkington:

> July 8th 1923 . . . I have been working very hard. Lady Howard de Walden's party on the 12th is I think the last musical engagement for me this season . . . The heat here yesterday was something terrible, & it seems funny to hope the sun will not shine much, but really we do feel like that, especially in this small house.

Thomas and Margot Howard de Walden's parties were famous for their music, their style, and the food served at them. Seaford House, their London home in Belgrave Square (now the Royal College of Defence Studies) was spectacular. As a young man in 1902, Thomas had bought an onyx mine in South America and shipped its entire stockpile of stone back to London on the Howard de Walden shipping line, to create at Seaford House an onyx hall, with a marble and onyx inlay floor and a double staircase with Ionic pillars in onyx. The house had been commandeered by the Government during the war, and when it was handed back he had modernized it and restored it to its former glory. The chef was a byword, his creations supplemented on party nights by crates of farm produce and hothouse fruits brought to London by train from the family's estate in Wales, Chirk Castle.

For Margot's musical events, fifty or more guests would assemble in the high-domed interior hall, from which they climbed the staircase to a circular gallery, off which led the reception rooms. She was a warm and generous person, "an unaggressive tonic", according to the socialite writer and diarist Lady Cynthia Asquith – "like a delicious soap, she really braces one". She was also good enough an amateur singer to sing from time to time in the concerts which she arranged. Drawn by Margot's personality and the glamour of the surroundings, many of the greatest figures in the musical world came to the Howard de Waldens' house: Karsavina danced there;

Stravinsky came to hear his music conducted by Anthony Bernard; Thomas Beecham brought part of his orchestra; and on 12 July 1923 Violet came to play the harpsichord.

Guests packed Seaford House that evening, and with no change in the weather the heat was oppressive. Violet played on a small stage at the end of the white-and-gold ballroom to an audience seated on neatly lined rows of gilt chairs, the large windows thrown wide open and the pink taffeta curtains drawn back to let air into the room. Supper afterwards was in the mahogany-panelled dining-room, which had a wooden ceiling painted with flowers. As the guests wilted and the ice cream melted, Margot joked, somewhat impenetrably, that by incorporating into the programme a piece for the flautist Louis Fleury, as well as the Ravel Septet, which contained a part for a harp, she had made an "exquisitely cool concert". At times like these, Violet became nostalgic for the days when she and Gordon had maintained their own luxurious house in London, and she had not been obliged to cram her diary with summer engagements. She kept up her morale, however, by reflecting that there were grounds for expecting a substantial revival of their fortunes in the not too distant future. Old Mrs Woodhouse, now in her nineties, was very frail; she was unlikely to live much longer, and Gordon was her only son.

# XII

## *How Can You Live in a House Like This?*

GORDON'S MOTHER DIED in the late summer of 1923. She had reached the age of ninety-three, still living with her two plain daughters, Ella and May, in Burghill Court, Gordon's childhood home in Herefordshire. Serious-minded, narrow in her views, charitable and selfless, Mrs Woodhouse belonged to a world utterly different from that in which Violet moved. It was now twenty-two years since she had resolved to cut Gordon out of her will, on learning about Bill from Dorothy, and having seen at first hand how Violet treated her son. Nothing in the intervening period had served to make Mrs Woodhouse relent. Indeed, as time went by she had been, if anything, increasingly hurt by her son's neglect; she was perplexed and disappointed that he had had no children, little suspecting Gordon's own part in that; and as she learned of his financial difficulties and Violet's bizarre household, which he apparently maintained almost single-handed, she had come to disapprove more and more of his way of life. Mrs Woodhouse attributed all Gordon's failings to his subservience to the profligate Violet, who had turned out to be the very opposite of the daughter-in-law for whom she had once so ardently hoped.

When the will was read, it transpired that Mrs Woodhouse had bequeathed the bulk of her fortune to Ella and May, leaving Gordon only £1,000. Burghill Court itself, however, was entailed, and so reverted to him automatically on her death. A few days after the funeral Gordon took Violet to stay there, and for a short time she was in two minds as to whether or not to persuade Gordon to take on the place. Judging by a letter to her youngest brother, it did not occur to her to consider the feelings of Gordon's sisters, who had lived at Burghill all their lives.

Burghill Court, Hereford.
*Sunday August 12, 1923.*
Dearest Roland,
I want you to come and visit us here. I am sure you would like it, &

really I can't make up my mind if I should not like for us to live here, & in any case you must come up & see it as if we make up our minds to sell it, there may never be another chance: We shall probably be here for the rest of this month . . . This house is such fun in a Victorian way & very comfortable. We can put up Williams [Roland's chauffeur], & if Dorothy likes to come & her maid – do try and persuade her . . . The bedrooms are lovely, big and comfortable, only baths in the rooms, but I personally don't mind this. There are lots of servants, & I believe she would like it. Anyhow my dear you must come & soon please.

Much love from Violet.

I want your advice, for I cannot make up my mind if we might live here.

When Violet eventually decided that Burghill Court was not for her, the two sisters, determined to keep the estate as their mother would have wished and having a sense of responsibility towards the servants, felt obliged to buy the house back from Gordon. With this additional capital Gordon's financial troubles were temporarily much alleviated. Nevertheless, for Violet and her *ménage*, it was time for a council of war.

The very fact that Violet and Gordon had even contemplated a move to Herefordshire was an indication that Armscote's days were numbered. Quite apart from anything else, it had too many sad memories. The house would always remind Violet of the war and of Max, who had loved it more than any of the others. It was here, too, that she had been living at the time when she had believed that Denis was dead, and when her relationship with Bill was under strain. Perhaps a change would bring back their past happiness. Bill, too, was ready to give up Armscote and move to a new house. He could hardly make ends meet with the farm, and wanted more land, as well as a more challenging garden. Gordon could just about afford either a house in London big enough for Violet's entertaining, or a grander and less ramshackle country house than Armscote, but not both. He was content to fall in with whatever Violet and Bill decided; if it were up to him, though, he would opt for the country every time. Violet quickly came to a decision and went into action. Within two months Armscote had been sold, and Violet had found and bought a house, of considerable charm and beauty and with a proper farm and a large garden, some thirty-five miles away. She wrote excitedly to Roland:

Dearest Roland,
*19th October, 1923.*
. . . We have bought a house!! Quite beautiful on a tiny scale: The

sort of house that Sybil[1] would go mad about: It is 700 ft up on top
of the Cotswolds near Stroud, William and Mary, panelled! . . . It is
called Nether Lypiatt Manor . . .

This was their final destination – Violet, Bill, Gordon and Denis were to
make Nether Lypiatt their home from 1923 until the ends of their lives. A
house of rare beauty built in 1701 by Charles Coxe, a Chief Justice of the
Great Session, on the site of a fourteenth-century manor house, it looks
from the north-facing front like a French château perched on top of a
Gloucestershire hill. Its classical proportions and elegant finish come as a
surprise after the rough stonework and rather jumbled aspect of the gabled
sixteenth-century Cotswold houses in the neighbourhood. The front courtyard is enclosed by railings in which are set delicate iron gates. From the side,
or from across the valley, the house has a lonely and menacing appearance, the
more disconcerting for its being isolated, far from the nearest village. Its four
storeys brood over the countryside below, higher and darker than the front
façade would lead one to expect. On the east side, low barn-like outhouses of
Cotswold stone lead to the farm, on the west is a two-acre walled garden. The
back of the house looks down upon precipitous beech woods, thick with blue-
bells in the spring, where wild garlic grows in abundance. At the foot of the
valley Violet could pick out the overgrown route of part of the thirty-mile-
long canal, first conceived in Charles II's reign and built in the eighteenth
century, which had once formed a link between the Severn and the Thames.
A hundred yards from the house she discovered what she was sure was the
site of the original manor, and when visitors came she would trip round
showing them the outlines of the kitchens and living rooms.

Where the garden ends, a path plunges down another part of the woody
escarpment to a twenty-foot high grey stone obelisk, which bears on its base
the inscription:

> My name is Wag, that rolled the green
> The oldest horse that ever was seen
> My years they numbered forty two
> I served my master just and true.

This monument – erected to the memory of Judge Coxe's horse –
symbolized for the locals one of the more benign of the many ghostly
presences which inhabited Nether Lypiatt. Long after his death, Wag was
said to gallop around the estate at night. Legend also has it that he used to
walk unattended to the neighbouring town of Stroud, carrying panniers and

1 Sybil Assheton-Smith, an attractive woman who was keen on Roland. Violet hoped in
vain to get Roland to take more interest in her.

a shopping list, and calling on the tradesmen, who would fill his baskets with his orders. He was said, as well, to be charged with rolling the lawn, which he would do without human assistance, neatly turning as he reached the edge to pull the roller back along the next track of grass.

A more sinister tale concerned the local blacksmith, who had been commissioned by Judge Coxe to forge the iron gates for the courtyard. The work was interrupted when the blacksmith was arrested, tried and convicted of sheep-stealing. The presiding judge was Coxe himself, who passed sentence of death, but postponed execution until the gates were finished. The blacksmith spun out the time by making the ironwork as intricate as possible; then in revenge, he cursed the house, incorporating a deliberate mistake of symmetry into the design of the gates, subtle enough not to be easily noticeable, but still visible to anyone who compares carefully the upper right corner with the upper left. Many local people continue to believe the house to be cursed; and in the three centuries of its history, it has never yet passed from father to son. To Violet, although she was proud of the legend of Wag, malign ghosts were a forbidden subject (she claimed this ban was so as not to frighten off the servants, but in reality it was due to her own superstitiousness), and it angered her if anyone spoke of them in her hearing. It was a bad start to a weekend if, as often happened, visitors who stopped to ask the way of one of the local inhabitants found themselves directed to the "Haunted House".

Violet adored Nether Lypiatt. Before the war, the house had been occupied by a farmer, in whose hands it had suffered grave neglect. The iron gates had been removed, but fortunately were found stacked in the barn. The main staircase was in pieces, and most of the extensive panelling broken when Corbet Woodall, the immediate predecessor of Violet and Gordon, acquired the house in 1914 and brought in the architect Peter Morley Horder to repair and modernize it. Horder's restoration was much admired by Violet for its sensitivity, and she was more than happy to leave his work untouched. Before she died, she was twice to furnish and decorate the house from top to bottom. Initially, however, from 1923 to 1926, Nether Lypiatt had an empty feel. There was not enough furniture from Armscote to fill the house and, despite Gordon's inheritance, she could not afford to complete all the rooms in the way she wished, or to maintain more than a handful of servants.

The focal point of Nether Lypiatt was its burnished wood staircase, which rose uncarpeted all the way to the attic, where Lily had her quarters with the two Pekinese dogs, keeping them tucked away until Violet wished to see them, like children in the nursery wing of some great house. On the ground floor, the hall was panelled in chestnut and the sitting-room wainscoting was mellow beech. The most beautiful room was the drawing-room which, facing south-east, and stretching the length of the house, was illuminated by light pouring in through its four large windows. Spacious bedrooms took up the first floor. Violet and Bill chose the two south-facing rooms, connected by an interlocking bathroom. Gordon was on the other side of the landing. Crystal Richards, the daughter of the farm bailiff, was taken on to do housework at Nether Lypiatt one summer holiday when she was fourteen, and was sent to dust and sweep the bedroom of "Madam". Puzzled by the lay-out, she returned to the servants' hall and asked why Major Barrington's room was where Mr Woodhouse's should have been. The servants replied with knowing laughter, and it was not until she went home for lunch that she received a vague and embarrassed explanation from her mother.

Bill was a capable farmer, and it had been Armscote's intrinsically uneconomic size, rather than his own inefficiency, which had made farming so unprofitable there. He had started to take an interest in cattle breeding, and saw encouraging potential at Nether Lypiatt both for arable farming and for rearing a pedigree herd of cows. But it was, of course, the garden which was the real outlet for his energy. He had served his apprenticeship at Southover, and his artistry had matured at Armscote. Lypiatt's more dramatic setting was precisely the framework he needed for what was to become his masterpiece, and the creation of the garden there became a life's work, described by Isabel Armitage, a neighbour who watched its evolution over twenty years, as a "never-ending weaving of a tapestry in nature".

Shortly before Gordon bought Nether Lypiatt, Corbet Woodall had planted a lime avenue in the walled garden. This tightly knit line of trees, which cast a deep shade through which mere speckles of light penetrate even on the sunniest of days, met at its end a huge sycamore, which stood like an altar at the end of a cathedral nave. As Bill continued Woodall's work, planting up the western side of the house, he took up the ideas he had discussed with Lawrence Johnston at Armscote and divided the area into four compartments with a medlar or mulberry tree in the centre of each. Yew seedlings from Hidcote were laid out in parallel lines thirty-three yards long, eventually growing into cliff-like hedges; beneath these, linked by grass paths, Bill planted wide overflowing herbaceous borders; close by he made a tapestry hedge by mixing box, ash, yew, beech, holly and hornbeam, which divided the flower garden from the kitchen garden.

At Hidcote Lawrence Johnston now had a companion in Norah Lindsay, whose creative gardening imagination was second only to that of Gertrude Jekyll, with whom she had worked. Norah had left her husband Harry, who, according to her great-nephew John Julius Norwich, was "not very nice", one of his not so innocent pastimes being the photographing of young girls in the bath. In 1895 Norah had started her famous garden at the Old Manor at Sutton Courtenay in Oxfordshire. Today the garden has gone: Norah kept no notes or sketches of it, and the only surviving record of its beauties is a descriptive article which she contributed to *Country Life*. When Norah had become short of money, Nancy Lancaster had suggested that she should set up professionally, beginning by laying out Nancy's large garden at Kelmarsh Hall in Northamptonshire. This Norah did, and for the next fifty years she devoted herself to her own and her friends' gardens.[2] Bill was not, of course, a client, but he spent hours exchanging ideas with her and with Lawrence Johnston, despite the distance from Hidcote to Stroud. Much influenced by Norah's way of letting flowers overflow and spill into each other up walls, into water and round trees and shrubs, until they eventually drifted off into wilderness, Bill achieved a similar effect in his own huge herbaceous borders.

Norah had an eccentric dress sense, and according to her niece Diana Duff Cooper, often wore tinsel and leopardskin with baroque pearls and emeralds. Witty and entertaining, she had been an immensely popular hostess at Sutton Courtenay and was readily incorporated by Violet into life at Nether Lypiatt. She was musical, and played the piano; Gordon was glad to see that she also took a keen interest in food, and added several of her menus to his recipe book; and, like Bill, she combined her love of gardening with a talent for drawing and painting.

Another source of inspiration to Bill in creating the garden at Nether Lypiatt was Harley Butt, who had returned to his native Gloucestershire with his wife and two children in 1920, three years before Violet's arrival. At Hyde, immediately above the village of Chalford, close to Nether Lypiatt, Butt had bought a house and seven acres of steep, tumbling hillside. Here, not more than a mile from where his family had lived in the sixteenth century, he was creating a garden and an arboretum, a silent refuge from his terrible memories of the war, in which he had served as a private soldier. Placed geographically in the heart of the rural region made its own by the Arts and Crafts movement, Butt's arboretum carried the marks of the movement's philosophy both in the simplicity of its design and in its conscious connection between personal fulfilment and manual labour. With his own hands, refusing help even from his two daughters, he made a path, incorporating wooden bridges and low stone walls, which skirted water

2 For example, Godmersham Park for the Trittons, Cliveden for the Astors, and Port Lympne and Trent Park for Philip Sassoon.

gardens and descended beside streams and waterfalls from the higher lime-stone outcrops through carpets of wild violets and anemones into the rich loam of the Chalford valley below. On either side of the path stood trees – Persian ironwood, Japanese maple, magnolia, weeping spruce, mulberry, wingnut, hornbeam, bamboo, American red cedar and scarlet chestnut – all identified in tall, narrow lettering cut into lead labels attached to steel rods spiked into the ground. The centre of the woodland was marked by a wild service tree, which bore bitter pear-shaped fruit.

Harley Butt and Bill liked each other from the moment they met. Bill's garden diary shows Butt's influence on his plans for adding trees to the wood below the house – there are numerous notes such as "seen at Butt's – corylus colurna [nut tree], taxus fructa luteo [yellow fruited yew]. Have ordered." Later, when Bill was planning a blue border at the west end of the garden, his diary refers to elegant shrubs from Butt's garden like the Himalayan perovskia, with its prominent spikes of lavender-blue flowers and contrasting silver-white foliage. Butt, who could not drive a car, often walked the two miles down to Chalford and up the equally steep hill to Nether Lypiatt on the other side of the valley, and his young daughter, Rachel, would sometimes accompany him. Even as a small child she was acute enough to notice that her father never spoke of the war, and to see how Bill loved to escape the rarefied atmosphere indoors to discuss gardening with him.

In retrospect Bill Barrington and Harley Butt can be seen as two of the foremost gardeners of their day. Little of Bill's work remains, since most of his planting was uprooted when the house was sold out of the family in 1958, but photographs in *Country Life,* and others taken by the gardening writer Peter Coats testify to how glorious the Lypiatt garden once was. Harley Butt's arboretum still – barely – survives. It is both thrilling and sad to visit this secret sanctuary today. Wild and overgrown, its seven acres contain half-hidden paths weaving through undergrowth, thicket and bramble, between the enormous fully grown trees which rise up and spread out in golds, reds, yellows and greens, only a few hundred yards from the main road between Stroud and Cirencester.

Having passed her last years in a state of semi-consciousness, Violet's mother died in 1923, the same year as Gordon's mother. Yet again James Gwynne's contorted will came into play. May had been left a life interest in Folkington and in James's money, but not in the rest of his real estate, which constituted the bulk of his fortune. The properties were due to follow their preordained and complex path of succession, but the money was to be disposed of by May "in accordance with James's wishes". Nevile hoped, unrealistically, that the wrong he had suffered at James's hands would now be righted, but Rupert and Roland would have none of it. The key provision in the will, so far as they were concerned, was that James had wished his estate to pass in trust first to Rupert, then to Rupert's as yet unborn male heir, then, if Rupert died without having fathered a son, to Roland, then to Roland's male heir, who – since it was now quite clear that Roland was homosexual – would never be born, then to the sisters in order of seniority. Subject to any arrangement which Rupert and Roland might make between them, that was that.

Rupert, the family expert on law and tax, proposed that he himself should stay at Wootton, and Roland at Folkington, but that otherwise each potential inheritor should renounce his or her contingent claim in return for a sum of money. To be effective, the scheme required that all the parties should agree. Violet, who needed the cash, signed up, as did Roland and Eva, but Dorothy changed her mind when, after Roland forced her to leave the main house at Folkington, Rupert refused to allow her to charge to the estate the cost of repairs to her farmhouse in the grounds. In 1924, before the row with Dorothy was settled, Rupert died and everything therefore passed to Roland. Thus it was that, in the end, Violet received virtually nothing from either of her parents.

Unable yet to do without her professional earnings, Violet continued her career in London, mixing public concerts with private appearances and making several broadcasts for the BBC.[3] In his memoirs, *Early Stages*, Sir John Gielgud describes how he and his leading lady, Gwen Ffrangcon-Davies, were summoned to smart parties throughout their 1924 London run in *Romeo and Juliet*. Of one occasion, at Mrs Bertha Stoop's house at Wandlebrook, he writes: "A rich lady who lived a little way out of London invited us to play the balcony scene on her lawn one Sunday night . . . Mrs Gordon Woodhouse, dressed in purple scarves and a turban, was playing Bach and Mozart on the harpsichord when we arrived, and the drawing room was crammed to suffocation . . ."

In London, the musical high point of 1924 was to be a concert on 18 November at the Aeolian Hall, in which Violet and Pablo Casals were to play together for the first time in public, in a programme devoted to Bach. Casals, by now generally acknowledged as the world's greatest cellist, was at the height of his fame in England, having performed regularly over the last four years with all the major British orchestras. As a young boy, he had discovered in a shop a battered Grützmacher edition of Bach's six suites for

3 Appendix 3 contains a list of known broadcasts.

unaccompanied cello, before he had ever heard them performed. It had been the crucial discovery of his life. As he worked through them, he realized that he had found the music that was closest to his soul, and during the next twelve years he practised them every day in seclusion. He started playing the suites in public at the turn of the century, but even after they had become his hallmark he never approached them without reverence, humility – even fear. "Bach is the supreme genius of music," he wrote. "This man, who knows everything and feels everything, cannot write one note, however unimportant it may appear, which is anything but transcendent. He has reached the heart of every noble thought, and has done it in the most perfect way."

Casals had never before given a concert with the harpsichord, and when he wrote to Violet on 14 August he professed some diffidence about his lack of practice, and asked her to include one of the Bach suites in the programme. He was honoured, he said, to be playing with her, but:

> ... the reason I have not replied sooner (for which I apologise) is that I could not make up my mind about which suite for cello to choose – especially whilst on holiday, during which time I have neglected my instrument, so much so that I am almost afraid to pick it up again; it seems to me extraordinary that I could play a Bach suite and incomprehensible that I have ever been able to do so. But since I have heard that everything is arranged I am throwing myself into it, and I beg you to add to the three works already mentioned the suite in C Minor.
>
> Please accept my deepest respects, dear Madam, and my admiration for you as an artist.
> Pablo Casals.

The concert had been initiated by Rubio, who took immense pride in bringing together his two greatest pupils. In one of his characteristic letters to Violet he gave his approval to the addition to the programme of the Suite for Solo Cello in C Minor:

*19 August 1924*
Dearest daughther [sic] Violet
I am very pleased to hear about you and Casals.
The suite in C minor

... most noble and mysterious note of dark Rembrandt! A sort of deep lament of such intensity that makes one hot and cold! – the Sarabanda is one of the most aMazING!

I hope you practice regularly

God bless you too

Your loving father, A Rubio.

A month before the concert, Rupert Gwynne died. His health had been deteriorating slowly since 1922, but the end came with surprising suddenness when his heart and kidneys failed. He had just been appointed Financial Secretary to the War Office and there was talk that he might even be destined for the Cabinet. Nobody took his death harder than Violet – for her Rupert was like a twin brother, she used to say – but she possessed the self-discipline of the true professional. Desolate and still in mourning, she hid her pain, took comfort from Casals's warm and generous personality, and threw herself into the lengthy rehearsals he always required, working, as it was said of him, "for the good of the composer, for the glory of music".

On the day of the concert Violet did something she would not usually even have considered: she asked Rupert's eldest daughter, Priscilla, to join her in the green room before the performance. In her heart, Violet was privately dedicating her own part in the concert to Rupert's memory as well as hoping to give Priscilla consolation and pleasure. The fourteen-year-old girl, a little gauche, swished past Casals as he was tuning his cello, knocking his finger with the flap of her blue serge coat and breaking his concentration. Casals, who had never managed to conquer his stagefright, exploded, and for a moment refused to go on stage. Violet was appalled. Beckoning to Mary Stanton, who was hovering in the background, she told her to take Priscilla back to the auditorium as quickly as possible.

The critic of the *Observer* thought Casals was not quite at his impeccable best:

> Even the great Casals cannot ride his single wheel without one or two side-slips, and a squeak just here and there in the suite reminded us that the first cellist in the world, when he essays six consecutive feats of unrelieved solitariness, goes in terror of his life . . . What a treat it was when, the lonesome stunt accomplished, the cellist called in the harpsichordist and the two of them gave us the D major sonata! Here, at last, was contrast – a beautiful curving, deep brown line on a shimmering, silvery background . . . as to Mrs Gordon Woodhouse's playing in her solo, the D major Partita, one could listen for hours.

The critic of *The Times*, however, was bewitched by both players:

> The ideal interpretation is when each artist is as individual as it is possible to be inside a common purpose. In the two sonatas of Bach in G and D for violoncello and harpsichord one felt this strongly. It had all the air of a conjuring trick, too; first the G major was played and we were left wondering how it was all done; then Mrs. Woodhouse played a Partita to show there was no deception, and Mr. Casals a suite to assure us there was no connection with the evil one, and then they did the trick again with the D major and still we could not make it out.

Since the war, Violet's household had become less cohesive than it had been before 1914. She had to concentrate on her professional performances, which meant spending more time in Denis's house in Chelsea, while Bill and Gordon had first to keep Armscote running on reduced staff and then, after 1923, to begin the work at Nether Lypiatt. Once the decorators were finished, Lypiatt was comfortable, despite its relatively sparse furniture, and Bessie, the cook, whom Gordon had brought from Armscote, was producing food as delicious as ever, albeit with simpler and less expensive menus. Initially, there were rather fewer visitors than at Armscote. Violet had not yet had enough time to get to know many of their neighbours, and in Lypiatt's early days most of her guests were from London.

The only people living locally who were already known to Violet were the architect Detmar Blow and his wife Winifred. In his youth, Detmar had been a friend and disciple of the writer, architect and social reformer John Ruskin, the pre-eminent art critic of the nineteenth century, and the poet and designer William Morris, one of the founders of the Arts and Crafts movement, to which Ruskin lent his support. Blow had made his name as the architect of the so-called "timeless" house, built with local materials and in vernacular designs so as to give the impression of having always been there. Before the war he was enticed away from his architectural career by the fabulously rich Bendor, second Duke of Westminster, to become his chief architect and *homme d'affaires*: the terrible moment of his fall from favour still lay far in the future when he had come with his wife and children in 1913 to live near Painswick, one of the largest and most unspoilt of the Cotswold villages. There, a few miles north of Stroud, he started to build his own house, Hilles, on a rough piece of ground with a spectacular view overlooking the Severn valley. Too old for the army, he had worked on the house day and night throughout the war (by searchlight at night, risking suspicion of being a spy), until it was ready for Winifred and their children.

Winifred, born a Tollemache, was Denis's first cousin, auburn-haired and fine-featured, a strong character with a formidable presence and a chin to match. Widely read, she knew Latin and let it be understood that she could read Greek. She relished the Arts and Crafts world into which her husband had brought her, carving out a position for herself as a patroness of the movement and turning Hilles into a centre for musicians, writers and artists. Charmed and fascinated by Violet, Winifred set about introducing her to the neighbourhood, and soon persuaded her to play for the Painswick Music Club, which had been founded by Winifred's protégé, the young composer Gerald Finzi, and a Painswick neighbour, Jack Villiers.

Among Violet's earliest visitors to Lypiatt from further afield was the recently knighted Sir Ronald Storrs, now Governor of Judaea, who in 1925 brought with him his friend Private "Shaw", the alias assumed by Lawrence of Arabia.[4] Few people in the twentieth century, or in any other age, have attained the romantic stature of T.E. Lawrence, whose account of his own exploits in the Arabian desert during the war describes him almost single-handedly winning over the Arabs to the British cause, then leading them in a breathtaking series of guerrilla attacks against the rail communications of Germany's Turkish allies. A scholar, archaeologist and traveller, with a profound knowledge of the Middle East, Lawrence was perfectly suited for the post of military intelligence officer with the Arab Bureau in Cairo, which he had joined late in 1914. In 1916 he had entered the Arab Revolt as a liaison officer with the forces of the Emir Faisal, with which he had fought throughout the campaigns against the Turks in Arabia and Palestine. Just how much is true of the tale told by this complex and tormented man will never be known. What is certain is that Lawrence had the world at his feet after the war, acclaimed as a hero, offered influential appointments, and basking in the intimate friendship of the great – Churchill, E.M. Forster and Bernard Shaw. He sat frequently to portraits by Augustus John, but chose to spend his time cloaked in the false modesty of anonymity. "I want to forget," he said, "and be forgotten."

Nevertheless, a yearning for the simple life and an appreciation of what he called "fine and distinguished craftsmanship", especially in printing, were genuine qualities in Lawrence, as was a love of music. He had an extensive collection of gramophone records, which he was to take with him when, in

4 In 1922 Lawrence had enlisted in the Royal Air Force as "John Hume Ross", but a year later, after his identity became known, he left and joined the Tank Corps as "T.E. Shaw". In 1925 the RAF allowed him to return as Aircraftman T.E. Shaw.

1926, the RAF posted him to the North-West Frontier of India (in October 1928 he would write from Miranshah to a friend in England: "Mrs Gordon Woodhouse was playing a little scrap of Bach on her harpsichord, via my gramophone, the afternoon your letter arrived here. I try and carry two or three of her records about with me."). At the time when he first visited Lypiatt with Storrs, he had just finished his masterpiece, *Seven Pillars of Wisdom* (printed privately in 1926), the story of his part in the Arab uprising. As he walked up the steps with Violet, he asked her, "How can you live in a house like this?" Violet carried on as if he had said nothing, but Gordon overheard the remark: "I think he meant he prefers a tent," he said afterwards.

Another visitor was Ethel Smyth – now, since 1922, Dame Ethel Smyth – whose music was beginning to be performed more often. Although she and Violet had been seeing each other far less than they had before the war, their friendship was quite strong enough to survive both these intermissions and Ethel's habit of falling in love every few years. Since 1919 she had been carrying on an "unutterably happy" affair with the writer Edith Somerville, whom she brought to stay at Lypiatt in September 1925 after a concert at the Three Choirs Festival, which that year was held in Gloucester. The main purpose of the concert was to resuscitate Ethel's Mass, written more than thirty years earlier (and performed only once, in 1893), with the composer herself conducting. Ethel tried to enlist Violet as one of the stewards, which would have meant her being on a money-raising committee during the festival, but Violet refused. Secure and confident in her own judgement, she had strong ideas about how music should be performed: the Three Choirs Festival did not meet her exacting standards and Violet would not compromise, even for one of her closest musical friends.

> I do not try to convert others but I feel so strongly against the Festival Style of any old music (which they always do) with quantity instead of quality, 3,000 instead of 300 voices, that it is like asking a Catholic to be a Protestant to make me actually pretend to encourage it, when I am wild against it. I personally believe in years to come no-one will think of playing Bach on pianos with monster orchestras to great mammoth choruses, any more than they would dress up a Botticelli picture in clothes like Queen Mary's. When you realise that in the Passion Music, the *lute* was intended to be heard among instruments, and that the Harpsichord accompanied the recitatives with its wonderful arpeggio running, sweeping chords, you can imagine that to me, steeped in the beauty of all that intention, the

vulgarity and disgusting vibrato of the modern organ is revolting. I believe I should adore the *Messiah* done properly, and not got up like Elgar's *Pomp and Circumstance*. Yet at Gloucester they have since the War spent £4,000 on ruining that lovely old organ!

Ethel had arrived at Lypiatt with Edith Somerville immediately after the concert, elated by her success – "I had a triumph . . . the choir informed me I was the best conductor they ever had." Edith's departing gift for Violet was a disgusting Irish herbal recipe for rheumatism, with instructions to take a wineglassful cold every morning. During her stay she spent most of her time in bed, writing, liberally staining the red silk bedcover with black ink, which Violet made no effort to remove. As an admirer of the three collections of *Experiences of an Irish R.M.*, the stories which had made Edith's reputation (written under the names of "Somerville and Ross" in collaboration with her cousin, Violet Martin), Violet treated the stain as a badge of honour, to be pointed out to subsequent guests as proof that they had been placed in the same bedroom in which the famous author had once slept.

No one knew better than Violet the healing powers of music, the special magic she could work with her instruments in the intimacy of small rooms. When her friend, the architect George Crawley, was dying of throat cancer in 1925, she took her clavichord to play Bach to him at his house in Chelsea Park Gardens. It was to be his last day of consciousness. Violet set the clavichord at the end of the bed while his family and his friends clustered round. Crawley's wife later recalled how he lay in the midst of them "looking like Francis of Assisi. Over him was spread a piece of blue Spanish silk on which lay just one beautiful red rose. No one who was there can forget the peace of that morning. As the soft notes of the clavichord came to him he looked absolutely happy. Bach was always to him the music of his heart . . . and on this day it seemed to bring him comfort." For Violet, to heal herself, however, was more difficult. The Painswick Music Club concert for 1925 coincided with the anniversary of Rupert's death, and the pain of her loss swept over her during the period of seclusion for rehearsals. "The wound is still very deep in my heart," she wrote to Roland.

Although they were not to know it, Violet's concert-going audiences in London were on the point of losing her in her prime. Her superlative professional performances, which had started immediately after the war, had lasted only eight years. They were brought to an abrupt end by a bizarre chain of events which enriched Gordon and which is still the cause of bad blood today – a double murder, and a series of financial accidents and coincidences which would have been found melodramatic in the pages of a shilling shocker.

# XIII

*Murder in the Black Mountains*

LONG BEFORE THEIR mother's death, Gordon's sisters Ella and May Woodhouse had shared Burghill with a cousin, John Drinkwater, the son of the British Vice-Consul in Naples. By a quirk of Italian law at that time, foreign children domiciled in Italy became Italian citizens on reaching the age of seven. To avoid this fate John's father farmed out his children with relations in England, and in 1901, shortly before his seventh birthday, old Mrs Woodhouse had volunteered to look after John permanently. Ella, aged forty, and May, thirty-two, brought him up like a younger brother, and from that day forward he always thought of Burghill as home.

The household in which John Drinkwater had spent his childhood was dominated by women. When he first arrived he was put at the top of the house in the care of a nanny and a nurserymaid. The kitchen was the province of the cook and two scullerymaids. Having inherited their mother's thrifty and dutiful code of behaviour, Ella and May dressed in clothes that reflected her stiff sense of propriety, with skirts brushing the ground, long sleeves, lace cuffs and matching lace collars. They wore their hair scraped back from the face into a tight bun, of which Ella's was held in place by a crescent-shaped starched lace cap pinned firmly behind each ear.

In 1908, when John Drinkwater was fourteen, a new coachboy arrived at Burghill. Charles Houghton, a former Dr Barnardo's orphanage boy, was twenty-four, with pleasant looks which were only slightly marred by somewhat haggard, undernourished features and his premature baldness, which made him seem old for his years. As time went by he worked his way up to become the butler, his new status entitling him to pinstripe trousers, stiff white collar and shirt, black jacket, and a black waistcoat, to which he added his own fob watch and chain. As the household's sole indoor male servant, Houghton was enlisted by the Woodhouse sisters to help discipline John during his adolescence, which in practice meant beating him in the stables at the end of the drive if he were caught lying or misbehaving. Houghton

207

was essentially a kindly man, however, whom John came to see as a father figure and later as a genuine friend. The Great War and John's marriage soon afterwards to a young Australian girl, separated them, but did not bring their friendship to an end. In all, Houghton served the Woodhouse family devotedly for eighteen years, earning their absolute confidence.

After Mrs Woodhouse's death in 1923 and the unfortunate episode of having to buy back their own home from their brother Gordon, Ella and May lived contentedly at Burghill for the next three years. They kept the house much as their mother had left it, its large Georgian rooms crowded with ponderous Victorian furniture – mahogany sideboards, armchairs and sofas upholstered in dark velvet and braid, and tables swathed in heavy material beneath spotless cloths of white linen. Photographs, porcelain, miniatures in silver frames and bric-a-brac stood everywhere. Ella, the elder sister, was a forceful personality and ran the place to a strict regime. Fires were never lit after 31 April or before 1 October. Food rationing, which had been introduced nationally early in 1918, had ended in 1921, but Ella continued it on a voluntary basis: every day, immediately after morning prayers, she would dole out to the staff portions of jam, butter and sugar from the larder, before planning the meals with the cook. If there were guests staying, they too were allotted their rations.

May was an altogether gentler character. Repressed, quiet and shy, she arranged the flowers every morning in the room beside Ella's office which served as the flower pantry. The two sisters combined their weekly devotions at the local church with a sense of responsibility for the poor, the sick and the elderly. They were often to be seen carrying baskets laden with home-grown produce, visiting cottages all over Burghill village. Within this confined and simple world, far from the mockery and palpable boredom which they engendered in Gordon and Violet, the sisters inspired love and reverence, not least from their own servants.

Ella and May had made wills bequeathing all their property to each other, but both were no longer young – by 1926 Ella was sixty-five and May fifty-seven – and they had to provide for the disposition of Burghill after their own deaths. Like their mother, they disapproved strongly of Violet's influence on Gordon. They were Christian souls, but that did not stop them resenting the unfeeling way in which Violet had contemplated expelling them from Burghill and taking over the place herself. There was no question in their minds of leaving their brother a single penny of their money, only for it to be squandered by Violet – and, for all they knew, to be spent by Bill and Denis, who had usurped Gordon's role as her husband. The contrast with their favourite cousin was telling. John Drinkwater, now a naval officer of thirty-two, conventionally married and with two small children, kept in constant touch with them, writing regularly and often visiting them at Burghill with his young family when he was on leave. In the summer of 1926 Ella and May made their choice, instructing their solicitor, James Calder, to draw up new wills in favour of John, to be ready for signature before they went away on holiday, as they did each September.

Two weeks before their departure, they learned to their dismay that Houghton, their trusted butler, had secretly taken to drink. Precisely when he had started no one ever knew – like all butlers, he had the key to the cellar. The war, during which he had served on a hospital ship, had brought him new experiences and altered his perspectives. On his return, while remaining loyal and grateful to the Woodhouses, he nevertheless felt trapped in the narrow community life of Burghill. Trusting and unworldly, Ella and May suspected nothing until Houghton seemed to undergo a character change, becoming increasingly unreliable, and sometimes frightening the female servants with his violent moods.

Houghton spent the afternoon of Sunday, 5 September 1926 at the village pub, drinking "scrumpy", the local home-made rough cider, after which he returned to serve the sisters their evening meal. He carved and offered up the meat without mishap, but while handing round the vegetables he stumbled and dropped the dish. Smelling alcohol on his breath, Ella and May suddenly realized the cause of his recent strange behaviour. Panic-stricken, they reacted impulsively. Ella, as always, took the vital decision. Houghton, she told May, must leave their employ at once.

It was an anxious moment for the two sisters. Since John Drinkwater's departure, Burghill had once again become a female preserve. Dreading a stormy or emotional scene in which Houghton might threaten them or break down and plead to be allowed to stay, they cabled a message asking their cousin and neighbour, Ernest Jackson, to come and join them, so that a man could be present in the house. Jackson came at once, and on the morning of Monday, 6 September Ella summoned the butler to the library. With May sitting silently beside her and Jackson close at hand in the next room, Ella gave Houghton a week's notice to quit.

The rest of the day passed off uneasily, but without untoward incident: Houghton carried out his duties normally, though he did not appear for dinner that evening. On the Tuesday morning he waited as usual on Ella and May at breakfast. Beneath the surface, however, he was by now desperate. Burghill was the only home life he knew, and he could not imagine what would become of him after his dismissal. He had an ally in Ernest Jackson, who was fond of him and believed that his loyalty and length of service gave

him every justification for expecting to end his days at Burghill. In the hope
of giving the sisters a reason to reverse their decision, Jackson planned to try
to persuade the butler to "sign the pledge" and give up drink for good. As
a first step, he asked Houghton to make his gun ready, intending to have a
quiet word with him in the park later in the morning, on the pretext of
going out together for some casual shooting.

After morning prayers on Tuesday 7 September, Ella and May went about
their daily household tasks – Ella going to her office, May to the flower
pantry to arrange chrysanthemums, dahlias, roses and sweet peas. Ernest
Jackson went upstairs to his own room; he had left home in a hurry after
receiving the sisters' cable and had letters to write. Suddenly a loud explosion
echoed through the house, followed seconds later by another. The servants
rushed towards the sound, with Jackson close behind them, running from his
bedroom headlong down the stairs. They found Ella Woodhouse lying
motionless on the stone-flagged floor of the passage between her office and
the kitchen. She had been shot in the back of the head from a range of two
yards and had died instantly. The wound had bled copiously and blood was
already beginning to seep into the cracks between the stone flags. Further
down the passage lay May Woodhouse, still breathing but mortally
wounded. She had come from the flower room on hearing the first shot and
had seen Houghton aiming the gun at her. Her right hand, which she had
put up in instinctive self-protection, was in ribbons, and there were shot
pellets in her throat. She died within minutes of her sister.

Jackson's first thought was to arm himself. He strode to the gun room,
seized and loaded a second gun, and started to search the house. Reaching
the butler's bedroom, which overlooked the back yard, he found the door
locked. Groans came from inside. Jackson despatched a servant for the
police and stood guard outside. When the police finally burst into the room,
they found Houghton slumped awkwardly in a wicker chair. He had cut his
throat with a razor, but was still alive. On the floor lay Ernest Jackson's
double-barrelled shotgun, which was kept in the butler's pantry and had for
many years been on permanent loan to Houghton for shooting rabbits and
pigeons in the park during his afternoons off.

The following day Gordon, in a state of shock, went over to Burghill with
Violet, who wrote to her brother Roland to tell him of what had happened:

Nether Lypiatt Manor, Stroud, Gloucestershire.
*9th September 1926.*
Dearest Roland
Gordon thanks you so much for your wire. It is indeed a dreadful

tragedy and one feels it is so extra terrible that Charles, our old and valued servant, should have done it! We feel so sorry that he did not succeed in killing himself, poor man. It appears that he did it in anger because they gave him notice, he having lately become drunk, rather drunk, & apt to be rude to them, and difficult with the other servants. He actually shot them with a gun, one outside the kitchen and the other not far off, after breakfast when Ella had gone to see the cook. They both must have known what he meant to do, because both had put up their hands to try & protect themselves, poor things. We went over to Burghill yesterday, & poor Gordon felt it very much. O Roland how dreadful it does seem. And today several people have actually come up here from the press, *Daily Mirror* etc & tried to ask questions! . . .          Much love from V.

John Drinkwater, stationed at Portsmouth, learned of his cousins' death from a friend who had seen the noon edition of the *Evening Standard* on the day of the murders. He set off immediately on the long journey to Herefordshire, arriving late at night to find the house deserted. The summer of 1926 was exceptionally hot and the large low-silled windows of the billiard room were wide open. He stepped inside. The two sisters, covered by white sheets, were laid out on the billiard table. There was not a servant to be seen anywhere, all the indoor staff having fled except for the late gardener's wife, Mrs Nunn, who was in her cottage in the grounds. John found a whisky bottle and drank himself into a stupor. He never fully recovered from that night alone at Burghill.

The popular press pursued the story relentlessly, milking every sensational aspect for all it was worth. None of the departed servants returned to help cope with the flood of wanted and unwanted visitors – police, undertakers, solicitors, relations and, worst of all, reporters and photographers. Mrs Nunn, however, was heroic. She looked after Gordon, Violet and John Drinkwater, made cups of tea for the press and the police, shepherded morbid sightseers off the premises, and cleaned up the gory mess that Houghton had left in the downstairs passage and in his own room. In gratitude, Gordon vowed to care for her "as if she were one of his own family"; many years later, when she was old and ill, he was to be as good as his word.

Over a thousand people attended the sisters' funeral service on Saturday 18 September, the stately prose of the local newspaper, the *Herefordshire Times*, reflecting the esteem in which they had both been held:

Simple and beautiful, in keeping with the lives of the two unfortunate ladies, was the double funeral of the Misses Elinor

Drinkwater Woodhouse and May Gordon Woodhouse, the victims of the Burghill shooting tragedy . . . Every resident in the district, from the oldest to the youngest, and from the richest to the poorest seemed to be present . . . Slowly and sadly the procession wended its way from the scene of the tragedy through the avenue of over-hanging boughs . . . tall trees rustled a mournful adieu out on the main road lined by sorrowing cottagers.

Behind the biers walked Mr. J.G.Gordon Woodhouse, the sole surviving immediate relative . . . At the rear of the funeral cortège was the deceased ladies' favourite pony, drawing a carriage full of floral tributes . . .

The remains of Miss May Woodhouse were left in the church while those of her sister were taken to the grave . . . On the ledges were brightly coloured dahlias, the favourite flowers of the two ladies . . . After the committal service, the clergy and private mourners returned to the church while workmen erected a stone slab, in readiness for the second burial in the same grave . . . The villagers filed past the grave casting loving and sorrowing eyes on where their "ladies bountiful" slept . . . most pathetic of all was the way in which the oldest of the employees lingered by the graveside, weeping unrestrainedly. From the church floated the solemn strains of the organ, heavy with grief but expressing in music "thoughts which lay too deep for tears". When the sun went down the ladies were left alone with the flowers that so fittingly symbolised the beauty and saintliness of their lives.

However beautiful, simple and saintly the reflections of the congregation, the thoughts of the nearest relations were taken up by less worthy matters. Ella's and May's new wills in favour of John Drinkwater had not been signed, and were therefore not valid. Their old wills, in which they had left their entire estates to each other, were the only legally binding documents. Gordon, as next of kin, was once again entitled in law to succeed to Burghill, as well as to the rest of his sisters' fortune. As for John, not only had he lost the two cousins who had brought him up, but the murderer had been his childhood friend, and a final twist of fate had cheated him of his rightful inheritance. After the funeral, he and his wife Edith returned to Burghill with Violet and Gordon, hoping against hope that Gordon might honour his sisters' last wishes as expressed in their draft wills. It was still not too late to agree a revised settlement. Sitting beside Edith Drinkwater in the open carriage, Violet soon dispelled any illusions. To this day, the Drinkwater family tradition has it that Violet's only words were, "I am sorry about it, my dear, but you see, I like pretty things."

James Calder, the Woodhouse family solicitor, spoke to Gordon, advising him that he was morally, even if not legally, bound to give up Burghill to John Drinkwater. Gordon was shaken, but Calder's appeal to his better nature was wasted unless Violet consented. She did not, and Gordon refused to budge. Violet wrote again to her brother:

Nether Lypiatt Manor, Stroud, Gloucestershire.
*13th September 1926.*
Dearest Roland

Thank you for your sympathy. I fetched Gordon back yesterday. He was awfully upset & broken down, & the funeral was an ordeal for him. You can imagine, policemen, crowds, the disgusting low press feeling. I turned my back & walked sideways to prevent the camera-man getting him, while he held his hat over his face, poor dear. We have all been so very fond of Charles that we can't help feeling so dreadfully sorry about him, & yet it was such a brutal act to shoot those two poor defenceless women. Roland, he sent Fan-Tan [Violet's Pekinese] a rabbit only last month for a birthday present, & was so devoted to Gordon & such a faithful servant. He must have gone mad for the moment. And I believe poor Ella had really spoken very nicely to him, & was trying to get him another place.

As the two left everything to each other except some legacies, & died so near to each other, Gordon will probably inherit most of it as next of kin. Strange isn't it. He will have to pay 2 death duties I suppose. He does deserve to have it, poor old pet, don't you think? Only I wish they had meant him to have it. I imagine he should have a clear £1500 a year more anyhow. He said I could tell you about this, but you will not mention it to anybody else will you? For nothing is definitely known as to the money at present, or what they left exactly. The horror of it all has upset him a good deal, & I feared for him at the funeral, but today he seems brighter. He intends to go back tomorrow for two days, & then Burghill will be shut up till the wills are proved. I wish he had not got it under such sad sad circumstances. Poor dear Gordon. Much love dearest Roland.                    Violet

If this was the end of the story of the Burghill inheritance, it was not quite the end of the butler's story. He wrote from prison to his closest friend, the under-gardener at Burghill:

Prisoner number 260. Gloucester Prison.
*24th September 1926.*

Somehow I wonder what I have done to be here and it seems to me like a dream but am afraid it is to [*sic*] true. I have had such a nice letter from Mr Gordon which has made me feel more cheerfull also lots of letters from friends etc. . . . I expect the threshing will soon be on. How I should love to be with you for it (never again. I am longing for the final settlement and with the help of God I will be a man to the last) . . . It is the first time for years I have not got Harry's potatoes up. I wish I was in the garden doing it now. I do a lot of reading of books never before could I settle to them. But now I will read twice over if a good one.

As the day of the trial drew nearer, Houghton wrote to his friend again:

*19th October 1926*
Dear Jack, I am longing for 4 November to come. It does seem a long trying wait and I am feeling the strain every day . . . Mr and Mrs Woodhouse sent me a lovely basket of fruit. Oranges, plums, pears, bananas and about 2lb of beautiful slab cake. It was very nice of them and they have offered to send me more. I may say I have enjoyed it very much.

The trial of Charles Houghton for murder was held at Herefordshire Assizes on 4 November 1926. He pleaded not guilty to murdering May, but guilty as charged to the murder of Ella. Defence counsel raised as an extenuating circumstance that Houghton had suffered from epilepsy in childhood, to which his sister testified. But the medical officer of Gloucester Prison and Ernest Jackson both gave evidence that the accused appeared to be perfectly normal. Houghton himself made a full confession – he had felt an uncontrollable surge of anger towards Miss Ella, he said, but had been taken by surprise by Miss May, and had never meant to kill her. The trial was all over in a day; Mr Justice Swift donned the black cap and passed sentence of death by hanging. John Drinkwater, James Calder and Ernest Jackson each tried to help Houghton, visiting him in prison and attempting to arrange an appeal on the grounds of his epilepsy, but the condemned man refused to co-operate. He felt that he deserved his punishment, and that his place was with the two Misses Woodhouse, who had always been so good to him.

Violet moved heaven and earth to obtain a reprieve. For a month she could talk of little else. As the date of the execution drew near, she redoubled her efforts. She was convinced that Houghton was a fine and decent person who had been driven by drink and despair to an utterly uncharacteristic act, to which the civilized response was merciful leniency. She persuaded the Bishop of Gloucester to visit him in gaol. She tried to make

Gordon, Violet and Bill at Southover Manor, soon after Bill had moved in to form a *ménage à trois*.

Violet with her dog, Puppet, in the garden at Southover Manor.

Gordon, Bill, Max and Violet under the mulberry tree at Southover Manor,
with Adelina Ganz. By now it is a *ménage à cinq* (Denis is in South Africa).
But was Adelina also a lover?

Violet's first harpsichord, which was adapted for her by Arnold Dolmetsch in 1899 from the seventeenth-century original by Thomas Culliford.

Dolmetsch also built a small clavichord for Violet in 1912, enabling her to ferry it from Armscote to London by car.

The Bloomsbury art critic, Roger Fry, wrote Violet a fan letter and made an oil sketch of her in 1922.

Violet and her Gaveau clavichord – people came from all over Europe to hear her play.

This photograph appeared in the first issue of *Music and Letters* in 1920 accompanying an article by Violet on early music.

Adelina Ganz, daughter of the impresario Wilhelm Ganz, who accompanied Violet and Gordon on their honeymoon.

When the composer Ethel Smyth met Violet in 1908: "a friendship which I knew was going to be one of the chief joys of my life took root".

Christabel Marshal, who fell desperately in love with Violet and schemed to prevent her marrying.

Radclyffe Hall, who wrote the first lesbian novel and dedicated a book of erotic poems to Violet.

Denis Tollemache, taken prisoner by the Germans in 1917, sent Violet this photograph from his prisoner-of-war camp in Freiburg.

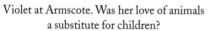

Violet at Armscote. Was her love of animals a substitute for children?

Photograph of Bill, Max, Violet and Gordon at Armscote, taken by Denis. The First World War was about to shatter their idyllic life.

Violet played in public with Casals in 1924.
He was then acknowledged to be the world's greatest 'cellist.

Violet, the first musician to record on the harpsichord, in the recording studio at Hayes in 1920.

Sachie, Edith and Osbert Sitwell – three "elongated peacocks" who adored Violet and illuminated the London artistic scene between the wars. Violet and Sachie revived hitherto neglected works by Domenico Scarlatti.

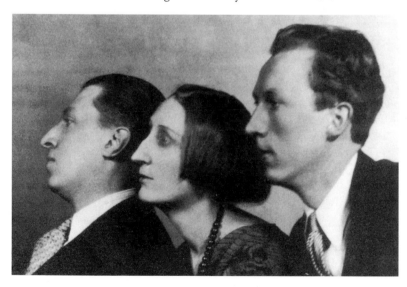

Burghill Court, where Gordon's two sisters were murdered by the butler.

Gordon's sisters, Ella and May, with their cousin John Drinkwater, to whom they were intending to leave their fortune.

Houghton, the murderer. He had served his victims faithfully for nearly twenty years.

One of the many newspaper reports following the murder of Violet's two sisters-in-law.

Nether Lypiatt Manor. In the the top right corner of the gates is
"the Blacksmith's curse" – the non-repeated motif of the iron whorls.

The garden at the back, which leads down through precipitous woods,
past an obelisk commemorating a ghostly horse, to a hidden canal.

Early in 1919 Delius wrote to his friends in Paris: "there is one really artistic salon – Mrs Woodhouse – a real artist – who plays the harpsichord most beautifully." Three months later he wrote this piece for Violet.

Bill Barrington's drawing of the wing at Nether Lypiatt

Violet with her revered teacher, Rubio, who compared her playing favourably with that of Pablo Casals.

Violet in the drawing room at Nether Lypiatt, the house in which she spent the last twenty-five years of her life. She is playing her Dolmetsch harpsichord

This photograph of Violet, taken by Alvin Langdon Coburn, was kept
by Bill in his wallet during the First World War.

Under Diaghilev's influence European fashion went oriental. Bill Barrington, who spent the last part of the First World War in India, returned with dazzling garments for Violet's already exotic wardrobe.

Gordon petition the Home Secretary, but relations and friends convinced him that there was nothing more to be done. Calmly resigned to his fate, Houghton wrote a last letter to the under-gardener, Jack, at Burghill.

*26th November 1926.*
This is just a few lines to say I am going on very well and I still eat and sleep well . . . I still get some nice letters . . . I must say all seem kind and nice to me and you would be pleased to hear the Bishop of Gloucester came to see me last Tuesday and we had a nice chat. I thought it was kind of him to come.

In December 1926, at the age of forty-two, Charles Houghton was hanged at Gloucester Prison. John Drinkwater became an alcoholic; and died in 1971; to this day his son – who became a successful barrister – is bitter about the way in which the Drinkwaters were treated by Violet and Gordon. Gordon, however, became a wealthy man, and was able once again to keep Violet in the manner to which she was accustomed.

# XIV

*Artists of the Golden Valley*

WITH THE SHOOTING of the Woodhouse sisters and the subsequent trial making headlines in all the national newspapers, local gossip about Lypiatt reached a peak of intensity. Children in the neighbouring farms spoke in hushed voices as they passed the house. They were told by their parents never to refer to the murder at school: but murder was not the only scandal. Violet was still a relative newcomer to the area and, despite the onset of middle age, her private life excited endless speculation. What was the secret of her attraction? How did she manage to keep each of her men bound to her? Which, if any, did she sleep with? How vast was the fortune into which, through Gordon, she had come? Since nobody knew the answers to any of these questions, everybody was free to air his own theory.

The war and its aftermath had led to a considerable relaxation in conventional morality, and the number of people who refused to receive Violet began to dwindle. For those who were uncertain what attitude to take towards her, it was helpful that Denis's cousin, Winifred Blow, had shown not the least sign of disapproval; indeed, Winifred's friendship with the Lypiatt household set the tone in the neighbourhood. The stand-offish were soon disarmed, for it was hard to maintain a censorious demeanour when the atmosphere around Violet was so harmonious. Unspoken questions about sex lurked in many of her acquaintances' minds, but even her friend and confidante, Winifred, did not really know the truth. Just once, towards the end of their lives, Winifred plucked up the courage to ask what her men did about "it". Violet replied firmly – but whether honestly or mischievously it is impossible to tell – " Oh, they could go to Gloucester for that sort of thing."

As memories receded of Max's death and of how badly Bill had hurt her, life at Lypiatt became as cheerful as it had been at Armscote before the war. With Gordon's second inheritance came a sense of liberation. At last they were able to finish the interior at Lypiatt and to build a second wing on the east side of the house, balancing the proportions of the façade (to ensure the blending of the new addition with its surroundings, the lower end of the southern garden wall was cannibalized for its stone, losing two feet in height). They could also afford their own place in London again, and chose a house in Brompton Square, principally for its music room. Violet resumed her shopping with enthusiasm. A letter to Roland in December 1926, thanking him for a Christmas present, gives a glimpse of the scale of the pampering which Gordon's family, in their wills, had sought so unsuccessfully to staunch.

> Gordon has given me four great volumes, a lovely scarf, diamonds
> and pearls from his family and a 20 Austin Saloon Landaulette . . .
> From Bill I have a lovely golden shawl and a book and from Denis
> a sable squirrel coat with beautiful velvet outside.

Violet brought to the task of furnishing Nether Lypiatt a taste so idiosyncratic that Osbert Sitwell used to claim he could always recognize something that had once been hers even after it had found its way into someone else's house. There was a homogeneity about her furniture, her paintings and her objets d'art which created the illusion that they were all the work of the same artist, regardless of their period or place of origin. Even she, however, could not redecorate both Lypiatt and Brompton Square single-handedly. Norman Wilkinson, now designing productions at Stratford-upon-Avon, had recently become a neighbour of the Blows in Painswick, and Violet promptly enlisted him as her consultant and assistant.

The large drawing-room at Lypiatt was the first to be tackled. Wilkinson taught the local workmen how to stipple the panelling in pale duck-egg green and to drag the floorboards in cream, allowing a hint of the natural wood colour and grain to show through the paint. In this room Violet kept her musical instruments, with drapes thrown over them to shield them against changes of temperature or humidity (the clavichords, the most fragile of her instruments, were always covered in paisley shawls). Although Bath was her main shopping town, the whole area around Nether Lypiatt was full of antique shops, and there she bought Turkish carpets and eighteenth-century furniture – lacquered chairs and walnut tables – and added to her already considerable library of poetry, early music, and French, German and English classical literature. Books lay around everywhere, many restored or re-bound at Bayntun's in Bath, the old editions adding richness to the rooms.

In the first-floor bedrooms, whose cool colours contrasted with the warm burnished wood of the landing off which they led, there stood four-poster beds hung with sumptuous curtains and canopies. Gordon's was in a pale chintz of birds and twisting flowers; Bill's, a magnificent Queen Anne bed, was in white embroidered satin and dark blue plush; for her own, Violet chose a mellow brick-red cotton moreen, the curtains lined in a richer, darker red and braided with yellow bands and tassels. Denis, ever a shade more spartan, and a shade less integrated into the household than the others, slept in a smaller four-poster bed, hung in a sober glazed cotton with autumnal leaves, in a room on the second floor, next to the spare rooms.

Through the Blows, Violet soon discovered the fabric designers Phyllis Barron and Dorothy Larcher, who had formed their partnership in the early twenties. Their farmhouse on the edge of Painswick was situated at the end of a lane which divided the garden in two, one side being dedicated to plants used in making dyes. The house's stable block had been converted into a workshop, with an indigo vat for hand-dyeing and an area for hand block printing. When visitors came, Barron, the more extrovert and entertaining of the two, would often add a bohemian touch by asking the men visitors to supply some of their urine, a valuable constituent of certain colours.

The rectangular rhythmical patterns of Barron and Larcher's designs had been inspired by Dorothy Larcher's journey to India before the war, and were quite unlike anything else being produced in Britain at the time. The subtlety of their colours appealed to Violet. Besides, it fitted her sense of values to be sifting through hand-woven cottons, organdies and linens in a rural village setting, looking for materials for the house and fabrics to send to her dressmakers to make up into scarves, shawls and dresses. Many of her wraps were kept in a chest in the hall at Lypiatt, from which, summer and winter, Violet would take her pick as she set off out of doors.

Every morning before breakfast, Violet's two Pekinese dogs were brought to her on leads, and she would take her exercise by walking with them at a fast pace twice round the walled garden. It was a good way to immerse herself in the detail of Bill's garden plans. She had the branches of the trees at the top of the beech wood cut back to open a view across the valley to the church at Bussage. Seeing and liking the new summerhouse of some close neighbours, she ordered one exactly the same, which she put in the south-west section of the garden and filled with wicker chairs, silk cushions, jugs, china, and silver witch balls. Violet named it "Little Lypiatt".

Bill and Gordon ran the small estate together from the office they shared with Denis on the ground floor. Their desks were each piled high with paperwork: Denis's was the tidiest, the orderly desk of a military man. It was a cosy room, its atmosphere a cross between a studio, a London club and an officers' mess. Ash lay a foot deep in the open fireplace. On a table by the door back copies of *The Times* were stacked against the wall. The shelves were lined with Gordon's books on antiques, Denis's on military history, and Bill's on architecture and gardening. In one of the lower cupboards Gordon kept jigsaws, a stamp collection, and a heap of Edgar Rice Burroughs's Tarzan novels. Bill experimented with collages, papier mâché and paintings, and made models of classical buildings (he particularly admired Inigo Jones) on the Elizabethan oak table. Gordon kept piles of Christie's catalogues and magazine cuttings about wine, food, furniture and country house sales. The office doubled as the smoking room; after meals, if there were no guests to entertain, the men would settle into their comfortable armchairs with their pipes and cigarettes. It was a sedentary existence and only Denis, who, still in his early forties, was a dozen years younger than the others, took the trouble to keep himself fit by jogging round the farm or hunting with the Beaufort. As Colonel of the 7th Hussars he owed it to his regiment not to allow himself to get out of condition.

Almost imperceptibly, Gordon's stature within Violet's household had grown. He had turned himself into a connoisseur of wine and antiques, and had also become extremely well informed about current affairs. Under his direction hospitality at Lypiatt became an art form. He took charge of the produce of the orchards and vegetable gardens, ordered the food, and organized the menus with Bessie. As the dishes were brought into the dining room he would preside over them, making sure that the courses were properly presented and checking the success or failure of each new recipe. Whoever came to the house, whether a six-year-old child, a gauche adolescent nephew, or the grandest of London friends, Gordon would lay on their special dish or their favourite chocolates; and he was never without huge raisins and rare marsala wines from the Woodhouse vineyards in Sicily. Sometimes, on a sudden whim, Violet would give the kitchen staff the evening off, sending them down to the cinema in Stroud with her chauffeur and car. When that happened, Gordon himself would do the cooking.

Considering that the house was not on the electricity mains, it was surprising how seldom hitches occurred in the kitchen. Lunch was always served promptly at 1.30 pm after the servants had eaten. Isabel Armitage still remembers the vegetables in subtle sauces, the exotic casseroles, the blackcurrant ice cream in frost-encrusted silver bowls, and Floating Islands, one of Gordon's own specialities: white-of-egg puffballs sailing like baby clouds over a pale rich crème vanille. He kept a stiff-backed blue notebook, into which he inserted newspaper cuttings and handwritten recipes from friends, and he was one of the first to buy Lady Jekyll's *Kitchen Essays* which, judging by the heavily annotated copy in the author's possession, he put to frequent use.

In a letter to the author describing her first visit to Lypiatt in the summer of 1928 Tamara Talbot-Rice, the wife of the Byzantine scholar Professor David Talbot-Rice, captures the atmosphere of the house:

I was young, moneyless, unknown in Gloucestershire, married to a younger son of a Gloucestershire squire whose parents did not know the Woodhouses and who had still to make his name. Worse still, I was Russian. At the time and at this place this was synonymous with being a bolshevik, in its turn synonymous with being a barbarian. David had known Violet at any rate since 1921, possibly earlier. He had adored her from the first. He had a great love and understanding of music, could easily follow complicated scores, but played no instrument. Knowing his devotion to Gordon Woodhouse and admiration for Bill Barrington, it was with considerable trepidation that I allowed David to take me to Nether Lypiatt. On arrival the beauty of the façade enchanted me and the objects we passed as the butler led us to the drawing room were very much to my taste.

On entering the drawing room I was confronted by three surprising figures. One was a minute, Dresden-like creature with nothing of the shepherdess about her; she was wearing the most individualistic yet beautiful clothes I had ever seen and since I had recently spent three years working in the world of Parisian haute-couture I was not easy to impress; her Cromwell-shaped patent leather shoes, though not in accordance with the day's fashion, were equally elegant and distinctive. Sitting behind her at a desk was a round-shaped man with a touch of the Pickwickian in his appearance. The third person rose from a window seat as we entered; he was tall, and very thick; hair sprouted unattractively on his face yet he was immensely attractive. The whole set-up, the three people, the furniture, books, objets d'art and pictures, regardless of their very different dates and origins, all savoured of the eighteenth century; so, I was soon to find, did the immensely lively and wide-ranging conversation, Violet's of a distinctly Rabelaisian kind.

I was warmly received. The food was delicious, the conversation stimulating. We were persuaded to stay on after luncheon to see over the house and exquisite garden and grounds. We stayed to tea, and after it I, who had heard some of the greatest musicians of the period, found myself listening with astonished delight to the harpsichord and clavichord being played to perfection. When we finally left, new horizons had been unfolded before me; my attention had been directed to the beauty of England's gardens, the quality of the English love of nature and the countryside, and to a culture which, whilst being essentially English, was also eminently European and also classical. The perfect day was enhanced by an invitation to return in two days' time.

On discovering that I had never been to Bath, Violet decided that we would pay a weekly visit. David and I were to drive to Lypiatt from Oddington, arriving as near 10.30 as possible. We then transferred into Violet's car with her chauffeur at the wheel. Her knowledge of Bath seemed to me complete. On each occasion we concentrated on a different section of the town, Violet pointing out the houses in which everyone of interest in the 18th and 19th centuries had stayed. We never failed to visit Angel's antique shop and second-hand bookshop before going to the Grand Pump Room Hotel, where Violet gave us lunch. I don't think she greatly liked going to restaurants but all three of us adored the Grand Pump Room; though the food was not particularly good, the service was attentive and the visitors included several old ladies who looked and dressed like Queen Mary. They delighted us and set Violet reminiscing. Her conversation sparkled, sometimes her tongue ran away with her, but even at her most acid she was always amusing and that seemed to render her asperities less cruel. After luncheon we invariably visited a couple of shops specialising in costume jewellery; Violet seldom emerged without some rather exotic-looking creation. Our visit to a cinema was the culminating event of the afternoon; we all delighted in the cinema. On the drive back to Lypiatt we often talked cinema. On arrival, over drinks, Violet would entertain Bill and Gordon by playing on the harpsichord the tunes we had heard that afternoon at the cinema. After dinner Violet would return to her instruments, this time to enthral us with items from her classical repertoire.

Violet had been a cinema addict from its earliest silent days. She much preferred it to the theatre, and was quite willing to sit through any number of dreadful short supporting pictures to see a repeat of a feature film that appealed to her, like Charlie Chaplin's *The Gold Rush*. Her niece, Elizabeth David, who herself was to grow into a most impressive woman and to gain fame as a writer of cookery books and a pioneering influence in raising British culinary standards, recalled being taken by Violet to the cinema as a young girl:

> It was soon after my father died, in 1924, that I first got to
> know Aunt V. . . . she decided that I and my sisters, as her late
> brother's orphaned children, must be cherished and entertained. She
> had recently discovered the cinema, and took us to see Douglas
> Fairbanks in the silent version of *The Thief of Baghdad*. I remember
> it still as a magical experience, with that white horse gliding through
> the sky. Once was enough for me to remember it for a lifetime, but
> Aunt V. went to see it day after day, accompanied by Uncle Gordon,
> Uncle Bill, and any other honorary uncles who happened to be
> around to be gathered up into her Rolls and carried along to the
> cinema. That was her way. Once she'd found something special she
> wasn't going to drop it. Same with her men.

Violet was given to obsessions, and in the mid-twenties she was gripped
with a sudden passion for Admiral Nelson. Elizabeth David remembers
"driving in Violet's huge car – a Daimler or a Rolls? – through Trafalgar
Square when the gentlemen rose to their feet and took off their hats to the
Nelson Column. Aunt V. then told me the story of how some museum
which had been presented with the hat which Nelson was wearing at
Trafalgar had committed the scandalous sacrilege of sending it to the cleaners. 'Imagine, Lizzie, that hat had the sweat of Nelson's brow on it, and they
actually sent it to the cleaners.'"

Violet became an authority on the life of Nelson, reading every book
about him she could find and acquiring an extensive collection of relics. She
came to know practically all the leading naval historians who wrote on the
Napoleonic era, as well as many of the admiral's descendants, including
the Lord Nelson of the day. On her trips to Bath she would sometimes
visit the grandson of Nelson and Emma Hamilton, whom Bill persuaded to
sell him one of Lady Hamilton's jewels, which Bill wanted to give as a
present to Violet. In a bedroom at Lypiatt she installed an octagonal wardrobe covered with a rare old English chintz printed to commemorate the
victories of the Nile, Copenhagen and Trafalgar. She took to playing sea
shanties and would occasionally conclude a recital with a stately version of
"Rule, Britannia!", to which Nelson used to be piped ashore. Such was her
infatuation that one of Bill's nieces (who was convinced that Violet and Bill
were never lovers in the full sense of the word) believed that, in a mystical
way, Violet had dedicated her virginity to Nelson.

Violet was also going through a period of musical obsession – in this
instance with Mozart. She had retained her interest in spiritualism, and

believed that she was subconsciously in some form of otherworldly communication with the composer. In February 1927 a fellow spiritualist, the Hon. Eleanor Brougham, a formidable spinster, invited Violet to tea. Also invited was the young historian Steven Runciman, who recorded the occasion in a letter to the author:

> Baba Brougham, as we called her, was in her forties, looking like a big-boned but well-bred cart-horse (but with very elegant legs: which annoyed Cecil Beaton, who thought they did not fit her body.) Baba was a highly cultivated lady, who knew "everybody" – well in with the royals, especially the Connaughts; and whenever Queen Ena of Spain came to London, she acted as her lady-in-waiting. Baba's link with Violet was spiritualism. I remember it being the main topic of conversation between the two of them, with me listening in silence. I thought Violet fascinating. Not only was she a consummate artist, but she was beautiful, combining a fey quality with an almost porcelain neatness, and remarkable physical strength and control. She had great personal charm and was not without humour, even when talking about the supernatural. I remember her being very amusing about the rather sinister ghosts at Nether Lypiatt.

After Violet left, Baba Brougham told Steven Runciman the story of the Mozart sonata:

> Violet's story was that she was one day idly improvising on the harpsichord when she found herself playing what was undoubtedly the first movement of a sonata, and she went on, without pausing, to play a second and a third movement. It was all so vivid that she was able to play the whole work again and to write it down. It was certainly, she thought, a work by Mozart, but it was something that did not appear in his published keyboard music, all of which she knew. So she firmly believed that it was dictated to her by Mozart's spirit. She never played it in public, but she used to play it to friends. It was a charming work, which you would have guessed was by Mozart, for at that time she was so possessed by him that, when she was improvising, she inevitably produced a work that Mozart might have written.

Walks in the surrounding hills and valleys or further afield were a central feature of the Lypiatt way of life. Violet would roam for miles with Bill, Gordon and Denis, scouring the countryside, which was then still largely untouched by the changes that were taking place elsewhere in England, eliciting local knowledge and amassing a storehouse of indigenous history and folklore. In the evenings they would pore over books together and read passages aloud to each other – *Highways and Byways in Oxford and the Cotswolds* by Frederick Griggs, Paul Fisher's *Notes and Recollections of Stroud*, and Francis Duckworth's *The Cotswolds*.

Closest to home were the villages of Througham, Miserden, Slad, Oakridge, Bussage and Sapperton, where Violet soon came to know the group of architects, potters, furniture makers and designers (including Barron and Larcher) known as the "Artists of the Golden Valley". In a dilapidated Elizabethan house at Pinbury two of William Morris's Arts and Crafts disciples, Ernest Gimson and Sidney Barnsley, had established a rural community of craftsmen dedicated to the idea of rejecting the machine age in favour of a reversion to art "made by the people, and for the people, as a happiness to the maker and the user". Their spiritual home was Daneway, an untouched fourteenth-century house just below Sapperton, where the Fabian socialist Emery Walker, founder of the Dove Press and T.E. Lawrence's printer, lived with his ungainly daughter Dorothy. Violet already knew Emery Walker through the arch-Fabian Bernard Shaw, but her first meeting with Dorothy was electric, rendering Dorothy an instant casualty of Violet's mesmeric effect on women. Ten years later, after the death of Mary Stanton, Dorothy Walker was to succeed her as Violet's secretary, assistant and general factotum. After Lawrence's return from India at the beginning of 1929, Dorothy, conscious that her connection with the most glamorous and legendary figure in Europe would stand her in good stead with Violet, used to bring him frequently to Lypiatt; in a letter she described him standing "quite still" without moving at all, all the time – for about an hour", intent on the wonder of Violet's playing.

While Violet was not tempted by the romantic socialism of Barnsley and his community, she shared their appreciation of Cotswold building, and identified with their love of nature, their originality and their uncompromising artistic standards. It appealed to her irreverent eye for humbug, however, that only the reasonably well off could afford the beautifully made furniture and textiles that came out of the workshops of the Artists of the Golden Valley, and that, for all their egalitarianism, they were not averse to accepting the patronage of rich and fashionable sponsors. Notable among these patrons was the painter and art connoisseur William Rothenstein, who had lived in the neighbourhood intermittently since 1908 and had become absorbed in its life, painting landscapes, or portraits of carpenters and thatchers, and staging plays annually in Oakridge village hall. In 1927, feeling that he had been producing the Oakridge plays long enough, Rothenstein found a successor in William Simmonds, an immensely talented sculptor and puppeteer who had followed the Barnsleys to the district.

The poetry and imagination of William Simmonds's puppet dramas left a deep impression on his audiences: so much so that when the Blow children were entertained one Christmas with Norman Wilkinson's crude commedia dell'arte figures, they were, to everyone's embarrassment, utterly unconvinced. Simmonds deployed all his extensive gifts in his shows, not only carving the puppets and designing the sets, but also inventing the plots, which were characterized by observation and gentle humour. The puppets were naturalistic and intricately made – a pantomime horse which divided in two, revealing another puppet inside the rear end; a puppet artist, which would paint a portrait on stage; an Archangel Gabriel, whose heavenly hair was made from tiny wood shavings and whose body was clothed in dozens of small oblong leather flaps, to allow the wings freedom of movement. In the intervals puppet scene-shifters moved props and discussed their work in broad Gloucestershire accents. Simmonds's wife, Eve, hand-stitched the costumes from cloth coloured with home-made dyes, and accompanied the stage action on her spinet or virginals. Altogether the dramas created a magical miniature world of English country life. Rothenstein spread their reputation in society circles, and backed William financially so that he could set up as a professional, with a regular annual three-week London season at the Grafton Theatre and occasional special performances at the Art Workers' Guild. Before long, the Simmonds puppet shows were doing the rounds of the grand country houses, including Eaton Hall in Cheshire, which belonged to Detmar Blow's patron, the Duke of Westminster.

Violet often went to see the Blows at Hilles and became attached to their children, remembering their birthdays, giving them imaginative presents at Christmas, and taking trouble to enter their world of plays, gymkhanas and improvised handicap races (Gordon providing the jockey caps). That they were related to Denis, and that she had no children of her own, further endeared them to her. It was at Hilles that she first met the Simmondses; she had gone over for lunch and tea with Winifred on one of the children's birthdays. Winifred and Detmar had arranged a puppet show as a treat, and initially Violet watched simply out of friendliness. The curtain parted to reveal an old soldier and sailor from the time of the Napoleonic Wars sitting by a shop in the street of a seaport, singing songs and chatting with passers-by. Suddenly this tranquil scene was interrupted by the arrival of the press gang, striking terror into the town's young men. Violet was enthralled by the dialogue and by the beautifully observed delineation of the characters, the pathetic unsuitability of the recruits, the bent and shrivelled bodies of the pensioners, the coarse, aggressive gestures of the gang.

The Simmondses were a self-contained couple, epitomizing the calm still centre of the Arts and Crafts movement. They looked the part – Eve, with her fringe and short bob, her grey hair pressing flatly against her cheeks; William with stocky frame and gentle face, which radiated goodness and *joie de vivre*. Their cottage stood in the middle of a field surrounded by steep hills and woodland, and could only be reached by a narrow footpath. Eve, who had acquired a better than amateur knowledge of plants and flowers, and possessed a fine eye for colour, had converted the stretch of rough grass by the front door into a diminutive garden of considerable charm. Next to the cottage stood a small barn which served as William's studio.

Apart from his skill as a puppeteer, William Simmonds was also a gifted sculptor. He drew his subjects from nature, making himself familiar with the conformation and the character of every horse in the neighbouring farms, and always knowing where a particularly fine-looking goose or hare was to be seen. His acute observations were expressed in minute detail in his pieces, carved mostly in wood, sometimes in alabaster or ivory. His talent was enough to induce Rothenstein's art-critic brother, Albert, to list him alongside Jacob Epstein, Wyndham Lewis and Paul Nash as one of the outstanding British artists of the inter-war period.

Violet built up a large collection of his work – a hedgehog which scuttled and swayed when pushed along the ground, a cluster of leverets, a portrait of one of her Pekinese carved in boxwood, with ebony eyes; large owls, several cats and life-size mice. She often wore on a cord round her neck a gold-painted carving of a chestnut leaf, inside which nestled a tiny wren. Her two most prized Simmonds pieces were an eighteen-inch-high, full-length figure of Lord Nelson, and a black mahogany cat resting with clenched toes, sphinx-like and self-absorbed, on a red cushion.

It is clear from Eve Simmonds's pocket diaries that from their first meeting she fell victim to Violet's magnetism. The same age as Violet, she treated her like a goddess and devoted hours of her time to pleasing her. Eve's needlework and embroidery, which she exhibited at the Arts and Crafts Exhibition Society in London, were very much what Violet wanted:

> I gave Violet a sleeveless embroidered jacket on her birthday. I think it was soon after that I must have started on the bonnets for Violet . . . I had made a black muslin bonnet for her on the lines of an old cotton sunbonnet for the garden, and she was so delighted with it that she was constantly saying "Do make me a new bonnet!"

I counted that over the years I must have made about sixteen.

Eve's sparse diary notes refer exclusively to Violet, recording visits to the cottage, invitations to Lypiatt, and Violet's failure to keep a promised appointment or to make a promised telephone call. Violet arranged that the Simmondses should spend part of every Christmas day at Lypiatt, as well as William's and Violet's birthdays in March and April (Eve's, for some reason, did not qualify). In return, Eve made sure that William showered Violet with his sculptures, drawings and elaborate toys, only occasionally fussing that some of the animals, scattered on floors and shelves all over Lypiatt, were too casually treated. When Violet left for London, Eve would sometimes catch a train and contrive to bump into her in the Brompton Road, in the hope of being whisked off by her to a film or invited to supper at Brompton Square. Violet knew, however, when and how to keep her different friendships in compartments. Despite their artistic gifts, she made no attempt to mix the simplicity of William and Eve Simmonds with the worldliness of Ethel Smyth, let alone the mannered urbanity of the Sitwells. On the other hand someone such as Tamara Karsavina, whom Violet could trust to appreciate the Simmondses, would be escorted to their cottage as soon as she set foot in Lypiatt.

Although Violet was at last secure enough financially to be able to give up performing professionally, there remained one final London concert before she did so. Early in 1927, Ibbs & Tillett booked her for a recital in the Grotrian Hall on 29 March. She included in her programme, for the first and only time, the piece Delius had written for her immediately after the war. Most critics regard it as virtually unplayable on the harpsichord, but in this, her final appearance, Violet made a gallant effort to prove them wrong.

The reviewer for *The Times* gave as much weight to Violet's traditional repertoire as to her playing of the Delius:

> ... Mrs. Woodhouse's technique is so brilliant as to recapture entirely the air of elegant virtuosity of the period. The sparkle of the instrument justifies so much more than the heavier tone of the piano the flashing passage work that is to be found in Bach, Mozart and Scarlatti. Mrs. Woodhouse's programme was drawn entirely from these composers, except the modern piece by Delius. This is true harpsichord music, though conceived from the entirely modern point of view, which is interested in what may be called the colour effects of block harmony. Delius's sweet, cloudy harmony, plus the

sparkling tone, gave the effect of shot silk, and showed that the harpsichord ought not yet to be regarded as an obsolete instrument whose possibilities have been fully exploited.

Another critic wrote: "Segovia on the guitar, Lionel Tertis on the viola, Casals on the 'cello, and Violet Gordon Woodhouse on the harpsichord may be classed together as the four who can distil from these instruments the purest musical essence."

Among those who heard Violet that evening was the Parsee Indian composer Kaikhosru Sorabji. As music critic of *The New Age* he wrote one of the most perceptive reviews that Violet was ever to receive:

That very great artist Violet Gordon Woodhouse gave one of her much too infrequent public performances at the Grotrian Hall on Tuesday the 29th. The work of this rare and exquisite artist has been known for many years to music lovers and cognoscenti, and it is only comparatively recently that she has become known to a wider public of concert goers – and if demonstration were wanted that in her we have one of the greatest living masters of a keyboard instrument, it was given in all completeness at this recital.

The superb elasticity and spring of her rhythm, the elegance and distinction of her phrasing, the magnificent crispness and precision of her technique, the delicate sense of timbre values, these things are not surpassed by any English-speaking musician whose medium of expression is a keyboard instrument. Her rallentandi are models of perfection, her quasi-rubato so perfectly balanced and rounded, so utterly free from exaggeration, that one is hardly conscious of its momentary relaxation of the rhythm. On the other hand there is in Mrs. Woodhouse's Bach-playing none of that metronomic woodenness that is supposed by some, entirely erroneously, to be the indispensable ingredient for playing this music. Nor does Mrs. Woodhouse attempt to "humanise" Bach after the manner of some of our inferior young women, who play him as though he were a Mendelssohn Song Without Words, or rather, it should be said, as if they thought he were. Her Italian Concerto and G minor Toccata were superbly great Bach playing, dignified, moving and expressive, and of a broad sedate beauty, completely free from any pompous pedagogic didacticism or stiff-limbed collegiate pedantry.

Equally beautiful was her playing of the C minor Fantasia of Mozart, a work which one has often detested when played upon the piano, but which she, upon its own instrument, made to sound perfect . . . I exhort, wheedle and cajole all readers to take the very next opportunity of hearing this wonderful musician, even if it be only by means of the wireless; and to those who possess gramophones I commend all her records – there are about a dozen – in *His Master's Voice* catalogue, particularly the two Bach Fugues in E minor and D minor, and that record containing a wonderful detached Prelude in E flat by the same composer.

Sorabji also sent a private letter to Violet. Asking her to excuse him for addressing himself to her directly, he wrote that "in his public capacity as a critic he had paid tribute to her incomparable art", but that he felt something more was now due.

Last night more than ever your recital was a revelation of a whole world of profundities, of subtleties of phrasing and manner that not only are never approached but exist as far beyond and above the conception of the ordinary platform performer as four dimensional space beyond the notion of a not very intelligent preparatory school boy hearing the multiplication table – and it was not for nothing that, as I have been told, that transcendent genius Busoni often spoke of you as one of the greatest living keyboard artists.

One thinks one has said all there is to say about such playing, such clairvoyant musicianship, such alchemistic magic of true quality blending as yours. And after, one realises that *all* is unsaid, that the only possible description of your playing is your own playing. I pray of you to accept, Madame, the most profound and respectful homage of a fellow musician.

Paradoxically, Violet's retreat to privacy came at the very moment of the triumph of all she stood for musically. By the late 1920s, after long years of struggle, the revival of baroque music had been assured by Arnold Dolmetsch's assiduous scholarship and Violet's matchless interpretation, while the improving technology of gramophone recording was making music available to the masses. But Violet, strong enough in character to be immune to the lure of easy fame, was determined to go her own way. From now on, with the rarest of exceptions, she played only to intimate audiences in library, study or drawing-room. "These audiences," writes Richard Luckett, the great Cambridge music scholar, "consisted of the most influential and discriminating artistic figures of the time. Where their testimony of her genius survives, it is unanimously approving. The remarkable thing is that so little has been set down about her. Yet this is confirmation of her privacy; it was not in the nature of the experience she offered that it should invite public promotion."

Distanced, by her own choice, from the musical capitals of Europe, and freed at last from financial pressure, Violet might easily have allowed her technique to slip, but her daily working routine remained unchanged. Straight after breakfast, which followed her morning walk, she would practise and study for at least three hours without fail. Moreover, far from fading, her reputation, if anything, gained lustre from her inaccessibility, as word of Nether Lypiatt's beauty and its welcoming hospitality spread to the artistic centres of Europe.

Apart from the central figures in Violet's circle who are met again and again, whether in London, at Lypiatt, or earlier, at Armscote – the Sitwells, Ethel Smyth, Dolmetsch, Rubio, Arbós, Arthur Waley and Lionel Tertis – others, such as Delius, Vaughan Williams, the composer William Walton, Thomas Beecham, Bernard Shaw, Siegfried Sassoon, Diaghilev, Karsavina and Ezra Pound, recur frequently in her musical life; and at one time or another almost all the greatest performers of the first half of the twentieth century played with her publicly or privately, including Casals, Busoni, Sarasate, and the Spanish classical guitarist Andrés Segovia. She was courted by monarchs and society hostesses, and her friendship was sought ardently by women whose talents would be even better known had they lived in a less male-dominated era – women like Radclyffe Hall and Christabel Marshal. Still others went to hear her play at home of whose visits we know little more than the books or letters they left behind in gratitude, or the fainter trace of an anecdote or an admiring mention to a mutal friend. Among these were philosophers and men of action, poets and painters, writers and actors: Lawrence of Arabia, Aldous Huxley, Isaiah Berlin and Bertrand Russell; Wilfred Owen, Robert Graves and T.S. Eliot; John Singer Sargent, Rex Whistler, Picasso and Rodin; Rudyard Kipling, Virginia Woolf, Edith Somerville, Arthur Symons and Kenneth Clark; Ellen Terry, Moira Shearer and John Gielgud; and, of course, the cream of the world's conductors and composers – Rachmaninov and Stravinsky, Albéniz and de Falla, Bartók, Henry Wood and Bruno Walter.

This, then, was Violet's milieu, traditionally English to the core, but open to talent of every kind and linked extensively to European culture. It had little in common with the iconoclastic urban outlook of the "Bloomsberries", who were too cliquish and too modish for Violet's taste. She preferred the idealistic egalitarianism of the Arts and Crafts movement to the fashionable socialism of the Woolfs; her favourite reading was from the poets and chroniclers of ordinary life, and of the countryside –

A.E. Housman and Thomas Hardy. She could be entirely modern, but rejected anything that smacked of modernism for its own sake. For her, the cult of the clavichord grew naturally from the poetry of her own life at Lypiatt, a life devoted to a vanishing idea of harmony. There was, for her, no sharp dividing line between the deep study of Bach and Scarlatti and the country-house life of her men, in which farming, gardening and fox-hunting were the daily fare. And if this seems strange to us today, it is principally because something stranger has come to replace it – the uprooted culture of the modern city.

# XV

*Riches in Abundance*

I
N 1930 ETHEL SMYTH fell in love yet again, this time with Virginia
Woolf, the novelist, critic, and luminary of the Bloomsbury Group.
Virginia and her husband Leonard ran the Hogarth Press, a small publish-
ing house which they had founded in 1917. In 1928 she had published
*Orlando*, a novel in homage to her love for the writer and celebrated
gardener Vita (the Hon. Victoria) Sackville West, followed a year later by
*A Room of One's Own*, an essay on women and writing which later became a
landmark of the feminist movement. She was struggling with her new novel,
*The Waves*, when Ethel appeared on the scene demanding her attention.
"An old woman has fallen in love with me," she wrote in February – "it is at
once hideous and horrid and melancholy-sad. It is like being caught by a
giant crab." Embarrassed that her friends might think she returned Ethel's
feelings, Virginia frequently derided her behind her back, ridiculing her
appearance and her by now considerable deafness. Nevertheless, in its lop-
sided way theirs was an intense love affair of a kind, for Virginia was
profoundly impressed by Ethel, and basked in her admiration.

Ethel very much wanted the new object of her idolization to hear Violet
play, but Virginia was more curious than tempted. Six months into their
prolific correspondence she wrote to Ethel, who was again staying at Lypiatt:

> Tell me all you do – in spite of my inaccuracy, every fact is valuable to
> me: time of getting up, bath, breakfast: scraps of talk, stray ideas,
> what you wear, read, eat; if you dream . . . have you a sitting room;
> how furnished; wine for dinner? Mrs. Woodhouse; and think about –
> what? – and feel – what? And what does your future look like? Also
> your past . . . [I] gape like a baby cuckoo for Ethel's words.

Virginia remained evasive about visiting Violet, adopting her habitual tone
of ironic condescension towards people who moved in grand circles:

> Mrs. Woodhouse. Would you convey to her, if she did ask us, and it

was not only your frantic anticipation that she would ask us, our grateful thanks; because it was very kind in her; and would you say how much I hope to meet her, and perhaps one day to come – one day soon I hope – to Nether what's its name – I love other people to have those houses, mats, tables, chairs, pictures, china and tapestry over the 4 post bed, with lavender in the chamber pots and biscuits in a box shd. one wake hungry in the night: other people I like to have them, not myself.

It was to be another year before Ethel finally succeeded in bringing Violet and Virginia together. Hoping she had laid the foundations for a friendship, she scrawled a pencilled note to Violet while travelling in a train after a private concert at Brompton Square in March 1931. "They were simply bowled over. L.W. said the grandeur of every single thing you played 'the superb music going on all the time'. Virginia said 'Of course you won't believe it what I, unmusical as you think me, got out of it – but I tell you I know Leonard has not enjoyed music like that for ages'. – I knew you'd make friends – that you belong in the same cage."

Virginia sent Violet in thanks a copy of her essay "Dr Burney's Evening Party", the exquisitely told fantasy of a disastrous encounter between the brilliant aristocratic poet and roué, Fulke Greville, and Dr Johnson, in the house of Dr Charles Burney, the eighteenth-century musicologist and Scarlatti scholar. It was a perfectly chosen present, but the relationship between Virginia and Violet was doomed to be stillborn from the outset, for their worlds were miles apart. Much as Ethel adored Virginia, she was goaded to write of her in her diary: "She is arrogant, intellectually, beyond words . . . of religion she has no conception. Her views, and the views of all the Bloomsbury group, about it are quite childish. Also their political views. They think all aristocrats are limited and stupid, and swallow all the humbugging shibboleths of the Labour Party . . ." Ethel's dismissive summing up of Bloomsbury was unkind – but then Bloomsbury was itself unkind, and few of its leading lights were more cynical than Virginia Woolf. It was only Ethel Smyth's starry-eyed vision of her two heroines that made her imagine that Virginia and Violet could ever have formed a genuine friendship.

For the last few years Violet and the Sitwells had been less in touch with each other than any of them would have wished. Violet had been preoccupied with Nether Lypiatt and her professional career, while Osbert and Sachie had been travelling and pursuing fame. Paradoxically, it had been the disastrous production of their musical entertainment *Façade* in 1923 which had launched the Sitwells on their way. The score, by the impoverished young composer William Walton, who was by then living with Osbert and Sachie in Carlyle Square, was based on syncopated jazz rhythms; the action, if such it could be called, consisted of Edith declaiming her own poems in a staccato delivery through a megaphone from behind a screen. The performance was meant to be comical, but Edith kept losing the beat and giggling, and by the time it was over the bemused audience had become thoroughly disenchanted with its amateurishness.

Osbert had turned the fiasco to advantage by exaggerating the hostility of the reaction. A scandal was a perfectly satisfactory outcome – the fate to avoid was being classed as a bore. The English, he claimed, were impossibly philistine; the newspaper critics had insulted the Sitwells in their sacred role as artists; he and his family now went about in fear of physical assault. A few months later Noël Coward's revue *London Calling* had opened, in which there was a sketch featuring the "Swiss Family Whittlebot" – an absurdly pretentious trio bearing every resemblance to Edith, Osbert and Sachie. Coward's show had been a huge success, and had brought the Sitwells the extra publicity they craved. Despite its initial failure, *Façade* had soon become part of the artistic fabric of the twenties, and its second, carefully rehearsed, production in 1926 had been a resounding success.

While Edith wrote poetry and Osbert lorded it over the cultural scene, Sachie had begun to make his name as an art historian, publishing *Southern Baroque Art* in 1924 and *German Baroque Art* in 1927. Together, the three Sitwells epitomized the post-war decade, a charismatic and seemingly inseparable trio of elongated peacocks bound to each other by taste, breeding and blood and surrounded by youthful admirers. The bindings had loosened, however. The beginning of their separation had been Sachie's departure from Carlyle Square on his marriage in 1925 to the materialistic and socially ambitious Georgia Doble, who claimed all the attention which he had once given to Osbert, and on which Osbert had come to be excessively reliant. In 1927 Georgia gave birth to a son, Reresby; thereafter, although Edith and Osbert were eventually to live together, it was increasingly as individuals rather than as a family that the Sitwells made their mark.

Their renewed friendship with Violet coincided with this period in which the Sitwells were starting to drift apart from one another. In 1932 Edith Sitwell left England to be near the Russian artist Pavel Tchelitchew, a much younger man with whom she had long been in love. Tchelitchew, a nobleman who had fled Russia during the Revolution, had settled in Paris with a group of neo-romantic painters who were exhibiting there. It was a difficult relationship, and Edith frequently returned home. In the late summer of 1933 she and Osbert were at Badminton, not far from Violet's house, helping their cousin, the Duchess of Beaufort, to entertain Queen Mary – always an exacting assignment and sometimes an expensive one, since the Queen expected to be given any object to which she took a particular liking. Violet lent Lily to Edith as her lady's maid, and from Badminton, the royal visit over, the Sitwells moved on to Nether Lypiatt. On their first evening, Violet invited W.H. Davies and his wife to dinner, having discovered that they were living near by at Nailsworth. "Fancy two celebrities of our note living so close and not knowing it!" wrote Davies in reply. Meeting again after such a long interval, at least fifteen years, they had much to talk about, and the party stayed up late into the night. Edith and Davies were the last guests to go to bed, exhausting Violet by keeping her up until two in the morning.

Next day, as chance would have it, John Drinkwater telephoned to ask if he might bring his wife to lunch. This was something he did from time to time, maintaining contact with Gordon and Violet in a manner which might be characterized as "keeping-on-good-terms-in-spite-of-everything". Ever since the murder of his cousins he had had his eye fixed firmly on Gordon's will, hoping that, having no children of his own, Gordon might in the end do the right thing by the Drinkwaters after his death. This particular visit, however, had more attached to it than Violet and Gordon supposed. John's alcoholism had begun to get the better of him. His financial affairs were in chaos, and he wanted Gordon to "lend" him money – money which, in his view, belonged to him anyway. When she learned of his intentions, his wife refused to accompany him, and John shoved his fourteen-year-old daughter, Diana, into the car instead. Terrified by the sophisticated atmosphere at Lypiatt, Diana nevertheless took in every detail of her two and a half hours there. She had been brought up frugally in naval quarters and had not seen lobster before, nor asparagus, nor lamb cutlets decorated with white paper ruffs. The tastes, too, were a revelation. The rack of lamb was so succulent it was almost sweet; peaches and nectarines lurked in a hot soufflé, whose froth rose up and overspilled its dish; and there were quantities of chocolates, nuts and coconut pyramids.

Diana spoke not a word at lunch. Violet, her tiny, fairy-like figure adorned in beehive layers of mauve velvet, and Edith, huge, white-faced after her late night, and tented in heavy, flowing black garments, appeared to her like two outlandish witches. After coffee, John Drinkwater asked to speak to Gordon alone. Diana's time in the drawing-room with Violet proved to be too short for her to listen to any music her hostess might play. Quite soon she was summoned by her father who, grim-faced, hurried her into the hall to leave. The journey home was in silence – John's request for money had been turned down by Gordon.

There was little traffic on the roads in the 1930s, and journeys by car were something to be enjoyed, rather than endured. Violet's household made frequent expeditions, sometimes being dropped off for walks and picnics, and then picked up again at a prearranged rendezvous, by the full-time chauffeur whom Gordon now employed. Among their favourite destinations were the nineteenth-century Italian garden of the Gorst family, who owned the village of Castle Combe; the formal seventeenth-century Dutch water gardens at Westbury, on the far side of the Severn, with their canals and yew hedges; and the rather ghostly seventeenth-century Oxfordshire village of Great Tew. Osbert and Edith, too, had their preferred places, where Violet would take them to shop or to sightsee – Angel's antique shop and Bayntun's second-hand bookshop in Bath; the church at Lydiard Tregoze, an eighteenth-century estate near Swindon, which contained the St John family's ancient tomb with its sixteen lifelike effigies of members of the first baronet's family; and Sezincote House, built by Samuel Pepys Cockerell between 1798 and 1805, the history of which particularly appealed to Osbert because it had "provided the theme on which King George IV and his band of landscapists and architects had founded . . . the Royal Pavilion at Brighton".

Violet wanted to take the Sitwells to see Winifred and Detmar Blow, but since early 1933 they had not been receiving, having become virtual recluses after Detmar had been accused of embezzlement by his patron, Bendor, Duke of Westminster. Hurt beyond words by the false accusation, as the Blows maintain, or in guilty confusion, as the Westminster camp made out, Detmar repaid £25,000 and suffered a nervous breakdown, from which he scarcely recovered before his death in 1939. To this day, the Blow version of events is that Detmar was given cash freely over the years as compensation for abandoning his lucrative career and accepting a small salary to look after Bendor's business affairs. But it was hard for him to prove his innocence, for the documentation of gifts and expenses had been kept to a minimum.

Towards the end of the Sitwells' stay in 1933, Bill's glamorous niece, Lorna Brooke, was invited to Lypiatt for the day. After lunch she was asked to entertain Osbert while Violet had a session with her chiropodist, who had come down from London. Having finished her treatment, Violet could find the pair nowhere. Searching the house and garden, she eventually tracked them down to "Little Lypiatt", the summerhouse, where they were ensconced in animated conversation. Violet was not at all amused, and Lorna, who strongly suspected that Osbert had a preference for men, of which her hostess was presumably as aware as she was, was nevertheless made to feel that she had encouraged one of Violet's beaux to make a pass at her.

After that first visit, Osbert came frequently to Nether Lypiatt, and his recollections of the house and its inhabitants were surrounded by a halo of romance. For him the house was

the colour of a guinea-fowl's plumage, standing on the top of a steep hill near Stroud, above the valley of the Severn. This old palace in miniature – for such, with its complex architectural organisation of iron grille and of gardens and outhouses as formal as a fugue by Bach, it seemed – constituted a perfect setting for [Violet]. Beyond the world of music stood the farm . . . and the orchards and kitchen-gardens. These factors helped to tinge the general atmosphere with a sense of the unvarying English traditional background; orchard and farm and potting-shed overflowed, as it were, into the lower storey of the house, into the more masculine rooms, comfortable studies and smoking rooms, where, among the pieces of solid 1790 or 1800 mahogany and well-worn carpets and chairs, had strayed baskets of apples and pears, shallow wicker trays of walnuts, even, occasionally, vegetables, – a turnip or a carrot, – roots of flowers, a piece of brass, so that by the content of the room, even coming out of a trance in a vacuum, you could judge of the season outside by these traces of the earth's fruits dropped from the cornucopia of some English Goddess of Plenty. The rooms above, superbly panelled and richly coloured, seemed always to be filled with sun – though I thought, sometimes, with the vanished sun of another age, which glowed also upon the garden. With its high yew hedges and stone walls, with its exquisite dark-toned flowers – for example bergamot, moisia roses, columbines in various shades of night and flowing water, and among the shrubs a honey-scented ceanothus, the spicy blossom of which was the colour of Violet's hair, and another that was hung with shapes like small red lanterns – it provided endless pleasure for hostess and guests. Here, before going up to the drawing-room to practise, she would walk, straight and supple, swift as a wind, round the confines, so as to breathe the sharp, hilly air; or she might take you . . . to see her feed the Italian green lizards that would flash with emerald fire as they flickered at her out of the interstices of the loose grey walls in which they lived, beneath the green grass terraces. Or, again, she might run you at great speed to feed with sugar Cupid, a young and most handsome

Herefordshire bull that might have been drawn by William Blake (so impulsive in her generosity was she to all living things, that once when, on a dark and cheerless day of winter a guest asked "where is Violet?", a witty friend, Norah Lindsay, who was also staying in the house, replied, "O she's out buttering the lawns for the birds!").

On 12 September 1933, Lord Barrington died, aged eighty-five. As the eldest son, Bill succeeded to his father's title and to what remained of the Beckett estate. Although he had finally been forced to agree to the sale of the big house, he had managed to safeguard much of his inheritance from the depredations of his stepmother and the incompetence of his father, and in the circumstances he came into more than he had expected. When the removal vans appeared at Lypiatt, bringing his possessions from Beckett, Violet put the best china and eighteenth-century furniture in the drawing-room, and invited William and Eve Simmonds over for a picture-hanging session. There were a number of Barrington family portraits by distin-guished artists – Kneller, Reynolds, Romney, Lawrence and Leighton – and they decided that the best place for these was up the staircase. The rest of the furniture and the less good pictures would have to go to London, together with a few of Gordon's and Violet's pieces which had been displaced to make way for Bill's.

Now that the three oldest members of the household had reached their sixties, they had come to find the tall, narrow house in Brompton Square rather tiring. They therefore sold it, and bought a flat in Porchester Terrace, convenient for Paddington station (the main-line terminus for trains to Gloucestershire) and with rooms large enough for Bill's bulky furniture. In the summer of 1934 the new flat was ready for its house-warming party.

That same year a Jubilee Festival was organized in honour of Ethel Smyth's seventy-fifth birthday, for which Thomas Beecham offered to conduct her two large works, choral and orchestral respectively, *The Mass in D* and *The Prison*, at the Albert Hall on 3 March. Although Ethel was by now stone deaf, she could hardly bring herself to admit this even to herself. In her autobiography she pretended that she had been able to hear the concert well enough to know that Beecham had "rendered the music as I had never hoped to hear it; and what is more, as if he himself loved it". Beecham's sympathetic conducting meant much to Ethel, for she greatly admired his musicianship and was acutely conscious of his previously lukewarm attitude to her compositions.

There are two revealingly different accounts of the Albert Hall concert – revealing because they show why Virginia Woolf and Violet could never have become friends. Virginia, scrutinizing Ethel where she sat in the Royal Box, made cruelly mocking notes of her jerky movements and her blunder in rising to her feet at the wrong moment, misled by her deafness into believing that the National Anthem was being played. Since the recent death of her rich sister, Mary Hunter, who had hitherto always provided the post-concert entertaining for Ethel's special guests, Ethel had been left to fend for herself. On this occasion she took her group on to a Lyons' Corner House, where they all paid for their own tea and buns. Virginia's lips curled as she made her diary entry for the day: ". . . and so to Lyons . . . that sordid crumby room . . . all rather strident and obvious amid clerks and shop girls."

Violet's reaction to Ethel's big event could scarcely have been in sharper contrast. Writing to Dorothy, she was full of pride in Ethel's achievement:

> 38 Brompton Square *4 March 1934*
> Darling Doll,
> I expect you will hear from Miss Hudson about the concert yesterday. It was a great success & Ethel & the Queen sat side by side in the Royal Box! looking very fine. We went to a sixpenny tea at Lyons by Ethel's request after, & it was very amusing. I was with Beecham, Sir Hugh Allan [Professor of Music at Oxford and Director of the Royal College of Music], Virginia Woolf, Vanessa Bell [a painter, and sister to Virginia], Lady Diana Duff-Cooper,[1] etc. Such a wonderful mixture, & who but Ethel could collect such a distinguished company at Lyons 6d tea! Lady Lovat was there too, & Lady Maud Warrender & Lady Cunard & goodness knows who else. Sir Hugh Allan said to me "This is the maddest tea-party since the Mad Hatters" or something to that effect . . . Ever so much love darling Doll from V.

In October 1935 Ethel came to stay at Lypiatt again, after a visit to her ear specialist in Bath. As usual Virginia pursued her with a letter ". . . I was told you were off somewhere in the country with Mrs. Woodhouse (please convey her my respectful homages). Ought we to buy the Scarlatti records?". Afterwards Ethel wrote to Violet the saddest of thank-you letters:

> I can never tell you how adorable it was of you having me – and letting me feel I shouldn't wear you out by my deafness. It touched me to the marrow. And I think of all you made possible for me . . . it

---

1 Lady Diana has been met before – as the beautiful debutante Lady Diana Manners, and as Norah Lindsay's niece. Her husband, Alfred Duff Cooper, later Lord Norwich, gained fame in 1938 for resigning from the government in protest against Neville Chamberlain's policy of appeasing Hitler.

made my heart ache to think I am cut off from what is my most overwhelming musical joy – your playing – but I won't dwell on that. Only don't think that because I say nothing . . . well, you know.

Bath was a popular health spa in the thirties, and Elinor Glyn, the green-eyed writer of highly successful, rather steamy romantic novels, who had gained notoriety in 1907 by featuring illicit passion on a tiger skin in her book *Three Weeks*,[2] soon followed Ethel and Denis there. Now aged seventy-one, she was staying at the Grand Pump Room Hotel, resting and trying to recuperate from an unpleasant operation. She had managed to gain an introduction to Violet, who invited her to Lypiatt, sending a car to collect her and complaining half-jokingly to Eve Simmonds that her house was turning into a convalescent home.

There was a chameleon-like quality to Elinor Glyn. Although she was a woman of poses, there were many sides to her personality: her case, in fact, was not so much one of faking a character as of choosing between several equally genuine alternatives. The persona she adopted now was gay, witty, brave and sophisticated, as she assured Violet that her cure had progressed splendidly. She was captivated by her visit to Nether Lypiatt, and hoped to sustain the new friendship by inviting Violet back to her house in Connaught Place, where the drawing-room was self-consciously littered with tiger skins. She wrote:

> Most Charming of Violets! Once more today, the scent of freshness & sweetness & love was in your atmosphere – no wonder everyone adores you! So gracious & so gentle. I was so happy in my day with you on Sunday, & again this afternoon, & I do thank, thank you for your being so kind to me. What fun we had looking at houses! & indeed someday I hope the dream will come true . . . Again every grateful "thank you" & every blessing from your new friend Elinor. Thank Lord B. [Bill] for so nobly driving me on Sunday! Remember it is a "date" in London. My telephone is Paddington 8918.

Next it was Denis's turn to go to Bath for a cure. By far the fittest of Violet's three men, Denis was still exercising daily at Lypiatt by jogging round the farm and woodlands, but he became unwell and was ominously prescribed "ray treatment". Violet often went with him to Bath in the Daimler, and was profoundly relieved when the treatment, which exhausted Denis, seemed to have effected enough of a recovery for him to discontinue it.

2 "Would you like to sin / With Elinor Glyn / On a tiger skin? / Or would you prefer / To err / With her / On some other fur?" Anon 1907.

Now aged sixty-four, Violet was beginning to feel her age. For the first time, she found herself looking back at her life. While spending the Christmas of 1935 in the flat in Porchester Terrace, she wrote to Dorothy: "You are right about the past, & how sad it must be to look back & I find myself shrinking from doing so now; a cowardly thing. How lovely it was to be young! Darling Dorothy, how much I do love you, & wish you well, & I hope to see you before long. I had some lovely presents & am so pleased to have dear Bill, dear Gordon & dear Denis with me." For some years she had been dyeing her hair. Dorothy did not at all like the result. "She has ruined her fascinating looks by making her hair blue," she complained to her diary, and later: "I seem to aggravate V. who is as cold as her steely blue hair." This dramatic shade, described by Osbert Sitwell as ceanothus-coloured, was a source of wonder to children. Some thought it quite natural that a person called Violet should have violet-coloured hair, but Bill's great-niece, Annabel Brooke, found it frightening. One evening, when Annabel was staying at Lypiatt, Violet came to her bedroom to say goodnight. She was dressed in an elegant crinolined dressing gown, her blue hair flowing out around her shoulders and down her back, ready for re-pinning. Annabel dived under the sheets, only to be dragged out by Lily and told to behave. Violet, so used to being able to charm children if she wanted to, suddenly saw herself through a child's eyes. For once in her life disconcerted, she said to Lily "Leave her – she likes to play at hiding in bed," extended a hand to Annabel in a gesture half way between a wave and a dismissal, and went to dress for dinner.

If Violet momentarily thought that her best years were behind her, she was mistaken, for 1935 was the year which marked the rejuvenation of her musical inspiration through the influence of two people, the instrument maker Tom Goff, and her old friend Sachie Sitwell.

Tom Goff had been taken to hear Violet play the harpsichord at Ovington Square in 1920, when he was still an undergraduate reading law at Oxford. Her music, her appearance and her conversation had left an indelible impression on him. Six years later Herbert Lambert, a well-known photographer and amateur clavichord maker, who lived near Bath, took him to Nether Lypiatt to meet her again. After playing to them for an hour on the harpsichord, Violet went over to her clavichord, which Tom had not seen in Ovington Square, and played the first of Bach's forty-eight preludes, the prelude in C Major from Book 1 of *The Well-Tempered Klavier*. The sound of that infinitely delicate piece as Violet coaxed it from the clavichord was to change his life:

Looking back on that afternoon, it seems to me that her touch . . . was most tender and exquisite . . . Certainly I thought I had never heard a more wonderful and more moving sound than that which her fingers drew from that frail web of golden strings. I was like the monk in the mediaeval story, who went forth from his monastery one day in spring and heard the lark singing in the heavens and listened spellbound. Then, when the song was finished he went to the monastery. But all the old faces which he had known had vanished. Time for him had stood still, and a century had passed while he listened to the song. Indeed such a spell was cast on me.

On the way home, Tom announced to the amused but dismissive Herbert Lambert that he was going to give up his career at the Bar and learn how to make clavichords. He was immoderately proud of his ancestry, being a direct descendant of King William IV, and the idea that he might turn himself into a full-time artisan struck his friend as bizarre. Undeterred, Tom set about his long apprenticeship in the craft of cabinet-making, attending a course near Bath while at the same time staying in Lambert's house and learning as much as he could from him. Moving back to London, he went on to enroll in adult joinery classes provided by the London County Council. When he told Joseph Cobby, the teacher to whom he was assigned, that it was not bookshelves he wished to make but clavichords, Cobby stared at him in astonishment and replied: "I have waited all my life for someone to say that to me." Eventually they set up a workshop together, becoming famous as pioneers in the making of early instruments, which they designed to be beautiful pieces of furniture in their own right, taking as much care over their appearance as over their working parts – the underside of the lids of their clavichords were decorated with inlaid inscriptions, or with paintings by contemporary artists like Rex Whistler, Oliver Messel and John Piper.

Violet recognized in Tom an artist after her own heart. The clavichord is the supreme keyboard instrument of personal expression, and Violet felt that she had been made for it. She had long played it in her drawing-room, usually after the harpsichord, but she had never possessed an instrument which gave her total satisfaction. In 1935 she found in Tom Goff's new clavichords depths and subtleties previously undreamt of. Later, as her physical strength diminished, even the harpsichord came gradually to yield first place to the clavichord in her affections.

Gentle, donnish and friendly, immaculately dressed in quiet suits (the trousers always with outside seams) and waistcoat, Tom was also shy and touchy, and could be over-sensitive about his art. Violet would sometimes make fun of him behind his back. But if she did not always sufficiently appreciate him, Tom's admiration for her was boundless. He described his first encounter with Violet as having been "as if one of the immortals had come to earth and was playing upon an instrument peculiar to the genius of such a being, and one could no more say that one liked or disliked the sound than one could have gauged the effect on more mortal ears of the lyre of Phoebus Apollo." There was a scholar in Tom as well as a romantic, and his analysis of Violet's technique, the fullest one extant, is a masterly exposition of her methods.[3]

By a fortunate coincidence, 1935 also saw the reappearance of Sachie Sitwell in Violet's life. Having spent the immediate post-war years pursuing his love of architecture, Sachie had become enmeshed in cosmopolitan "smart" society after his marriage to Georgia. Georgia was bored by Weston, Sachie's manor house in Northamptonshire, and was only interested in London and the endless parties given by the "bright young things" of the twenties and early thirties, such as the Hon. Stephen Tennant (Lord and Lady Glenconner's son), Cecil Beaton, the photographer, and Cynthia and Oswald Mosley (she the daughter of Lord Curzon, formerly Viceroy of India, and Foreign Secretary from 1919 to 1924; he a Labour MP and soon to become Britain's most prominent fascist). By 1935, filled with a sense of spiritual malaise, Sachie had returned to his lifelong passion for music, completing biographies of Mozart (1932) and Liszt (1934). He dedicated his next book to Violet, *A Background for Domenico Scarlatti*. She later confessed that it was another four years before she read the book properly, but her letter of gratitude showed that his gift marked the point at which she realized for the first time that Sachie placed Scarlatti on the same high plane as she did.

With this exchange there began a musical relationship which in the end was to become as significant to Violet as her relationships with Dolmetsch, Rubio, Ethel Smyth and Tom Goff. With Sachie alone was she able in her last years to share her deepest ideas about music; and when war came again, it was to Sachie above all others that she would turn for the solace of music, as they embarked together on an extraordinary odyssey in search of forgotten works of Scarlatti.

> Porchester Terrace W.2. *January 1935*
> My Dearest Sachie,
> It gives me the very greatest pleasure to think you should dedicate your book on the glorious Scarlatti to me, & how delighted I am

3 See Appendix IV.

that you should be the one to write it . . . that you should be the one to see that Scarlatti had his proper seat with the immortals . . . I sometimes feel that Rubio and I are the only persons engaged with music who realise that Scarlatti is equal to anyone within his own sublime limits and limits are so necessary to Art, don't you think? I really worship him, & often resent harpsichord players generally not able to play him properly, & piano players with no respect or imagination, & of course the brilliant orchestral writing is utterly wasted on the piano . . . Thank you so much . . . I mean to give a concert at the Wigmore Hall March 5th & wish you were coming but I think it unlikely

Much love & many thanks for the honour from Violet.

The forthcoming concert to which Violet referred was to be a public recital, her first for years, in which she would play with Lionel Tertis,[4] perhaps the greatest viola player of the twentieth century. After nearly a decade out of the public eye, and spurred on by renewed energy at the thought of giving another concert, Violet took on an ambitious programme, playing pieces by Handel, Giovanni Battista Martini, Mozart, Baldassare Galuppi, Giuseppe Tartini, Scarlatti, Georg Philipp Telemann, Nicolo Antonio Porpora, Vaughan Williams, Kalnis, Poulenc and Marin Marais. Once again, as had happened with her concert with Casals, Violet more than matched her fellow artist. The music critic of *The Times* thought that "everything was exceedingly well played, though one felt that the viola's tone was sometimes too dry, especially on the top string. The viola tone seemed, too, to take off some of the sparkle of the harpsichord, which sounded better in the solo music."

Recording technology had made significant advances in the thirties, and it is a minor tragedy that Violet never returned to the studio in these years. This was partly because of her return to quasi-amateur status, but more because, as Harry Haskell put it in *The Early Musical Revival*, "the gramophone companies . . . simply gave the public what it wanted to hear." Describing Violet as "Landowska's most formidable rival", Haskell writes that her few recordings have stood the test of time "remarkably well", and laments the "lacuna in the historical record" which has deprived future generations of the sound of her impressively "magisterial technique and grand manner".

When Violet did appear in public, it was usually for charity. In the

---

4 In 1938 Tertis came to live near Lypiatt and often played with Violet in her drawing-room. He must have achieved a gentle, muted effect, for Eve Simmonds thought his viola and Violet's clavichord "very well balanced and beautiful together".

summer of 1935 Lady Londonderry, one of the great political hostesses of the day, persuaded Violet to play a harpsichord programme in aid of one of the many good causes which she supported. This was followed by a recital in November at Lady Wimborne's. Much to the annoyance of Osbert Sitwell, his protégé William Walton had recently fallen in love with Alice Wimborne and had moved into her Chelsea mews house, deserting Carlyle Square where Osbert had looked after him for sixteen years. A talented pianist and a great beauty, Alice Wimborne lived in perfect infidelity in her husband's magnificent William Kent house behind the Ritz in Piccadilly, where she arranged concerts and recitals of exceptional quality, in which Violet regularly performed.

On 5 May 1936 Violet agreed with Kennedy Scott, the conductor, to support the ailing Bach Cantata Club by holding a harpsichord concert at the Royal Academy of Music for a token fee of fifteen guineas. She played Bach's French Suite in G and the Partita in B Flat. The *Daily Telegraph* commented:

> To hear Bach played on the harpsichord is at all times refreshing, but especially so when the music is presented with the nice discrimination and deftly unobtrusive skill that distinguish Mrs Woodhouse's performances. It was delightful to hear all the resources of contrasted colour used with such aptness and imagination, and to note the subtle variations of tempo – a true rubato – that left the essential rhythm unimpaired.

Violet's mastery was founded on intensive practice, which she never allowed to lapse into routine or mechanical exercise. In the late thirties she was increasingly working in private on the relatively few known works of Domenico Scarlatti, transferring them to the clavichord. It was, however, on an occasion when she was practising Bach on the harpsichord that Osbert Sitwell was able to observe her without being seen or heard, and without disturbing her concentration. He had risen early one morning at Lypiatt, taking his papers into the drawing-room to read in a corner before breakfast, and when Violet came down she did not see or hear him. She opened the harpsichord, raised and pegged the lid, methodically removed her bangles, rings and bracelets, softly commanded her Pekinese to lie down on the rug, sat down and began to practise. "So intent was she on the job before her," wrote Osbert,

> that of phrasing and re-phrasing a fugue of Bach's over and over again, that I was able to remain, enthralled, in the room for over an hour while she engaged in an astounding personal combat. I have never been more interested than in this process of wrestling with

an angel audible, if invisible; a struggle to which she perpetually reverted, renewing the attack from a different angle, and not ceasing until she had achieved a victory whereby she had mastered every thought and feeling that the greatest of European composers had expressed within the strictest bounds of his art.

On 28 February 1938 Violet was in London for the eightieth-birthday celebrations of her old mentor, Arnold Dolmetsch, whose family had invited a large number of friends from his past to the Art Workers Guild to listen to music composed or arranged by Dolmetsch between 1888 and 1936. The French Ambassador made an appreciative speech in recognition of Dolmetsch's services to the artistic life of France. Dolmetsch's response was ungracious. As the Ambassador bent to take the insignia of the Croix de la Légion d'Honneur from their case, Dolmetsch visibly shrugged and audibly "humphed", as if to say "and about time, too". The occasion was further marred by his own speech, in which after a perfunctory expression of gratitude, he vented his bitterness at the many imaginary injustices he had suffered over the years.

The Simmondses had also come up to London for the Dolmetsch party. On the following day Violet took them off to a retrospective exhibition by Sickert,[5] and then to a performance of *Robert's Wife*, a play starring Edith Evans. They were accompanied by Gordon and Bill, who were congratulating themselves on having dodged a heavy musical occasion and an unpleasant speech the previous evening. One of Violet's most attractive traits, however, was to see only the best in her friends, and she wrote warmly to thank Dolmetsch, singling out for special praise his early composition "Il est ressuscité", a hymn inspired by the first sound of the bells after their silence throughout Holy Week.

54 Porchester Terrace London W2 *7 March 1938*
My dear Arnold
I have been intending to write to you ever since this day last week, but was waiting to be able to suggest a day to drive to see you and bring that bottle of brandy from Gordon! But I have been longing to tell you what an immense pleasure I experienced in listening to the programme of your music. I came away feeling excited, happy and much moved by the really golden beauty and originality and freshness of what I had heard: and the divine sound of the Easter hymn: I cannot imagine how you managed to make that effect! The

5 Walter Sickert (1860–1942), English Impressionist, noted for his London interiors, whose work was much admired by Osbert Sitwell and Violet.

contralto song "Sweet Bee" was so moving: and of course, Hark Hark the Lark, both so exquisitely orchestrated and played in such a fashion by Carl! [Dolmetsch's son.] Now I should like to have Records of those three pieces immensely if they are done. I did not see anyone when I came away to ask. I think you should have another concert of your compositions. Several more!

I never expected to hear such music, and I was touched and moved to the heart, and *I am not easily stirred* !! I felt exalted. And musical Emotion is like religion. There is nothing like it in any other art. Now some day before long I hope to suggest coming down to [see you in] Haslemere.

My love to Mabel, and thank you dear Arnold for making me feel such enthusiasm and pleasure. Your affectionate Violet.

Having discovered that Osbert was popular with Queen Mary as someone to entertain her, his cousin Mary, the Duchess of Beaufort, would invite him to Badminton whenever the Queen came to stay there. After a while the role of courtier would pall, and he would move on with relief to stay with Violet. In the late summer of 1938 Violet was at a spa in Wales with Bill, Denis and Gordon, taking a cure for rheumatism, when on a sudden royal whim Queen Mary expressed the desire that Osbert should take her to see Nether Lypiatt. Mary Stanton had died in June and Dorothy Walker, who took her place, had not yet moved in, so it was left to the three servants who lived in − the butler, the maid and the cook Bessie − to look after the Queen. Bessie wrote an affectionate letter to Violet afterwards giving a full description of the visit:

> . . . everything went off so well, my dearest Madam . . . what a moment of nerves but She said Good afternoon to us and Captain Sitwell came in with her and I gave your best love to say how very sorry you were not to be here and Queen Mary spoke up and said I am sorry too . . . she admired your little round Nelson wardrobe and wanted it opened and she admired the gold pictures in your room and also the model of his lordship on the cupboard . . . I think it was her lady in waiting said tell me I see so many of Nelson's things about, why? I said you admired him so and what he did . . . she asked to go in the garden she really had a good look at things . . . I know you will be pleased it all went off so well madam dear,
>
> Yours very affectionately Bessie.

Given Queen Mary's notorious acquisitiveness, Violet's absence proved fortuitous for her Nelson collection and for her "gold pictures", which were actually collages of Venice made for her by Bill. But Queen Mary had missed what she had chiefly wanted, which was to hear Violet play, and the visit led to a summons to Buckingham Palace in the autumn. There Violet played not only for Queen Mary but also for her daughter-in-law, Queen Elizabeth, and for Queen Elizabeth's two young children, the Princesses Elizabeth and Margaret. Violet afterwards wrote proudly to Dorothy:

> 54 Porchester Terrace, W2 *Nov 1938*
> Darling Doll,
> I think the affair went off very well, and that I played as well as I could have, on the old harpsichord which belonged to Handel. Anyhow they seemed to think that they would like me to come again. The Queen [Elizabeth; now the Queen Mother] looked, and was, quite charming, and the two little princesses SWEET, with beautiful manners, and the little one was very excited and enthusiastic, and Princess Elizabeth quieter, but charming and beautifully mannered, and delighted with the harpsichord. They do not seem the least spoiled, and sweet and gay, and the Queen also. Prince Paul of Serbia was there to listen, and seemed so intelligent, and Lady Nunburnholme, and Lady Victoria Wemyss,[6] Lord Gerald Wellesley, Captain Streatfield and Tom Goff. I thought how pleased Papa and Mama would have been!
> Much love my dear Violet.

As 1938 drew to a close, forebodings of a new world war were in the air. The Prime Minister, Neville Chamberlain, had returned from Munich waving a piece of paper, an agreement to cede the German-speaking part of Czechoslovakia to Hitler in exchange for a promise of "peace for our time". But there was widespread anxiety that appeasement might not succeed, and Violet was tormented by her memories of the Great War – the death of Max Labouchère, Bill's ordeal in Mesopotamia, Denis's narrow escapes. The thought of a new generation undergoing what they had suffered filled her with fear, and brought back in a flood her old feelings of anger against warmongering politicians. These feelings were no doubt stronger in Violet, with her emotionally naive character, than in others, but the conviction that "it must never happen again" was widespread throughout the country, and did much to undermine the possibility of a robust foreign and defence policy, which ironically would have been by far the best safeguard against Hitler's aggression.

6 Woman of the Bedchamber to Queen Elizabeth, and a godchild of Queen Victoria, she died in May 1994, aged 104.

The year of 1939 started normally enough – a New Year puppet show at the Simmondses' cottage with eleven guests from Lypiatt; the Rothensteins coming over for lunch the following week; journeys into Cheltenham to the cinema to see David Selznick's *The Prisoner of Zenda* and Greta Garbo in *Ninotchka*; Dorothy Walker's annual Boat Race party in April, given at her father's house on the Thames at Hammersmith, but taken so naturally under her own wing by Violet that most of the guests assumed that she was the hostess; and visits from Tom Goff and Sachie Sitwell. The whole household moved to London as usual for May and June. But already Hitler had invaded what remained of Czechoslovakia in March, and Britain and France had felt obliged to give a guarantee to defend Poland. As the summer drifted on into July and August, Violet at last accepted that war was inevitable. On 25 August, she asked Dorothy Walker to make arrangements for all her musical instruments to be transported to Lypiatt for safety.

# XVI

*Wrath and War*

O N I SEPTEMBER 1939, Nazi Germany invaded Poland; at the same
time, Russia, which had signed a secret "non-aggression pact" with
Germany, invaded eastern Poland. Two days later, Gordon, Bill and Denis
gathered round their wireless set to hear Neville Chamberlain announce
that the British ultimatum to Germany to withdraw from Poland had
expired, and that Britain was therefore at war. Violet could not bring herself to listen. Her experiences from 1914 to 1918 had left her with such an
indelible horror of war that she was unable to come to terms with the fact
that there was a vast difference between taking arms against Hitler's Nazis
and fighting senselessly against the Germany of Kaiser Wilhelm II. She was
overwhelmed by a sense of impending destruction, not only of life but of the
cities of Europe, the buildings, sculpture and paintings, the rich and diverse
civilization which she had loved from childhood.

Violet shared with the two Sitwell brothers a profound admiration for
German culture. In her youth, Leipzig, Berlin and Vienna had been her
musical Meccas; and her mind had been filled for over fifty years with the
genius of Bach, Mozart, Beethoven and Wagner. Her first piano teachers,
Winter and Beringer, had steeped her in that peculiarly German tradition of
apprenticeship, in which art or scholarship is passed from generation to
generation, as the pupil graduates to become in turn the master. Long after
the outbreak of war, she was not ashamed to tell people that she would have
been proud to have been born a German.

Although one of Violet's most appealing characteristics was the intensity
of feeling with which she expressed herself about every idea under the
sun, her vehemence against anything that smacked of jingoistic militarism
now struck even her greatest admirers as unbalanced. Having been set on
a pedestal by her own family, and accorded almost regal status by Bill,
Gordon and Denis, she had grown accustomed to saying and doing whatever she liked without having to exercise much self-control. Since Max's

death nobody had stood up to her, and now that she had become fearful of losing everything she held dear, her misery and her blind faith in the harmonizing effects of German music had driven her to look elsewhere than to the Germans for the main responsibility for the disaster which was about to befall the world. She believed that the greater culprits were the soon-to-be-deposed Prime Minister, Neville Chamberlain, Hitler's most implacable opponent, Winston Churchill (now First Lord of the Admiralty once more, the position he had held at the beginning of the First World War), and the Marxists, whom she vaguely associated with Judaism. Germany had been provoked beyond endurance in 1919 by the punitive Treaty of Versailles, its very survival threatened by the rise of Communism; war itself was the ultimate evil, visited on the innocent young by incompetent or malign non-combatants – that, at least, was Violet's doctrine, much of it derived from the Sitwells and magnified as it passed through the prism of her own feelings and preconceptions.

Ethel Smyth was one of the few who might have had the authority and the sense to set boundaries to Violet's wilder notions, but she would not tackle the problem. Engrossed in the last volume of her own memoirs, she avoided all mention of politics with Violet and wrote instead merely of music, expressing her gratitude for the help Violet had always given her, from the time when, in May 1908, Violet had talked the London Symphony Orchestra into performing "On The Cliffs of Cornwall".

Violet was temporarily out of touch with Edith and had not seen Sachie since the summer, but she wrote to Osbert at Renishaw, the Sitwells' large, cold eighteenth-century family home in Derbyshire: "Isn't this shocking! Do let me have a line to say how you are, and how dear Sachie and Georgia . . . & so soon the visiting moon looks down upon another horrible abyss." She was reassured that she still had at least one kindred spirit:

> I was so thankful to get your letter. Norah Lindsay is staying here & is suffering from an attack of roaring Patriotism mixed with the terror of Peter's going to war. Her conversation is full of go-till-we-drop bellicosity which I do not believe she really feels. Osbert, it is just like a kind of drunkenness which is so catching.

Edith had been summoned back from France by Osbert (she would spend the rest of the war with him at Renishaw), while Sachie had been allocated home defence duties near Weston, his Northamptonshire home. In October 1939 Sachie received from Violet what was to be the beginning of an intense correspondence.

If we are alive in February we might meet, but it is a long time ahead. The war & all to do with it seems so terrible & it makes one wild, & each day people in authority almost seem to wallow further & further, & to see less & less reason, & of course make it more & more difficult to stop.

Her letter swept on to music, her sole hope of consolation. It was four years since he had sent his book on Scarlatti to her, but she wrote without embarrassment:

Oh Sachie, today I took from the shelf your book upon Scarlatti. I have never read it only just glanced at a page. And I must tell you that it is simply Fairyland opened before my view, so miserable with this senseless and appalling war. A whole dream world of splendour and sumptuous beauty and pictures of music is now in my mind and soul. I am so delighted I never read it till now . . . Shall I try and bring a clavichord and play you the last really glorious Scarlatti [piece] which you gave me? . . . I had much rather read as you write than anything by a dull expert. I have never been able to read the lives of musicians. Did you see in the paper the other day, that a great many books are to be printed extra in braille, as so many blinded soldiers are expected. Does not that make one feel beyond weeping? I think you are the most magical writer . . . in the world on the subject you handle in so superb and subtle a fashion . . .

Alerted by the devastating attacks of German Stuka dive-bombers on Spanish cities during the Spanish Civil War in 1937 and 1938, and lately on Polish cities, the Home Office swiftly ordered the closure of theatres, cinemas and concert halls to avoid giving crowded targets to the Luftwaffe. As in the First World War, the livelihood of musicians was an early casualty, and the music-loving population turned to the wireless. Nevertheless, on 8 November Violet defiantly gave a concert at the Assembly Rooms in Bath, devoting the first half of the programme to the harpsichord and the second half to the clavichord. Stimulated by some new Scarlatti music Sachie had sent her, she chose predominantly baroque composers, crossing off Mozart's Sonata in C Major from the printed programme and substituting two additional pieces by Scarlatti. At the request of Tom Goff, who was by now established in London with a workshop in his house in Pont Street, Violet advertised in bold print that she was playing a clavichord made by T.R.C. Goff and J.C. Cobby.

After the rapid fall of Poland, cynically carved up by Hitler and his new ally Stalin, there followed six months of quiet preparation by all the combatants known as "the phoney war". A British Expeditionary Force went to

France, and there, with its French allies, awaited Hitler's next move. Since air raids were expected on London at any time, Violet's household remained at Lypiatt, their lives pervaded by an unreal air of normality. Near the turn of the year Bill's niece, Lorna Brooke, who lived near Bath, asked Violet and Bill to stand as godparents to her recently born twins. Violet accepted, having long since forgiven and forgotten the incident when Lorna had spent too long alone with Osbert in the summerhouse at Lypiatt, but she assumed that she need not bother to attend the actual christening – and if she was not going to attend, she had no intention of letting Bill go either. Lorna, however, was not afraid of Violet: she insisted they both came, though she had a moment of irritated regret when Violet made one of her grand entrances, stayed for less than half an hour, and left with Bill, Gordon and Denis clamped to her side.

The Cotswolds were officially designated a "safe area", but the domestic machinery of war ground systematically into operation. They were advised "How to Protect the Home", issued with gas masks, and supplied with a guide entitled *Things to do in an Air Raid*. Ration books dropped through the letterbox. The winter of 1939/1940 was unusually severe, with snow and frost so deep that the narrow Cotswold roads became impassable to all but army vehicles. Overnight birds froze to the trees. Christabel Aberconway,[1] who had lent Bodnant, her house in Wales, to evacuees, braved the weather to come to Lypiatt in January 1940, full of high spirits and refusing to succumb to war gloom. She found Gordon in fine form, blossoming as a raconteur – "nobody can get a word in," she wrote to Osbert.

Christabel Aberconway's visit coincided with the arrival of Violet's only nephew, John Gwynne. Although Violet had never been as close to Nevile as she had to Rupert or Roland, his son John had a special place in her affections. The family firm had thrived after Nevile had succeeded to the chairmanship, switching successfully to the manufacture of aircraft engines in the Great War and cars in the twenties. This had enabled him to send John to Eton and Oxford, despite having been excluded from his own father's will. In 1926, however, which was John's third year at Oxford, the firm had been hit hard by price-cutting and the growing popularity of mass-produced cars from manufacturers like Austin, Morris and Ford. Despite the protection against American imports afforded by a high tariff wall, business was difficult in the British motor trade, and the Gwynne car, losing its competitive position, was relegated to the status of a collectors' item (a Gwynne car owners' club still exists). Nevile and Bluebelle became hard up once more, while John, who had

1 Lady Aberconway, society beauty, friend of Osbert (but not of Edith or Sachie), patroness of the arts, and notorious troublemaker.

shown no interest in engineering and had intended to become a barrister, could no longer expect to support himself financially during the initial period of low earnings in that profession, and so was obliged to become a solicitor. He hoped ultimately to stand as a parliamentary candidate for Rupert's old seat in Eastbourne, but in 1939 he joined the army.

A fine-looking man, dark, charming and eccentric, John was a courageous horseman, with all the Gwynnes' love of the countryside; he was also extremely fond of music, and one of Violet's most uncritical admirers. He, too, could do no wrong in her eyes. And now, like Max and Denis and Roland twenty-five years before, he was about to be sent to France. Violet was not quite sure what he was to be doing, but she did know that it was secret, and likely to be dangerous. Later she would learn that he was in the Special Operations Executive, which undertook hazardous and clandestine missions in enemy-occupied countries. Christabel wrote to Osbert that, although John's impending departure was "an agony for Violet . . . she is being even more enchanting than usual".

Early in January 1940, taking William Simmonds with her to turn the pages and soothe her nerves, Violet made a clavichord broadcast for the BBC in Bristol, and then another in March. When Osbert wrote to congratulate her on the second broadcast, she replied inviting him to come and stay, bringing with him Edith and his boyfriend, David Horner. "I am getting desperate about the war & almost ready for anything" she wrote. "I even begin to hate Chamberlain and Halifax."[2] She asked W.H. Davies to come for a meal to see his old friends, but as he was too ill to make the short journey to Lypiatt, Violet's party drove over to visit him. Alone for a moment with Osbert, Davies told him that he was in such pain that he would "like to turn over on my side and die".

In April and May 1940 the war began in earnest. German troops invaded Denmark, Norway, Belgium and Holland in a crushing series of lightning attacks. Churchill replaced Chamberlain as Prime Minister, hopes of stopping Hitler in north-east France crumbled as the German armour ripped through the French defences, driving the Allied forces before them or cutting them off, and threatening to isolate and destroy the British Expeditionary Force. In June Paris fell, and on the 22nd France surrendered. Driven back to the Channel coast, between 27 May and 3 June, 200,000 British and 140,000 French soldiers were miraculously evacuated from Dunkirk, abandoning their transport and heavy weapons, but saved by an armada of naval and merchant vessels, small fishing boats, pleasure craft and

2 Lord Halifax, the Foreign Secretary, had been Chamberlain's main pre-war supporter in the policy of appeasement.

even sailing boats. With invasion seemingly imminent, Anthony Eden, Churchill's Minister for War, who would soon be reinstated as Foreign Secretary (from which post he had resigned in 1938 in protest at the Government's policy of appeasement), broadcast an appeal for men between the ages of fifteen and sixty-five to volunteer for local defence. Bill and Gordon were just too old, and Denis was ill again, but all over Gloucestershire men bicycled, hobbled or walked to Stroud police station, where they formed long queues, patiently awaiting their turn to sign on.

While Stalin and Hitler plotted to divide Eastern Europe between them, Britain and her Commonwealth and Empire for a while stood alone against the combined forces of Germany and Mussolini's Italy (which had come into the war on Germany's side in May 1940), to be joined in 1941 by Japan as the third Axis power. France had collapsed and had been partitioned into occupied and unoccupied zones, with a collaborationist government led by Pétain, the veteran hero of Verdun; Spain's Fascist neutrality, too, was sympathetic to the Nazis; neutral America was friendly to Britain, but stayed aloof from military involvement. Between July and October, the Battle of Britain was fought to decide the country's fate, outnumbered Hurricanes and Spitfires taking on the German bombers and their Messerschmitt fighter escorts in a desperate attempt to deny the Luftwaffe the air superiority which the Führer demanded as a precondition for invasion. In September 1940 the Luftwaffe abandoned attacks on airfields and military targets in favour of night raids by large formations of bombers against the civilian populations of London, Coventry, Liverpool and other cities. The decision to switch targets proved to be a mistake, for civilian morale was not broken, the RAF was given a desperately needed breathing space in which to train fresh pilots and replace aircraft, and industrial production was less disrupted by night bombing, which was less accurate and more indiscriminate than the earlier daylight attack.

All this time Violet remained at Lypiatt, while month by month her world disintegrated. Dolmetsch had died in February. She told his son Carl that, in spite of her great loss, Arnold's spirit remained with her through his harpsichord, which she always played, its tone rich and beautiful. She reread his letters, adding to the packet a long and emotional one from his widow, Mabel.

*March 8th 1940*
Dearest Violet
Your kind and understanding letter brought me great comfort. I never realised before that it was possible that real *consolation* can

come through the sympathy of beloved human beings. As said Quantz[3] with regard to music:- "what comes from the heart touches the heart". I know that you were one of Arnold's oldest and closest friends and that there was an unseverable bond between you independent of time and changes. One thing I know will please you; and that is that after holding aloof from all organised forms of religion for so many years, (though profoundly religious at heart), last Autumn he re-entered the fold of the Catholic Church, and so he was able to die in peace with no secret regrets on his mind. He received the last rites while still conscious, and as he felt the imprint of the Cross upon his forehead he leant forward and I saw the sanctification revealed on his countenance. With his last respiration a beautiful smile overspread his face as though he saw some beatific vision. Then as a sacred and treasured duty I helped the nurse to prepare him for the burial.

From that moment onwards he grew more and more beautiful. His form became clothed in majesty and a soft smile of triumph lit up his features as though to say "I have done my work and attained my beatification". He was like a beautiful marble effigy and, having a strong feeling that although he had ceased to breathe, he was still cognisant of what was passing around him, I used to go in and talk to him and tell him about every thing; and that we were going to have the requiem mass and that afterwards Rudolph was going to play the "Dead March in Saul" [Handel] on the organ. Also about the kindness of all the friends. And so up to my last view he remained lovely and beloved . He is buried in a little cemetery outside Haslemere amongst the woods; it is on the southern slope of a little hill. His tomb is in the centre, at the summit and beside it there is a natural spring. So we shall be able to water the flowers in his little garden quite easily. We intend to make a living museum of the room where he dwelt and worked. We shall keep his special books, instruments, bench and tools there and make music in there from time to time.

Well dear Violet I am glad to have told you all this.

Ever yours affectionately, Mabel

Then, in April, "Darling old Rubio was gone", aged eighty-six, a nostalgic reminder of the years of her youth, when Violet was learning her art at the hands of a master. Tom Goff had joined the Scots Guards and had been

3 Johann Joachim Quantz, the eighteenth-centuryGerman flautist and composer.

posted to Canada as ADC to the Governor-General, and in September W.H. Davies had finally died. Since petrol rationing made travel almost impossible, Gordon and Bill were the only two outside Davies's close family who were able to attend his funeral.

Lonely and cut off from her friends, Violet grew frustrated and spoke ever more immoderately against those she held responsible for the war. She now saw Churchill as the arch-enemy, and as the war's destruction became heavier and more widespread, so her hatred for him increased. She imagined feverishly that, had Chamberlain not been forced out of office, the policy of appeasement might have succeeded in restoring peace to Europe. The threat of defeat had stirred the majority of the population to a sense of resolution – Ethel Smyth had stoutly declared, two days after the fall of France, "of course we shall fight and win" – but Violet seemed to have slipped back a quarter of a century. She could not see clearly the barbaric tyranny and racism of the Nazis, nor Hitler's lust for conquest. All she could see was what lay directly within her own field of vision – the same patriotic fever, the same sabre-rattling, and the same absurd optimism which had sent Max to his death, and had led to the pointless carnage of Ypres and the Somme. To talk to Violet of a just and necessary war was to invite a dismissive tirade.

Echoes of the bombing occasionally reached the countryside. Constantly harried by the British fighters, the Luftwaffe's bomber pilots were in the habit of jettisoning bombs to lighten the aircraft when trying to get away, and Gloucestershire lay along the flight path to the shipyards of Bristol. In July a bomb had landed near Lypiatt at Birdlip; in September a German bomber was brought down at Oakridge Lynch, near the Rothensteins' house, by a Hurricane of the Kemble Defence Flight. The crew of four baled out, the church bells rang the alarm and a posse from the Miserden Home Guard, armed with pitchforks, arrested the Germans, who were relieved to be offered whisky and cigarettes rather than being summarily shot or skewered.

Osbert Sitwell had recently set to work on an open-ended autobiography, which eventually ran to five volumes (though there was a later addition, twelve years after the fifth volume had appeared). For the first volume, *Left Hand! Right Hand!*, Violet supplied him with some much-needed detail about Rubio, adding her comments as a professional musician. Hitherto Osbert had been spending his time editing *Two Generations*, a book about his antecedents, which he sent "to Dearest Violet in the hope that this book may take her away for an hour or two to a more agreeable and less stupid and cruel epoch." Take her away it did. "I can't tell you how pleased I am to get the book. The only possible way to keep at all one's reason is to try to go back, as you take one back, to the past."

Osbert's anger and sense of isolation were fully equal to Violet's – indeed, they spurred each other on to even greater heights of invective and anti-patriotism.

> *2 November 1940*
> Darling Violet
> . . . I have really been too furious to write to you, *even* to you. My temper is beyond words and I shall be in leper's corner soon . . . today, I see in the paper a letter from an old lady saying that The Women of England *demand* a war that will last for seven or eight years, so that the Germans shall *know*! Really, what *are* we to do? I agree with Hitler in thinking that Churchill is mad: he must be. How is it possible to satirize such a man, a man who stated only yesterday in parliament that even if no house were left standing, we should go on fighting, shoulder to shoulder? *What the hell*? And I am so tired of all melodramatic rubbish about "But let that Wicked Man Beware! He shall have *short* shrift . . . WE will go forward, undismayed, alone if necessary, and for years and decades, with death as our companion, disaster as our handmaiden, and devastation as our concubine . . ." It's too silly and sickening . . . I have started making notes for my own autobiography: but it will make you blush to see what I've said about you! I enclose two poems – or rather a poem and some fables. The first is rather depressing; the second is in praise of *morals* (how I hate that word). What can we do except stand there and be bombed? We can't throw them back. Bless you, darling Violet. Much love to Gordon and Bill and Denis, if he is with you, as perhaps he is?
>
> PS. It is no use *writing* sense about the war as no one will publish. Shaw wrote to me that he had even had an article refused by the *Daily Worker*! He added that when "this war has blasted and bombed itself to the nethermost hell, it will still fall short of what I think of it."                    Y'r devoted Osbert

While Osbert resorted to ranting escapism, Edith's way of coping with the war was to express herself in poetry. Feeling lonely at Renishaw (fond as she was of Osbert, she was never on really intimate terms with him), she began to write powerful poems full of Christian imagery – her "Still Falls The Rain", with its cathartic pictures of the Crucifixion, reads like an offering to the pain of those suffering under the 1940 air raids. While not exactly dedicating her poems to Violet, Edith used to write them out on lined paper and send them to her, with Violet's name at the top, before they appeared in print.

In a wholly depressing year for Violet, almost the only good news was the appearance in the autumn of John Gwynne's new girlfriend, whom he brought to stay at Nether Lypiatt. Patricia Morrison-Bell was a quiet girl of twenty-two, with dark pre-Raphaelite looks; her father was a Conservative Member of Parliament, her mother an Anglo-Irish aristocrat. She was musical and also discreet, observant and not easily scared, as befitted a junior recruit to MI5, the branch of the Secret Service which deals with security in Britain. At first Violet received her coolly, addressing her formally as Miss Morrison-Bell. When John remonstrated, asking Violet to call her Patricia, Violet replied, "I shall see if I like her first." The girls John had previously brought to stay he had generally been banned from bringing back, but by the end of the first evening the only question was when John was going to marry Patricia. From then on she was "Pattie" to Violet, and they became devoted to one another.

Patricia was invited to all Violet's recitals – or, rather, summoned, for Violet would brook no refusal, pretending she might forget the music if "Pattie" was not in the room. The first such occasions were three charity concerts held in quick succession that autumn at Upton Park, near Tetbury in Gloucestershire, which Kenneth Clark, then Director of the National Gallery, had rented for the duration of the war. Having been given special permission by the Home Office to open the National Gallery for music after its paintings had been removed to a cave in a Welsh slate quarry, Clark had arranged a number of lunchtime concerts there for the benefit of the Musicians' Benevolent Fund; enjoying his new role as a musical patron, he had encouraged his wife, Jane, to make use of the large hall at Upton Park for concerts to raise money for the RAF Benevolent Fund.

Violet practised hard for the first performance (on 26 October), trying out pieces on Eve and William Simmonds. The Clarks' eight-year-old daughter, Colette, hardly listened to the music as she lent over the gallery to watch Violet, so transfixed was she by "the purpliest hair she had ever seen". By the time the second concert took place, John had become engaged to Patricia. Violet wrote to her to congratulate them both and to wish them well:

> The recital is at the same house . . . I must tell you that it is not the
> harpsichord next time but the clavichord. But it would be so nice if
> you could come, & especially if you could come to lunch with us
> first? . . . I do hope you had a nice leave. I have always had a very
> special affection & admiration for John, & for the spirituality mixed
> with great manliness, which makes his character so fine, & I am so

glad he has been able to have the *good luck* to have such a lovely young goddess to understand him, & I do hope you will both be as happy as a fairytale.

The Sitwell nerve under fire was not the strongest ,[4] and when the city of Sheffield was heavily bombed, Osbert, six miles away at Renishaw, seemed to lose all sense of proportion. "The last raid on Sheffield was worse than any in London," he wrote to Violet. "Of course, it is a hideous town, but *hundreds* of people were killed. We have an unexploded bomb just outside our lovely 18th Century park gates, and I suppose they will go up. The noise was too appalling. How I hate Winston." To cheer him up Violet lent him a magnificent pair of marble figures of negroes. He might feel "in extremis with horror and boredom and bad temper" about the war, she said, "but I seem to be now in a continual state of nervous fury. Anything more brutally stupid, there surely never was . . . I get into such a rage, so often that I feel furious with almost everyone, even dear darling Norah [Lindsay]."

Ignoring Lily's urgent pleas to remain safely in the country, and undeterred by the news that a bomb had landed in the garden of their flat in Porchester Terrace, causing havoc to the building, Violet went to London at the end of January 1941. She was so lonely now that she was quite prepared to override Lily's fears and face the German air raids for the sake of seeing her friends and playing music in their company. From Claridge's she wrote to Osbert, begging him to join her: ". . . How I wish Sachie and Georgia were coming too." Christabel Aberconway encouraged Violet to scrounge enough petrol to bring her clavichord to London with her, and together they gave Osbert a post-birthday musical party in Christabel's flat, the first of what was to be an annual series of such birthday treats. A significant element in Violet's rage had been her feeling of uselessness and isolation in the country, combined with the realization, as she approached the age of seventy, that her powers must at some stage decline. Now that she was playing in London again, her frustration receded as her music once more became a refuge for others in their times of fear or despair.

If Violet felt the onset of age physically, she never lost her spiritual youth, or her ability to win new friends and disciples. Towards the end of the winter of 1940 an Australian musician in her twenties, named Valda Aveling, was brought to see Violet by Winnie de Polignac, who had been

4 In the Great War, Osbert's (notoriously difficult and eccentric) father had advised him that he was unlikely to undergo as terrifying a bombardment in the trenches as the naval shelling his mother had faced in Scarborough – but, if the worst came to the worst, Osbert should "retire to the Undercroft", have plenty of nourishing food and take short naps.

left stranded in London when war broke out, but was still as dedicated as ever to helping talented musicians at the beginning of their careers. Valda's account of this first meeting has a startlingly similar ring to the accounts of so many other musicians who, over the years, tried to describe the effect upon them of Violet's playing. As Violet sat at her clavichord, Valda felt immediately that it was her own musical understanding that was being put to the test. When Violet had finished playing, she approached Valda and saw the expression of wonder on her face. Taking both the girl's hands in hers she said, "I see you *do* understand." It was unquestionably a turning point in Valda's life:

> A whole new world opened up to me. She created a new sound. The clavichord is so completely different from the harpsichord. It casts a spell. It has total magic; and when I first heard Violet play, it was exquisite. I *was* spellbound. Her personality, her appearance and her playing were one and the same thing, you could not divide one from the other.
>
> Violet taught me all the secrets of her touch and the magic of her effects. How, in contrast to the harpsichord where you touch the instrument with your fingertips, almost like plucking a guitar, and must rely on speed, for there is no depth of tone, with the clavichord you must stroke the keys. It is the only [keyboard] instrument where you can make a slow vibrato . . . and if you press too hard it goes out of tune, or if you stretch the strings too hard they will break. All your dynamics are in the vibrato. She taught me how to break the chords, not just plonk, plonk, plonk your fingers down simultane-ously. [During my first lesson] we had just finished the lesson with the chords when Bill Barrington, who had been coming in and out of the room, returned and said, "It doesn't sound any different to me". I was appalled. I didn't know how he dared.

Returning to the country, Violet began to see more of the Clarks. She found their mixture of snobbery and fashionable socialism distasteful, and resented the fact that her talented friend, the artist Rex Whistler,[5] who had recently joined the Welsh Guards, was on active service, while Kenneth Clark had not only managed to avoid military service himself, but had also used his patronage to gain exemption, by having them classified as "war artists", for others such as Graham Sutherland and William Rothenstein's sons, Michael and John (characterized by Violet as "doing no kind of work

5 The painter, illustrator, and designer Rex Whistler, whom Violet had known well since 1930, joined the Welsh Guards and was killed in Normandy in 1944.

"doing no kind of work but their horrible pictures"). Nevertheless, Violet was grateful to the Clarks for their concerts, and for bringing to Lypiatt visitors to whom she could play. In March 1941 William Walton, Alice Wimborne, Sir Walter Monckton (then Director-General of the Ministry of Information, the government propaganda arm) and Loelia, Duchess of Westminster, came over with Jane Clark. The hot topic of conversation was a libel case, recently splashed over the newspapers, which had reached the courts the previous fortnight. The Sitwells had been outraged by an article in *Reynold's News* disparaging them as minor and passé cultural figures, and had sued. This trivial defamation earned each of the three Sitwells £350 (about £7,000 today) in damages, plus costs. Violet, aware how irritated Osbert had been by Walton's defection to Alice Wimborne, wrote him the sort of letter she knew he would like to receive:

> Willie [Walton] I thought seemed very self-conscious. Lady Wimborne looked so pretty and beautifully dressed. Willie said what a lot of money you had made, (and he was glad) and we shouted "not nearly enough". Bill is quite violent about it, and thinks you got very little for the disgraceful things said. Has Willie got rather conceited?? They asked me to go with them to Bristol to hear his concert, but I did not. I thought his children's things beautifully orchestrated, but they might be rather dry on the piano. He said he would send them to me for the clavichord. I think the Clarks are rather bores don't you? Denis is not very well I am sorry to say.

Denis was now, in fact, alarmingly ill. Suspecting in her heart that he had cancer, Violet refused to acknowledge the truth, telling outsiders that no doctor seemed able to diagnose his condition of high temperatures and "poor blood". Since she was terrified of death, and had the strange notion that his disease might be contagious, it took some courage to insist that Denis remain with her at Lypiatt. There she rearranged the ground floor of the south wing, making room for his nurses and preparing for his hoped-for recuperation. Intermittently throughout 1941 she believed he was getting better. In his periods of remission he would be well enough to become "quite jolly" with her, and would try to make her see sense about the war, only to lapse back into illness again.

Violet paid scant attention to Denis's arguments. Her opinions were by this time so seditious that the Sitwells were the only people with whom she could any longer be entirely frank. She told Osbert to burn her letters "as people had been arrested for much less"; and, much as she regretted doing so, she in return burned his. She looked forward eagerly to his visits. When Queen Mary was evacuated to Badminton in 1941 for the duration of the war, Osbert was twice summoned to entertain her. Violet wrote to him in May, teasing him that he might find the top room at Lypiatt uncomfortable after the luxury of Badminton – but "an abandoned talk is worth a good deal". She had been asked to make three harpsichord broadcasts – for the BBC's Overseas, Home and Empire services – and to make records of them; she hoped Osbert's stay would not be too much disturbed by the visiting BBC team.

Although she told Osbert that she felt "too old" to do the broadcasts, Violet nevertheless rose to the occasion. In July a large BBC van duly came through the iron gates and parked in the courtyard, backing up to the steps at the entrance door. A few yards away, in the summerhouse in the walled garden, the Simmondses, Bill and Gordon listened to the recordings, which came over clearly and delicately. At the end of July Violet wrote to Sachie asking him if he had heard her broadcast and thanking him for his latest book, *Valse des Fleurs*, in which his re-creation of a day in St Petersburg in 1868 had taken her "for a day or two into Fairyland which is what I have always hankered after all my life". It was too long, she said, since she had last seen him and, determined to remedy the omission before the onset of another winter without coal (which, like most other fuels, was severely rationed), she offered him and Georgia three gallons of petrol if they would come and stay with her.

# XVII

*My Poor Broken Limbs*

ON A FROSTY MORNING at the end of January 1942, Violet fell on a slippery path in the orchard at Lypiatt and broke her right wrist. Bill and Gordon rushed her to hospital to have it set. Walking unsteadily towards the casualty department, she fell again on the polished linoleum of a passage floor and broke her left arm. For a time it seemed that her playing career might be finished, but her iron will stood her in good stead and she refused to contemplate the possibility of a crippled retirement. Two weeks later William Simmonds found her in low spirits, but taking her misfortune with courage. With her right hand she could just move her fingers and managed to write to Osbert in pencil "My arms have been very unhappy & still are, & my once pretty hands look crooked, tho' the surgeon thinks they should become straight." Osbert's sympathetic letters and Edith's latest book of war poems, *Street Songs*, helped relieve her depression. It gave her particular pleasure that Edith was starting to enjoy a critical renaissance and that her poems were increasingly seen as speaking for their time. Violet wrote enthusiastically to Osbert: "What a poet she is: as poignant & as magnificent in spirit as the Elizabethans, plus her own terrific imagination & beauty, & compassion."

One of Edith's admirers had offered to buy her a property in Bath, and Violet hoped, briefly, that she might become a neighbour. House-hunting on Edith's behalf, with both arms in slings, Violet soon found "a treasure, with a delightful outlook at the back" in Gay Street, but Edith's psychological roots were at Renishaw and, although she bought the house, she never lived in it.

> I am so excited about 8 Gay Street, what an angel you were to go and look over it. Osbert and I are so grateful to you. We are certainly going to buy it.
>
> Alas, it simply isn't possible for Osbert and me to go and live in

the house for the moment. For these reasons: "They" are trying to commandeer the house here, not a nice quiet lot like the Admiralty, but a nasty crew of heavens knows what and we have a furious rush to get work done which *has* to be finished by the autumn. I have to get this thing on poetry done for Macmillan [the publishers].

Despite her broken limbs and her mounting anxiety over Denis, Violet went to London in February, again taking rooms in Claridge's, where Georgia and Sachie were staying. But Denis's condition worsened and Violet returned to be near him when he was moved to a private room in the hospital in Stroud. Praying for a miracle, Violet summoned a surgeon from London, Sir Crisp English, who took "a slightly less hopeless view than the local doctors". On 26 April Violet wrote to Osbert:

Denis hovers between death and life . . . Brave as we should know he would be: forgetting to find the words, & then laughing and saying "It doesn't matter really" but he was crying also. It wrings my heart when I think of it. And now I hear that Bristol and Bath were bombed . . .

On 1 May 1942, Denis Tollemache died, at fifty-eight by far the youngest member of Violet's household. Believing it improper to leave the bulk of his money to Violet, he left her £500 and a choice of any personal belongings "for the person who gives everything away to everybody". The rest he bequeathed to the upkeep of Helmingham, on condition that its occupant should not be Roman Catholic. He was buried in the tiny family churchyard in the park at Helmingham, where Violet, Gordon and Bill placed a memorial tablet inscribed:

To the memory of Denis Tollemache D.S.O. sometime Colonel of the 7th Hussars born 1884. This tablet was erected by his three friends.

Violet found it impossible to believe that Denis was gone. "I have had this beautiful friendship & love for 50 years ever since he was a little boy and he has never failed me," she wrote to Sachie. She asked Osbert, who was due to come to Lypiatt on 1 June, to write something about Denis for *The Times*.

Osbert, I know I was the person he loved only, in the world, & had done ever since he was a boy of 8 or 9 years old & I feel very sad in my heart. He left here a lovely stick by William Simmonds, with a little otter carved on it, & I am sure he would like you to have it. He was one of the greatest gentlemen in the world, & one of the most

steadfast & true. And Sir Crisp English said he was the bravest man
he had ever met.

Osbert obediently wrote an obituary, which he sent to Violet and she
forwarded to Ethel Smyth, though in the end it was not published. Violet
wrote to thank him for ". . . the most rare & beautiful appreciation of beloved
Denis, you have just said what no-one else could have, & in a way no-one else
could have put it, & I am grateful to you from the *very depths* of my heart."

Violet also wanted Ethel Smyth to compose a piece about Denis, but she
made excuses – she was herself recovering from a bad fall, she said, and "I
have not yet written about Virginia!!".[1] Her scrawled letter, in frail handwriting, asked Violet to understand that Osbert's piece had put better than
she ever could all that she might have written of Denis's chivalry and his lifelong reticence about his wartime experiences. "I didn't really *know* him and
saw him so seldom. I mean I think it would be almost cheek for me to write
about him, as I can't go an inch below the surface and should have to be select
about what called forth chiefly my admiration – his angle towards you."

Violet was by now was utterly despondent, convinced that the war was
bringing civilization to an end. Edith tried to comfort her: "How little we
have left to us, excepting what is *all* for you and me, music and poetry. They
can't take that away from us." Ethel Smyth reflected bitterly on how strange
it was that "the nation that produced the Mass in D [of Beethoven] and the
St Matthew Passion [of Bach] is now leading the way back to barbarism!".

Violet, however, conscious that to protest against Hitler was futile, and
clinging to the idea that peace might somehow still be saved, turned her
anger on the British Cabinet, those "gangsters" and "bestial fools". While
there were some who indulged Violet's outbursts, on the grounds that a
genius was permitted to say what she liked, others came away furious, and
her words did irreparable damage to several friendships. Gordon and Bill
would sit in silence through her arguments and tirades, unless appealed to
by Violet, in which case they would unfailingly support her. Violet was
particularly irritated at the way Norah Lindsay stuck to her views about the
war: "I am so fond of her, it really is too disgusting, that shocking two pence
coloured cheap, vulgar, gobbling patriotism, not really patriotic at all."
Tamara Talbot-Rice, stung by Violet's excuses for Hitler and her criticism of
Churchill, reacted with sharp retorts, but

a glance at her face invariably silenced me. She who had for so long
been ageless now looked old, worn and lost. Her world was disinte-

1 On 28 March 1941, in a final collapse of her always fragile mental health, Virginia
Woolf had committed suicide.

grating, many friends had died, she worried over her nephew, John, her wonderful intellect was becoming clouded; now she was out of touch whereas previously, for all her idiosyncrasies, there had been no generation gap between her and any of her friends.

As the war went on Violet became more eccentric. In her private life she had become, if it were possible, more autocratic than ever. Earlier in the year Bill had arranged for his niece, Joan Brooke, to come to Lypiatt as his "land girl"(the Government drafted land girls to replace men who had gone to the forces, in order to keep up agricultural production). Violet was pleased at the prospect of adding to her staff. "How useful it will be and she can act as chauffeur sometimes" she wrote to Roland. Born and bred in the country, Joan was hard-working and down-to-earth, and had never before met with anyone like Violet. It was like working for the Tsarina. The indoor servants were under instructions from Gordon to keep special quotas of butter, milk, cream, eggs and poultry for "madam". Away from the house, the farm ran smoothly unless Violet decided to make one of her tours, dressed in black sheepskin coat, red mittens and woollen or taffeta bonnet, interfering in everything to do with the animals. "No", she would say, countermanding Bill's orders, "the calves will *not* be killed. They will *not* be going to market." Then with an imperious, "let them run loose, let them be free", she would fling open the doors of the henhouse, allowing the birds to scatter, clucking, into the distance, for Joan laboriously to gather up later. These were the only occasions on which anyone ever saw Bill angry with Violet.

Bill's farm manager, Bert Richards, however, took Violet's behaviour in his stride, accepting that that was how madam carried on and making the necessary arrangements to adapt to her ways. His daughter remembers him explaining that Violet loved mice so much that she charmed them to run up and down her arms. If Bert knew that she was due to make a tour of the farm he would shut the cats behind a special partition he had built in the loft, and wait philosophically until she had passed.

By July 1942, chocolate and sweets had been added to the rationing list and nearly all food was in short supply, a predicament which brought out the inventive in Gordon, who somehow always managed to keep alive Lypiatt's hospitable atmosphere. He searched everywhere for under-the-counter supplies and made up imaginative recipes using leeks, cabbages and root vegetables out of the Lypiatt garden. When, to protect the crops, new government regulations ordered that rabbit numbers should be reduced to no more than two per acre, the guns came out and rabbit casserole became one of his specialities. Even "Beckett Plum Pudding", a raisin pudding named after Bill's favourite nursery treat, stayed on the menu as Gordon eked out his pre-war stock of marsala raisins from the Woodhouse vineyard. Those of Bill's and Violet's nephews and nieces who had the good fortune to be evacuated to Gloucestershire would look forward greedily to an invitation to lunch, and the luxury of a meal such as other children could only dream about. When the Brookes came over from Bath, Gordon produced a cream trifle with macaroons for them, followed by pyramids of triangular black treacle sweets from Holland wrapped in gold paper, and chocolates hidden in silver snuff boxes. They could not help noticing that Violet's place was laid with her own tiny silver knife and fork and her own silver dish containing butter – everybody else, of course, had margarine.

In other ways, too, the old magic remained. One visit to Lypiatt that summer left an imprint on an impressionable child, Bill's great-niece, Annabel Brooke, which remains as clear to her today as fifty years ago. After ringing the bell and being ushered into the hall by the butler, she and her brother and sister were enveloped in a mysterious paradise. On the left stood walking-sticks on whose handles scuttled ivory mice. Wooden animals peered out from under chairs or stretched themselves in front of a marble fireplace. Dark portraits looked down from the walls. In the drawing-room, where the sun streamed in through the four windows, Violet was waiting, attended by "Uncle Bill", tall, elegant and immaculate in trousers of a wide check pattern, and the friendly, untidy Gordon. Breaking away to greet the children with exclamations of pleasure, Violet rustled and tinkled in buckled shoes with pointed toes and red heels, her long blue silk dress gathered in layers, her shoulders draped with a flower-embroidered, silk-tasselled cream shawl, her glass ball earrings, filled with pink liquid, cascading down on filigree chains to frame her neck.

While the grown-ups talked, Violet kept the children quietly immersed in large books with page after page of pictures of exotic birds and flowers. There was a square cardboard book with a hole in the middle which unfolded, concertina-fashion, into panoramic scenes from the Great Exhibition. Another cardboard book, half the size, opened out to show pictures, painted by William Simmonds, of the animals at Lypiatt. Then there was a musical box which played sparkling, but unrecognizable, tunes; and a Toby jug which, when picked up, played "D'ye ken John Peel?" A sturdier latched box, bound in red leather and resembling a giant bible, contained a two-scale keyboard in ebony and ivory, which could be played with the assistance of an accordion-shaped hand-pump. This was the "Bible Regal Organ", copied for Violet by Tom Goff from an original that had been taken out to the trenches in the First World War.

After lunch Violet rang her bell and called out "Bring in the children," whereupon two groomed, shining, bushy and bustling Pekinese were led in from their "flat" by Lily. It seemed to Annabel as if the dogs had a nanny all to themselves. Violet's Pekinese, which were either named after bees or given Chinese names suggested by Arthur Waley, invariably accompanied her from Lypiatt to London and back again. If one of them fell ill, Mr Board, a London vet, was sent for; and if Lily complained that the weather was too wet for walking, Violet would pronounce that the Pekinese would get bored without an outing and would summon the chauffeur, Law, to take them for a drive in the Daimler. Reclining on silk cushions in the back seat at the ideal height from which to gaze through the car windows at the world outside, they would then circle Lypiatt in state (or, if they were in London, Hyde Park) without getting their paws wet, while Gordon and Bill turned a blind eye to the fact that petrol was rationed and almost unobtainable. To Violet, the life-span of her dogs never seemed long enough, and whenever a death was imminent she would cancel all her engagements.

Outside on the terrace at teatime Violet handed out mealworms from a box under the step to three large lizards with hooded yellow eyes who slithered up expectantly from under the flagstones. Over Violet's blue figure, over the flashes of green and yellow-ochre-grey stone, spread the shade of a thirty-foot-high cotoneaster, its branches, heavily laden with berries, making a great splash of bright red. The garden, having matured over twenty years, was full of compartments to explore. Yew hedges divided it into a series of "rooms", leading to the lime avenue, dark and gloomy, the perfect place for games of hide-and-seek. At the bottom of the beech wood lurked the overgrown canal. Among the trees stood the gravestones of three generations of Violet's Pekinese, each carved by William Simmonds and inscribed with a dog's date of birth and an affectionate phrase of farewell. In another part of this forest Annabel came across Wag's obelisk; walking back through the garden, she found the summerhouse with its shimmering witch balls and piles of dark green, maroon and silver grey cushions strewn comfortably around the floor. To return home was to leave fairyland and go back to reality.

At the beginning of July 1942, Gordon learned that old Mrs Nunn, who alone of the Burghill servants had not run away in horror on the night of the murder of Gordon's sisters, was no longer well enough to look after herself. True to his promise, he took her in to Lypiatt, installing her on the top floor with a nursing sister, helped by a rota of three assistant nurses. The sister lived *en famille* and was encouraged by Violet to bring her fifteen-year-old daughter to Lypiatt for five weeks in the summer holiday. It would have been hard to know that there was a war on, so self-contained was the household, and so full of happy and harmless incident. Sprawled across "Nunny's" bed, Bill played solitaire with the schoolgirl, and tried unsuccessfully to teach her how to tie a knot in a cherry stalk with her tongue, while Violet raced her down the stairs, giving her the inner handrail side but beating her by three steps. In the lime avenue Bill showed her bees lying on their backs, drunk with nectar; one day he completely took her in with a practical joke, when he propped himself up against the wheatsheafs disguised as a tramp. When Lily went away on holiday, Violet kept her hat on, being unable to do her own hair. She kept fit by walking with Dorothy Walker eight fast circuits a day round the kitchen garden, her still swollen wrists hidden by embroidered frills at her cuffs.

In January 1943 Violet set off for London, where she borrowed a clavichord, since she found it too difficult to transport her own from Lypiatt. There she gave a round of private performances and caught up with old acquaintances. Her life now increasingly revolved round the Sitwells. She had, however, been distracted by her injuries and by Denis's death, and had underestimated how strained the relations between the brothers were becoming. Osbert got on badly with Georgia, and Sachie had no time for David Horner. In the circumstances it was somewhat tactless of Violet to write to Osbert telling him that she took more pleasure in playing to Sachie than to anyone: "What a poet he is, & what an imagination in music. More than anyone almost, except Rubio, I have ever met. Ethel Smyth is a great appreciator, or was, of how music should be played, & the imagery & wonders, but Sachie is quite amazing, & I know he suffers from his sensitiveness, like I do, & the horrors of never being understood."

Osbert was, in fact, making plans in which Sachie was to play no part. With a sudden surge of energy, he told Edith that they must resume their roles as champions of the arts. The time had come to do something to keep civilization alive; they would organize a poetry reading. Up to a dozen poets agreed to take part in the event, and the rehearsals in March went well. At the reading itself, the following month, such eminent figures as John Masefield (then the Poet Laureate), Walter de la Mare and T.S. Eliot were thoroughly co-operative, but Dorothy Wellesley (known to them as "Egeria") was tiresome. Violet, who at the last moment was not well enough to attend, was regaled afterwards with Edith's description.

Renishaw, *April 1943.*

Darling Violet,

I should have written to you yesterday, but we have been having MORE than a spot of trouble with a certain Egeria, about which I will tell you presently.

But first let me say . . . I do hope you are better, dear Violet. It is wicked that you of all people should ever be ill, be in pain, or anxiety. It is an unnatural thing, not right in nature: that is how I see it. Because you were born to be happy, just as you were born to make other people happy – and do.

This is *private*. The reading was a huge success, but there was an appalling scene after it. D.W. denounced me, hit Harold Nicolson,[2] and was finally taken away. She sat on the pavement in A. Bond Street, B. Bruton Street, and C. outside the Hyde Park Hotel, where she was staying. She also wrote a letter to the Queen, which has been got away from her. Poor wretched woman. I am more sorry for her than I can possible say, but she really is an egoist. She seems to think that she was the only person who was nervous or who was going to read. My life for weeks was quite impossible, as she had to have letters written to her by every post. Sometimes I would have three letters by each post (six daily) all changing her mind.

I tell you this because OF COURSE you will hear, otherwise I wouldn't tell you because of being unkind to her, which I don't want to be. You will hear because nobody talks of anything else.
Oh dear Oh dear!

Having told you all I have to tell, I send you a new poem. Osbert says he likes it better than anything else I have written. I wrote it when I was in London, about a fortnight ago.

Osbert and I were talking of you with an enthusiastic love and admiration, to Dr. Gordon Bottomley. Some of his poetry is like you. Best love, and all my thoughts, how I hate and loathe to think of you being ill and suffering in your heart and mind. It is all so wrong – like this terrible thing of those young people all going away – all adding to the burden of your heart. Oh Violet, it is dreadful. Your affectionate Edith.

Her wrist and arm healing and her musical spirit reawakening, Violet set about re-establishing her musical salon in London. She did not like being beholden to Christabel Aberconway, and Claridge's made an unsatisfactory base, so she made Gordon sell the flat in Porchester Terrace and take a lease on a flat in Mayfair "quite pretty, tho' small . . . rather exquisite". As always when she had acquired somewhere new to live, Violet was excited, and she

2 The diplomat husband of Virginia Woolf's inamorata, the gardener Vita Sackville-West.

spent the summer decorating and organizing the removal of furniture from Porchester Terrace to Mount Street.

In July the Sitwells' father, Sir George, died. "I know the charming tolerant humour with which you regarded your father had affection and understanding in it," Violet commiserated with Osbert. This time, however, her words struck quite the wrong note. Osbert, like Sachie and Edith, had very little fondness for his eccentric father, and all three had been awaiting his death for two years. Relief, and expectant anticipation of a substantial inheritance, which would bolster Osbert's finances and rescue Sachie's and Edith's, were swiftly overtaken by anger when they found that Sir George's presumed fortune had disappeared. Osbert replied grimly to Violet's letter.

> Renishaw. *14 August 1943*
> Darling Violet,
> . . . my poor father's affairs, this is not for general knowledge, are in a state of pitiful confusion. He has obviously been swindled out of his fortune. He had large sums in Switzerland (about 70 or 80 thousand). It looks – but we cannot tell for certain yet – as if it has disappeared entirely. His will was vindictive, but the money was not there. Everything is left to Reresby and Francis [Sachie's two sons] over Sachie's head – and Sachie, who, poor Darling, never under-stood business, may very well be ruined. It looks as if he and Georgia will have £400 (I haven't told anyone but you this) a year to live on, with of course Weston rent free but an expense! . . . I am really terribly worried over Sachie . . . What has happened is that my father lost all the Trust Funds of Weston (about £20,000 out of £30,000) gambling in the 1929 slump. He would not admit it, and paid an extra missing income out of his own pocket, without telling anyone. Reresby does not know his "good fortune" but if the Swiss money's there, he will be far richer than Sachie. It's all a very great distress and worry but don't tell anyone but Gordon and Bill.
> Edith has been left £60 a year! She isn't at all grateful.
> In fact life is a nightmare.
> Do you know it takes as much time and work to be done out of a fortune, as to inherit one . . . All my time now goes to business (I can't work) and all in order to be poorer . . . I think Bill had a good deal of this from his step mother so he will sympathise.
> I long to be talking to you instead of writing.
> > Your Osbert.

Although they had each disliked Sir George in different ways, their shared resentment of him had formed a strong bond between the three Sitwell children; now that he was dead, Sachie and Osbert redirected their resentment against each other, and particularly against each other's partners. Osbert's hostility towards Georgia, hitherto reasonably well concealed, turned to open warfare, and despite his professed concern for Sachie, who was, admittedly, incompetent in financial matters, the only practical help Osbert gave him was a loan of £500. As for Sachie and Georgia, they came to detest David Horner, whose influence on Osbert they mistrusted. Osbert took the impoverished Edith in at Renishaw, but otherwise did nothing at all for her. In 1939 Sir George's Swiss trust, administered by the Banque Populaire Suisse, had held investments worth over £71,000, but by the time of his death this had mysteriously shrunk to just over £10,000. The nominal beneficiary of the trust was a former cashier of the bank, a fact which gave rise to all sorts of suspicion and led to the bank reluctantly offering £20,000 in compensation, which Osbert pocketed for himself, giving nothing to Edith or Sachie.

Violet, however, was deaf to their discord. Once she had made a friend-ship her code dictated resolute loyalty. Full of sympathy over Sachie's predicament, she set herself to raising his morale and finding pragmatic ways in which to tackle his money problems. She offered him the use of her new flat – "only can you cook? Just a breakfast?" Another idea occurred to her – why should not she and Sachie, during the winter months, give fort-nightly clavichord recitals of Bach, Scarlatti, early English music and Mozart, with talks by Sachie and "extremely expensive tickets"?

By far the most musical of the Sitwells, Sachie turned for comfort to Violet's uncomplicated friendship. There was, however, more than that: he was fascinated by her and could not see her as old – she seemed to him barely to have altered since the day when, at the age of twenty, he had first met her. Her hair was no longer black, but everything else about her gave the impression of youth. Her delicacy of build, her light, fragile and elegant figure, her quickness of movement, her spontaneous conversation and her strong personality combined to mesmerize him. "She was a phoenix. Hers was fire, all fire," Osbert wrote after her death. Her eyes escaped the cloud-ing of old age, remaining large, dark and clear, and reflecting all the variations of her moods. Sachie revelled in her instinctive emotions, which carried her into loving, hating, stubbornness, impulsiveness, compassion and generosity. Having endured moments of despair in her own life, and believ-ing these to be the fate of all creative people, she was able to offer help born of experience to Sachie's deadened spirit.

It was by no means a one-sided relationship, however, for Violet responded to Sachie's attention with an Indian summer of fierce artistic intensity, as he drove her to master new and ever more taxing pieces, and unlocked the last undiscovered chambers of her genius. She began to play with a depth of understanding which even she had never previously attained.

> *August 1943*
> Dearest Sachie
> I cannot thank you enough for your letter; forced up from the heart of such a poet as you are. If you could know what it means to me to be understood, & that the clavichord should be understood for the marvellous instrument it is!! I shall always be grateful for having had dear Rubio's certain belief that I was a very good interpreter of the best music, & now YOU! & how delighted I am that you admired Paderewski so much! I heard him as a young girl, the first time he ever played in London, to an empty hall, & it was like a living fountain to me. Much the greatest, in fact stupendous pianist I have ever heard . . . Thank you for every word of that wonderful letter,
>      Your very affectionate Violet

Finally installed in Mount Street by the autumn, Violet invited the eighty-seven-year-old Bernard Shaw to tea. She had known him for nearly fifty years and had watched him evolve from *enfant terrible* to the second most famous man in England, by now more or less equally celebrated for his wit, his plays, his austere dietary convictions, his freethinking socialism, his opposition to the war, and his patriarchal beard. She asked Sachie to join them.

> 11 Mount Street Mayfair W1  *24 November 1943*
> Dearest Sachie,
> THANK YOU for your letter. Your letters are one of the chief joys of my artistic life, which is so unthought of by the Public & the Privates . . . I am looking forward with delight to see you the day after tomorrow: Bernard Shaw intends to come & when I sent a message to say I thought you were coming, he sent a message back saying "Sachie Sitwell and the Clavichord will suit me very well." A quarter to four will you come, for he wishes to go away before it is dark. From your very affectionate Violet.

Intent on gathering material for his autobiography, Osbert inserted himself, too, into the tea party. His fifth volume, *Noble Essences*, published two years after Violet's death, devotes a chapter each to ten people he considered to be among the most remarkable he had known. The chapter on Violet contains a cameo of Shaw's visit.

. . . the scene is pitched on a wide upper floor in Mount Street, on an afternoon of late autumn; to be precise about 3.45 p.m. on 26th November 1943 . . . Both my hostess and I shared a great admiration for Shaw, and for his courageous attitude towards the war . . . I made my appearance at the flat punctually at 3.45 to find Miss Emery [i.e. Dorothy] Walker at the window, watching for Shaw in the direction of Berkeley Square – for, at the age of 87, he had announced his intention of arriving on foot from his flat in Whitehall Court, situated some two miles away on the Thames Embankment, and she wanted to be ready to meet him at the door . . . A moment or two later, tall and straight as a tower he could be seen striding buoyantly along the empty street below . . . In a few moments he had entered the flat, and at once his full, Irish voice . . . poured into the room its resonance, bringing with it a tremendous sense of personal energy. Except when being played to he talked the whole time. Almost as soon as he arrived I remember that someone – perhaps myself – mentioned to him the raids, for bombing was reaching its climax, and Shaw remarked:
"I hate all this destruction. Every time a bomb falls on Berlin or London it kills a number of young Europeans: a fact which, as an old European, I deplore."
But he scarcely looked an old European, and I recall that . . . when I said how glad I was to see him plainly in such good health, he replied:
"At my age you are either well or dead . . ."
When Violet Woodhouse was about to begin, Shaw would not sit in the armchair that she, with her usual grace and quickness of movement, had pulled for him near her . . . Instead he chose a chair with a long, stiff back, and sat very upright in it . . . almost touching the instrument, while she played Bach and Scarlatti to him. His eyes watched the keyboard and his long bearded face had assumed an expression [both of] solemnity and of mockery, if this be not a contradiction in terms, as well as that of benevolence which the giant classical masters never fail to summon up in the hearts of all lovers of music . . .
When Mrs. Gordon Woodhouse stopped playing, we had tea and Shaw began once more to talk. Now he would not speak of the

war, but confined himself to telling us of Sir Edward Elgar, and how the famous English composer had liked to play, over and over again, the gramophone records made by Cicely Courtneidge and Jack Hulbert [popular entertainers], alleging that in them he found the secret of the perfect use of rhythm . . .

At 5.30, after eating two pieces of toast and butter, he set off again on foot for home. It was dusk now, but though there was an almost complete blackout, and he had brought no torch, he insisted on returning alone, as he had come, and we could only watch him walking into the darkness.

Violet wrote describing the same occasion to her sister Dorothy:

My Darling Doll,
Bernard Shaw was extremely amiable, & extremely talkative. I asked Osbert & Sachie Sitwell to come also, & B.S. started off by saying everyone told him how well he was looking, & seemed surprised, because he had lost his wife just lately, but he says tho' he was very fond of her, it had been a burden for 4 years, & so now he finds it a relief! He then turned to Osbert & said "Was your father a nice man?" Osbert said "No!!" A strange conversation wasn't it. He was pleased with the clavichord & said I played a Bach prelude like a poem, etc. But I think him aggravating as a musical person; too over intellectually minded perhaps. I should have begun to quarrel with him perhaps if he had stayed much longer. I have broken off here, for Rex Whistler came to see me, & then Tony Ganderillas, & I must go and wash my hands for supper. Dear & beautiful Winnie Polignac died during the night before last, & O, I am so grieved. She was so exquisitely musical & I loved having her here. She will be a great loss to the musical world & dear Ethel will be sad I expect. She was a great & passionate friend of hers in the old days, much love Darling Doll from your devoted V.

Two weeks later, Sachie wrote to Violet, for the first time pushing her hard to learn more Scarlatti pieces. On 1 December Violet replied apologetically that she had brought none of the music Sachie had sent her to London. From now on, however, Domenico Scarlatti was to be her consuming interest.

# XVIII

*Late-Flowering Passions*

ORN IN NAPLES IN 1685, Domenico Scarlatti was an exact
B contemporary of Handel and J. S. Bach. In the 1940s, when Violet and
Sachie began their quest to reach a full understanding of his work, he was
much less well known than his prolific father, Alessandro, whose operas,
masses and cantatas had brought him fame and a six-page entry in the 1928
edition of *Grove's Dictionary of Music and Musicians*. By contrast, Domenico
rated a single page, largely devoted to his travels to Venice, Rome and Spain,
his musical bibliography, and his reverence for Handel, together with such
peripheral matters as his gambling, his corpulence and his hand-crossing
technique at the keyboard. Of the genius which Violet detected in
Domenico's work, the only hint in *Grove* is a quotation from his father's
letter of introduction to the patron of music Ferdinand de' Medici: "This
son of mine is an eagle whose wings are grown; he ought not to stay idle in
the nest, and I ought not to hinder his flight."

As Violet immersed herself in Domenico Scarlatti, her spirit soared and
made her proof against the exhaustion which afflicted so many in 1944, as
the war stretched into its fifth year. She and Sachie already knew probably
as much of Scarlatti the man as there was to know. Long before the two
had met, Violet had acquired an old edition of Dr Burney's four-volume
*General History of Music* (1776–89), which treated extensively of the Scarlatti
family, and Edward Dent's *Alessandro Scarlatti: His Life and Works* had been
given to her by a friend in 1907. Relying mainly on the same two books
for his biography of Domenico, Sachie had fleshed out the few known
facts about the composer and given them colour by a method which
Violet greatly admired, that of taking fragments of information about
the musician's life and placing them within the historical contexts of
eighteenth-century Italy, Portugal and Spain, the three countries in which
Scarlatti had lived. Re-creating street life from his study of the paintings
and architecture of the time, and drawing on the letters and memoirs

of Domenico's contemporaries, Sachie had produced a convincing, if enigmatic, portrait. As for Scarlatti's music, Violet had to rely on the scant material collected by musicians over the years. She owned copies of the *Essercizi* and the sonatas published in London by Scarlatti's English friend, Thomas Roseingrave, but neither she nor Sachie possessed the Alessandro Longo volumes, published in 1910, which contained 545 harpsichord sonatas, the great bulk of his sonata *oeuvre*.

That so little was known of Domenico Scarlatti's intriguing and powerful personality only added to his allure. There had always been a Scarlatti cult of a kind, especially in England, but the musical public had long been rationed to hearing only a handful of his sonatas. Since the playing time of these was never more than two or three minutes in length, it had become the fashion for one or two to be set at the beginning of a programme, as an introduction to what was considered weightier material. The mystery surrounding Scarlatti was heightened by the fact that his greatest music, composed during the last years of his life, was not written for public consumption but for one person, his royal patron, the Portuguese Infanta Maria Barbara, later Princess of the Asturias, and still later Queen of Spain.

Maria Barbara and her husband Fernando lived in a strange, sequestered world, moving like clockwork dolls between their five palaces with their court at pre-ordained times of the year. She suffered from severe melancholia, as did most of the Spanish royal family, and she found in music – and especially in the human voice – her only solace. She composed music and was a skilled harpsichordist, and Violet and Sachie took on the challenge of discovering all they could about her opera productions, her festivals and her musical instruments. They also researched the story of another member of the Court, Scarlatti's friend the castrato singer "Farinelli" (his real name was Carlo Broschi), whose matchless voice had conquered Europe before he had been brought to the Spanish Court in the hope of curing the seemingly irreversible depression of Maria Barbara's father-in-law, King Alfonso.

It was in 1944 that Violet and Sachie came to realize that they could never properly understand Scarlatti's music, with its breathless pace, its variations of expression and mood – exultant, joyous, dark, cryptic, unsettling – until they had heard a broader range of his work, and arranged it into a rational framework. It was obvious that the sonatas differed widely in expression, but that some were linked to each other, not only by their tonal schemes but also by a multitude of other devices. As a first step, Sachie was determined that Violet should develop as large a Scarlatti repertoire as possible.

Violet's Mount Street flat was, however, less exclusively devoted to music than Maria Barbara's palaces. Sometimes music-loving guests would bring philistine husbands or wives, who would be ushered into the study and offered a drink. It was the task of Gordon and Bill to entertain them there, and to keep them well away from the sacred rites of the music. There were occasional lapses. One evening, during the post-concert supper in the dining-room, Bill's niece Lorna Brooke was in the course of telling Violet how much she had enjoyed her playing of a Bach partita when crashing sounds of rough chords filtered through from the adjoining room. The table froze. After a few whisky and sodas, Lorna's husband, who had not seen a harpsichord before, had given Gordon and Bill the slip and was trying out the instrument. Violet did not make light of the affair. She sent dramatically for her tuner, Henry Tull, who was still audibly repairing the damage when the last guest left for home.

James Lees-Milne, the biographer and diarist, visited the flat in 1944 to collect Winnie de Polignac's friend Alvilde Chaplin, with whom he was much taken (they later married), although she had a husband at the time, the zoologist and musician Anthony Chaplin. As a literary man, Lees-Milne was brought to the music room rather than the study. He wrote in his diary entry for 2 February:

> Mrs. Gordon Woodhouse full of conversation. She was seated at the clavichord when I entered. After Alvilde joined us she turned to another clavichord made by Tom Goff. She played a Bach prelude, and I thought how lovely. After some more I decided that the instrument was too thin. I needed more volume to be satisfied. When I remarked that I could not claim to be really musical, she stopped. She talked about her house Nether Lypiatt, and called in Lord Barrington who showed me his sepia drawings of the house. He is a sweet, friendly, simple creature, and I would suppose not up to her exacting intellectual level.

Two weeks after Lees-Milne's visit, the bombing of London was resumed with Hitler's new "terror weapons", the pilotless V1s, known as "buzz-bombs" or "doodlebugs". "I don't like to think of you being in London," Sachie wrote, himself having returned to Weston.

> If it goes on, do go back to Lypiatt. What about the Scarlattis? Have you managed to borrow them? Do *please* see to it. It would be so *wonderful* if you could look at one or two more of them; particularly the "hunting"[1] one, and one or two of the Spanish ones,

---

1 K477/L290 (Ralph Kirkpatrick, *Domenico Scarlatti*).

the Bourrée d'Aranjuez;[2] and the ones which are in guitar style. Do please do this. It is the only thing I can think of that interests me; everything else is so deadly, now.

Lily, petrified by the buzz-bombs, had already persuaded Violet to leave London. With her left wrist still causing her pain, Violet told Sachie that, although she had stopped working, "if anything could induce me to set about more Scarlatti it would be you." Finding, however, that the wrist grew worse without exercise, she forced herself back to practising. By April she had mastered the two Scarlatti pieces which Sachie had insisted she learn. One of these, which she called simply "the very beautiful one", for a time obsessed her, and she became convinced that no player since Scarlatti himself had understood as she did how to express the pageantry or the passion of his music. Although the sonatas were "more gorgeous on the harpsichord, they seem more desperately and unbearably beautiful and architectural on the clavichord and more like going back into a fantastic and strangely inhabited world". One night, pining for an audience, she was reduced to asking Lily to listen to three pieces, as neither Bill nor Gordon, nor even Dorothy Walker, would appreciate them. She wrote incessantly to Sachie. It was uncertain when they would next meet, but she had agreed to take her best clavichord to London for a recital to the Churchill Club on 6 July. Would Sachie be there?

The Churchill Club had been sponsored by the Prime Minister's future daughter-in-law who, as the Hon. Pamela Digby, had married Randolph Churchill in 1939 (now, in 1996, she is the Hon. Mrs Averell Harriman, United States Ambassador to France). The club had been established in 1943 for American soldiers newly arrived in Britain, and especially for those among them who were culturally minded and wanted a place in which they could escape the mess atmosphere when not on duty. A temporary centre had been provided for them in Ashburnham House, Westminster, where they could borrow books and listen to music and lectures. To Violet's relief, since she felt sullied by having agreed to play at a club bearing the Prime Minister's name, she discovered that Jane Clark, who had taken charge of the cultural programme, had already signed up Osbert and Edith for a poetry reading the night before the recital. Jane's attachment to the title of "Lady Clark", five years after Kenneth Clark had been knighted, gave rise to some amusement. "Does Jane Clark sign herself to you as she does to me 'Yours sincerely Jane Clark (LADY CLARK)' in large letters?" Osbert

2  K377/L263 (Kirkpatrick, op. cit.).

enquired of Violet. "You must come, *please* to our reading, and we'll be naturally at your recital."

A smile at the Clarks' expense was, however, no more than a diversion in a generally grim year. Ethel Smyth's health had been failing for some time. Early in May her resistance finally gave way and she died, aged eighty-six. Violet had not long before had a lively correspondence with her, sending her £5, which Ethel had spent on a train ticket so that her brother might visit her. That exchange of letters was no consolation, however, and although Violet had long been expecting Ethel's death, when the news came, she was not prepared for the sense of shock and bereavement which overcame her. For a while she was quite unable to reconcile herself to losing one of her greatest friends, a friend who had once been in love with her, and who had proved so loyal over thirty-four years. She felt a profound melancholy, "not nostalgia which I like but Black Dismals, as stark as the kitchen sink".

Fortunately, Violet was too engrossed in Scarlatti and her Sitwell life to sink into a prolonged depression. Osbert and Edith had by now worked themselves up into a state of fury and agitation over their father's will and the circumstances of his death. They believed that the embezzlement of his fortune had almost certainly culminated in his murder at the hands of his beneficiary, the ex-cashier of the Banque Populaire Suisse, Bernard Woog, aided and abetted by his English wife Olga, who together had looked after Sir George during his last years in Switzerland. When Edith sent Violet her newly published anthology, dedicated to Violet and inscribed "For the great and beloved artist . . . this the first copy to appear with Edith's love", she took the opportunity to keep her abreast of events:

> . . . Osbert and I are feeling a little battered by these latest revelations about father. We have just been reading through certain letters from the man who has got all his money, and in whose house he dragged out the last years of his life – they are HORRIBLY sinister in the light of what we now know. They have a giggling, gloating atmosphere . . . letters were written to us, imploring for help, and were then found torn up by this man. Then there is the most curious passage about the old man insisting on having food when he is in the bath . . . the nurse says he never did. What does this mean? I think I know . . .

As this drama rumbled on through the spring and into the summer, Edith, who had become a full-blown celebrity once more, and was clearly enjoying it, made several forays to London, where she entertained royally at the Sesame Club in Grosvenor Square. Using her wit, charm and gift for friendship to catch the tide of admiration while it lasted, she set herself to building up a fresh network of allies and admirers. She saw in Violet and her clavichord the ideal vehicle for reminding the new generation of poets of the link between music and poetry. Wanting to reserve for herself the role of hostess and patron, however, she plotted to lure Violet out of Mount Street to the Sesame Club.

Sachie, meanwhile, could think of nothing but Scarlatti and Violet. He now saw that the haphazard way in which they had been tackling the sonatas would no longer suffice; it was essential that they have a fuller edition of the scores so as to be able to set them into some order. "I have just written off this morning," Sachie wrote in May,

> on two attempts to get you the complete Longo edition. I only hope they will be successful. It is wonderful to think you have begun on more Scarlatti. Do *please* try and get on with a few more of them. If only we could get that Longo edition, then we can identify all the Spanish ones, and the others too! I want particularly to hear the guitar ones, which are said to be like Spanish "flamenco" music, and the Catalan one, which may be a Sardana, a wonderful sort of local dance.

Violet would have liked to have recorded her playing of Scarlatti, and she had maintained her connections with the gramophone companies; but because of government control of chemicals needed for the war effort, materials were almost unobtainable and even an anonymous fixer calling himself "Mr. Smith", whom Sachie knew, had been unable to procure a supply of shellac. The restrictions did not, however, apply to the BBC, which wanted Violet to record some pieces by Scarlatti's pupil, the Portuguese organist and composer Carlos Seixas. Some early English music was to be recorded at the same time, which, to Violet's annoyance, an Austrian performer, Alice Ehlers (once a pupil of Landowska), had been asked to play. "Why not ask the only English player of the sort!?" she remarked to Sachie. "But I don't at all wish to do the Seixas, so we can be as grand as we like with them, and you might perhaps talk with them, yes?" "I am perfectly furious about Mdme Ehlers", replied Sachie, "what does she know about English music? It wouldn't even matter if she could play, but she can't! Really they are such a pack of fools at the BBC."

In spite of there being more than twenty years' difference in their ages, by the summer Sachie and Violet were acting as if they were in love. Sachie planned to see her every day of his short London holiday away from his

Home Guard duties in Northamptonshire.

> I am longing and living for the 4th July . . . for the concert, and will come as you say the next day . . . it will be lovely to have dinner afterwards . . . And Darling Violet you will be playing some other time, won't you, because it is the only thing I look forward to. I will either post the Scarlatti to you or leave it at Mount Street when I have arrived . . . Do write to me again. I love to see your handwriting on the envelope. And I do hope you are working. There is so much for you to do; and I believe you are playing better now than ever.

Knowing what a hard taskmaster Sachie had become, Violet experienced a certain fear when he gave her all the volumes of the Alessandro Longo's Scarlatti edition, instructing her to learn between twenty and thirty pieces. She would put off starting each new sonata until she had braced herself for the ordeal. If only she had been twenty years younger; and how much more difficult it was to play them on the clavichord! The Scarlatti scholar, Ralph Kirkpatrick, states that none of the sonatas were originally written for – that is to say, improvised and perfected on – the clavichord. Violet was, therefore, attempting something previously untried. The pieces posed immense technical problems, with extended leaps, glissandi, arm rebounds and hand-crossings; it was not for nothing that Scarlatti himself had been considered a supreme virtuoso even in his early years as a composer of church and theatre music, long before he had attained his highest powers in the privacy of the Spanish Court. To play the sonatas as she wished, Violet had first to master these technical difficulties, and then to enter into Scarlatti's spirit. It was all the more extraordinary to her that, while his instrument of composition had been the harpsichord,[3] which she had employed almost exclusively for his music before 1937, he sounded "so terrifyingly coloured and so descriptive with a terrible and passionate logic" on the clavichord.

Violet was convinced that only she and Sachie properly appreciated the genius of Scarlatti, whom she considered the equal of Mozart and Bach. Tom Goff refused to count him as a great composer, while Anthony

---

3 Author's note: I have followed Kirkpatrick and other scholars in asserting that Scarlatti composed his sonatas only for the harpsichord. According to Richard Luckett, however, citing the work of recent scholars in the Spanish royal archives, there were clavichords in the Infanta Maria Barbara's possession; and several unexplained oddities in the principal texts strongly suggest that Scarlatti also wrote for the clavichord – a remarkable confirmation of Violet's musical instincts.

Chaplin, though Violet respected his musicality, and though he much admired Scarlatti, was, she wrote, content to "maunder and wallow for hours on end" and did not feel "as if he must die if the pieces are not properly performed". Having played so much with Arbós and Rubio as a young woman, Violet had also come to believe, with some justification, that no one living, and certainly no Anglo-Saxon, was capable of interpreting Spanish music as she could. These early mentors of hers had reflected in their own compositions the popular styles of the different regions of Spain. In her approach to Scarlatti's compositions in the Spanish idiom she therefore brought to bear a unique understanding of the hidden springs of his artistry – the fusion of Italian formality with Spanish vernacular rhythms.

Back at Lypiatt, without the stimulus of London and missing Sachie, the person who made her feel most alive, Violet fell into gloom. With petrol so scarce she had fewer visitors, and in any case took little pleasure in the company of those who made the effort to come. The youngest Blow daughter arrived in a pony trap, bringing with her an officer on leave. Others came by bicycle. All were treated to the same disconsolate reception, even her nephew John. "I got bored with Alvilde and then with dear John Gwynne who came, altho' I love him," Violet wrote to Sachie.

> You spoil me for all those listeners. I think you are the most musical person I know, and fastidious which is so necessary and so unusual. I have begun two most lovely Scarlattis, difficult, and I think neither of them marked. One is a regular guitar technique and the other simply exquisite, rather like heavenly and melancholy Bells, with astonishing complicated accents in the middle about ten times.[4] It reminds me of "I long to talk with some Old Lover's Ghost who died before the God of love was born" [a line from John Donne's "Love's Deity"]. I also read that the clavichord was much in use in Italy about the Scarlatti times, and there is even a picture of an Italian one, or two, one about a hundred years earlier than the other, and I feel that the clavichord is able to take us into where all past years are, more than any other vehicle in the whole world. It is like looking or getting into where this life and music and sounds are still going on somewhere, somehow. And Sachie, you really are the medium in many ways, who has shown me how to find this wonder, for I feel it to be a magic, a dream, and how much of it is your doing? Who knows?

At long last it seemed that the war might be nearing its end. By mid-

4  K27/L449 (Kirkpatrick, op. cit.).

August 1944 the Allies had fully consolidated their landings in France and were making good progress in rolling back the German armies. The Russians were advancing rapidly on the Eastern Front. However, the hopes were premature. Germany was far from surrendering, despite the flattening of its cities and the destruction of its armed forces, and with the prolongation of the war Violet found she needed Scarlatti in order to maintain her emotional equilibrium. Having mastered four new pieces, she now had a repertoire of eighteen sonatas. Sachie, however, was not satisfied. "Do please not stop. Do begin again and learn more, so that you have them ready for when we all meet in London. They must be part of our private peace celebrations. Like you do I grieve every moment the war goes on." A month later Georgia mistakenly told Sachie that Violet had learned eighteen new Scarlattis. Excited, but somewhat doubtful, he wrote urging her, if it were really true, to make the figure up to twenty-four. Her playing was his sole pleasure. "You are the ONLY living master, great and small. Because some of the things you play are in a sense the largest, Chesapeake and Shannon, for instance; or the Midsummer Night's Dream, which makes me almost cry to think of it. I am simply longing to see you, Darling Violet."

"I fear I have not learned 18 new Scarlattis!" Violet wrote on 22 October.

> I told Georgia I now knew 18! But since then I have partly learned a Wonder, and I have begun another. I cannot express to you how astounding some of these new ones are. It makes me feel almost ill to think upon them, and I sometimes think it is like a silent restoration, what I have been doing, for they are almost terrifying, as I think I said, so dramatic, and if one can only have the judgement and self-sacrifice to play them safely enough, they are like strange and fantastic dreams and visions of the past, full of trappings and sparklings, and ceremonials, courts and very melancholy. There is another Castrati[5] one which makes one feel how easily Scarlatti could beat even poor old Mozart, right off the field, and much more simple, but alas! also much more difficult.

Arriving a fortnight later in London, Violet wailed from Mount Street: "O Sachie here I am, and where are you? I have seen [Arthur] Waley and the Babyook [Beryl de Zoete], and how I wish you were here. The date for the clavichord at the Churchill Club is fixed for the 30th [November] . . . I thought to give an entire Scarlatti Programme perhaps." Sachie came to Violet's performance at the Churchill Club, but on returning to Weston he found that he missed her, and he even showed signs of being jealous of

5 Written for Farinelli.

Anthony Chaplin, an enthusiastic clavichordist. Sachie urged her not to lend Chaplin the Scarlatti volumes, but to open them herself and find something new: "You must not mind my mentioning it . . . it has been the most wonderful sensation of the last five years . . . and I love and admire you more than ever."

Tom Goff, who, after Canada, had served in South Africa as an attaché to the High Commissioner, Sir Evelyn Baring, returned to England at the end of 1944. There was no war work for him in London, and he was soon demobilized. Contacting his old partner Joseph Cobby, he managed to derequisition his house in Pont Street and started up his workshop again on the top floor. The two craftsmen prepared themselves to build six new instruments, including another clavichord for Violet. Wood was virtually unobtainable – the Board of Trade was keeping back supplies for the repair of war damage. Tom was refused a private licence, but was rescued by the painter Henry Lamb (who had once exchanged one of his pictures for one of Tom's clavichords), who was able to obtain planks of beech, lime and mahogany through a businessman who was sitting to him for a portrait.

Violet invited Tom and his mother to Lypiatt in January 1945. Though delighted to see him back, she found a week's visit too long. For all his dedication to music and to instrument-making, Tom was not a natural musician. He had no innate feel for rhythm, for the rise and fall of a phrase, or for harmonic progressions and resolutions. When he was young he had acquired a mechanical level of competence, but no more than that. Yet he aspired to something beyond his reach – to be regarded as an artistic performer, if not perhaps to concert standard, then at least of a skill sufficient to demonstrate the quality of his instruments. Given Violet's ultra-perfectionism, she was predictably irritated when Tom trespassed on her ground, and the lessons she gave him were a breeding-ground for quarrels. She felt he had no understanding of what she was trying to convey. Worse, he could not combine his reverence for Bach with an appreciation of Scarlatti. For his part, Tom complained that she was corrupted by Scarlatti, a charge which in Violet's eyes betrayed insensitivity verging on insanity. "If one could hate Bach, he would make me!" Violet moaned.

Heaving up first one shoulder and then the other, and making a slipshod scurry at the end of the Bars, and playing half a fugue solemnly, because he is unable to do the rest. For goodness sake destroy this letter at once, dear Sachie! He is furious with Scarlatti for writing a Glissando, and with me for playing it. Did you ever hear such a thing? How could I spoil the clavichord doing it so gently? And I told him he spoiled the clavichord, forcing the tone till it is quite out of tune, because he is totally unable to make a vibration. He said I was too severe. All the same I am really fond of him, and he does make beautiful instruments, but why, O why, does he wish to be a Virtuoso!

Despite his absence on war service, Tom's reputation as an instrument-maker had become well established, but he had a wider ambition. In spite of all Dolmetsch's pioneering work, it was still unusual for authentic instruments to be used in concert halls for programmes of seventeenth- or eighteenth-century music. Tom was determined to ensure that they should be regarded as an essential part of the proceedings rather than a quaint archaic option. He urged Violet to broadcast more, to play in more harpsichord concerts, and to add amplifiers during her playing, so as to increase the popularity of his clavichords. She, on the other hand, thought the idea of amplifying the clavichord ludicrous and would have none of it. In the cause of his crusade he shamelessly exploited both his musical and his society contacts; and by the 1960s few dared perform eighteenth-century works with solo or continuo keyboard parts other than on a harpsichord.

While Tom excelled at making the relatively simple clavichord, of which Violet had five at her death, his harpsichords were less successful. Neither a scholar nor a natural craftsman, he had come to his profession late in life and had acquired his knowledge of the traditional methods of construction somewhat over-rapidly. Like his clavichords, his harpsichords were visual works of art, veneered in burr walnut and inlaid with tulip wood, box and ebony. To give them extra sturdiness and reliability for the concert hall, he built them with aluminium frames; in addition, in an attempt to make them more powerful than they should be, he increased the weight and tension of the stringing. These liberties detracted from the tone; without them, however, he could not have done as much as he did to advance the popularity of the harpsichord.

Before the war Violet had tried out Tom's first harpsichord, made in 1937, but had found it insufficiently expressive, since at that stage he had not yet incorporated a technical device which, at her wish, Dolmetsch had added to her own instrument.[6] Many years later Tom claimed in a BBC broadcast that, once he had adopted her suggested alterations, Violet thoroughly approved of his pieces and "drew forth every sound of which harpsichords

6 Half hitches, allowing the pedals controlling the registers to be set in different positions to enable the strings to be plucked more loudly or softly.

are capable". This was a lapse of memory, however, for although he modified his first harpsichord in 1939 (and his twelve post-war harpsichords all included the new feature), after Violet's death in 1948 he lamented in a letter: "I grieve and grieve that she could not have lived long enough to play on my harpsichords, which I was only just beginning when she died."

The wintry months of the beginning of 1945 dragged on. In February Bill became ill. It was probably only an acute case of flu, but Violet was extremely anxious and asked John's wife, Patricia, who was a devout Christian Scientist, to pray for him. Although Violet did not herself become a Christian Scientist, when Bill's fever abated she told Patricia that it was her faith which had "poured back health into him". She herself had moved away from the Church of England by now, but as she approached the end of her life, she was still searching earnestly for different paths towards spiritual truth. She even explored Eastern religions: after reading *Peaks and Lamas* in 1945, she entered into a long correspondence about Buddhism and Tibetan philosophy with its author, Marco Pallis.

By this time London was under a new form of attack from the V2, a supersonic rocket which differed from the V1 in that it arrived at its target before it could be heard or detected, whereas the noisy V1 signalled that it was about to fall by the sudden cutting out of its engine. Lily's terror of both types of flying bomb confined Violet to Lypiatt, where she received a fairly constant stream of visitors who managed to overcome the difficulties of transport. Osbert twice sent the young literary critic and poet Henry Reed, a recent protégé who had reviewed Edith's poetry favourably, to lunch with Violet. "I like him so much, so sensitive, and such an interesting eye," she wrote. She wondered, too, since Denis had left her a little money, whether Osbert's friend John Piper would make a drawing of Lypiatt[7] and decorate one of Tom's clavichords for her. Osbert also wanted a Goff clavichord and told Violet that he had sent Tom "that book of mine, with a sycophantic dedication, in order to try and get the clavichord out of him. I think he is fanatical . . . why can't he like both Scarlatti and the great Bach?"

Osbert had isolated himself again at Renishaw, in order to complete the final volumes of his autobiography. Nevertheless, he was put out that Sachie had, as he thought, taken advantage of his absence to usurp his position, with Violet. Osbert felt as close to her as ever, and as part of his effort to re-establish their former intimacy represented himself as Sachie's financial protector, which was far from the truth at this stage (though later Osbert was to help Sachie by buying his interest in Weston from him, while allow-

7 Piper's painting of Lypiatt is at Renishaw. It appears in Osbert's chapter on Violet in *Noble Essences*, (1950).

ing him to live there rent-free). "You'll never know how much I love your playing, or how much your friendship, which has seen me through *two frightful* wars of absolute idiocy, means to me," he told her. "I long to see you. I love you far MORE than Sachie does, if possible, and only distance and having all Sachie's worries to deal with prevents me from doing anything I want to."

In the spring of 1945 Sachie's wife Georgia left for Canada to visit her mother. Theirs was an open marriage, which had permitted each of them to conduct a string of affairs, mainly with members of "smart society" (though Georgia had recently had a liaison with the Chief Constable of Northamptonshire). Violet always adopted a scrupulously affectionate manner towards Georgia, but there was neither real warmth nor, surprisingly enough, any jealousy in their relationship. Georgia, who much preferred the *beau monde* to music, seldom accompanied Sachie to Mount Street, and her six-month absence in Montreal now freed him and Violet to concentrate more intensively than ever on their exploration of early music. Violet had made contact with the organist and Scarlatti scholar, Richard Newton, who brought to her attention an edition of five Domenico Scarlatti sonatas published by Gerstenberg in 1930, including one which is printed only as a fragment in the Longo edition. Newton would have lent it to her, but he mistrusted the post and was afraid that any remaining copies in Germany might have been destroyed by the Allied bombing: so he sent her tomatoes instead, accepted an invitation to Lypiatt and consulted her about the restoration of his eighteenth-century Hitchcock spinet. Violet had also been researching into other composers, and had found two more forgotten pieces of exceptional quality, "a beautiful short piece by [Michael] Praetorius, and a *marvel* by Alessandro Scarlatti – a slow aria with a figured Bass,[8] and it has almost made me feel like a creative artist for a short time, trying to fill it in, although Alas I am so far from being one."

Meanwhile Hitler's defences were collapsing at last, as Russian troops approached Berlin and the Allies crossed the Rhine to sweep through Germany from the west. The advancing armies now had their first harrowing encounters with the Nazi death camps, the Russians at Auschwitz, the British and the Americans at Buchenwald, Belsen and Dachau. On 30 April Hitler committed suicide in his bunker in Berlin, and on 8 May Germany surrendered. In London, a vast crowd in the Mall celebrated jubilantly in

---

8 In the seventeenth and eighteenth centuries, harpsichord accompaniments were not written out in full but were represented by a line of bass notes, leaving the player scope for invention, but requiring a thorough knowledge of harmony.

front of Buckingham Palace, where Churchill, standing on the balcony beside the King and Queen, acknowledged triumph with his cigar and his famous V-for-Victory sign. A month later, in his own words, "all our enemies having surrendered unconditionally or being about to do so, I was immediately dismissed by the British electorate from all further conduct of their affairs." Churchill's defeat in the July election by the Labour Party under the leadership of Clement Attlee was partly due to the way the armed forces cast their votes. To Violet it seemed like a belated, but none the less welcome, recognition of her own hatred of war.

Violet was in London for most of June, freed at last from Lily's constant nagging to go home to escape the V-bombs. On the 27th, following one of Edith Sitwell's Sesame Club lunch parties, she performed a number of Scarlatti pieces, including the three she had discovered with Sachie – the "Portuguese", the "guitar" and the "hunting" sonatas.[9] Grosvenor Street, however, where the Sesame Club was situated, was not an ideal venue for the clavichord. One of the guests that day, John Gielgud, remembered that her playing was almost drowned by the roar of the passing traffic, though it is possible that he exaggerated. The critic John Russell wrote to Edith afterwards that on the night of the concert he had been unable to sleep, so excited was he by Violet's music.

Sachie visited Lypiatt towards the end of July, at the same time as Arthur Waley and his constant companion Beryl de Zoete. They went sightseeing, and sat up after dinner talking into the small hours, but above all they went to hear Violet play. For Arthur Waley, now an oriental scholar of international renown, who had first heard her as a schoolboy in 1905, memories came flooding back, and he dedicated a short story[10] in the December issue of the *Cornhill* "To Violet Gordon Woodhouse in gratitude for fairy music". At the end of the visit Violet, Gordon and Bill drove Sachie back to Weston, which Violet had never before seen. If she were not so old, she wrote afterwards, she would love to visit the place four times a year now that she realized how close it was – it had the most romantic interiors she had ever seen.

In August, the war finally ended when Japan followed Germany in surrendering unconditionally, after atomic bombs (secretly developed by the USA in a race against time with Germany) had been dropped on the cities of Hiroshima and Nagasaki. Politically out of step with the vengefulness of the day, Violet was furious to learn that the Australians were

9  K504/L29, K28/L373 and K477/L290 respectively (Kirkpatrick, op. cit.).
10  "Monkey", an imaginary additional chapter to the sixteenth-century Chinese novel of that name which Waley had translated in 1942.

clamouring for the Japanese Emperor to be hanged. "The Mikados have been in line for 800 years, have they not? As to the Atom Bomb! Did you read Dean Inge's[11] fine article about it? He is a brave man." But she preferred talking about music. She wrote enthusiastically to Sachie about a rare old book which she had found in Bayntun's:

> I actually found my lovely old edition of Dr. Burney's Travels, in two volumes, and I feel I may be impelled to start again working, as it is so fascinating. I fancy Dr. Burney had rather bad taste in music, but that does not matter. How exciting about his meeting with Caffarelli[12] as an elderly man, and his still wonderful singing. He seemed to really prefer the works of Ph. E. Bach to John Sebastian. Very strange. Do you remember his description of the beautiful flute playing of Frederick the Great, and his lovely palaces? And the description of Aless. Scarlatti, and Hasse, and Galuppi?"[13]

More visitors came to Lypiatt in August and September. John and Patricia Gwynne brought Prince Fritzi von Preussen, a grandson of Kaiser Wilhelm II, together with his wife Brigid, a Guinness brewing heiress. A man of charm, correctness and self-discipline, Fritzi embodied many of the characteristics which Violet most admired in Germans. Shipped to Quebec in 1940 as an enemy alien, he had been interned in a railway shed, where he had slept in a bunk bed and become the camp leader. The following year he had been released and returned to England, no longer considered a threat to national security but required to work as a farmhand outside Wantage. Shortly after the von Preussens had left, Tom Goff arrived, but he proved to be a distracting visitor. Violet told Sachie, "his playing is so awful – like a Daddy-Long-Legs capering on top of a gold mine without any purpose and you know there never can be one – and so conceited poor thing – always wanting a lesson! And attempting such difficult pieces. But the first is the last as the Bible says, and all is wrong."

Capable of great generosity towards other artists, Violet gave short shrift to musicians in her own field. She complained of Myra Hess's "thumpings" on the piano, and of Lucille Wallace's "mechanical thumpings" on the harpsichord. Even the young were not immune. On one visit, the

11 The "Gloomy Dean", the eighty-five-year-old anti-war Dean of St Paul's, a distinguished scholar who also contributed weekly articles to the *Evening Standard*.
12 An eighteenth-century castrato second in fame only to Farinelli, Caffarelli earned enough to buy a dukedom.
13 Johann Hasse from Hamburg and Baldassare Galuppi from Venice, both eighteenth-century composers.

Detmar Blows brought along a confident and highly talented youth, Antoine Geoffroi Dechaume, who nonchalantly sat himself down at her harpsichord and began to play to the assembled company. With wordless disapproval, Violet froze him to a standstill. Kathleen Long, the pianist, who revered Violet's playing, once tried to compliment her by saying that she and Casals had gifts which set them apart from all other performers. Violet was not as flattered as Kathleen Long might have hoped. She felt she already had a clear appreciation of her own standing in the pantheon of twentieth-century performers, and she reminded Kathleen that Rubio had once said that he had taken more pleasure in teaching her than Casals.

Edith persuaded Violet to play at the Sesame Club once more in October. "It was an exquisite, beautiful afternoon, and one that gave the greatest happiness to everyone who was there," wrote Edith afterwards.

> The only sad thing was, that everyone wanted it all over again, and then still all over again. What strange varieties of experience, to be sure. In some ways the Scarlatti seems as if it had been written by a bird – but in others you hear the human heart beating. It was so wonderful to hear the Bach – so great, and abolishing human petty miseries. I am sure if only people could hear more music, they would be GOOD, in the real sense of the word, and wise, as Plato said people would be if they studied the movements of great planets . . . Tom [T.S.] Eliot was bitterly disappointed not to be there to hear you. But there was a young poet there, who had not had this wonderful experience before – George Barker . . . he was really in a dream when he left.

The first of Violet's new clavichords arrived at Mount Street with Tom Goff in February 1946. Christabel Aberconway, who had been making mischief as usual by passing on criticisms which Violet had voiced about the painted design, also arrived and managed to patch up the row. Violet was thrilled with the instrument, so she was in forgiving mood. Its tone was "as beautiful as Seraphim". She had found a motto for the flap – "Time will run back, and fetch the age of gold". "Would you believe it Tom wished to put it into Latin! An English poet like Milton, and so extraordinarily beautiful and suitable for an English clavichord and I hope to be played on by an English person. I found out that he did not like the word 'fetch'!" The contretemps was soon over – "So till the Next Great Dispute, things are perfect between him and me."

At seventy-five, age was making Violet hypercritical – age and the realization that her circle had dispersed, never to return. Norah Lindsay, who had blotted her copybook by her patriotism in the war, came under renewed attack. She admired all the wrong people, socialites like "the Beattys [the Earl and Countess, David and Dorothy] , the Trees [Ronald and Nancy, a transatlantic couple] and O Dear, it is when she gets artistic that she is hard to bear". Norah's attitude towards the Duff Coopers[14] also failed to give satisfaction: she boasted about "Dear Duffy & Dear niece Diana . . . & Bill asked severely what made them disgrace their son by getting him sent to the Nuremberg trials." Next it was the turn of Siegfried Sassoon. Violet found his new volume of autobiography, *Siegfried's Journey*, dreadfully dull, as she told Osbert. "That self-deprecating candour might be interesting to him in a diary, but is not attractive reading to others surely. And I am sure I don't look like a French Marquise! And you are not a bit like yourself. The poor thing can't be the least entertaining or descriptive." Norah Lindsay was, however, irrepressible, and Violet was too fond of her, and found her too entertaining, to allow the occasional argument to damage their friendship. After the Nuremberg row, wrote Violet,

> she bobbed up again quite quickly: she does amuse me: she looked simply killing with a rather tight, old, shiny cloth long coat, & a regular cock-a-doodle of artificial camellias pinned on to the sable or fur collar, & a toque with almost everything on it except a dead pheasant, & in a very jolly temper: I can't help liking her, tho' I know she is dangerous. She saw Sachie & Georgia here, & called out "Well, Sweeties" as if they were a couple of cockatoos, & after the way she went on about Sachie a little while back! Anyhow she is such a jewel compared to Churchill, whom she adores!!

Violet's mood was much improved when she received a message inviting her to play for Queen Elizabeth and her two daughters at Buckingham Palace on the Royal Family's Ruckers double-manual harpsichord. Tom Goff, who considered himself a friend of the Queen, was characteristically annoyed that it was not he who had been asked. Violet felt that he should be recognized, "even if he was behaving like a Prima Donna of the Nineties", and asked Osbert to praise his clavichords extravagantly to the Queen. Violet was unusually nervous on the afternoon of her performance. She was playing an unfamiliar instrument – albeit one maintained and tuned for the Palace by Tom – and she no longer quite trusted her musical memory, as she had in her prime. In the event she need not have worried, for the Yellow

---

14 Duff Cooper was now British Ambassador to France. He and his wife Diana had allowed their sixteen-year-old son, John Julius, to join some diplomats who had stopped off at the embassy on their way to the trials of Nazi war criminals at Nuremberg.

Drawing-Room provided a setting for her of the kind she had always found most perfect. As soon as she began to play her fire returned, and Princess Elizabeth and Princess Margaret enjoyed an evening which they both remember with pleasure to this day.

In the spring of 1946 something happened which threatened to shatter Violet's reviving equanimity. Sachie fell violently in love with Moira Shearer, a beautiful young red-haired ballerina who was beginning to make her name at Covent Garden. Born Moira Shearer King, she was twenty and Sachie forty-eight when they met. He had first seen her at a matinee of *The Sleeping Beauty*, after which he had written her an admiring letter; a month later, he had taken her to lunch at the Maison Basque in Dover Street. Presents, letters and books showered down on her home in Hammersmith, where she lived with her mother. Sachie's passion went unrequited, but Moira enjoyed his company even if, as a down-to-earth Scots girl who prided herself on her brains, she was distinctly irritated that his casting of her as a demi-goddess apparently required her to be treated as not only ethereal but also mindless.

Sachie could not make a secret of his discovery. As with the works of art he so loved, the exquisite Moira had to be shared – not necessarily with Georgia, but certainly with Violet. But how was Violet to react? She could hardly compete with a woman scarcely more than a quarter her age, yet her feelings for Sachie had run very deep, and he had come to mean as much to her as the four men with whom she had lived. Now she had to choose between retiring in misery or incorporating the newcomer into her own life. It was not a difficult choice. If she was hurt, she did not show it. Besides, Moira was a fellow artist. Violet elected to carry on as if Sachie's romance were the most natural thing in the world.

Five days after Sachie's first lunch with Moira, Violet went to see her dance at Covent Garden. She professed to be ecstatic and planned to go again as soon as possible. "I think her entrancing, and of a radiant quality on stage. I am wild to have a Ballet of 'Farewell Miss Julie Logan'[15] with her as the enchanted heroine . . . and have invited her to supper after the ballet."

Moira Shearer remembers Violet coming regularly to the ballet with Sachie, Gordon and Bill, frequently taking her back to Mount Street afterwards for supper.

> She was tiny – very neat and birdlike, her hair coiled closely to her head. She had bright penetrating eyes and very quick movements

---

15 A story by J.M. Barrie, the author of *Peter Pan*.

and she was somewhat autocratic . . . it was clear that Violet ruled Gordon and Bill Barrington entirely. Everything in Mount Street revolved around HER . . . I was struck by her strong, almost masculine personality – no obvious femininity of manner, no wiles or charm of that kind. She was always centre stage, straight-backed and imperious. Gordon and Bill were like shadows in her wake . . . I was twenty and fascinated by the ménage. Of course I was curious about their relationships – Sachie was much amused by my curiosity but guarded to the point of clam silence. I always hoped to see some little sign of affection between them but never did.

To the young Moira, Violet seemed to reign over her coterie like an empress.

Before or after her delicious suppers she always played – her instruments were in the largest room and little chairs were placed ready for her audience. It was extremely ceremonious; we seated ourselves, there was absolute silence and she entered, almost severely, neither looking at nor speaking to anyone. Her playing was lovely – very exact and classical, which suited her favourite Bach and Scarlatti perfectly. I think her only forays into modern music were some charming pieces by Albéniz and Granados. These I specially liked – they suited the sound of the clavichord so well. I wish I had been older, bolder, and could have suggested Debussy – maybe a little Poulenc – but I didn't dare, and if I had I don't think I'd have got very far!

Later in the summer, in July, Violet invited Sachie and Moira to Lypiatt, where Arthur Waley and Beryl de Zoete were enjoying an extended stay. Violet told Osbert that Sachie was like a doting parent with Moira. So, too, was Violet. She arranged for her chauffeur, Law, to give Moira driving lessons in the field opposite the front gates, and did everything possible to make her stay enjoyable. While most people were in awe of Arthur Waley, Beryl was variously thought of as a worthy consort for the great man, a witch, or an object of ridicule. The Sitwells were in the third camp, especially Edith, to whom Beryl's tactless, gushing personality had supplied an easy target over the years. Violet had previously been more charitable, but now she joined in. "I wish you could have seen Beryl in her sunbathing attire which she wore most freely before the farm labourers," wrote Violet to Sachie. "She looked rather like a stout coolie." With her startling red hair and large body, Beryl was no longer a beauty. "Will you tell Georgia that Beryl said she did not like to be left too long alone with Old Ovid[16] at Cameo Corner, because he became amorous. It tickled my fancy as I looked at Beryl. When will anyone be safe?"

Violet had been consistently extending her range for fifty years, and despite everything she continued to do so with apparently undiminished energy. In the summer of 1946 she wrote to John Gwynne: "I have been trying to learn an elaborate *Concert Fantaisie* by Haydn. I do like the Scarlattis so much better than Haydn & Mozart, tho' I fancy I play them better (Haydn & Mozart): they seem so much more at the surface, lovely & graceful tho' they are. This piece was one of von Bulow's[17] great concert pieces & is arranged by him for the piano." Her musical memory, once so exceptional, was less secure than it had been, and her wrists still needed treatment. It was, however, only she who was aware of any decline in her powers. Mrs Otto Kahn, the wife of the chairman of New York's Metropolitan Opera House, suggested that Violet should tour America with her harpsichord and clavichord, and found the perfect way to tempt her, by stimulating her competitive spirit. "She says I should knock spots off Landowska which made Sachie laugh: she is really very nice and seems as if she would arrange everything. I do not know how to cure my memory or my stiff neck or stiff fingers, or rather wrists. O Dear."

The idea of a contest between Violet and Landowska was appealing: it reminded Sachie of the contest between Scarlatti and Handel in 1709, arranged by Cardinal Ottoboni, in which the two players were adjudged equal on the harpsichord, but Handel was declared the victor because of his superiority on the organ. In New York Violet would surely be the winner, if only because of her great superiority on the clavichord. In the end, however, she regretfully refused the invitation. The thought of matching herself against the only player who had ever approached her own level of performance on the harpsichord (she never had a peer on the clavichord) was overtaken by the realization that she might no longer be able to do herself justice.

Had Violet been in her prime, it would in fact have been Landowska who had most to fear from a direct comparison. Richard Luckett cites with approval the expert opinion of John Ticehurst, a professional harpsichordist whose career was tragically shortened by an accident to his fingers, who kept careful records of his observations at concerts of early music in the 1920s,

16 Moshe Oved, the owner of the London jewellery shop Cameo Corner, was susceptible to flirtatious women.
17 Hans von Bülow, the celebrated late-nineteenth-century conductor and pianist.

when Violet was in her fifties and Landowska in her forties. Ticehurst dismissed Dolmetsch as lacking in technique and preparation; he found Landowska technically very accomplished but mechanical as an interpreter (an effect, he noted, enhanced by her instrument, a Pleyel); but he had no reservations about Violet, and would have agreed with Osbert Sitwell that ". . . though the mention of ancient instruments might to some minds carry the suggestion of a certain preciosity, she completely rid them of this peril: her fire burned their rind away, and revealed the flaming core of all music."

Although Violet could be severe at times, she was invariably sympathetic to those in distress. In August 1946 Violette Leconfield, the estranged wife of Lord Leconfield, "latched on" to her, as Violet resignedly put it, begging for help to get her out of a pauper's asylum, where she had been incarcerated for nine months following a nervous breakdown. Her truculent and selfish husband, relieved to have got rid of her, and having been embarrassed at her propensity for wandering around stark naked, never visited her, and failed to realize that she had recovered despite her forbidding surroundings. Although they barely knew each other, Lady Leconfield's plight touched Violet's heart, and by the middle of October Violet had extracted her and brought her to Lypiatt.

> Poor thing! She seems to me so dreadfully sane! Full of intellectual knowledge, & grinding all she reads thro' a sort of mental mincing machine, quite without imagination or anything of interest, except lucidity, & who cares for all that? . . . Still I am so exquisitely pleased to see her free, after all that shattering Bedlam, & full of admiration for her courage. She might have left Petworth [her husband's grand estate in Sussex] & all its pomposity only yesterday.

The baptism of a new Tom Goff instrument gave Violet the opportunity to pay an unusual compliment to Moira Shearer. She invited several people to tea. When the lid of the clavichord was raised, it revealed a painting by Oliver Messel of the Palace Garden scene in the first act of *The Sleeping Beauty*, with Moira running through the colonnade. On the last day of 1946 Moira's mother, who had heard Violet play earlier in the summer, wrote thanking her for her kindness to her daughter. Moira had had a momentous year, she said, enriched by the new friendships she had made in Violet's Mount Street circle, and above all "by the belief that so great an artist as Violet had shown in her". The letter was like a farewell. Moira went on to fame as the star and *première danseuse* of the celebrated Powell and Pressburger film, *The Red Shoes*, but she was never to see Violet again.

# XIX

*Time Will Run Back and Fetch the Age of Gold*

THERE IS AN OMINOUS entry in Dorothy's diary for the first month of 1947:

*January 11* Telephone rang and it was Dorothy Walker from Lypiatt to say V. was far from well & asked me about the diet I had when I was so bad in my liver and brain, but neither of us could hear, except a word here & there, so after V. tried to speak they rang off. Oh I do hope she hasn't anything really bad but at her age & if she is wasting it is such a bad sign & one gets really apprehensive. I have had a strange horrid fear hovering over me for a day or two. I wake feeling something dreadful is going to happen and my mind is obsessed with the future & its miseries.

Dorothy's premonition was all too accurate; although Violet did not know it, for Bill and Gordon had been persuaded by the doctor to keep the truth from her at all costs, she had cancer of the liver.

Darling Sachie,
Thank you so much for your letter. The doctor now tells me that I have been having jaundice (a slight attack) and he thinks I have a gall stone, but O Sachie, I hope this is not true. Do you not think he might be wrong? He says I must eat as much as I can, for I am so thin. I think I do not like him very much – We go to London tomorrow. I think I would almost rather die than to have an operation. I have not up to now had any violent pain and I thought one had such dreadful ones with a stone . . . My very best love to Georgia. Bill gave me such a charming little velvet jacket for Christmas by Patou and I have not worn it once.
     Your devoted Violet.

My legs, when I get out of the bath look like the Gobi desert, all ripples of wrinkles!! You know!

Cynthia Jebb, the wife of the politician and diplomat Gladwyn Jebb (later Lord Gladwyn), had known Violet since the end of the First World War, when she first had started attending Violet's musical Sunday afternoon teas and had been "thrilled at entering this milieu where I met . . . all sorts of people I longed to know". When she heard that Violet was ill, she paid her a visit, recording in her diary on 23 February that her friend had "a form of jaundice which goes on for ages", and that, although Gordon had begged her to stay only a short time, Violet was on such good form that she had stayed an hour. "I was admitted to her presence as to the holy of holies . . . she lay on a couch in front of the fireplace in which burned two electric fires full on. She was in black and red, with an enormous paste cross, and looked very wonderful, though she said she was dying." No doubt recalling Violet's extraordinary behaviour during the war, Cynthia Jebb added, "She is a great artist and therefore I suppose that her prejudices, lack of patriotism, and malice, must to an extent be forgiven her. She lives in a world of her own, surrounded by adulation, but when one hears her play clavichords, one is moved by her mastery and passion."

When Violet spoke of death to Cynthia Jebb, she was testing the effect on herself and on others, of saying the unsayable. Would the reaction to her statement confirm her suspicions, or would it give her the reassurance she craved? Would saying the words out loud make the truth easier to bear, if it were as bad as she feared? Christabel Aberconway encountered Violet as she wrestled with these questions, though it was not until a year later that she confided to Gordon and Bill, in a letter written to them both:

> . . . I think Violet knew: at one time anyhow. Then, her supreme courage, and her *will* to live for your sakes, made her obliterate the knowledge. Shall I tell you about this now? If I don't, I probably never shall, and I long for you both to have every memory of her.
>
> After she became ill, I was once with her alone, she lying on the sofa in front of the fire in her room. She turned and said "My Darling Christabel, you don't think I am going to die? And do I *smell* as if I am going to die? I am so frightened." With every power in my spirit and mind I vowed to her that she *was* going to get well. I expended all my vitality in assuring her of this.
>
> Then I went away for a while to Bodnant. On my return she asked me to come to luncheon. She was seated at the dining room table with her back to the light when I arrived. You both didn't come in for a little while. Violet looked at me, a little sternly. Then

she said "You were wrong in what you said to me. I *know* now. But do not speak of this to me or to anyone. Now I want to show you Lear's drawings of himself and his cat Foss."

You can imagine my distress during that luncheon – and afterwards. Indeed, I came to feel that Violet so much wanted to put her own knowledge away from her, that I was a reminder to her of that knowledge, and that I gave her no strength or vitality, indeed that my presence wasn't good for the new design she had created for her last months with you both.

This may be, you will say, imagination on my part. To me it is wholly true . . .

Violet went with Bill and Gordon to Brighton for several weeks in the summer of 1947, surrounding herself with books and hoping against hope that the sea air would do her good. William Simmonds, deeply unhappy about her illness, wrote to her there; others visited her – Tom Goff, the Sitwells, her brothers Roland and Nevile, the latter with Bluebelle. By early September her health was deteriorating fast. Although finding it difficult now to walk, she wanted to see Sachie more often and returned to London in October, booking him and Georgia for dinner at the Savoy Hotel. By December it was clear that Violet was close to death. "It makes me miserable to think of it. I think apart from Edith she is the most wonderful woman I have ever known", Sachie wrote to a friend.

Violet spent the last months of her life in Mount Street, but her mind was full of vivid images of Lypiatt, especially the garden and the walks outside. She behaved with fortitude; up to the end she never gave the impression of being an invalid and as her body faded her vitality and spirit seemed to glow more strongly, and her character softened. Bill and Gordon watched in helpless sorrow, Bill trying to cope through withdrawal and painting, while Gordon busied himself with ever more solicitous efforts to conjure up from the household's meagre rations delicacies for Violet to eat. Dorothy's diary describes what turned out to be her last meeting with Violet, who had been driven down to Folkington for the day to make her farewell:

*November 25th 1947.*
In many ways this has been a wonderful day – Glorious sun, and very cold wind. I suppose my last time of Darling little V. & the impression of *great* courage, a gentle sweetness and love I never saw before; we had such a happy time & when I said goodbye, and opened the gate for them to drive thro' & saw the last of them the tears would come. She looked more ill than one could imagine, and an almost

frightening strange colour, her frightful thinness, and her wonderful bravery and her sweet and touching ways; it is heartbreaking; she was so adorable to Miss P [Dorothy's housekeeper, Miss Plomley]. And me, so loving. Gordon the most unselfish, kindest person and Oh how thoughtful. Bill was very restless, and I imagine very unhappy. They came about 5 to 1. Roly arrived with cocktails and a delicious spaghetti dish to begin with. My contribution to the feast was my small salad, onion sauce, veges and chocolate mousse; Gordon brought dressed crab, a huge pile of sandwiches, rolls etc. & for us tomorrow some halibut . . . we had a small delightfully leisurely lunch. Bill went off early to sketch the barn.

To hide the terrible colour of her skin, Violet wore a veil. Her fear of death was extreme. When Patricia went to visit her in London during the weeks before Violet died she would say, in a pathetic voice, which wrung Patricia's heart, "Pattie, *stop* me from dying". In her bleakest moments mad perverted music danced in her mind. Just before the end she cried out to Sachie:

Help me drive the devilish noises of music out of my head. I feel like Tom of Bedlam – "The Flaming Drake and the night crow make music to my sorrow". I have got such appalling anaemia and low blood pressure and have to drink so much and the only happy moments in my day are when I sink into a lovely drunken sleep after gin drinking, much ordered by the doctor, has begun to act. Do you think we shall ever have a picnic at Great Tew?

Sachie tried to keep Violet's attention away from her illness, taxing her with more undiscovered music. Three weeks before she died, weak as she was, she was still playing:

11 Mount Street *December 1947*
Darling Sachie
Just to tell you there is a toccata in your music [Scarlatti] which is the most tremendous marvel I think I have ever heard in its way; very Spanish, and I shall fear never to be able to play it; I have never tried anything so difficult – the Spanish idiom is very strong and the rhythm really magnificent. Another one is quite exquisite and goes on the kind of gaiety with which Bach sometimes almost breaks one's heart. I am so excited and I was feeling as if it would set my teeth on edge to even touch the keyboard these last days. Guitars, Castanets, loud harsh sounds in this wonderful place and, it is strange to say, seems as if it must have been

intended for the clavichord.

If I could ever play it.

Unwilling though she was to speak of death to anybody other than
Patricia, Violet was making her last dispositions. She had several nieces and
two sisters, but at the very end she decided to leave her collection of jewellery
outside the family. She had promised them to Patricia, and on another occasion to Elizabeth David, but she changed her mind a few days before she
died. Sachie had been her passion for ten years and she wished him to have
something beautiful to remember her by. Violet's last letter was to him:

Darling Sachie,
I mean you and Georgia to have the jewels, and there is no-one in
the world I should more wish to possess them – you keep your
things and do not send them to the Caledonian market [a street
market in London]; and you like real jewellery and not false and I
consider myself very lucky to find you to have them both. Osbert is
coming to see me this afternoon and I intend to tell him I wish to
have them made with an heirloom and that I wish Georgia to have
them now, unless I wish to borrow them back, and I may add a
lovely little diamond collar to them – they are insured for the
moment very much below their value . . .

Although Nether Lypiatt belonged to Gordon, he had always told Violet
that it was up to her to decide who should eventually have it when they were
all departed. The house might well have gone the same way as the jewels -
according to Sachie's son Reresby it was promised to him. But John
Gwynne had also been told several times that he would inherit it, and in the
end he did. It was perhaps Violet's way of making restitution for James
having cut Nevile and his son John out of his will so many years before.

In her unpublished history of the Gwynne family John's sister, Kit Ayling,
gives a haunting description of the last visit she paid to Violet before
she died.

It was a strange evening; Gordon and Bill sitting there like unhappy
ghosts while Violet held us all with her magnetic power. We had
been told that she must not tire herself, and really should not play at
all; in any case we should try and leave early. This proved to be quite
impossible. After dinner (which she scarcely touched) she said she
was going to play, as Alan [Kit's husband] she knew, appreciated it,
and for two hours we sat round her and were no longer conscious of
time. Almost at once she turned to Scarlatti, and it did not seem
fanciful that she was possessed by his spirit; I know I have never

been more conscious of strange forces around me. She still had her remarkable looks, and her eyes glowed in her dead white face; but we were transplanted from the physical sphere and no longer noticed personal details. Gordon's and Bill's feeble protests were swept aside as if they had never existed. I think that she herself felt that she was possessed; it was certainly a very remarkable demonstration, and as we left the flat and walked into the dark of the streets we both had the impression that we had been in the presence of a great vital force. It had seemed to me that the atmosphere had been charged with electricity.

On 8 January 1948, aged 77, Violet went into a coma. Dorothy's thoughts were all with Gordon; her repressed love for him and her resentment of Violet's role in his supposed lifelong suffering came to a head in her diary entry the day after Violet's death:

*January 10 1948*
. . . Gordon's announcement of her death in *The Times* today is his last tribute in not saying "wife of": The story of that triangle if told would be too tragic to bear or believe; Gordon's martyrdom at the beginning. I realised it as perhaps no-one else, for I was so fond of him, and saw his misery; it is better perhaps not to think back how gay and cheerful he was in those days, loving hunting, cricket & dancing & then Bill came; but before Violet's marriage Violet had ruined Gordon's future, but 'tis best perhaps to stop, for it is wrong to speak ill of the dead, and V. was a genius in her way, and can't be judged.

For five days and nights Bill and Gordon took turns to stay by Violet's side until she was placed in the coffin and taken to the church in Folkington. There they again kept vigil, in turn, throughout the night until the funeral the next day. Even at such a time Gordon deferred to Bill. Bill accompanied the coffin as the chief mourner, Gordon following behind clutching a tiny bunch of violets which he threw into the grave. Roland organized the lunch afterwards at Wootton. In her diary, Dorothy paid her last tribute to the dead sister in whose shadow she had lived for sixty years.

*January 14 1948*
A strange day like a dream, far more than real. It is night now . . . it will soon be over and more like a dream than ever. The gale fell . . . at 7.40 a.m. I went to the church. It was almost dark. The 4 long candles by V's coffin which was covered in flowers. The church was

full of flowers and just the altar lit; Roly and Bill & no-one else. Mr.
Mall in white vestments read the communion service beautifully and
I took communion for the first time for many years; Roly, Bill and I
went up to the grave but it was still covered up. I came home and we
had breakfast . . . Mr. Tom Goff came . . . So utterly different to
what I imagined; how often Violet has written and talked of him. He
was terribly overcome & said Violet was the most wonderful genius;
he is devoted to her. God rest Darling Violet's soul. What a unique
personality hers was. She fascinated old and young, men and women;
she seemed to cast a spell over people, and Oh, how brilliant.

Bill and Gordon were kept busy in the days following Violet's death
answering letters and making arrangements for the funeral at Folkington
and the semi-private memorial service a week later in London at Grosvenor
Chapel, South Audley Street. For the music at the memorial service they
chose predominantly Bach, with a ground base by Scarlatti at the end of the
service. Dorothy, who now never left her farmhouse at Folkington, missed
the service. Gordon wrote to her, describing the Archdeacon's address and
telling her who had attended – mainly family and close personal friends.

The letters were too many to count, most of them to Gordon, as etiquette
required, but some to Bill and some to both of them. Osbert Sitwell wrote
on the day of Violet's death:

. . . Tom [Goff] telephoned me an hour ago – and I have not heart
to break the news to Edith. One can only be thankful that, the
illness having reached the pitch it did, Violet has gone: but it is not
of her, but of you, and of Bill, that one now thinks – and she would
think if she were here. The blow after so long a strain must be
appalling for you – but how wonderful you have been all along, and
what comfort to Violet! I suppose she was about the most extraordinary and wonderful being one will ever meet. I am grateful to
her for so many things and among them that, coming to hear her,
I got to know you. For you know, dear Gordon, that we are all
*devoted* to *you*: but that makes it worse now, for we worry as to your
present condition. Do take care of yourself. And do stay in London
at present. Oh, what an awful loss we have all suffered! When I
think of that vivid, beautiful creature, so unlike any one else, and
with her unique gift, not only of music, but of understanding,
I could go on weeping . . .

The same day Osbert's companion David Horner also wrote:

*9 January 1948* Renishaw.

My dear Gordon,

. . . You have indeed much to comfort you in the memory of so many years of devotion to her, and it was a devotion wh. she appreciated and on wh. she depended. You have had an unique experience for Violet was entirely unlike any other person. Her absolutely personal point of view about everything; never accepting second-hand ideas; her intense love of beauty of every kind, whether it was some exquisite music she had discovered or a lovely piece of silk, her devotion and loyalty to her friends; her enthusiasm; her extraordinary deep passionate feelings; perhaps one can combine all these sides of her character into the one word "genius" . . . Violet's generosity knew no limits. She would always lavish her musical genius and always play the music wh. she knew had particular, personal appeal. The memories of many hours at Brompton Square and Porchester Terrace come to me, as I write, and nothing can take those memories from me . . . from your ever affectionate David.

Bill took responsibility for Violet's gravestone. He wrote to Roland to tell him that he had been giving careful consideration both to the stone in the churchyard and to the memorial tablet in Folkington Church. He would not ask William Simmonds to undertake the carving, as he could only work on inspiration and could seldom respond to commissions; so he recommended a firm in Stroud. The headstone should be in stone or slate. He and Gordon "thought that Violet should have her own particular V inside a lozenge with *no* crest or coat of arms – then the inscription".

Bill went on to tell Roland that two spaces were to be left on the stone, one for Gordon's name and the other for his own. His mind had gone back to their earliest years with Violet on the Sussex Downs. Since they both intended to be cremated, there would be "no messing about Darling V's grave" because both his and Gordon's ashes would be "blown by the wind on the turf at the foot of the downs". Two days later Bill wrote again to Roland to let him know that he, Sachie, Osbert and Tom Goff were collaborating on the wording for the memorial tablet, which should be *Much more personal* and laudatory of her music and personality and affectionate but that will require much more consideration and their agreement will be difficult to arrive at. Osbert suggests that their part of it will take some time to do." The final wording is inscribed on a tablet in Folkington church: "Born with a rare genius for music, her playing of the harpsichord revealed a forgotten world of beauty and imagination; and the echoes of her music will sound forever in the hearts of those that loved her."

*The Times* printed a comprehensive obituary, contributed anonymously by Sachie Sitwell. A shorter supplementary note was supplied by Vere Pilkington, who concentrated on her playing:

> There has died one of the greatest musicians of our time . . . No one who heard her can ever forget her playing. Legends have grown up about her . . . She had an unbreakable gypsy rhythm which is given to few in a generation, a tautly strung tight-rope from which she could never fall: no conception was too grand to be embraced in the compass of her instrument, no phrase so humble that it could not be moulded with infinite care. Her phrasing was that of a bowed instrument, and in former years it was to Rubio the cellist that she went for final approval of her line. The subtlety of her playing was infinite and her clarity perfection; and yet when she began to play one forgot that music was made up of notes and became spellbound and entangled in a golden web of purest sound . . .

Sachie attempted the wider story of her life, in a long piece which was somewhat cut by the editor of *The Times* (the excerpts below are taken from Sachie's unabridged text):

> The death in London of Violet Gordon Woodhouse after a year's illness has removed a musical genius whose art was entirely unique in that she excelled upon both harpsichord and clavichord, a duality of expression which it has been given to no other player to emulate, let alone achieve . . . her personality was as magical as her music. Her force of character was such that could extract the last ounce of love and fidelity from her household and her friends.
>
> . . . As a young girl she was present at Paderewski's first London recital. Jean de Reszke and Sarasate were the other musical idols of her youth. Of the last of those she has often spoken to the present writer, and it may be that her approach to music was from a Spanish rather than Teutonic angle.
>
> . . . For many years it was her practice to invite her friends to her house and to play to them, and of the quality of these performances it would be impossible to speak in measured terms for . . . she was the equal of any player that ever lived. No-one who has ever heard her will forget her as a player of Bach . . .
>
> . . . in later years she took more to the clavichord, which in her

opinion was the most beautiful solo instrument ever invented. Her playing of little pieces by the Elizabethan composers was on a par with her rendering of the suites and fugues of Bach. In course of years her repertory became fantastic in scope and size. She was incomparable as a player of folk songs. She played Mozart in a manner that brought tears to the eyes . . . and hearing her . . . play the "Farewell song" from *Il Seraglio*, I was reminded of Keats, who wrote that after hearing an air by Mozart, he could not sleep all night.

The little pleading tones of the clavichord were all fire when she played "Scots Wha Hae" or the sailor's song "Chesapeake and Shannon". In later years the beautiful instruments made by Mr. Thomas Goff were a joy to her, and perhaps her playing was never better than in these last years when she made Domenico Scarlatti her special study. Upon an afternoon only two years ago she played to the writer all the Scarlatti that she knew for two hours and a half until she had counted forty and more sonatas and lost count – an incredible performance that proves her power of memory. One can never hope to hear again such a performance of Scarlatti . . . She would have chosen, probably, to be remembered for her Scarlatti and for the slow and mighty sarabandes of Bach. It is an appalling thought that we will never hear her play again, or go with her, which was her relaxation, to Tchaikovsky's *Sleeping Beauty*.

The only consolation in the loss of so rare a being is the thought that such persons were ever born . . . Even so, music was but half of her life. The other half was given to her family and her friends.

Sachie also wrote a posthumous prose poem to Violet[1] and told Gordon that he was "absolutely broken, so I can dimly imagine what you are going through . . . I can't think how we shall any of us feel the same. The poor darling was so wonderful and unique in every way . . ."

Two months later Osbert started work on the essay on Violet which was to form a chapter in his autobiographical book *Noble Essences*. When the piece was finally ready in August 1949, Gordon wrote unemotionally to Dorothy, to whom Osbert had written asking for material:

You ask if Osbert S. is conceited, I should say the answer is Yes. They are a curious family, fight amongst themselves but woe betide anybody casting aspersions on any of them, then they hang together and go for you tooth and nail. Yes he still has that castle nr. Florence

1 Printed in Appendix IV

and goes there quite a lot. I have not read much of his latest book yet but am looking forward to the next one, with a long chapter about Violet. I have read the manuscript & am not entirely pleased with it but it is Osbert's life, after he knew her, with a few dates of her early life which I was able to supply.

George Bernard Shaw did not write to Gordon until five months after Violet's death and then, perhaps remembering their exchange at the gathering in November 1943, wrote in highly original terms:

4, Whitehall Court, London SW1 *16 June 1948*
Dear Mr. Woodhouse,
When I became a widower in 1943 I was inundated with letters sympathising with my grief and loneliness. As I was not grieving, nor more lonely than I wanted to be (people who grieve soon forget or make a luxury of their grief; and I have a gift for privacy), these kindly-meant messages were not at all welcome; and I never inflict them myself. I hope it is not too soon to send you a line as one widower to another to say that I rejoice in her memory as I am sure you do.

After a successful marriage when one of the two goes I believe it is always a surprise to the survivor to find how much their lives were governed by one another. For 45 years I had to sing every night to please my wife, and be in bed before 11. Since her death in 1943 I have not touched the piano; and I am never in bed until after past 12. To give her a holiday from housekeeping I sailed round the world and drove my car from Cornwall to the Shetlands and all over Europe. Now I never dream of travelling: as to loco-motion I am more of a tree than of an animal. She was nomadic. The funniest part of it was the rush of women to achieve a rich widowhood by marrying me. I was reputed to be fabulously rich; and at 87 I could not live long. Many handkerchiefs were thrown. You will probably have plenty of offers of the devotion of a lifetime to the tenderest care of you if you have not had them already. If not now, when you are older. Lypiatt Manor is a tempting address. So beware.

Meanwhile you will be as surprised as I was by the change to bachelor habits . The things I should never have done but for my marriage were all to the good. Two – the right two – can live better than one.

The footing I seem to be assuming with you is the work of Dolly

[Dorothy], whom I have known from her childhood.
Don't dream of answering. G. Bernard Shaw

Gordon and Bill continued together at Nether Lypiatt for three more years, living much as before. Bill carried on with the flower garden and the farm – he was president, in 1949, of the Stroud Agricultural Show, and won prizes for his Hereford heifers. Food rationing continued, and Gordon devoted himself to the vegetable garden and the fruit. The year after Violet's death he described the garden to Dorothy as

> looking ghastly – everything dried burnt and brown but I have a really good crop of gooseberries, and of black and red currants, and Morello cherries. A very poor crop of apples. Hardly any vegetables, peas, r-beans, carrots, turnips a failure. Potatoes small little things generously given to the pigs. I made 16lbs of butter yesterday & I am bottling today. Have lots of sugar, thanks to supplies coming from Barbados. Shall have plenty of figs; don't forget to gather yours half ripe before the birds get them.

Isabel Armitage remembers Gordon clothing all the pears individually in muslin cloths to protect them from the wasps, giving the trees a ghostly appearance as the daylight faded.

In their self-effacing way, Bill and Gordon both assumed that Violet's friends and admirers would drift away once she was gone, but among the host of her visitors had been many who had come to feel close to the two men in their own right. Those who made the effort to keep in touch were struck by their composure and by the way that independence had brought out something new in them. Not that they forgot Violet: on the contrary, they turned her bedroom into a shrine. Visitors were now taken there on arrival. Her brushes and personal objects were laid out exactly as when she was alive, and a William Simmonds carving of a fox was placed on her pillow. A few of her smaller possessions were selected as tokens for the servants or posted off to relations and friends. Bill's niece, Daphne Celey-Trevilian, received a Nelson heirloom and a trunk of Violet's silk underwear, which she still has to this day. Moira Shearer was rather upset when an old box, with a trinket inside, arrived containing no message.

Until his own death Gordon sent Dorothy flowers to take to Violet's grave on all her anniversaries.

> *November 5th 1948* To take 2 lovely nosegays Gordon sent up, to Violet's grave. This is the anniversary of their engagement in 1895; it is (to me) almost unbelievable seeing what Gordon went through,

that he cares to remember what surely must have been the most tragic step in his life. Is he a saint?

A year after Violet's death her gravestone was finally installed: "May 18th 1949 I went up to see V's stone. I am very disappointed in it & it might have been put up by a heathen or pagan, not a word or suggestion of God."

In 1951 Gordon fell seriously ill. Bill arranged for nurses to look after him night and day, while Dorothy, awaiting his end, confided her feelings to her diary:

> *March 12th 1951.* Two P.C's from Bill this a.m. saying Gordon was ill – haemorrhage & other things, Oh I am so sorry . . . what a life of marvellous goodness & selflessness no one will ever know.

> *March 22nd 1951.* Then from Lypiatt came a little Rosemary and 2 Christmas roses, so took that up to V. Dear Gordon packed the box himself.

A month later, knowing that he was dying, Gordon summoned the servants to his bedside to say goodbye. That night he faded away. Bill, now quite alone, wrote to Dorothy:

> Nether Lypiatt Manor Stroud Gloucestershire.
> So my dearest Dorothy Gordon our dear and very old friend has gone to the better lands. He quietly passed away this a.m. I think he was very pleased to go thinking himself a bother to his nurses.
> He will be *very* quietly cremated & his ashes brought to Folkington & placed beside V's one day.
> What a wonderful generous character. Dear Dorothy another link with our past. Yours ever Bill.

Gordon left Bill the right to go on living at Lypiatt, together with the remains of the lease of 11 Mount Street and a life interest in all its contents. He also left him his Austin and his Ford van.

> Nether Lypiatt Manor Stroud Gloucestershire. *April 16th 1951*
> My Dearest Doll,
> I intend coming in to see you for a moment on Monday. Law [Bill's chauffeur] and I are bringing Gordon's ashes down and expect to arrive about 2.30 with some flowers for my Darling little V's birthday. Poor dear Gordon he didn't really want to go,

he looked upon me as a sacred fruit in his care. He really was a
most *wonderful* character . . . Darling Dorothy how sad times are.
I have a nice nurse staying with me till Saturday for company.
Yrs. Ever Bill.

On arriving at Folkington Bill and Roland went off to scatter the ashes.
Dorothy missed Gordon dreadfully and was sad that there was no service,
only a prayer said beside Violet's grave. A year later, looking back, she
could not help comparing him favourably to Bill: "April 23rd 1952 . . . how
different Bill is from dear Gordon, I suppose no-one but me has any idea
as Gordon sent all the flowers etc for me to put up there & Bill has never
sent one."

The Sitwells, however, did not desert Violet's memory. Each year for six
years on the anniversary of her death they put a notice in *The Times* – "In
loving memory of Violet who died January 9th 1948, 'Time will run back,
and fetch the age of Gold'." In addition Osbert would hire a car to go to see
her tablet, composed mostly by him, and to visit her grave with Dorothy.
It pleased Dorothy to find that Osbert was "devoted to Gordon" and after
Gordon's death she found comfort in exchanging with him memories of
the man she loved.

The close-knit family which had defined Dorothy's horizons and in
which Violet had once shared centre stage with her father at Folkington was
now dispersed beyond recall. Reggie had died in 1938, honoured in Canada,
English in his ways to the last, his family so hurt and alienated by his
father's ostracism that they only once returned to Britain. Eva, too, had died
before the war, childless and pre-deceased by her husband Charlie, who had
gone bankrupt and left her in poverty. Roland had become degenerate and
was being blackmailed by, among others, his butler: the trustees of James's
estate failed to prevent him from dissipating his entire inheritance, which
James had intended to preserve in trust for future generations of Gwynnes.[2]
Nevile and Bluebelle lived to a happy old age, Nevile dying the same year as
Gordon, aged eighty-three, at his farm ten miles from Folkington, while
Rupert's daughter Priscilla lives at Wootton to this day. Dorothy herself was
to die in 1958 at her farmhouse at Folkington, after finding at last the male
companionship she had always craved in "Mr H.", whom she nursed until
his death from cirrhosis of the liver.

Nether Lypiatt was too big for Bill alone. Unable to find anyone congenial
to share it with after Gordon's death, he bought a house in Sussex, making

2 Roland was to die in 1971. Earlier his doctor had been the notorious Dr Bodkin
Adams, acquitted of multiple charges of murdering rich and terminally ill patients.

way for John Gwynne to move into the house he had inherited. Over the next four years, however, their relationship collapsed completely. Bill was distressed that John decided to put Nether Lypiatt up for sale after Patricia separated from him (plans for handing it to the National Trust with John still living there fell through): but it was a dispute over the inscription of Gordon's name on Violet's gravestone which caused the greatest bitterness. When Gordon died, Bill instructed the stonemason to leave a space for his own name immediately below Violet's and above Gordon's, as though he, rather than Gordon, had been her husband. John objected violently and the ensuing row rumbled on for years, ending with a severance of all communication following two letters from John to Bill in November 1955.

Nether Lypiatt Manor *9 November 1955*
Dear Bill,
. . . I find it very terrible that this curse should have come upon us all . . . One thing I must however say: I always recognised the special relationship between you and V. And your mutual devotion; and I respected and accepted it absolutely. What neither I nor others have felt *at all happy about* since she went has been your carrying it so far as to request that *your name should appear between hers and Gordon's on the tombstone in the very churchyard where she and Gordon were married*. I would like to know whether V. ever expressed any such wish – that your name was to appear between hers and Gordon's; otherwise I think I should tell you now I shall use one day my influence with Roland and the Bishop of Chichester to have the following words inserted after her name:
AND HER
EVER LOVING HUSBAND
(Gordon)
I believe her relations would be profoundly relieved and your own would not be sorry . . .

Temporarily unhinged with grief at the breakdown of his marriage, John was prepared to use any argument which came to hand: he invoked the biassed Dorothy to his cause and suggested that Bill's meddling with the tombstone had put a curse on Nether Lypiatt, which only the proper wording on the stone would dispel. What hurt Bill most was the implication behind John's claim, quoting Patricia, that at the end it was to Gordon, not Bill, that Violet had turned for comfort.

Nether Lypiatt Manor *16 November 1955*
Dear Bill

. . . You say *I frustrate the wishes of my benefactors.* By benefactors, I presume you include Gordon. I have discussed this matter on more than one occasion during the last 4 years with V's nearest surviving relation [Dorothy] who knew Gordon better than anyone else outside. She was of the opinion he was a most wonderfully unselfish and self-effacing character and he would have agreed to your suggestion about the tombstone only because you wished it. I do not think V's other nearest relation [Roland] would dissent from this opinion. As to V's own wishes, Patricia told me when I got back from Germany it was always Gordon she wanted with her at the end. The whole thing undoubtedly preyed upon Patricia's mind without knowing it especially, as I have said, during the months she was at Lypiatt . . . Till then I attached little importance to it, but since then, so much inexplicable misfortune has befallen others as well as myself, I have felt I cannot do otherwise than do something about it . . . John.

Bill died in 1960. His nephew and heir, Patrick Barrington, followed Bill's instructions written in 1948 to his executors that he should be "cremated in the most simple way with no memorial service or other ceremony and no flowers and I also wish my ashes to be distributed at the foot of the downs to the south side of Folkington Church . . . by C.F. Law".

Three months later, John Gwynne wrote to Patrick Barrington about the inscription, but Patrick, a vague and eccentric man, did not reply, and in the end John had his way. Gordon's name was raised from the foot of the gravestone to a position just below Violet's, while Bill's name was carved underneath, where Gordon's had once been. It was a fitting end to the ambiguity surrounding their intermingled lives: a mystery which none of their contemporaries ever completely unravelled and in which, despite a thousand clues, some part of the truth must always remain undiscovered.

# FAMILY TREES

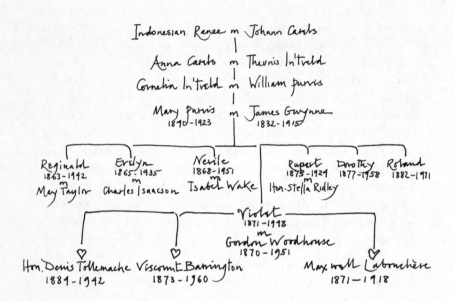

Indonesian Renee m Johann Carels

Anna Carels m Theunis In'tveld

Cornelia In'tveld m William Purvis

Mary Purvis m James Gwynne
1890-1923          1832-1915

Reginald          Evelyn          Nevile          Rupert    Dorothy   Roland
1863-1942        1865-1935       1868-1951        1873-1924  1877-1958  1882-1971
m                 m               m                m
May Taylor       Charles Isaacson  Isabel Wake    Hon. Stella Ridley

Violet
1871-1918
m
Gordon Woodhouse
1870-1951

Hon. Denis Tollemache   Viscount Barrington          Maxwell Labouchère
1884-1942               1873-1960                    1871-1918

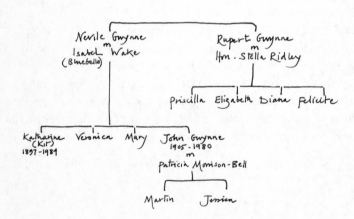

Nevile Gwynne                    Rupert Gwynne
m                                m
Isabel Wake                      Hon. Stella Ridley
(Bluebell)

Priscilla  Elizabeth  Diana  Felicite

Katharine   Veronica   Mary   John Gwynne
(Kit)                          1905-1980
1897-1989                      m
                               Patricia Morrison-Bell

Martin     Jessica

# APPENDIX I

Letter from Arnold Dolmetsch, dated 31 December 1911:
3, Rue de Laudience, Fontenay sous Bois

Dear Mrs Woodhouse,
I should have liked to answer your very interesting letter immediately. But I could not, for I knew my answer to be rather long.

Mrs Landowska's knowledge of the clavichord is based upon her attempt to play upon a small "gebunden" instrument, in bad condition, which belongs to her friend, and mine, Jules Ecorcheville, the eminent musicologue. She concluded from her own unskilled playing upon an unplayable instrument that Bach's music can not have been intended to sound that way. And I agree to it so far! She, therefore, began a very active campaign to prove . . . what you wrote to me about. She has written many articles in French and German, misquoting texts, giving out wild statements, drawing illogical conclusions, with such apparent authority, persuasive eloquence and cleverness that many people believe it. I know, however, some of the leading French musicologues, who do not take her quite seriously. I was in America, and only echoes of this came to me. But, now, the clavichord is here, and a Clavichord player too, a man who knows, who really has got together all the facts. And it is going to be quite exciting, for she has compromised herself so far that it will be a problem how she can extricate herself. And yet, she has no other alternative, for I am just now taking the question in hand. I cannot debate the whole thing here, for it would take many such pages as this. I will only say this: At the time of Bach, there were "bundfrei" clavichords with two strings to EACH note, sometimes three, with compass of 5 octaves, covered strings in the bass. Even with two keyboards and independent Pedals of 16 ft. tone. See "Jacob Adlung" (1699–1762) Musica Mechanica Ongaedi. Paragraph 571–572, 573–579, 581–582, 593–602. It is in the British Museum, I think. A copy is in my hands. See also CPE Bach "Art of Klavier Playing". Mattheson's Orch 1 Part iii Sect. 4 and other contemporary authorities I can give you. In the 18th century, in Germany, the word "Klavier" meant in a General sense, all the instruments with keyboards and strings. But, in common language, Klavier meant Clavichord. The Harpsichord was designated by the words Clavicymbel, Clavicembals, Cembalo, CLaVESSIN, or CLAVESin and Flugel.

The word Klavier passed later on to the square pianos, and the word Flugel to the Grand Pianos.

When Bach wrote for the Harpsichord, he always made it clear by some one of the special names. When he wrote Klavier, he meant Clavichord. Although, in most cases, there is no reason why this music should not also be played upon the Harpsichord. Mme L. argues that no clavichords were in Bach's possession at his death. I say that the first and most valuable number of his inventory (see Spitta's Bach) is a Clavichord with several Keyboards and Pedals. It is called "I Complete (fourniet) Clavier thu 80". This is followed by 4 "Clavesin's" valued from 50 to 20 thu. These of course are Harpsichords.

It is further mentioned in Chap VI of the succession preserved in the Leipzig archives that J.S.B. gave during his lifetime to Joh. Christian Bach, his youngest son, 3 "Claviers with Pedal". Were these also Harpsichords? He would then have possessed 8 Harpsichords, and not one Clavichord! No, common sense and the understanding of the words say that he had 4 Clavichords and 4 Harpsichords.

After my playing the Clavichord at a concert here on December 20th, one D. Heinrich Moller, representative of one of the foremost German papers came to tell me that my playing of Bach on the Clavichord was enough to disprove all that Madame L. said. He asked me to write about the Clavichord for his paper, and offered to arrange a performance in Berlin. I have been too busy to follow this on. But I am writing to him tonight. I had a thundering success that night! And also last Friday in the "Salon du Figaro" (Dec 29). I think the Clavichord to be an immense success here. Now about YOUR Clavichord. Last Tuesday 26th, the lacquer being dry, I expected a painter to do the inscriptions. He did not turn up. Upon enquiry, he is most seriously ill, not expected to recover. He is old . . . On Wednesday I got another one. He started the work but I did not like it. So I washed it off the next day – now I have got a GOOD ONE. He will have finished on Thursday evening. I shall varnish over the gold Friday, and Saturday Jan 6, the Clavichord will be put in its special case and sent to you. This delay is maddening, I know. But it cannot be helped. We have had uncommon bad luck.

Your kind invitation to see you at Armscote House is very tempting, and I hope I shall be able to avail myself of it. But, I cannot say positively yet. My visit to England is for "business" first, although I hope to get some pleasure out of it also.

Mrs Dolmetsch sends her kindest regards to you, and I remain yours very sincerely,

Arnold Dolmetsch

# APPENDIX II

Letter to Violet Gordon Woodhouse about Bach's clavichords

The Professor of Music,
St. Patrick's College,
Maynooth, Dublin                                              22.12. 1912

My Dear Mrs Woodhouse,
Last May when passing through London I went to the British Museum to look up some of the quotations in Mr Dolmetsch's letter – which I return herewith – and ever since I have been trying to write to you about the matter, but could not find the time and energy – indeed I often had time but no energy, but whenever I had a little energy, some more pressing work had to be done.

These quotations do prove that in Bach's time there were "bundfrei" clavichords. But on the other hand the fact that none of these instruments has come down to us would seem to show that they were not very frequent. It should be observed, too, that in those days Clavichords were called "bund-frei" when there was a string for each natural Reg. See Arling i.c. Par. 579.

Dolmetsch maintains "when Bach wrote klavier, he meant Clavichord" but he gives no proof for that. He says himself on the contrary, "the word klavier meant in a general sense all the instruments with keyboards and strings".

As to the question how many Clavichords Bach possessed, Dolmetsch exclaims: "Common sense and the understanding of the words say that he had 4 Clavichords and 4 Harpsichords." I am sorry to say this appeal does not convince me. I am afraid in D's case the wish is the father of the "common sense".

It may be mentioned further, that while Bach's contemporary Quantz speaks of his art of Cimbals playing, there is no testimony during his lifetime connecting him with the Clavichord.

Observe also that he did not make use of the "Bebung", that peculiar Clavichord effect. On the other hand he evidently calculated on the fact that the lower strings of the cimbals sound for a considerable time, which those of the Clavichord do not, c.f. e.g. the final Prelude in the 48.

I am just starting for Stanbrook and perhaps I may, during these Christmas holidays, have the pleasure of accepting your kind invitation to

come to your house. Would Monday 30th inst. do or Tuesday 7th Jan?
With kind regards also to Mr. Woodhouse
Yours very faithfully,

H. Beverunge

# APPENDIX III

Some known BBC broadcasts by Violet Gordon Woodhouse

*12 December 1924.* An hour-long radio programme for the BBC compiled by
Philip Heseltine entitled *Old English Ayres.* Five singers took part, with
Violet on the harpsichord (see *Philip Heseltine* by Barry Smith).

*13 November 1925.* Dorothy's diary: "Now I have to sit up late to hear sister V.
playing the harpsichord at 9.30 when I like to be getting to bed." Music
unknown.

*10 November 1926.* Mozart Fantasia and "two little things by Bach" (letter
from V.G.W. to Roland, November 1926).

*13 June 1929.* Harpsichord Recital at 9.35 pm. Music unknown. Dorothy's
diary: "V's playing came through beautifully."

*3 January 1940.* Clavichord recital.

*8 March 1940.* Clavichord recital recorded in Bristol on 25 February.

# APPENDIX IV

## LITTLE DARK MAGICIAN OF THE CLAVICHORD
### (*To Violet Gordon Woodhouse*)

Of which wonderland of music
    I tried to write the best I could,
With always at back of my mind
    "The little dark magician of the clavichord",
A dear friend I loved, and heard play for thirty years,
    who was no musical pedant and not a scholiast,
But with a memory
    amounting to total recall of music she had ever known.
A player beyond equal in Bach and Mozart,
    and in sonatas by Domenico Scarlatti

But besides all this,
    and more than all else perhaps,
In her unimaginable rendering of little pieces
Of which the effect would be totally lost
    if played upon a piano;
Such as, old songs
    Like "Dover Camp", or "Tell me, Daphne", of Giles Farnaby;
"Chesapeake and Shannon", a sailor's song;
    "The Willow Song" from Verdi's Otello;
Or "Scots wha hae", this last
    more spirited than were believable;
In all of which
    she must have resembled, I think,
In effect, however different in idiom,
    that forgotten virtuoso of the cymbalon,
And been thereby twice over,
    Amongst the greatest of solo players there has ever been.

I believe the secret in her performance
    of these little encore pieces in such perfection
Being the impeccable gradations
    And the study of a lifetime, of tone and timing only attainable, it may be,
On the clavichord, which she called
    "The most beautiful solo instrument ever invented."

*Sacheverell Sitwell*

# APPENDIX V

In August 1968, Tom Goff recorded for BBC Radio an analysis of the methods by which Violet achieved her memorable effects. Short extracts from his broadcast have been quoted elsewhere in this book, but the piece is worth reproducing in full, since it constitutes the valedictory of a refined musical sensitivity to Violet's genius.

*Violet Gordon Woodhouse – Her Playing of the Clavichord*
by Tom Goff

Today I have a very vivid impression of the manner in which Violet Gordon Woodhouse played the clavichord. As it must be with all the greatest experiences in life, the hours which I spent listening to her music will gain in value and significance as the years go by, but some of the impressions, which are so clear to me now, may well become blended with others. Therefore I should attempt to record the detail while it is still fresh in my mind.

It was in 1920, while I was at Oxford, that I was first taken by a friend to Gordon Woodhouse's house. The house stood on the east side of Ovington Square. I can most clearly see the drawing room on the first floor, filled with a dozen or more friends, sitting in every attitude of attention, while the winter afternoon merged into dusk and Violet played upon the harpsichord. Beginning with a pavan of Byrd, she played a series of pieces for the harpsichord by eighteenth-century composers and then passed to folk dances and transcriptions of her own devising. This was the first occasion on which I heard the instrument to the making of which I have since given a great amount of my time.

I often ask my friends the questions "What did you think when you heard the harpsichord for the first time?" "Did you like the sound at once?" Or "Is it an acquired taste?" Now that I know the sound of the harpsichord so well and I try and recapture my own first impressions, the answers to these questions interest me. But when I carry my mind back to that afternoon, over twenty-five years ago, I can obtain no very clear answer in my own case. I do not think that the sound of the harpsichord cast the same spell upon me as did the sound of the clavichord; for, if I found the clear tones of the plucked string so satisfying, why did I not at once seek by some means to acquire a harpsichord? Or why did I not then devote myself to the playing of this superb seventeenth- and eighteenth-century music on the instrument for which it was composed?

I think that these questions can only be answered by trying to judge the effect on my imagination of the character and personality of the player herself; but how can I do this, without calling to mind the image of Violet Gordon Woodhouse, as I first saw her? There was a kind of magic about her appearance, the sound of her voice, the way in which she crossed the room, indeed in all her movements; everything was so alive, so imbued with an ardour of purpose and resolution; yet, she was so slight, so fine, so exquisitely drawn; but I think that she had in her eyes something of the divine fire, and that they spoke of another age and another world. One Christmas I told her the story of *Farewell Miss Julie Logan*. In Barrie's story Miss Julie Logan, abandoned by Prince Charlie after she is supposed to have succoured him in the hills, haunts the glen and comes to the Manse and poor Mr. Yestreen can never forget the magic of her coming. Her spirit, a compound of fire and humour and affection, never lost its hold on his imagination. So it was – or at least so it seems to me that it was – when anyone came to be acquainted with Violet Gordon Woodhouse; the spell, wrought by her music and her conversation, held them so that they could never forget her.

I suppose that the full impression only came to me in later years; but, when I look back to my first visit to the house, I see that the effect was already there and that the enchantment of her appearance, her amazing mastery of the harpsichord, with the rich variety of sound which she drew forth from the instrument, all combined to impose an unforgettable impression on my mind. I cannot say whether on first hearing I thought the sound of a harpsichord unusual or beautiful or disturbing, because the whole experience was not to be measured in the usual terms of daily life. One of the immortals had come to earth and was playing upon an instrument peculiar to the genius of such a being, and one could no more say that one liked or disliked the sound than one could have gauged the effect on mortal ears of the lyre of Phoebus Apollo.

I only heard Violet Gordon Woodhouse play once more that year. It was an evening in July and in the summer twilight a few candles were lit and then, opening the harpsichord, she played the first octaves of the C Minor Fantasie of Mozart, the sixteen foot tone of her harpsichord providing a noble foundation to the fabric of beauty and majesty which came into being under her fingers.

It was some years later that I first heard Violet Gordon Woodhouse play the clavichord. I was staying near Bath and [a friend] took me over to Nether Lypiatt Manor. After playing to us for an hour or more on the harpsichord, she went over to her clavichord, which I had not seen in Ovington Square. She sat down at it and played the first Prelude of the 48 [i.e. Bach's *Well-Tempered Klavier*]. Sometimes, when I have discussed her clavichord playing with friends in these later years, they have suggested that her beautiful mastery of the instrument was explained by her increased love of the clavichord and her concentration on its possibilities in these last years. But, looking back to that afternoon, it seems to me that her touch was most tender and exquisite and her performance equally without a flaw. Certainly I thought that I had never heard a more wonderful and moving sound than that which her fingers drew from that frail web of golden strings . . . The idea that I should ever make such instruments would have struck me as fantastic; for what skill and knowledge and love, or so it seemed to me, must have gone to produce an instrument which under Violet Gordon Woodhouse's fingers could so touch the heart. But perhaps the seed of great experiences in life are often sown in secret, to germinate and come to fruition in the course of time, and I suppose that I carried away that afternoon some longing which, even if I had never known Herbert Lambert, might have reached fulfilment by some other means.

Since that afternoon in 1926 I have often heard Violet Gordon Woodhouse play on the clavichord, and each time that I have heard her I have been possessed with a kind of amazement. The motion of the first experience has endured, and therefore it is difficult to analyse an art so spontaneous and so convincing. But I fear that in a few years all the things which she herself said to me about her playing, and the impressions which I received from contact with a great and unique artist, may not be so clearly in my mind as they are today. Therefore I should endeavour to set down something new and at least give permanency to some written shadow of a wonderful reality.

First of all I believe that anyone would have been impressed with the great vitality of her playing, which seemed at one with her appearance and her character and her conversation. Her playing could not but be alive and vivid, because her spirit entered into and lived in her music; and all the thousand voices of her intellect, the voices which found an echo in the poetry of Traherne and Crashaw, rejoiced in the solemn enthusiasms of Mace and recalled a multitude of obscure and wonderful quotations, sang to her and through her to those who gathered to listen to her. Playing, she was as a creature bewitched. In *Farewell Miss Julie Logan* her first appearance is heralded by one incident. The violin, the playing of which the Minister has forsworn as being out of keeping with the serious character of his office, seems, when he opens the cupboard, to press itself into his embrace, so that he cannot choose but play it and draw from it every tone of which it was capable.

I have so often made an instrument, played it for weeks, come to believe that I was acquainted with every quality in its compass; and then I would take it to her and hear it, as it seemed to me, for the first time. If my clavichords now sit, muffled in covers, silent and unplayed, they have had their glorious hour. Under her fingers they came to life and spoke to the heart of things, which are enduring and unforgettable. I can compare them to a flint, on which was struck the imperishable spark of her genius. On them she must perforce perform, with all the passion and beauty which was her nature.

Often it has been said that genius is entirely spontaneous in its manifestations. I believe that this is true. I think that this is the reason why when one hears some phrase, which one has known for years, played by a great artist, one says: "Of course; it could not be played otherwise," and its true meaning seems to be clear to one for the first time. On the other hand, listening to another great artist, one seems to be aware of many fine calculations, planned subtleties and ingenious contrivance. In Violet Gordon Woodhouse's playing, all seemed inevitable. Her inspiration spoke with a voice which could not be denied, and one listened to her and was convinced. And when one asks, why did she see it in this way and no other, one is baffled by the mystery of genius. Speaking of *King Lear* a friend said to me "How could Shakespeare have sat down in cold blood and written:

> Thou'lt come no more,
> Never, never, never, never, never

and summed up for all time the feeling of the human being confronted with the supreme facts of loss and death?" May it be that in the case of one of Shakespeare's genius, but to feel the emotion, the words must inevitably rise to his lips?

Perhaps it is not altogether fanciful to find something of the same kind in Violet Gordon Woodhouse's playing. It was inevitable that these passages should sound as they did when she performed them, because the music of her being allowed her no alternative. Her ear spoke to her and her fingers drew from her chosen instrument all that love or grief could find to utter.

I think it was this sense of spontaneity which explains something which so often surprised her hearers. One might ask her about some piece in the Fitzwilliam Virginal Book or a composition by one of the lesser eighteenth-century composers, which seemed on a superficial view lacking in interest, and she would play it to one. And, immediately, out of what had seemed to be dry bones, a new and thrilling work of art had come to life. Everything was in place, each phrase acquired a new eloquence, the ornaments, which had appeared the embodiment of eighteenth-century convention, became pregnant with beauty and imagination, and one was confronted with something new and convincing.

One incident comes back to me. I do not suggest that the music of Mendelssohn should be played on the clavichord, but once, after seeing a performance of the *Midsummer Night's Dream* and hearing Mendelssohn's music, I transposed the opening of the Overture from its original key of E major to D major so as to bring the first semiquavers within the compass of my clavichord. Then, thinking that it might amuse her, I left the manuscript with Violet Gordon Woodhouse. A week later, when I came to see her she played to me an enchanting transcription of the *Midsummer Night's Dream* Overture, adorned with the most exquisite harp effects, and performed it with such ecstasy and high spirits that she seemed to bring the veritable magic of Shakespeare and his fairies down to "this dim spit which men call Earth". And to those who heard them, how completely convincing were her other transcriptions, such as those of the air of Ophelia in Verdi's *Otello*, or "When I am laid in earth", or "Hunsden House" and many others.

Another matter of wonder to me, as I came to know Violet Gordon Woodhouse better, was the extent of her repertory and her power to learn anything by heart and retain it indefinitely. I would speak of some piece and, although she had not played it for years, she would sit down at the clavichord and play it with perfect accuracy and certainty. I have followed with the music and wondered that she could recall the least detail, produce every ornament and observe every rest. I imagine that there has never been a great artist who was less worried by the effort of always playing from memory than was Violet Gordon Woodhouse.

In saying this, I would not wish to suggest that all her music was evolved without effort. I believe that she had worked very hard at the piano in her youth. Certainly her commanding technique suggested that this had been the case. During the years in which I have known her, I think that she practised the clavichord for two or three hours a day. In her view the clavichord was the hardest keyboard instrument (I do not think that she was considering the organ in this statement). She thought that the clavichord made greater demands on the performer than even the harpsichord. Nothing could be disguised. Everything must needs be perfect. It was because she believed so ardently in the supreme qualities of the clavichord, with all its subtle range of gradations of tone, that she passed so much time practising and perfecting every phrase which she played upon the instrument.

I think that it would be fair to say that the thing to which Violet Gordon Woodhouse attached most importance in clavichord technique was the necessity to secure the most perfect legato. She would say to me "Bind the notes". On the other hand, her staccato, when she chose to adopt it, was beautifully calculated and effective. It was not as short as the piano staccato. She would play the note short and yet leave it with the utmost care. Occasionally she would adopt a deliberate staccato in certain passages written high up in the treble. For example, in the Prelude in E minor of the First Book of the Forty-eight she would separate each note in the treble voice, giving each phrase an extraordinary eloquence and importance.

I connect her feeling on this point with her devotion to the art of the great singers of the past such as Jean de Reszke. The bel canto figured so largely in her own playing. She would play a high note in some air pianissimo and it gained an emphasis which held the listener's attention. She would allow the voice of the clavichord almost to vanish into silence and then allow a note to reach one's ear as if it were a voice from another world. Thereafter her phrases flowed on, one succeeding another, full of decision and passion, and one would ask oneself, how long could so wonderful a cantabile be sustained, ever touching and persuasive. Who, having once heard it, could ever forget her playing of the Adagio of the Mozart C Major Sonata? Or the Saraband in the English Suite in G Minor?

She used the vibrato, the most beautiful and characteristic effect on the clavichord, with great discretion. Her finger appeared to be balanced on the key for an instant, as near the front of the key as possible, and then to be exerting the slightest increase and decrease of pressure. According to her view, the key must be depressed, before this slight increase and decrease of pressure was applied. To stretch the strings to the extreme limit in one downward movement was calculated to produce that exaggerated sharpening of the pitch which is so ugly in clavichord playing.

Vere Pilkington has written of Violet Gordon Woodhouse's exquisite and subtle sense of rhythm. While her tempi were usually conceived on broad and leisured lines, the ebb and flow of the movement remained marvellously flexible. Yet below the surface you felt that the pulse beat clear and unerring. Those who heard Chopin play the piano have described how he could vary the time in the manner which has come to be known as tempo rubato. It would no doubt be wrong to apply such a term to Violet Gordon Woodhouse's performance of music of an earlier period, yet to some degree there was the same suggested counterbalance of gain and loss in the measure against a background of fixed and defined rhythm. This is in accordance with what Miss Kathleen Long told me that Rubio, in an eloquent attempt on the English language, used to say to her, as I believe he also did to Violet Gordon Woodhouse, that in her playing there must be "more ansety and elstety". This "anxiety and elasticity" was present in every movement of her fingers as in every bar of her music. Moreover the fine effects which she achieved by very slightly anticipating or delaying the attack was also, I believe, the outcome of the teaching of Rubio.

Two examples of this method occur to me. I think of Violet Gordon Woodhouse's lovely performance of the Gigue from the first Partita in B Flat. I am sure that the sense of splendid and joyful movement was heightened by one small subtlety, the anticipation of the A and G in the fifth bar by the right hand. As an example of the eloquent effect which Violet Gordon Woodhouse achieved by slightly delaying her attack, I would recall her playing of the passage in the Prelude in F Minor in the second book of the 48, where the first theme returns. It is impossible to dissect great art, but it seems to me that her genius bid her pause for just that fraction of a second, in moving to the D Flat in the 58th bar, to permit the cry, that only the clavichord can utter, to reach the ear at that moment. For at this moment and at no other could this cry achieve its purpose. For then, above all, is the ear painfully alert to receive the impression and appreciate the wonder and sorrow of the music.

I doubt if there is any musical instrument, certainly no keyboard instrument, so endowed to emerge and vanish into silence as is the clavichord. Indeed, its quiet tones are never very far removed from that silence which Mrs Meynell calls "the very soul of life". The eloquence of that silence is very near, ready to round off the perfection of the phrase. I think that it was something of this feeling that explains the secret of Violet Gordon Woodhouse's phrasing. The voice emerged and vanished into silence, her pauses rounding off the beauty of her phrases.

I would like to give a host of examples of her phrasing, but perhaps I should confine myself to two examples. This was how she phrased the opening of the Gigue from the French Suite in G major:

[Tom Goff played at this point]

Then she phrased the opening of the Fugue in G major in the 2nd Book of the 48 in this way: [Tom Goff played]

I have heard this fugue played by many great artists, but I have never heard anyone else produce the effect of grace and delicacy which Violet Gordon Woodhouse achieved in this fugue, and who else has ever found that song, full of the most moving regret, in the running semiquavers of the final bars?

I do not think that anyone who ever heard Violet Gordon Woodhouse play on the harpsichord or clavichord will forget the beauty and eloquence of her ornaments. Under her hands they seemed to become a vital and essential part of the melody. I wish that I could set down some of the ornaments which she played in the Pavans of Dr John Bull. They clothed the music with a sombre and convincing brilliance; a vanished world came to life, instinct with ardour and tragedy of Tudor England. Last year Violet played to me the hymn tune "Mein Jesu was für Seelenweh", composed by Bach for the Schnellig Hymn Book. When I looked up the music, I found that the second part opens as follows:

[Tom Goff played]

Violet Gordon Woodhouse played the tune to me on the clavichord in this way: [Tom Goff played]

Certainly the melody seemed to gain a new beauty and poignancy from the turn and appoggiatura.

To achieve the effects which Violet Gordon Woodhouse required, she demanded the finest and most sensitive stringing, so that the clavichord should respond to the least bidding of her finger. To make instruments for her, as I have done during the last ten years, was the noblest education that an instrument maker could desire. Her ear was so sensitive that she could detect the increase of a thousandth of an inch in the diameter of a string. If you altered the gauge of the wire by one degree, she was immediately aware of the change. With regard to the keys, she [once demanded of me] a perfect evenness of a certain note: after I had re-examined the mortice of the key I did discover the minutest particle of glue adhering to the felt – her finger had felt what was not perceptible to the normal touch. As I have already said, there was no sound, I think, which these instruments were capable of producing, which she did not draw forth from them.

Thus I carry with me a vivid and radiant impression of Violet Gordon Woodhouse. If I close my eyes, I can see her sitting at the clavichord, her beautiful fingers rising and falling with the grace and speed which led W.H. Davies to write his enchanting poem to her. I would like to take leave of her, playing the lovely Scarlatti Sonata in F Minor (No. 285). She loved this sonata, which she said made her think of the story of Miss Julie Logan. The way she played the phrase:

[Tom Goff played]

comes back to me now. Then I was in touch with something in music which I shall never encounter again.

# VIOLET GORDON WOODHOUSE
## DISCOGRAPHY
by Alan Vicat

This listing shows all the known recordings made by the Gramophone Co. Ltd, and, with the exception of matrices HO5745 and HO5746 (octavina), all the items were played on the harpsichord.

The arrangement of this discography is as follows:
(a)  The first column gives the matrix number. The suffixes AE and AF were allocated to the recording expert Edmund J. Pearse. In practice these were also used by Fred Gaisberg, W. Sinkler Darby and others at Hayes. The Bb/Cc prefixes were used for 10in./25cm. and 12in./30cm. respectively, but, unlike the AE/AF suffixes, were both in the same single numerical series.
(b)  The second column shows the number quoted in the company's catalogues. Where a (*) is given this indicates that that take of the material was not published. In the case of Bb10523–2 and Bb10524–2 the (M) indicates masters were prepared and the catalogue number E516 allocated. The latter was then changed to B2790 in the cheaper plum-label series, but, for some reason, the proposed issue was cancelled on 24 August 1928.

I would like to thank Ruth Edge and the staff of the EMI Music Archive for kindly providing much information from the company's written records. Also Alan Kelly, who has assisted in many different ways and generously cast a very experienced eye over this; Peter Adamson and Malcolm Binns for sending tapes of recordings in their possession to confirm the identities of some of the discs listed here; and Raymond Glaspole who has also provided tapes as well as both discs and information. To all these I am indeed grateful.

Acoustic recordings made on 28 June 1920 by Fred Gaisberg at Hayes.
*10 in./25 cm.*

| | | | |
|---|---|---|---|
| HO5741AE | * | a) "L'Arlequine" (from 23rd Ordre) | F. Couperin (1668–1733) |
| | | b) Tambourin (from Suite in E Minor) | J. P. Rameau (1683–1764) |
| HO5742AE | * | a) "La Forlana" | Anon. |
| | | b) "Alman" (FVB 152) | T. Morley (1557–c. 1603) |
| HO5743AE | * | Sonata in D Major (probably L461/K29) | D. Scarlatti (1685–1757) |
| HO5744AE | * | Sonata in A Major (probably L345/K113) | " |

*OCTAVINA VIRGINAL*
| | | | |
|---|---|---|---|
| HO5745AE | * | "Nobodyes Gigge" (FVB149) | R. Farnaby (c.1590–?) |
| HO5746AE | * | a) "The Irish Ho-hoane" (FVB26) | Anon. |
| | | b) A Gigge. "Dr. Bulls Myselfe" (FVB189) | John Bull (c.1562–1628) |

*12 in./30cm.*
## HARPSICHORD

| | | | |
|---|---|---|---|
| HO4444AF | * | Fugue in D Minor (probably BWV948) | J.S. Bach (1685–1750) |
| HO4445AF | * | a) Prelude in E Flat major (probably BWV815a) | " |
| | | b) Gigue in B Flat Major (probably from Partita No. 1 B Flat major BWV825) | " |

Acoustic recordings made on 7 July 1920 by W. Sinkler Darby at Hayes.
*10 in./25cm.*

| | | | |
|---|---|---|---|
| HO5758AE | E203 | Three English Folk Dances: <br> a) "Newcastle" b) "Heddon of Fawsley" <br> c) "Step Back" | arr. C. J. Sharp |
| HO5759AE | E203 | "Nobodyes Gigge" (FVB149) | R. Farnaby (c.1590–?) |
| HO5760AE | E204 | Sonata in D Major (L461/K29) | D. Scarlatti (1685–1757) |
| HO5761AE | E204 | Sonata in A Major (L345/K113) | " |

*12 in./30cm.*

| | | | |
|---|---|---|---|
| HO4466AF | D490 | a) Gavotte in G major (Zimmerman D220) formerly attrib. to H. Purcell | (?Jeremiah Clarke, c. 1659–1707) |
| | | b) Prelude in E Flat Major (BWV815a) | J.S. Bach (1685–1750) |
| HO4467AF | * | a) "L'Arlequine" (from 23rd Ordre) | F. Couperin (1668–1733) |
| HO4467 II AF | D490 | b) Tambourin (from Suite in E Minor) | J.P. Rameau (1683–1764) |
| HO4468AF | D491 | Fugue in D Minor (BWV948) | J.S. Bach (1685–1750) |
| HO4469AF | D491 | Toccata in E Minor – Fugue (BWV914) | " |

Acoustic recordings made on 10 April 1922 in Recording Room No. 1 at Hayes (recording expert not given).
*10 in./25 cm.*

| | | | |
|---|---|---|---|
| Bb1202 –1 | * | Partita No. 1 in B Flat Major (BWV825) | J.S. Bach (1685–1750) |
| –2 | * | – Allemande | |
| –3 | E275 | | |
| Bb1203 –1 | * | Probably Partita No. 1 in B Flat Major | " |
| –2 | * | (BWV825) – Courante | |
| Bb1204 –1 | * | Probably Partita No. 1 in B Flat Major | " |
| –2 | * | (BWV825) – Minuets 1 and 2 | |
| Bb1205 –1 | * | Galiarda (FVB185) | John Bull (c.1562–1628) |
| –2 | E275 | | |

Matrices Bb1202–3 and Bb1205–2 were issued in France with the catalogue number P484.
*12 in./30cm.*

| | | | |
|---|---|---|---|
| Cc1206 –1 | * | Suite No. 5 in E Major – Theme and | G.F. Handel (1685–1759) |
| –2 | D645 | Variations – "Harmonious Blacksmith" | |
| –3 | * | | |
| Cc1207 –1 | * | English Suite No. 3 in G Minor (BWV808) | J.S. Bach (1685–1750) |
| –2 | D645 | – Prélude | |
| Cc1208 –1 | * | a) Polonaise in G Minor (prob. BWV Anh.125) | (?W.F./C.P.E. Bach). |
| –2 | * | | |
| | | b) March in D Major (prob. BWV Anh. 122) | " |
| | | c) Musette in D Major (prob. BWV Anh. 126) | " |
| Cc1209 –1* | | a) "Scotch brawl" | Anon. |
| –2 | * | b) "Gathering peascods" | arr. C.J. Sharp |
| –3 | * | c) Hornpipe | H. Purcell (1658–95) |
| | | d) "Bryhton camp" | Arr. C.J. Sharp |

Acoustic recordings made on 26 March 1923 in Recording Room No. 1 at Hayes (recording expert not given).
*10 in./25 cm.*

| | | | |
|---|---|---|---|
| Bb2742 –1 | * | "The Earle of Oxford's Marche: (FVB259) | W. Byrd (1543–1623) |
| –2 | E294 | | |
| –3 | * | | |
| –4 | * | | |

| | | | |
|---|---|---|---|
| Bb2743 –1 | * | "The Queenes Alman" (FVB171) | W. Byrd (1543–1623) |
| –2 | E294 | | |
| Bb2744 –1 | E295 | Galiarda (FVB255) | " |
| –2 | * | | |
| –3 | * | | |
| Bb2745 –1 | * | "Rowland" (FVB160) (Listed as "Lord | " |
| –2 | * | Willobies welcome home" in Lady Nevells | |
| | | Virginals Book) | |
| –3 | E295 | | |

Matrices Bb2743–2 and Bb2745–3 were issued in France with the catalogue number P467.

Electric recordings made on 6 April 1927 by George Dillnutt and D.E. Larter in Studio C, Small Queen's Hall.
*12 in./30 cm.*

| | | | |
|---|---|---|---|
| Cc10519–1 | * | Italian Concerto – Allegro | J.S. Bach (1685–1750) |
| –2 | D1281 | (BWV971) | |
| Cc10520–1 | D1281 | " – Andante | " |
| –2 | * | | |
| Cc10521–1 | * | " – Presto | " |
| –2 | * | | |
| –3 | D1282 | | |
| Cc10522–1 | * | a) Polonaise in G Minor (BWV Anh. 125) | (W.F./C.P.E. Bach) |
| –2 | * | b) March in D Major (BWV Anh.122) | " |
| –3 | D1282 | c) Musette in D Major (BWV Anh. 126) | " |

*10 in./25 cm.*

| | | | |
|---|---|---|---|
| Bb10523–1 | * | a) Sonata in G Major | D. Scarlatti (1685–1757) |
| –2 | M | | |
| | * | b) Sonata in G Minor | " |
| Bb10524–1 | * | Sonata in E Minor | " |
| –2 | M | | |

*12 in./30 cm.*

| | | | |
|---|---|---|---|
| Cc10525–1 | * | a) "Mal Sims" (FVB281) | G.Farnaby (c.1563–1640) |
| –2 | * | | |
| | | b) "Tell mee Daphne" (FVB280) | " |

Electric recordings made on 23 May 1928 by George Dillnutt, E. Fowler and W. Vogel in Studio C, Small Queen's Hall.
*12 in./30 cm.*

| | | | |
|---|---|---|---|
| Cc12989–1 | * | Sonata in D (Hoboken XVI/37) | F.J. Haydn (1732–1809) |
| –2 | * | – 1st movement | |
| –3 | D1589 | | |
| –4 | * | – 2nd and 3rd movements | |
| Cc12990–1 | " | * 2nd and 3rd movements | " |
| –2 | * | | |
| –3 | D1589 | | |
| –4 | * | | |

# BIBLIOGRAPHY

Aberconway, Christabel, *A Wiser Woman? A Book of Memories*, Hutchinson, 1966

Adlard, E., *Recollections of Edy Craig*, Frederick Muller, 1949

Allan, Mea, *William Robinson*, Faber & Faber, 1982

Asquith, Lady Cynthia, *Diaries 1915–1918*, Hutchinson, 1968

Ayling, Kit, *My Father's Family*, unpublished memoirs

Baker, Oliver, *In Shakespeare's Warwickshire*, Simkin Marshall, 1937

Baldock, Robert, *Pablo Casals*, Victor Gollancz, 1992

Baron, Wendy, *Miss Ethel Sands and Her Circle*, Peter Owen, 1977

Barrington, Charlotte, *Eighty Years On*, John Murray, 1936

Barrington, The Hon. Daines, *Miscellanies*, J. Nichols, 1791

Becker, Robert, *Nancy Lancaster*, Alfred A. Knopf, New York, 1996

Beecham, Sir Thomas, *Frederick Delius*, Hutchinson, 1959

Bell, Quentin, *Virginia Woolf: A Biography*, Hogarth Press, 1972

Beringer, Oscar, *Fifty Years of Pianoforte Playing*, 1907

Blain, V., Clements, P., and Grundy I., *The Feminist Companion to Literature in English*, Batsford, 1990

Blow, Simon, *Broken Blood*, Faber & Faber, 1987

Boxer, Arabella, *A Book of English Food*, Hodder & Stoughton, 1991

Bradford, Sarah, *Sacheverell Sitwell*, Sinclair Stevenson, 1993

Brittain, Vera, *Testament of Youth*, Virago, 1978

Brown, Jane, *Eminent Gardeners*, Viking, 1990

Buckle, Richard, *Diaghilev*, Weidenfeld & Nicolson, 1979

Burney, Dr Charles, *A General History of Music*, Volume I, 1776

Butler, Ruth, *Rodin*, Yale University Press, 1993

Carley, Lionel, *Delius: A Life in Letters*, Volumes I and II, Scolar Press, 1988

Cheltenham Art Gallery and Museum catalogue, "William and Eve Simmonds", 9 February–15 March 1980

Colles, H.C., *A Dictionary of Music and Musicians*, Macmillan, 1928

Cooper, Lady Diana, *The Rainbow Comes and Goes*, Hart-Davis, 1958

Cossart, Michael, *The Food of Love*, Hamish Hamilton, 1978

Crawley, May, *George Crawley: A Memoir*, privately published, 1926

d'Ariste, Jean, *Le Pau Hunt 1840–1914*

De Courcy, Anne, *Circe, The Life of Edith, Marchioness of Londonderry*, Sinclair-Stevenson, 1992

Delius, Clare, *Frederick Delius*, Ivor Nicholson & Watson, 1935

Dent, Edward, *Alessandro Scarlatti*, Edward Arnold, 1905

Dolmetsch, Arnold, *The Interpretation of the Music of the XVIIth and XVIIIth Centuries*, Novello & Co. Ltd, 1915

Dolmetsch, Mabel, *Personal Recollections of Arnold Dolmetsch*, Routledge & Kegan Paul, 1958

Drinkwater, C. H., *The Family of Drinkwater*, privately published, 1920

Duckworth, Francis, *The Cotswolds*, Adam & Charles Black, 1908

Evans, Roger, *The Years Between: The Story of 7th Queen's Own Hussars*, Gale and Polden, 1965

Fay, Amy, *Music Study in Germany*, Macmillan, 1886

Fellowes, Edmund H., *Memoirs of an Amateur Musician*, Methuen, 1946

Fisher, Paul Hawkins, *Notes and Recollections of Stroud, Gloucestershire*, Trübner and Co, 1871

France, Rachel, *A Century of Plays by American Women*, Richard Rosen, New York, 1979

Fuller-Maitland, J. A., *A Doorkeeper of Music*, John Murray, 1929

Fussell, Paul, *The Great War and Modern Memory*, Oxford University Press, 1975

Ganz, Wilhelm, *Memoirs of a Musician*, John Murray, 1946

Gascoigne, Bamber, *The Encyclopaedia of Britain*, Macmillan, 1994

Gibbs, J. Arthur, *A Cotswold Village*, John Murray, 1900

Gidding, Robert, *The War Poets*, Bloomsbury, 1988

Gilbert, Martin, *First World War*, Weidenfeld & Nicolson, 1994

Glendinning, Victoria, *Edith Sitwell*, Orion, 1993

Glyn, Anthony, *Elinor Glyn*, Hutchinson, 1955

Gray, Cecil, *Peter Warlock*, Jonathan Cape, 1934

Greensted, Mary, *The Arts and Crafts Movement in the Cotswolds*, Alan Sutton, 1993

Griggs, Frederick, *Highways and Byways in Oxford and the Cotswolds*, Macmillan, 1908

Gwynne Pumps Ltd, *Land Drainage Pumps*, 1943

Gwynne, Dorothy, *Diaries 1890–1952*, unpublished

Gwynne, Nevile, *Diary, 1882–1894*, unpublished

Hammerson, Michael, *No Easy Hopes or Lies*, London Stamp Exchange, 1991

Haskell, Harry, *The Early Music Revival*, Thames & Hudson, 1988

Howard de Walden, Marguerite, *Pages from My Life*, Sidgwick & Jackson, 1965

Jebb, Miles, *The Diaries of Cynthia Gladwyn*, Constable, 1995

Jekyll, Lady, *Kitchen Essays*, Nelson, 1922

Kennedy, Michael, *The Works of Ralph Vaughan Williams*, Oxford University Press, 1964

Klein, Harman, *The Reign of Patti*, Fisher Unwin, 1920

*Lady, The*, editions for 1893–1920

Laurence, Dan H., *Shaw's Music: The Complete Musical Criticism of Bernard Shaw*, Bodley Head, 1981

Laver, James, *Edwardian Promenade*, Hulton, 1958

Lawrence, T. E., *Seven Pillars of Wisdom*, Cape, 1935. *See also* Shaw, T. E.

Lewis, J. R., *The Cotswolds at War*, Alan Sutton, 1992

Ley, Rosamund, *Ferruccio Busoni, Letters to his Wife*, Edward Arnold, 1938

Longford, Elizabeth, *Wellington: The Years of the Sword*, Weidenfeld & Nicolson, 1969

Luckett, Richard, *The Revival of Early Music and the Suppositions of Cultural History*, unpublished

Mapleson, J. H., *The Mapleson Memoirs*, Bedford Clarke & Co., 1888

Marsden, William, *History of Sumatra*, "Printed for the Author", 1811

Massingham, H. J., *Cotswold Country*, Batsford, 1942

Masson, André, Perot, and Jacques, Tucoo-Chala, Pierre, *Le Pau Hunt aujourd'hui*, 1984

Masters, Brian, *Now Barabbas was a Rotter*, Hamish Hamilton, 1978

Mumby, Frank (ed.), *The Great World War*, Volumes I and II, Gresham Publishing Co., 1915

Ottewill, David, *The Edwardian Years*, York University Press, 1989

Oxfordshire and Buckinghamshire Light Infantry *Chronicle*, editions for 1914–18

Pakenham, Thomas, *The Boer War*, Weidenfeld & Nicolson, 1979

Pearsall , Ronald, *The Worm in the Bud*, Weidenfeld & Nicolson, 1969

Pearson, John, *Façades*, Macmillan, 1978

Philip, Robert, *Early Recordings and Musical Style*, Cambridge University Press, 1992

Powell-Edwards, Lieutenant-Colonel, *Sussex Yeomanry and 16th Battalion, Royal Sussex Regiment, 1914–1919*, Andrew Melrose, 1921

*Purvis Family History 1694–1988*, privately printed, 1988

Radclyffe-Hall, Marguerite, *The Forgotten Island*, Chapman & Hall, 1915

Richardson, Kenneth, *The British Motor Industry*, Macmillan, 1977

Robinson, William, *The Wild Garden*, John Murray, 1903

Ronald, Sir Landon, *Variations on a Personal Theme*, 1922

——, *Myself and Others*, 1931

Rothenstein, William, *Men and Memories*, Faber & Faber, 1932

Royal Sussex Regiment, *A Short History of the Royal Sussex Regiment, 1701–1926*, Gale & Polden, 1941

St John, Christopher, *Ethel Smyth*, Longman, Green & Co., 1959

Sarsby, Jacqueline, article in *Crafts Magazine*, May/June 1994

Schafer, R. Murray, *Ezra Pound and Music*, Faber & Faber, 1978

Scholes, Percy A., *The Oxford Companion to Music*, Oxford University Press, 1980

Seymour, Miranda, *Ottoline Morrell: Life on the Grand Scale*, Hodder & Stoughton, 1992

Shaw, Bernard, *Music in London, 1890–94*, Constable, 1932

Shaw, T. E., *Letters to Bruce Rogers from T. E. Shaw*, privately printed, William Edwin Rudge, 1933. *See also* Lawrence, T. E.

Sitwell, Osbert, *Left Hand! Right Hand!*, Macmillan, 1945

——, *Noble Essences*, Macmillan, 1950

Sitwell, Sacheverell, *A Background for Domenico Scarlatti*, Faber & Faber, 1935

——, *Southern Baroque Art*, 1951

——, *An Indian Summer*, Macmillan, 1952

——, *Southern Baroque Revisited*, Weidenfeld & Nicolson, 1967

Skidelsky, Robert, *John Maynard Keynes*, Macmillan, 1983

Smith, Barry, *Peter Warlock: The Life of Philip Heseltine*, Oxford University Press, 1994

Smyth, Ethel, *Female Pipings in Eden*, Peter Davies, 1933

——, *As Time Went On*, Longman, Green & Co., 1936

——, *What Happened Next*, Longman, Green & Co.,1940

Spalding, F., *Roger Fry*, Granada, 1980

Stuckenschmidt, Hans Heinz, *Ferruccio Busoni*, Calder & Boyars, 1970

*Survey of London*, Athlone Press, 1980

Tollemache, Lord, *The Tollemaches of Helmingham and Ham*, privately published, 1949

Tooley, M., and Arnander, P., *Gertrude Jekyll*, Michaelmas Books, 1995

Van der Straeten, *History of the Violoncello*, William Reeves, 1915

Vaughan Williams, Ursula, *R.V.W.: A Biography*, Oxford University Press, 1988

Venn, J. S., *Alumni Cantabrigienses*, Part II, Volume IV, Cambridge University Press, 1947

Waley, Alison, *A Half of Two Lives*, Weidenfeld & Nicolson, 1982

White, Gilbert, *The Natural History and Antiquities of Selborne*, 1836

Woodhouse, Gordon, *Dining-Room Recipes*, unpublished, library of the author

Young, Percy, M., *George Grove*, Macmillan, 1980

# INDEX